MEMOIRS,

BIOGRAPHICAL AND HISTORICAL,

OF

BULSTRODE WHITELOCKE,

LORD COMMISSIONER OF THE GREAT SEAL, AND AMBASSADOR AT THE COURT
OF SWEDEN, AT THE PERIOD OF THE COMMONWEALTH.

BY

R. H. WHITELOCKE,

PROFESSOR ROYAL OF WURTEMBERG.

LONDON:

ROUTLEDGE, WARNE, AND ROUTLEDGE,

2, FARRINGDON STREET;

NEW YORK: 56, WALKER STREET.

MDCCCLX.

[*The Author reserves the right of Translation.*]

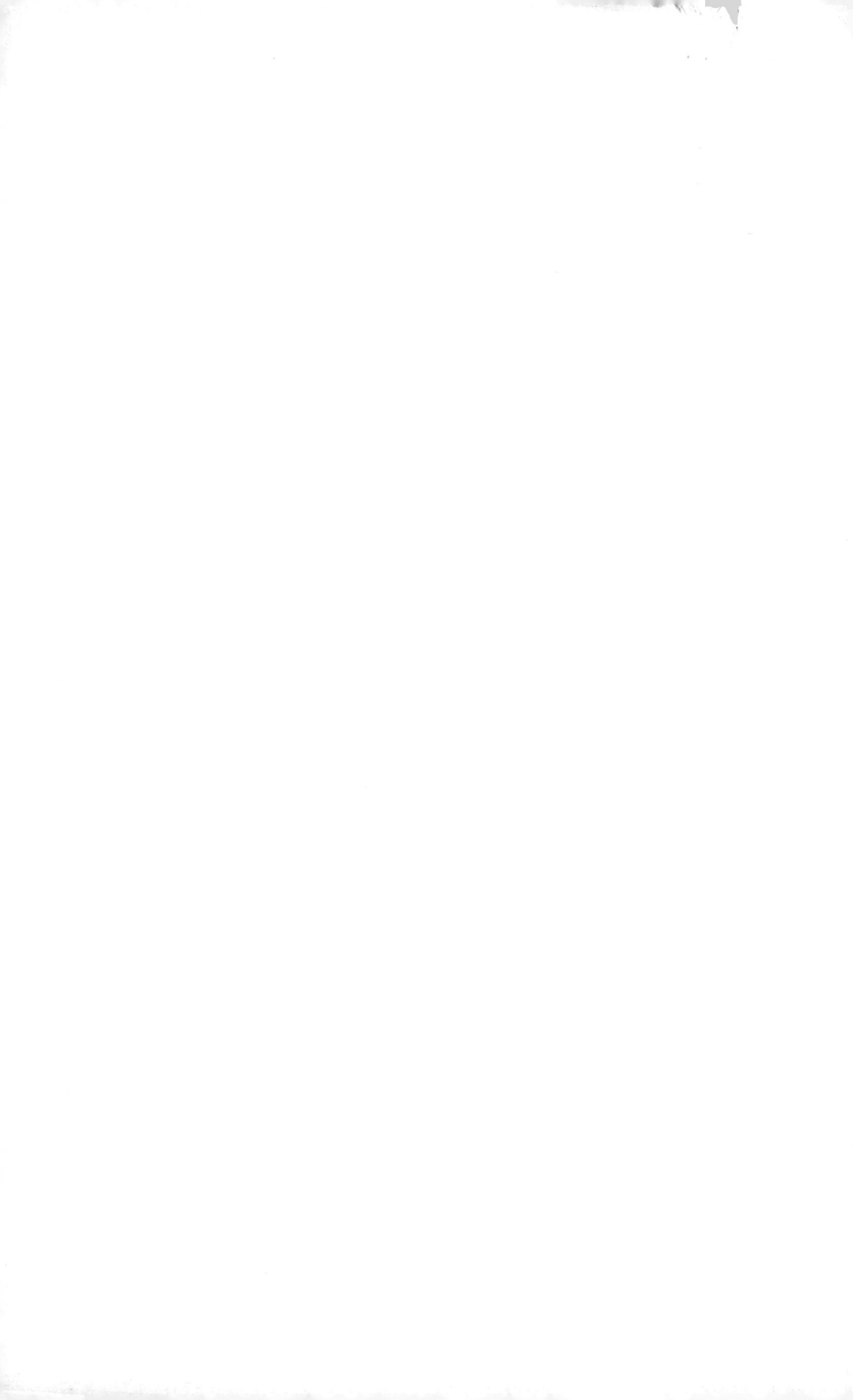

PREFACE.

FAMILIAR as is the name of BULSTRODE WHITELOCKE to the student of English history, both as an actor in many of the important scenes of the most remarkable epoch in our annals, and as the writer of that authentic record of the events of his time, entitled "Memorials of English Affairs," it seems, at first sight, singular that no complete memoir of his life should have hitherto been given to the world.

The true cause of this neglect, and of the want of a due appreciation of Whitelocke's character and services, in such meagre biographical sketches of him as have yet appeared, is to be traced, however, to the strong prejudice which, for a very protracted period since the Restoration, existed against the more prominent actors on the popular side during the Civil War and the Commonwealth. The awful retribution that befel the misguided monarch, whose tyrannical proceedings provoked their determined and relentless opposition, led, in conformity with a law of nature, to a reactionary feeling in his favour, and Charles I. accordingly came to be venerated by a numerous and influential section of the community as a royal martyr. Indeed, it is but just we should remember that most of his objectionable acts originated in mistaken convictions, religiously cherished, and that his tenacity in clinging to them was dictated by the proud spirit of a king who considered himself responsible to no man—reigning by Divine right alone.

This marked sympathy with the ill-fated monarch, and its concomitant prejudice against his successful antagonists, are visible in almost every literary production bearing on the subject, more especially in the historical and biographical works that appeared in the latter half of the 17th century, and during the whole of the succeeding one. But, in our own times, a better knowledge and a more liberal feeling have been gradually developed : justice has at last been rendered to Cromwell, especially, and his character vindicated from many odious charges.

From Whitelocke's intimate relations with the Protector, it was not surprising that he too should be calumniated and misrepresented. But, it is now time that a man whose example as a right-minded and steadfast patriot exercised no little influence on his contemporaries, and whose public measures entitle him to be regarded as a wise statesman— if not, indeed, as the founder of our present constitutional system of government—should no longer remain in comparative obscurity ; the time is come when an attempt may fairly be made to rescue his memory from both obloquy and neglect.

The patriotic statesman consoled himself, in his old age and retirement, with the belief that posterity would eventually do him justice.

The author of the present work thinks it right to say that he relies confidently, not on the arguments which he has found it his duty to use, but on the good works of the eminent man whose life is here portrayed, to secure for him that grateful remembrance which is due to all men who have served their country, at any epoch, both faithfully and well. It only remains for him to add, that the Memoir has been composed partly from printed sources, and partly from unpublished MSS.

R. H. W.

London,
November, 1860.

CONTENTS.

CHAPTER I.

1605—1623.

CHAPTER II.

1623—1626.

CHAPTER III.

1626—1628.

CHAPTER IV.

1628—1629.

CHAPTER V.

1630—1632.

CHAPTER VI.

1633.

CHAPTER VII.

1634.

CHAPTER XI.

1640—1642

CHAPTER XII.

1642—1644.

CHAPTER XIII.

1644.

CHAPTER XX.

1654.

CHAPTER XXI.

1654—1656.

CHAPTER XXII.

1655—1658.

MEMOIRS

OF

BULSTRODE WHITELOCKE.

CHAPTER I.

1605—1623.

Birth of Bulstrode, only Son of the eminent Judge, Sir James Whitelocke—His early Years—Is sent to Merchant Tailors' School—Commences the Study of the Law —Is entered of the University of Oxford, and favourably noticed by Laud, then President of St. John's, and by Juxon—Meets with an Accident while hunting, and quits the University—His singular Cure by a German Doctor.

THE subject of this memoir, Bulstrode Whitelocke, whose name is so familiar to the modern historian and student of English history from his oft-quoted "Memorials of English Affairs," first published in 1682, and who played so important a part during the brief but stirring period of the Commonwealth, was born on the 6th of August, 1605, in the house of Sir George Croke, his mother's uncle. It was situated somewhere in Fleet Street, and was probably near the spot where Temple Bar now stands; but at this distance of time it is extremely difficult to identify the site of any private dwelling in this quarter. The very Bar itself is comparatively a modern structure, having been erected in 1672, and is therefore not identical with that which the turbulent citizens of London were too apt to close, till Monk put an end to the practice, and the Restoration reduced it to a mere matter of form.

Bulstrode's father was James Whitelocke, then a simple *armiger*, or esquire, in virtue of his profession as a counsellor-

B

at-law, deservedly held to be a very learned man for the
time. He afterwards attained the rank of serjeant-at-law,
and was eventually raised to the dignity of a judge, on
which occasion he was knighted. James Whitelocke was
the youngest son of a younger brother, sprung from a very
ancient family in Berkshire, where they had long continued
to cultivate their estate without either wasting or improving
it. In those days the heirs to landed estates were seldom
prompted by feelings of ambition to extend their property.
They left the cares of money-making to their younger brothers,
who might follow professions, or turn merchants, or seek their
fortune by foreign adventure, if they pleased. The love of
money increases with its acquisition, as we all know ; not so
the love of broad acres, at least where luxury has not yet
found admission. Such was the case, at all events, with the
Whitelockes, for the size of their estate was considered to be
ample enough, and to constitute the patrimony of a gentleman. They had lands also in the counties of Oxford and
Buckingham ; and so late as the reign of James II., one of
their descendants still possessed part of the ancestral property near Wokingham, in Berkshire.

Young Whitelocke's mother was Elisabeth Bulstrode, of
Bulstrodes, in Buckinghamshire. This lady belonged to a
still older family than her husband could boast, for her
ancestors had lived there in a flourishing condition and in
the foremost rank of country gentlemen, untrammelled by
titles and courtly honours, for no less than fourteen descents,
being one more than James Whitelocke's pedigree could
show on parchment. Here also, as in the former case, impro-
vidence stepped in at last, and the vice of extravagance,
wholly unchecked by successive losses in later times, divested
the Bulstrodes (or Boustreds, as the name was sometimes
written) in the end of all their fair possessions.

The infant was christened in St. Dunstan's Church, Fleet
Street, on which occasion he had for his godfather his
paternal uncle, Captain Whitelocke, afterwards described by

his too partial nephew as a man of excellent parts and wit, but of a wild fancy. He named the child Bulstrode, at which the minister stopped, being startled at the somewhat taurine sound, and asked in a tone of dismay if they could not give the poor babe some other name. But the captain, a man of despotic mood, as godfather, without condescending to argue the point, allowed the good man a choice between the names of Elisabeth and Bulstrode, being resolved, he said, that the boy should have either the one or the other of his mother's names. The infant was accordingly christened with the old Saxon appellation, so doggedly insisted on by his uncle.

The same chronicler, who has recorded this baptismal scene, forthwith proceeds to moralise, and to repeat how this world of blossoms and flowers is in truth, despite its scenery, a mere theatre of labour and sorrow, and how the child, on emerging one hapless day from its cradle, must have unconsciously found it so.

At the expiration of one year—twelve months of milk and honey—the harsh expulsion from Eden ensued, and little Bulstrode was placed out at nurse, at a cottage near Woburn, in Buckinghamshire. The nurse to whose charge he was given had been a servant in his mother's family, and during her servitude had no doubt fared generously; but upon being married to a rustic had to content herself with the old simple Saxon diet of the peasantry, unpalatable enough where tender nurture was required.

Fortunately for the nurseling's intellectual and bodily growth, the mother paid frequent visits to the cottage, and soon perceived that the child was "neither well ordered nor dieted," as she expressed it. The nurse pleaded in justification, that it was "a testy child," and that she could not get it to eat its "shaffling broth, though she made it as yellow as a golden noble."

When the Saxons were rulers in the land, this term meant "lamb-broth," but since the Conquest it had gradually been used to signify a pottage stewed from young eels, and rendered unctuous with rusty bacon, which served to give the mess consistency and the much-prized colour.

The heir was forthwith conveyed back to Fleet Street, where he was taken out every day to inhale the fresh air in the meads and shady groves of the Strand, near the Maypole ("within the Libertie of Westminster"), or along the walks and gardens by which the pedestrian approached the mansions of our old nobility, who at that period loved the flowery banks of the clear and sparkling Thames.

His fifth year soon arrived, and memory began to dawn. He was then, so he said himself in after life—perhaps more philosophically, though less orthodoxically than he supposed —"in a kind of state of innocence, not knowing ill, nor so prone to it, as we become by the inclinations and temptations of a riper age;" and to this he is pleased to subjoin, "that to love and delight in such little children and their artless prattle is a testimony of good nature."

In the year following, the city air, wafted by an east wind to his abode, brought sickness with it, and his mother, who had proved his best nurse, now turned out to be his best doctor, using for her remedy some innocent decoction of balm or mint, or other herb possessing the virtue of leaving nature alone, and of not interfering with her healing power. "She did much good," said the pious and still grateful son, when speaking of this more than half a century later, "and practised great charity by her extraordinary skill in physic, whereby, with the blessing of God on her endeavours, she did many great cures in her own family, upon her sick friends and neighbours in the country, nay, most upon poor people, who had not means to gratify a doctor. Her only reward was their love and prayers, which she did never want." And he adds, admonishingly, to his daughters, "the like course is worthy of your study and practice."

Upon reaching his seventh year, his sturdy father, who had been one of the hardest students that Mulcaster ever reared at Merchant Tailors' School, and who was still fond of poring over the lumber of our mediæval laws, found leisure to argue with the fond mother, and overpower her with some Greek or Latin quotation respecting the value of time. The boy was put out to school. Long afterwards he justified this act of his father's by bidding his own children remember the Egyptian hieroglyphic for time—a serpent,—because Cyril says: "it is stretched out in length, and complicated in many circles, as the many series of days and years; it creeps tacitly away without any noise, nor can it be called back."

The chief reason with his worthy sire for considering this age the proper one for school was, it seems, because Hippocrates divides the age of man into seven parts, the first of which ends with the seventh year; a secondary reason he found in Varro, who makes a yet clearer division of the several ages—not that any other number could compete in propriety with the harmonious and mystic seven. So thought Shakspeare, and so thought the scholars of those days. Young Bulstrode was accordingly sent off to a boarding school, where he was to be educated after the fashion recommended by Paschalius. As our good laws are said by some sagacious modern declaimers to be the result of our pre-existing mal-administration, such as that which corrupted society in the reign of Charles II., so in like manner, just and liberal ideas spring up in youthful minds from the cruelty and injustice of pedagogues, and it has always been a favourite axiom with some ethical writers, that good comes out of evil. Reluctant to condemn this banishment from home, the memorialist takes refuge, like a true Oxonian, in authority, by relying on a passage of the great Bacon, respecting good observances, where he affirms, that "since custom is the principal magistrate of man's life, certainly custom is most perfect when it begins in young years, and this we call education, which is in effect but an early custom."

For the sake of this laudable custom, the boy was kept at school with the same severe and tyrannical master, who was accustomed to chastise his pupils a second time, should they ever fail to cry out on receiving the first castigation.

An accident occurred at last, which changed his destinies, by transferring him not to the sway of a milder potentate, but to a more eminent seat of scholastic discipline. The master of the school where he had been placed allowed great licence out of school hours, and neglected the old Roman custom of not permitting a boy of ten years old to walk through the city without some keeper to take care of him and restrain the rash impulses of youth. The boy found his way into a stable, being very fond of horses, when one of them with a sudden kick cut his upper lip asunder. Unskilfully treated by an ordinary barber-surgeon, he was removed home again, where his mother sewed the parts together with a needle and thread. The operation, though attended with prolonged suffering, was so successful in its results, that nothing remained to disfigure Bulstrode's face but a slight seam.

Had the blow fallen on his head, his life, he says, would have been in great danger, but the torment of the wound taught him due caution for the future.

Having accompanied his father to London, Bulstrode was placed by him at Merchant Tailors' School, where James Whitelocke had been educated himself, a school even then renowned for its good training and the sound learning it taught. Dr. Johnson sneers at the profession of a school-master, but the pedagogue was regarded in that age as something more than a merely useful member of society; and although the eminent masters who had thrown such lustre round this remarkable school had no hand in governing the nation, they did good service to the State by making many of their scholars fit to do so.

Here, besides his progress in "humane learning," his parents were very careful for his instruction in divine things, which is not to be wondered at, since his mother inclined to Puritanical views in religious matters. From boyhood he was accustomed by her to indulge in the utterance of pious sentiments. He has left not a few manuscripts on serious subjects, the fruit of his religious meditations and biblical studies in the original languages. In a future part of this work it may be considered advisable to cite a few passages culled from those writings, which show him to have been no contemptible Greek and Hebraic scholar, considering the age in which he lived.

On returning home daily at five o'clock after schoolhours, his father, who in his youth had worked incessantly till midnight, kept him close to his private studies, encouraging him by his own example, for he continued to the end of his life a hard and devoted student. Yet he was not so injudicious a parent as to deprive the boy of all exercise and recreation.

On attaining his thirteenth year the lad had grown into the favour of his master, and had secured the good-will of his schoolfellows. About this time an accident happened, which served to advance him yet higher in estimation, and which he himself, with the superstitious feeling of the age, deemed prophetical of his future fortune. There fell out a sore difference between the scholars of his own and those of Paul's school, which ended in a kind of civil war.* Whenever they met each other singly or in parties, the streets

---

* The boys did but imitate their elders at the Universities. Grievous were the discords that even then subsisted between the Northern and Southern scholars at Oxford, where dreadful conflicts were apt to break out between the Masters and the Undergraduates on points of discipline, or during contested elections. Dire was the scene in Cat Street during the vigils of St Kenelm, or between the regent cum non-regent masters and the commonalty of the scholars on the feast of St. Benedict; and it would appear from veracious chronicles, that it did not much matter what the saint's day was, when the opposing factions were bent on mischief. Similar brawls happened between the Company of Goldsmiths and that of Merchant Tailors, and the feud that estranged the Snips, or Scissors, from the Skinners, because one contended against the other for precedence among the Companies of London, still lives in the records of civic history. The Worshipful Company of Tailors formed a valiant fraternity of linen armourers, and Sir John Hawkewood was not the only knight of the shears to uphold the honour of the guild. We need not wonder then at finding the boys of their school so pugnacious.

of London were disturbed by savage and bloody combats. Strong beyond his years, our youthful hero was the head of his party, and manfully bore his part in these dangerous frays.

To suppress this intestine feud, and not unmindful of their peaceful and erudite monarch, who was well informed of all the incidents of the day in his "gude" town of London, the masters hit upon an expedient to heal the breach, probably suggested by our Scotch Solomon himself, who loved to interfere in small matters, while leaving the graver cares of state to his favourite "Steenie." An embassy was contrived for the purpose of pacification, and young Whitelocke was nominated *Princeps Legationis*. With a large train of his schoolfellows he accordingly marched through the streets to Paul's School, duly announced his arrival there, made his solemn entry like an ambassador into the school-room, where all the scholars and many other auditors were present, and was here received with many of those formal ceremonies that still delight diplomatists. He made an oration in Latin, which fortunately has not been preserved by the "Latiners" of the time; but it set forth the miseries of civil war and the benefits of peace, winding up with a proposition for steadfast amity, with a league offensive and defensive between the two republics. After a brief withdrawal he and his associates were readmitted, when they were answered by one of Paul's scholars in another Latin oration, in which the orator stated, that they had taken the amicable proposal into their serious deliberation, that they had found it acceptable, and had ratified it with their unanimous consent; whereupon some prefect called aloud, "*Plaudite*," and they were honourably dismissed. The event was looked upon as ominous, nor was it forgotten in after life.

The master of Merchant Tailors' School accustomed his scholars about this time to act and recite in public, with a view to impart confidence and courteous bearing, as well as

an aptitude for public speaking. When at home, young
Whitelocke was instructed in music, writing, dancing, fencing,
and short-hand. He became no unapt scholar in all these
various accomplishments, and was looked upon indeed as a
kind of prodigy.

When summer arrived, by way of reward for his diligence
and great progress, he was conveyed to Fawley Court, near
Henley in Buckinghamshire, an estate which his father had
purchased the year before of Sir William Alford. The stern
but useful lessons of scholastic discipline utterly failed him
here, and Bulstrode—an only son, the heir of this fine estate
—must have shown so strong a liking for natural recreation,
for woods and flowers and pure air, that it alarmed the
ambitious hopes of the father. The boy was accordingly
soon hurried up to town, and doomed to the study of the
law,—that too in the summer vacation, which made it all the
harder. His father, who was esteemed the fourth land-
owner in his county by virtue of his estate, happened to be
Reader of the Society of the Middle Temple, the labour and
charge of which is recorded in a MS. work of his own ; not
so the solid law and excellent learning to which he gave
utterance in that reading. The honour he shed on his
profession and the Middle Temple, together with the reputation he himself acquired, is, of course, studiously omitted in
his MS. narrative, and it was left for others to commemorate
his signal merits. The various professors of the law and the
different law societies desired and obtained copies of his
lectures. Indeed, it is quite evident from his brilliant career,
that the Reader had fairly earned his fame, and had by his
great learning disarmed the hostility of King James, who
watched the doings of lawyers, magistrates, and aldermen
with a most jealous eye. To this reading or lecture the
father admitted our young student of law as a member of
the Society of the Middle Temple. The reading term being
over, they both returned to Fawley Court, from which place
he was sent to Oxford to be entered of that university. He

was principally recommended to the care and supervision of Dr. Laud, afterwards so famous, who at that date was President of St. John's, and who in the same college had been the contemporary and early friend of his father. Here Dr. Laud discharged his trust with fidelity, and appointed Dr. Parsons, a physician, a discreet and learned person, to be the young man's tutor.

At the early age of sixteen his studies of philosophy and logic commenced, and were closely followed up; he took notes diligently, but did not ultimately preserve many of them for the use of his children, so many printed helps being available. Dr. Laud kept a strict account of his studies, had him constantly at his lodging and examined him privately. As for his tutor, this worthy man was not satisfied with merely reading to his pupil, but made it a rule to converse with him about the current topics of the day, treating him indeed as his companion.

Besides his university learning, he took pleasure in the study of history, particularly that of England. Some of his notes made at the college have been published, and may be consulted by any one curious in such matters, at most of our great public libraries where copies are kept. Whatever theoretical speculations he may have entertained on this head, the discretion of his tutor prevented him from uttering them. The laws were then so watchfully and jealously administered by the members of the Star Chamber, by the censor, and the king's attorney, ever alive to the treasonable nature of truth, that we need not suppose much of this then rare and contraband commodity was preserved at Oxford. Here too he frequented some music meetings, in which his proficiency made him acceptable. For his recreation abroad, he became acquainted with Mr. Juxon, originally a scholar of Merchant Tailors', then a commoner in St. John's College, who afterwards as Bishop of London attended Charles I. on the scaffold, and subsequently was made Lord Treasurer and Archbishop of Canterbury.

But at present Mr. Juxon was the humble parson of Somerton in Oxfordshire, seemingly happy and devoted to the agreeable sport of hunting, which he indulged in for the sake of preserving his health, that had become slightly impaired by intense study. Mr. Juxon taught him moreover some of the woodman's craft, and his pupil preserved to the end of his life a fondness for the sports of the field.

In his seventeenth year he was preparing to take his degree of B.A., when another serious accident occurred to him and put an end to his academic pursuits. By this time, Laud having been made a dean, was succeeded by Juxon in his presidency, whose new dignity caused him to eschew hunting in company with commoners now become his subjects. To supply his loss in the field, young Whitelocke associated himself with Master Wright, son of Sir George Wright ; Mr. Allen, afterwards Sir Thomas Allen ; Mr. Bennet, afterwards Sir Thomas Bennet ; and his brother, who became Sir Humphrey Bennet ; a Mr. Dixons, a Mr. Mayes, and several other young gentlemen of the same college. They maintained a small pack of beagles, and hunted in company, but were neither so careful nor moderate as when they were directed by older heads. Bulstrode's father tied him down to rather a short allowance, so that he was not rich enough to keep a horse, and hence he hunted mostly on foot, often walking six or ten miles to the place where sport was expected. Taking this violent exercise, he one day sprained his leg, and before it was quite well, sprained it again, when finding his powers exhausted, he lay down on the ground in a meadow near Islip. Here, weary to the last degree, he fell into a slumber, and slept for about two hours. On awaking, having lain so long on the cold, moist earth, his sprained leg was so benumbed and stiff that he could not stand, much less crawl from the spot to obtain help. Fortunately he carried a hunting horn, and with this he "wound a call," which soon brought his comrades to his side, fancying he had found sport. On seeing his sad state,

they procured a horse to carry him to the next town, and
from there he was sent in a cart to Oxford. Of course
Dr. Parsons put forth the whole of his medical skill, and
every physician in and around the "seat of all human
learning" was called in and consulted. All the advice that
these learned brethren could give was bestowed, all the
resources of their venerable art were employed, and much
physic, "many sweatings," such as would have attenuated
Hercules and annihilated a modern prize-fighter, together
with huge cataplasms were tried. The lameness grew only
the worse in the hollow of his thigh, and the torture
increased. He was lifted and carried by men from place
to place, from his bed to his seat, and when weary from his
seat to his bed again. The skill and science of Oxford
fairly broke down, and the power of medicine succumbed.
On this occasion the worthy Doctor Parsons seems to have
suspected as much, and did what he should have done at
first ; he sent word of the event, and described the case to
the sufferer's mother at Fawley Court ; she then instantly
sent the old coach for her son, with a bed and pillows inside
prepared for him. Into this he was stowed, and after a
rough journey of some hours reached home a sad cripple,
and was received on the threshold by his afflicted parents.
Although he was pronounced incurable by the Faculty of
Oxford, his mother was yet willing to be comforted ; she
was no admirer of Oxonian orthodoxy, and without loss of
time sent for one Dr. Mathias, a German by birth and
education, who, practising in London without any licence
from the Archbishop of Canterbury, was regarded in consequence as a quack by his brother Galens of England. But
he enjoyed much repute in London with the citizens, and
his skill was now to be put to the test in young Whitelocke's
case. After inspecting the leg, he said that nature had
formed a jelly in the hollow of the bone, in consequence of
the cold taken in the joint by lying on the damp ground
after the sprain. Having delivered this oracular explanation,

he set about the cure, first proceeding to write his prescription in broken English. In this he prescribed a liquor made from a large quantity of muscadine, to which there was to be added a fair proportion of ox-marrow together with various herbs, all of which, steeped in so much water, was to be boiled for a certain time. Then he caused a brick to be made red-hot in the fire. Slaking this in the liquor, he wrapped it in a napkin and applied it to the spot where the pain was most acute. As soon as one brick cooled, another succeeded it in the same manner and place; and this application was continued steadily for ten days every morning and evening.

The sufferer thus learnedly and gratefully explains the operation and its salutary effects in an account subsequently drawn up for the information of his children:

"The bricks first soaked up the liquor, which was strengthening and mollifying, and then by fumigation and infusing the liquor into the lame part, the pain in that time was very much assuaged and my strength renewed, so that I was able to go with crutches, and in a short time left them off. Then I walked with a staff, but in a little time I cast that away too, and was well cured. The particulars hereof I have inserted, in a thankful remembrance of God's goodness to me, and to admonish you, my children, to be careful to avoid the like mischiefs, and for a remedy in the like accidents, and for the credit of the worthy doctor."

CHAPTER II.

—◆—

1623—1626.

Resumes his Legal Studies, and has for Associates Hyde, Maynard, Palmer, and other
  Men of subsequent Celebrity—Cultivates elegant Accomplishments—Marriage
  of his Sister Elizabeth to Mr. Roger Mostyn—Forms the Acquaintance of Selden
  —Desires to travel abroad; advised to see "Crowland" first—Accompanies the
  Judges on Circuit—Accession of Charles I.—His arbitrary Acts—Arrival of the
  Queen—Adjournment of the Parliament to Oxford in consequence of the Plague
  in London—First Causes of Dissension between the King and the Parliament—
  Disgrace of Lord Keeper Williams—Coronation of Charles I.

AT the time of his recovery he was eighteen years of age.
He returned to London to be in commons in the Middle
Temple as before, and quietly set himself down to study the
common law. It was his good fortune to make the acquaintance at this period of many students who became celebrated
in after life, and whose names are familiar to every reader
of English history. There was Mr. Geoffrey Palmer, his
cousin, who was afterwards made a baronet and the King's
Attorney, Mr. Richard Solme, and Mr. Bartholomew Hall ;
Mr. Maynard, who was subsequently knighted, created King's
Serjeant, then Lord Keeper, and who lived to see the Revolu-
tion of 1688 ; Mr. Hyde, who became Lord Chancellor,
Earl of Clarendon, and the grandfather of two queens; Mr.
Tichborne, son of Sir Walter Tichborne ; Mr. Freake, son of
Sir Thomas Freake; Mr. Robert Hide, afterwards Lord Chief
Justice of the King's Bench ; Mr. John L'Isle, son of Sir
William L'Isle, who became one of the Commissioners of the
Great Seal in the time of the troubles, and met with a
melancholy fate in Switzerland ; Mr. Hoskins, son of Ser-
jeant Hoskins, with many more of the same society. Then

there were others belonging to the other Inns, as Mr. Grimston, afterwards Master of the Rolls ; Mr. Hale, the illustrious Chief Baron, and afterwards Chief Justice ; Mr. Fountain, subsequently a serjeant, with many others of less note.   Young as our Templar was, he took care to converse and associate with the best students, and gained no small advantage from his intercourse with these gifted men ; but ambitious also of mixing with the gay world, he perfected himself in fencing, dancing, vaulting, and riding the great horse, and thereby brought on a slight return of his former lameness, from which indeed he occasionally suffered for the rest of his life.   In music he grew to be quite a master, for his father Sir James, who was skilled in vocal music, and who had weekly concerts at his house in Fleet Street, caused his son and two daughters to be thoroughly taught this accomplishment.   At this period also he resumed his historical studies.

When he had reached his nineteenth year, his sister Elizabeth was married to the son and heir of Sir Roger Mostyn, of Mostyn, in Flintshire.   The bride's father gave her a portion of 2500*l.*, no inconsiderable sum in that age, and Sir Roger settled on his son a noble estate of 3000*l.* a year.   But the old gentleman allowed only a narrow provision for present maintenance and jointure, which caused his son to run into debt ; and our Templar, who reverted to this when an old man, was liberal enough to write : " It is an occasion of much prejudice to young men to be kept too strait, whilst their fathers are alive."   This was a great match for the quality and estate of the family ; but great matches do not always prove the most comfortable,—at least not in this case, for although the young man was of a " high spirit and good nature when out of passion, he was not well fixed, nor over kind."

Shortly after this event, Sir James Whitelocke was removed from his chief justiceship of Chester and the Welsh Marches to be a judge of the King's Bench.   This removal led indirectly to a contact with the great Selden, "that admirable learned man in his age." From him Bulstrode received good counsel and encouragement in his studies, and, although he does not own it, a great bias to his political opinions. Selden gave him at that early period some golden rules : "Not to neglect the study of men, but to be as often as he could in the company of 'ingenious'* and learned men, from whom he might gain as much by conversation as he could by the study of books." His second rule was : "That however late he should be in company at night, to read somewhat on his return home, so that there should be *nulla dies sine lineâ.*" The third rule was : "To be careful in the choice of what books he read ; not to waste his time about common, known, or impertinent matters, but to study the most profitable learning, that which is not ordinary— except in such points of law as are alike to all ; yet even in this to acquire a more special knowledge than what was commonly studied, not forgetting, of course, the useful and general points also." Fourthly : "That what he read and judged useful, to be sure and make himself master of it, not lightly pass it over, but to take such course and notes, that he might find it again when occasion required." Fifthly, and especially, he recommended to him the study of English history, of records, of ancient manuscripts, and to compare them with the year-books and printed histories, by which course both the one and the other would be the better under- stood. What a satire on our many careless compilations, dignified with the title of history ! How long shall we consent to be duped by ignorant and fulsome productions, composed, for the most part, for the purpose of misleading mankind by suppressing or distorting facts, by putting a patriotic construction on crimes, by glossing over vices, and by exalting mediocrity—to serve the ends of party ? But Selden did not confine himself to the mere bestowal of

---

* This word was commonly used for "ingenuous" by the writers of the seventeenth century.

advice, for he gave him lessons and general instruction in
the Oriental tongues and other branches of knowledge. The
veteran jurist liked the company of his junior so well, that
he allowed him the free range of his well stored library. Of
this privilege Whitelocke often availed himself, enhanced as
it was by the frequent enjoyment of the incomparably learned
conversation and direction of the owner. This proved a
source of contentment for the rest of his life, and was at
that time a decided furtherance to him in his studies.

In the midst of this hopeful course he was overtaken with
a "vain humour," as he quaintly calls it, which was allayed
by the wisdom of his father ; this was a desire to travel
beyond seas, and to gratify which he asked leave. The old
gentleman, who had never perhaps entered a ship in his life,
answered his son's request by telling him a tale, as he called
it, of the Lord Treasurer Burleigh, who when his son wished
to travel asked him if he had ever seen Crowland in his own
country. And when the son desired to know the reason of
such a question, the father replied, that in Crowland and other
parts of England there were rarities quite as observable, and
monuments of antiquity equally worthy of admiration, as in
any other part of the world. These he wished him to see
first. Our young law student understood the hint, and
therefore humbly asked leave, that in the first place he might
be allowed to travel in his own country. He even himself
suggested that as his father was on the bench, he might
obtain, through him, the favour of the other judges, and be
allowed to attend them in their several circuits. He pleaded,
that in this way he should be enabled to see all the principal
places and persons in the various counties, besides gaining
some improvement in the knowledge of circuit business
proper for his professional knowledge. His father liked the
motion, and procured the consent thereto of his brethren on
the bench. An old friend and neighbour, Sir Cope D'Oiley,
(of whose family estate Whitelocke became at an after period
the purchaser, but which King Charles II. compelled him to

c

re-sell in order that he might extort the purchase-money)
bestowed a good nag upon him,—a most acceptable present,
particularly at that time, for it was the first horse he ever
possessed—and the kindness of the act was indelibly
imprinted on his memory.

Being fitted out for his journey, he rode this year (1624)
two circuits, one in the Lent, the other in the summer
vacation. He was treated with much kindness and civility
by the judges, counsellors, officers attending circuit, and by
the gentlemen of the several counties, which "he could not
but remember with due gratitude to them." He carried
with him on his journey Camden's "Britannia" and Speed's
History with the maps ; in every place he compared the information contained in books with that which he received from
the respective inhabitants. By this course he gained a sound
knowledge of all that was really memorable ; and sometimes
when the judges were sitting long in one town, he would
make short journeys and meet them again at the next
rendezvous. All his notes are still preserved, and it is clear
from their perusal, that he kept up his knowledge of the
law by freely conversing at meals and other meetings with
the members of the long robe, where cases were constantly
put and technically discussed. Such practice must prove as
advantageous to a young lawyer as playing in a band to a
young musician, imparting in each case confidence as well as
nice tact. On his return he entered his twentieth year, and
performed some exercises at Motes in the house and Inns of
Chancery, according to the orders of the society, for his
degree of Utter Barrister. He found time for resuming
those accomplishments, that were at that time more highly
prized than perhaps they are worth, and gratified his father
by his constant attendance at his chamber in Serjeant's Inn.
In the evening, at the frequent music meetings given by the
father, his children were accustomed to sustain their parts,
and indeed often composed music themselves.

This year he went two fresh circuits, explored the forest

of Dean, and nearly lost his life by crossing the rapid river Wye with his groom and horses in a flat-bottomed boat ferried across by a woman, who used a singular sort of scoop to propel it. It was in this year also that he completed his abridgment of the whole history of England, " which," as he says, " though it were made and finished at several times, yet a good part of it was in this year." He recommended the perusal of this abstract many years afterwards to his children, observing, that " at this time the following notes of our public story, wherewith the ensuing annals are necessarily intermixed, will be the better and the more fully understood by you."

In Bulstrode's twentieth year King James I. died,* and at his funeral his successor, Charles I., *contrary to precedent* (a thing that somewhat shocked a common lawyer even at that epoch) was present ; and shortly after the Duke of Buckingham was received by the king into an "admired intimacy and dearness."

The question then at issue and agitating men's minds was, whether the late king had died a natural death or not. From much that appears in the "Liber Familicus" of Sir James Whitelocke, the reader might be strongly inclined to believe, that foul practices were resorted to, and that the fate of James I., in this respect, was somewhat analogous to that of Charles II.

The accession of the new king was signalised by arbitrary and illegal acts from the very beginning. There were general musters in all the counties, and 12,000 soldiers were levied. "Coat-money" and "conduct money" were ordered to be disbursed by the country, the sums to be reimbursed out of the Exchequer. Charles and his father's ex-minion, Buckingham, knew that these doings were deliberate violations of the English constitution. They knew that there was no intention of ever repaying from the Exchequer the sums thus extorted, but that, on the con-

* On the 28th of March, 1625.

c 2

trary, schemes were being proposed to the Lord Treasurer
for issuing a large amount of brass money to be compulsorily
current as silver.   Again, to increase the infamy of the act,
the troops so levied were to be sent to the Palatinate to serve
as foreign, not as English soldiers.   The King granted a
commission for Martial Law to keep those sold conscripts in
better discipline.   Our student was present at frequent
debates concerning these points of Coat and Conduct money
and this pretended Martial Law, when he heard the opinions
of his father, of the other judges and learned men who
debated on them, and he cautiously subjoins : "They much
improved my knowledge."

The King's marriage with the sister of the King of France
soon followed.   The ceremonial of espousals took place in
Paris, presided over by Cardinal Richelieu, with the highest
state, feasting, and bravery that could be displayed.   The
English people little dreamed, perhaps Charles himself did
not know (for Englishmen are willing to give him the benefit
of the doubt, to which the duplicity of his subsequent career
almost disentitles him) that the future Queen of England,
Henrietta Maria, had contracted a solemn obligation with
the Pope and her brother the King of France to educate
her children as Roman Catholics, and to choose Roman
Catholics only to be in attendance upon them.   Dejected
as the English people were at this period, it is difficult to
believe they would ever have suffered the Queen to sit as
consort on her husband's throne, if they had suspected this,
a fact which was first published in the form of a document
many years afterwards in the *Ambassades du Maréchal de
Bassompierre (tom. iii. p. 49).*   It became secretly known
to our future statesman before the accession of Richard
Cromwell to the Protectorate, and this serves to explain
much of his dislike to the restoration of the second Charles.

After the arrival of the Queen, under the escort of the
Duke of Buckingham, when some " extraordinary " solemnities and ceremonies were omitted, which the people charitably

ascribed to the plague at that time raging with increased violence, the King evinced his fixed purpose of subverting the old order of things. By his command, the Lord Keeper Williams convoked all the judges, and told them that His Majesty desired to change his style ; to use for the future that of " King of Great Britain " in all legal acts and proceedings, in acts of State and in different Acts ; he prayed the judges to consider of it, and to certify to him how this might be done. They all met, consulted together and agreed that it could not be done ; and they further informed the Keeper, through the Chief Justice Montague, that their predecessors having been asked their opinions on the same point in the first Parliament of King James I., had unanimously declared the same thing, with which judgment the Lords and Commons had concurred.* During the debates and discourses among the judges on this subject, at which great freedom was allowed in a confidential way, our student was also permitted to be present, his discretion being well known.

The parliament met at Westminster, and pressed the grievances of the nation, when the plague again interfered with their proceedings—conveniently enough as the young king supposed, for he adjourned the session to Oxford. It availed him but little, however, and equally so his attempt to keep the body of his own privy council in the dark as to the fact, that he had lent the *Vanguard* and seven other English ships to the King of France, compelling the mariners, notwithstanding their repugnance, to serve against the Protestants at Rochelle ; and although the latter sent him a petition to forbear, he imperiously and expressly commanded the vice-admiral, Pennington, to obey orders, which the loyal seaman reluctantly complied with. The Parliament, now at Oxford, justly incensed at this proceeding, fell foul of the Duke—whose conduct would appear to be

---

* The policy of the executive was right in this instance, but the nation had not been prepared to appreciate its importance.

inexplicable but for some secret attachment to the cause of
France—and they summoned Dr. Montague, one of the
King's chaplains, to the bar. The question of "Divine
Right" and absolute monarchy was at issue here, when of
course the bishops assured the king that should the Church
be once brought down below herself, even the Crown itself
would soon be impeached, and they further maintained that
his father, James, had approved Dr. Montague's opinions.
The truth of the latter assertion was disbelieved by the public,
but the knowledge we now have of James's character renders it not unlikely that the bishops spoke truth upon this
occasion. Be that as it may, neither party felt inclined to
yield ; the king would not grant redress, and as the
Commons would not vote supplies without it, they were
dissolved by commission.

An inexplicable course of policy now ensues. Notwithstanding the refusal of subsidies, the king prosecutes his
design of the war, equips his fleet for sea, makes a league
with the United Provinces against the Emperor and the
King of Spain, and issues a proclamation to recall the
children of recusants from beyond sea—a most intolerant
act, but only too much in accordance with the spirit of that
age. Then he fulminates against popish priests with singular
inconsistency, when we reflect that he had many in his own
palace, and recalls all Englishmen in the service of the
Emperor, the King of Spain, and the Archduchess. Such a
line of policy could only have been instigated by the duke
from passionate motives, and not from the king's pretended
sense of honour, because a late Parliament had induced his
father to side with the Palatinate and come to a breach with
Spain. Had the policy now adopted been really in behalf
of Protestantism, he would never have issued the orders he
did to the vice-admiral, Pennington ; and setting aside the
interests of his own people, whom Charles at this time most
thoroughly despised, it is hardly conceivable that he should
have oscillated between his affection for his sister in the

Palatinate on the one hand, and his love for his wife, who seems to have ruled him from the very first, on the other. Thereupon he sends out his letters to the lord-lieutenants of counties, touching a general loan of money to him, and gives warrants for the disarming of recusants. What crime had the latter class of persecuted persons committed—so few in numbers, so weak in influence? It was a vain attempt to divert popular indignation; for when the fleet was ready, and ten regiments, with Lord Wimbledon for their commander, went on board, and when it was divulged that the design was known only to the duke, not to the council, and that Buckingham himself did not intend to go, "the mutterings of the people became loud and general."

It is evident from the brief enumeration of these events in our student's diary—although he abstains as usual from all comment—how deep was the impression they produced at the time in the minds of rising men. As Bulstrode was even at this time bestowing great attention on our foreign relations, and was only restrained by deference to his father's wishes from visiting the continent, the mere recital of these and similar arbitrary deeds must have caused in his mind deep discontent, the more lasting because necessarily suppressed and concealed. Well, the expedition was disgracefully managed, and returned from Rochelle with ignominy. A universal clamour arose, the council itself examined the commander, and it turned out that the officers had no orders to fight. "This fending and proving little salved the honour of the nation," but to amuse it her merchants were prohibited from trading with Spain upon pain of confiscation of their merchandise, and the trained bands were exercised— not surely in expectation of another Armada.

In the meantime the plague raged in London to that degree, that 5000 persons died there in one week, and the disease spread rapidly to many places in the country. The demoralisation that usually ensues after the appearance of a pestilence had long begun. Henley-on-Thames, which was quite close to Sir James's house at Fawley Court, was infected, and at the village of Kemenham, opposite to his abode, the mortality was quite appalling. An entire family, consisting of Mr. and Mrs. Clutterbook, their children and servants, was swept away. Overcome with dread, for the nature of the pestilence was then even less understood than it is at the present day, the old gentleman acted, as many in later times did during the prevalence of the cholera. He kept his people retired at home and his doors shut, prevented all ingress, and if money had to be paid (for it was harvest-time), a tub of water was set without doors, the money first dropped into it, and then taken out by the parties who were to receive it. But by the time the intensity of the plague was somewhat diminished—when only 2500 persons had died in London during the week—it fell to the judge's turn to go to Westminster Hall and adjourn the Michaelmas Term from that place to Reading. Such an expedition seemed as fearfully fraught with danger as a visit to the fabled Upas-tree growing in the valley of death, and the judge for once stood in nearly the same predicament as a condemned criminal. Yet go he must, nor shrink from his duty.

It required great importunity on the part of the son to obtain his father's consent to wait upon him, which he generously averred he wished " on account of the danger," but in reality to cheer the old man. They came the first day to Horton, near Colnebrook, to the house of his uncle Bulstrode, and next morning early drove on to Hyde Park Corner, where they all dined on the ground with such meat and drink as they had brought in the coach. After the old heroic process of " filling themselves," and leaving the saddle-horses behind, they drove " fast" through the streets to Westminster Hall, where the officers were ready. The court was promptly adjourned, the judge returned, and they again reached Horton that night. A religious feeling of contrition in some measure justifies the panic then existing, for the annalist observes : "It was a sad spectacle to see the streets overgrown with grass, and empty of people. It was one of the woes denounced by God on those that break his commandments (Lev. xxvi. 22), that their highways should be desolate (Isa. xxxiii. 8 ; Amos v. 16). Alas! alas! thus it was in England for our sins, and we know not how soon it may be so again,* unless we earnestly repent of them." All were not so considerate as the young man, for many deemed it a visitation of God, who punished the king by vicariously chastising his people. This doctrine—a favourite one in all ages, has made many a leader undeservedly odious. No one seems ever to have suspected that the sin was that of general uncleanliness, of bad sanitary regulations, of miasma arising from an entire want of drainage and ventilation.

About this period an eminent prelate was disgraced—no other than the Bishop of Lincoln, the Lord Keeper Williams ; this was caused by his demeanour towards the Duke of Buckingham, at the Parliament in Oxford, and the offence was duly remembered. It did not cause much sensation, as the sheriff question was then engrossing public attention, and feeding the general discontent ; but it led to Laud's promotion and lamentable influence.

The term being kept at Reading, Whitelocke attended as reporter in the King's Bench, and went to the court almost daily from Fawley. On one of these occasions his frame sustained a severe shock by his overturning the coach ; for, "forgetting the story of Phaeton," he took it into his head to drive four lusty horses, without possessing the skill of a practised charioteer.

Political events continued to absorb his attention, and he now alludes to them in his Annals far more frequently than at first. He refers to the king having called another Parliament, because he found that the discontent of his subjects

---

* This prophetic supposition was correct, for a far more dreadful plague raged in London in 1664 and the two succeeding years.

increased, and points out that the old *ruse* was previously resorted to. The bishops were commanded to proceed against the Papists by excommunication, and the king gave out, hypocritically enough, that he had determined on leaving Montague to the Parliament, "to the great regret of Bishop Laud," who was now gradually creeping into the king's favour, since the disgrace of Williams.

The coronation of the king is fixed for Christmas-day, and commissioners are appointed to receive and determine claims concerning services to be done. Knights of the Bath are to be made, and proclamation made for every one having 40*l.* per annum to come in and receive the order of knighthood.*

A day of thanksgiving was kept for the ceasing of the plague in London and the outparishes, after it had swept away 35,417 persons. Henceforward fasts became very frequent and predominated over the festivals; but although proceeding from mistaken piety, they were at least sincere. Something of king-craft is visible in the selection of Christmas-day for the coronation of Charles; it was performed, as was generally supposed, with the usual ceremonies,† by Bishop Laud, but the king wore a robe of white satin,

---

* This occasioned Bulstrode to inquire into the point: why men should be summoned to take the order of knighthood, and he found that, generally, all tenants who held of the king, or of any mesne lord by knight's service, were both called knights, might be summoned by king's writ to take the order, and might be amerced, if they did not appear on the day appointed for that purpose. He has written three columns of legal notes about this service, but they are no longer of any value, as all the old enactments concerning knighthood were subsequently abrogated by the Act passed 17 Car. i. c. 20.

† This, however, was not strictly the case, for in Laud's diary, as brought forward against him at the trial, it appeared that he had altered part of the king's oath taken at his coronation, in a most material point about passing such laws as the people should choose, which he left out, and added a saving of the king's prerogative in the oath. In short, the king did not take the oath so fully as his predecessors had done, in order that when the parliament might tender to him any unpalatable laws for the royal assent, he might answer that he was not by oath obliged to confirm them. At that coronation, on account of the plague, he issued a proclamation, in which he promised to dispense with the attendance of those knights, that by an old statute were bound to be present at the ceremony. A few months after, he took advantage of their absence, and raised a vast sum of money out of their estates at the Council Board. When they pleaded the proclamation as their justification, they were curtly answered—that the law of the land was superior to any proclamation.

"because, *as some say*, purple was not to be had." This
introduction of the qualified term—"some say"—seems to
imply that such was not the true reason. Is there anything
papistical in white satin? And did the narrator suppose
that Laud or Buckingham had made some innovation with a
Jesuitical object?

A Frenchman once wrote a book to show that many of
the greatest wars owed their origin to trifles, and the historian who enters upon the analysis of any reign or period
fruitful of great results, cannot afford to neglect what at first
sight may seem a very trivial matter. Forms and ceremonies
that in modern times excite contempt, or at the best are
looked upon as the germs of solid rights and privileges not
yet developed, were then regarded as symbols or signs that
it might be impious to reason upon. Gog and Magog struck
mystic terror into the breasts of many of the citizens—the
presence or absence of a candlestick, and whether the candle
itself should be of wax or tallow were matters in connection
with which a great many venerable men were willing to endure
martyrdom ; and to this day your profane tallow is pro-
scribed at Merchant Taylors' School. It is sufficient to read
Laud's diary to see the great value he attached to what
would now be regarded as puerile and fantastic ; and even
the father of our Templar, in his old age, Sir James Whitelocke, the judge, a man in many things of the most liberal,
enlightened, and generous nature, made a kind of essay to
ascertain the disposition of his grandchild, then an infant in
its nurse's arms, that would shock a modern psychologist.
But this circumstance will be related in its proper place.
In reading the history of this period we must ever remember
that most of the ideas then prevalent as respects both public
and private life were based on the grossest ignorance and
folly. Folly itself was constantly dressed up in the garb of
wisdom ; it was personified at court in the person of a professional fool, whose rank, position, and usefulness surpassed
that of even many a modern official. Archie, the most cele-

brated of all, received a fee of 10s. from every new mad
knight, and must consequently have realised a small fortune
by every batch of them, from each of whom the heralds and
other court brethren of the fool extracted no less a sum that
44l. 17s. in the days of King James, himself a true personifi
cation of folly and misrule.

CHAPTER III.

—◆—

1626—1628.

Bulstrode chosen Member for Stafford—Charges made in Parliament against the Duke of Buckingham—Whitelocke joins in the Remonstrance against "Tonnage and Poundage"—Parliament Dissolved—Bulstrode called to the Bar—Proceedings in the Star Chamber—Disputes in the Royal Household, and Dismissal of the Queen's French Retinue—Abortive Expedition to the Isle of Rhé—Asssassination of Buckingham—Bulstrode's Quixotic Adventure—Treaty of marriage with Miss Willcox broken off—His Journey to the Western Counties—Extracts from his *Iter Occidentale.*

BUT another Parliament was now assembled, of which our young Templar was a member. Although still a mere law student, and unknown to fame, he was returned as a burgess by two boroughs, that of Stafford, and that of Brigge, in Yorkshire. At the former place his election was secured by the local influence of a Mr. Cradocke, and at the latter by that of Sir Humphrey May, the Chancellor of the Duchy, both of whom were his father's ancient and hearty friends. By parental advice he waived the representation of Brigge, and took his seat for Stafford, having for his colleague one Sir John Offley. He received good counsel, after assuming his new dignity, concerning his demeanour in Parliament, was told, no doubt, that he must not crow nor bray, and was exhorted to leave the gallery, which was then held to be the resort of mutineers, where he had hitherto taken his seat by the bye. As for his vote, this was left to his conscience, and it was seldom given to the court party ; but he refused to identify himself with any party or faction.

He looked upon the Parliament of England, he says, as

the best school in Christendom—was constant in his attendance—was frequently on committees—took notes of all that
passed, and bequeathed them as heir-looms to bear record of
how he acted.   Being an eye' and ear witness of all those
great transactions—involving as they did the future destinies
of the country—he was enabled to relate them with the more
confidence ; and this diligence procured him much knowledge, besides experience in public affairs.   He had to compete with many members of great abilities.   At that time
the House of Commons boasted of such members as Sir
Edward Coke, Sir Thomas Wentworth, Sir John Eliot,
Sir John Savill, Sir Dudley Digges, Sir Edwin Sandys, Sir
Robert Phillips, not to speak of Noy, Littleton, Selden, Pym,
Hampden, Hollis, and many others; a goodly array, of whom
many still hold high rank amongst England's worthies.

A few words uttered in this Parliament in a speech by
Mr. Clement Coke, formed the key-note of all that subsequently occurred.   The words in question made a lasting
impression, and the more so from their being brief and
pointed : " It is better to die by an enemy, than suffer at
home ! "   Such being the temper of the House and the
country, it may be supposed that the shallow king-craft of
the monarch—his pretended proclamations about Papist
recusants—his fine words about the honour and defence of
the land, which was being notoriously neglected, were clearly
seen through and appreciated at their proper value.

They were told that his Majesty had called them together
to make good laws, and to execute justice.   They took him
at his words, but reversed their order.   The supplies last,
the grievances first.   They complained, moreover, of national
disgrace ; of Popish influence now upon the increase ; that
the narrow seas were not guarded ; that pluralists were
allowed to be (meaning by this pre-eminently the Duke) ;
that honours and places of judicature were sold ; that ships
had been delivered up to the French; and, lastly, that three
subsidies and three fifteenths had been misemployed.   Now

the King knew, and his prime minister, the Duke of Buckingham, also knew, that every one of these complaints was well founded. Then the House ordered that the Duke should have due notice of what was intended, and that their complaints were chiefly referable to himself.

His Majesty did not attempt to refute these accusations; he alone was capable of redressing such grievances; and yet with a degree of fatuity, that baffles comprehension, told the House that they themselves must do so; that he would not permit any of his servants to be questioned among them, far less any of those that were in eminent place; he saw, he said, that they especially aimed at the Duke, and wondered what could have so changed their affections towards him. And then he threatened them in the following terms:—

"I would you would hasten for my supply, or else it will be worse for yourselves; for if any evil happens, I think I shall be the last that shall feel it." This prophecy was not however literally fulfilled, for he was certainly not the last. Everyone, even Sir Thomas Wentworth, who was not yet bought over to the crown, suspected that Popish counsellors had suggested the King's speech, and by his advice, as well as that of Selden—that of Noy too, one of the blackest king's attornies subsequently that ever prosecuted a truth-speaking Englishman—the House voted: "That common fame is a good ground of proceedings for that house."* Not that proofs were wanting to exhibit the corrupt conduct of the Duke and other eminent persons in place, but at that stage, it would have been cruel to betray the names of their witnesses, and expose them to the tender mercies of the Star-chamber.

A taste of what would have been their fate was given them by a message from the throne, that the King took notice of Mr. Coke's "seditious speech and Dr. Turner's articles

---

* A more dangerous maxim can hardly be conceived, for any wise man to act upon, but the blind spirit of party did not see what a two-edged weapon it might prove.

against the Duke of Buckingham, but indeed against the honour
and government of himself and his father." Stern passages
presently ensued, for neither side felt disposed to flinch.
The Earl of Bristol was impeached, and eleven articles
presented against him, ten of which were upon his alleged
Popish machinations in connection with the Court of Spain.
It was, however, not the House, but the Attorney-General
that accused him; not because he had been the transgressor
implied, but evidently in consequence of his having himself
previously impeached the all-powerful Duke.

The articles against his Grace were thirteen in number. Nor
was Lord Conway, the Duke's creature, forgotten, for he likewise had become implicated in the charge. Among the various
items, the Duke was stated to have frequented, when in Spain,
the services of the Romish Church; to have adored their
sacrament, and conformed to their rites. The fourth and
fifth articles were the most serious : That he procured King
James to write a letter to the Pope for the dispensation, and
to style him " Sanctissime Pater ; " that the Pope sent a bull
to the Duke to encourage him in the perversion of the Prince.
All this encouraged the Commons to act; and at a conference with the Lords, they brought their impeachment of
the Duke. It was managed by eight of their members, and
Sir Dudley Digges made a magniloquent peroration, in which
he compared the Commons to the earth and sea ; England
itself to the world ; the King to the sun ; the Lords to the
planets ; the Clergy to the fire (alluding, possibly, to the
odium theologicum) ; the judges and magistrates to the air ;
but the Duke of Buckingham to a blazing star.*

The Duke was further accused of having monopolised and
sold great offices ; of having bought the office of Admiral
from the Earl of Nottingham with the King's money, not his

---

* Because comets were believed to portend the ruin of kings, the downfall of states,
and great national disasters. See Milton's beautiful lines on the subject, which escaped
so narrowly the fatal shears of the censor. The comparison as a whole is not original,
as the reader may see by referring to that extraordinary composition preserved in our
English Bible as a sort of dedication to King James.

own; also those held by the Warden of the Cinque Ports and the Constable of Dover in the same way : that he had neglected his duty as Admiral, since the coasts were infested by pirates; that he had obtained by fraud and force the sum of 20,000*l.* from a ship called the *Peter* of Newhaven ; had extorted 10,000*l.* from the East India merchants, by arresting their ships ; had compelled other Englishmen to give into the hands of the French king the *Vanguard* and six other vessels, for the purpose of being employed, with the Duke's previous knowledge, against Rochelle ; that he had sold honours and titles, and compelled Lord Roberts by threats to pay 10,000*l.* for his title, which sum was paid ; that he had sold the office of Lord Treasurer to Lord Manchester for 20,000*l.*, and the Mastership of Wards to Sir Lionel Cranfield for 6000*l.*; that he had procured titles and pensions for his kindred and allies from the King ; that he had embezzled the King's money, and obtained large grants of the Crown lands for his own emolument—the gifts amounting, as far as could be ascertained, to no less a sum than 284,395*l.* Lastly, that the plaister and potions which the Duke caused to be given to King James in his sickness, justified "a transcendant presumption of a dangerous consequence."

The King, had the Duke been innocent of these charges, should have maintained his implied promise inviolate, given to the Commons at the opening of the session, in which he called upon them to execute justice ; and he should have remembered his other promise of allowing to the members the privilege of Parliament, freedom of debate and access to his royal person. Instead of so acting, as a prudent monarch would have done, he committed Sir Dudley Digges and Sir John Eliot to the Tower, went to the Lords' house and told them of it, adding, "that he could clear Buckingham of every one of the matters whereof he was accused." Likely enough to a certain extent, but only by acknowledging himself to be a *particeps criminis*, and an unconstitutional monarch.

D

Violent scenes succeeded rapidly, and the King embroiled himself also with the Upper House. But it must not be supposed that the whole country was quite unanimous in their opinion. The Universities of Oxford and Cambridge have generally been opposed to the people at large on questions connected with liberty of the person and freedom of mind. Cambridge acted consistently on this occasion, when the heads of the houses, to show their contempt of popular indignation, as well as their loyalty to the King, elected the Duke of Buckingham their Chancellor. The spirit of this act was precisely the same as that which prompted the sister University of Oxford, *inter alia* and at a later period, to burn some prose works of Milton by the hands of their common hangman.

The Duke of course denied the charges, did not exonerate the King from them assuredly, when he admitted that the money paid by the East India merchants had been received by his Majesty, and failed to perceive that whoever had the money, it was not the less on that account an opprobrious robbery. But, if innocent, why plead the general pardon of King James, and the new king's coronation pardon, as entitling him to the benefit of them? As for the sale of the King's lands for the royal purpose, this may have been partly true with respect to his own particular case, since it was notorious that the Kings of England, for many generations, what by treasons, constructive and accumulative, or simple and real; what by fines, forfeitures, and confiscations; what by presents, gifts, and bribes ;—had always plenty of land on their hands, which they were in the habit of selling in order to make up what was called in the language of the Exchequer, "the casual revenue." Edward IV. had at one period more than a fifth of all England in his possession, and Henry VIII. all the spoils of the Abbeys, with the exception of St. Katherine's. If Burleigh, the minister of Elizabeth, died seized of lands and tenements sufficient to fill a modern auctioneer's catalogue,—so the Duke must have reasoned, so

his master must have felt,—why should the Duke be singled
out for punishment, and exposed to the vengeance of a faction,
for doing what ministers and favourites had always done
with impunity before? Even the University of Cambridge
itself may have reasoned in this way.

I have dwelt at some length upon the preceding particulars,
for the purpose of showing the moral effect those scenes
could not fail to produce upon an ingenuous and ardent
mind, upon a young man just entering into public life. He
saw men like Selden, and indeed most others, opposed to
the corrupt practices of the court, and indignant at the
treachery, and the unscrupulous villainy of men in high places,
of those who should have been the guardians and shepherds
of the people. His part was therefore soon taken, and he
was henceforth to be numbered with the men of the opposition party. No man of honour could possibly be a minis-
terialist. He joined in the remonstrance made by the
Commons against the King's taking of tonnage and poundage,
"though not granted to him by the Parliament;" he concurred in their profession of attachment to his royal person,
but with their hope that he would not permit the Duke to
have any more access to him; and lastly, in their petition
that he would not dissolve the Parliament. They received
for answer that the King *would* dissolve it; and this he
accordingly did by commission, Thus "this great, warm,
and ruffling parliament had its period." Reviewing afterwards this part of his eventful life, Whitelocke says to his
children : "I leave this recital to you for an example, that
in all debates I was neither swayed by court flattery, nor
popular vanity, but only by that reason and conscience which
God had given me."

Whitelocke, now about to enter upon his twenty-second year,
retired into private life, and resumed his professional studies.
It was seven years since he was admitted a gentleman of the
Middle Temple, during which time he had studied diligently.
Having performed the accustomed exercises at Motes in the

house, and at readings in the Inns of Chancery, he, together
with several other gentlemen of his society, that were his
contemporaries, was called by the Benchers to the degree of
barrister-at-law, and honoured with the title of esquire.
Following the example of Selden, he enters, when recording
this event, into a somewhat tedious narrative about esquires
and titles in general. We may dismiss the first as possessing
no general interest at the present day, however valuable it
may be to the antiquary, but I am glad to discover remarks
in connection therewith, that reveal the liberality of his
mind. Thus there is one·passage, in which he admits, that
virtue is the best nobility ; another where he—a man of
thirteen proved descents by his father's side and fourteen by
his mother's—confesses that the nobility of blood is vile
except it be adorned with virtue. As for knighthood, he
says "it is often worne by many who never saw a camp nor
studied anything but pamphlets or playbooks, nor ever
served their prince or country, but who have lived at home
conversing with carters, or in London with lacquays and
black patches." Here is another on the same topic : " Let
a man's natural nobility be what it will, yet if he be poor, the
title of gentleman will hardly be allowed him, but if he be
rich, though unknown from where he came, the officers at
arms will easily be persuaded, for a gratuity, to afford him
the title and arms of a gentleman." Then with sentiments,
which he thought Christian, but which in reality are rather
Jewish in their practical working, he observes, " Let this, my
children, be your pattern, to uphold your gentility, to live
virtuously and to leave sin, without which no birth will make
one noble."

The administration of public affairs was now getting worse
and worse. The King institutes a sham and facetious
process, in the Star-chamber, against Buckingham, the accusation being precisely the same as that which the Commons
had made. The farce was carried on for some time, but
dropped before it came to a hearing. The Privy Council

advised the levying of tonnage and poundage, and to get
the ratification of it in the next Parliament ; a forced loan
was attempted by the agency of Noy (who considered
himself a great legal antiquary), but resisted by some
sheriffs as a case without precedent ; a benevolence was
required ; and then, as usual, when some great blow was to
be struck, a general fast was ordered.   It is astonishing how
long this piece of state-craft has served its turn ! It was
promptly followed, as intended, by commissions for musters,
with power of martial law, with the impositions of loans,
and the billeting of soldiers, whose outrages drove the
people to phrensy ; but were there not the clergy to preach
passive obedience from their pulpits, " That the King might
make laws, and do whatsoever pleaseth him " ? Six thousand
English soldiers, transferred from the States to the King of
Denmark ; all men that refused to lend money to the King
constrained to serve as common seamen on board ship ;
recusants allowed or compelled to compound—such form
parts of the disastrous picture that England now presented !

Nothing will better illustrate this picture, however, than
by describing briefly the discord, that prevailed in the King's
family at this time, the immediate consequences of which
occasioned humiliation to the country in its foreign relations.

The King, not satisfied with the rebuffs he had received
from both houses of Parliament, interfered also with the
management of his own household.   The French servants—
like commons and peers—remonstrated in their turn, and said
" that the King had nothing to do with them, he being a
heretic."   In the articles of marriage it had been stipulated
that the Queen should appoint all her servants; and now,
incensed at her husband's want of deference to herself in this
matter, she insisted on her right.   From some erroneous
conclusion in their political calculations, the Jesuit priests
attached to her Majesty's household, had also, about this
time, compelled the Queen to do penance by walking bare-
footed to Tyburn, near which spot lay the bones of certain

priests, formerly executed there, and regarded by their
living representatives as martyrs. Stung to the quick by
this accumulation of insult, the King sent back to France
the whole of his wife's French retinue, and with it a letter
of excuse to the French king. France, which could not
be expected to have much sympathy with England at that
particular period, resénted the act as a violation of the
articles of marriage. A private insult was offered to Cardinal
Richelieu, at the suggestion of some disgraced French abbot
residing at London, who found a Mr. Walter Montague too
ready to abet his design—that of embroiling this country in
a war with France. The chief pretence for making it was,
to assist our co-religionists of that nation, but one of the
causes was alleged to be the embargo laid on our merchant
ships in French ports. This made the war popular to some
extent, but unhappily the Duke of Buckingham caused
himself to be appointed general of the forces by land and
sea, with power to make knights and confer promotion. His
appointment alone sufficed to ruin the expedition, for no
man trusted him. He appeared off Rochelle with a hundred
sail of ships, and desired the inhabitants to join with him in
behalf of the French Protestants. There was every reason
for their so doing, if they had only had confidence in his
ultimate intentions, but apprehensive perhaps of being
eventually betrayed, they contented themselves with the
cautious reply : " That they were bound by union and oath
not to do anything without the consent of the rest of the
religion."

The Duke had sufficient military knowledge to discover,
that the island of Rhé, a strong and well provided place,
would suit his purpose better than the island of Oleron,
which was weak and ill-provided. He accordingly landed
1200 men on the former island, defeated the French opposed
to them, and then more slowly landed the rest of his army.
The delay was fatal, as it enabled the governor to obtain
fresh forces and provisions, the Duke being engaged in

publishing a useless manifesto respecting the causes of the war, and how the King of France had, contrary to his promise and agreement, employed English ships against Rochelle. The manifesto should have been made weeks or even months before, and copies of it should have been then distributed to the citizens of Rochelle. Had this been done in time, it might have regained their confidence. He was subsequently outwitted by the governor of the island, who pretended that he wished to send word to his master, the French king, and obtain his permission to surrender the fortress. In reality he had long since sent word—for supplies to be sent him, and these he promptly received. The Duke, on discovering his mistake, showed great vacillation of purpose. He too had sent for and received supplies, though inadequate to his wants. He now batters the citadel, then proposes to go away. Foiled again by the enemy, he attempts to storm the fort, is repulsed, raises the siege, and retreats to his ships. But he had made no provision for this, had constructed no works to cover his rear in case of a reverse. The result was, that the French inflicted so severe a blow as to cover the whole enterprise with disgrace.

The national discontent at home became universal, our very seamen grew tumultuous, but the Duke threw all the blame on his council of war—that convenient scapegoat. On this occasion the Parliament, previously acquainted by the King with their common danger, petition, first themselves, for a general fast, and then for redress of grievances, before granting a supply. As with the war, so with domestic concerns, the Duke made a Scotchman, by the name of Melvil, his second scapegoat, and assured the Commons that it was he who had said : " That the Duke intended to put the King upon a war against the commonalty, with the assistance of Scotland and the like ; and that Sir Thomas Overbury had poisoned Prince Henry by his instigation."

Rochelle being still besieged, and the inhabitants having changed their minds, the Duke was appointed to go with the

fleet and relieve that place in the following year. Whilst
sojourning at Portsmouth he was stabbed to death by
Lieutenant Felton, a political fanatic. His death did not
change the fortunes of his master abroad, for the expedition
signally failed ; nor did it rally the affections of the English
people to the crown, since no change of measures or system
on the part of Government ensued.

But our young barrister was eschewing politics and law
for a short season, and about to commit himself to a very
silly adventure. He had an intimate friend in the temple,
one Mr. John Pyne, who was deperately in love with a lady
in Dorsetshire and her fortune, which was considerable in
land. The lady returned her lover's affection, but being at
her uncle's house, and the latter wishing to keep her
unmarried, because he was in hopes of securing her estate,
to which his children were entitled by reversion in case of
her leaving no nearer heirs, kept her in a kind of restraint,
and debarred her from Pyne's attempts. The latter
acquainted his friend Whitelocke with the state of the case,
and demanded his active assistance in his behalf. Dissuasion
being useless, he with other friends went down in a coach to
a town near the uncle's house. A consultation was there
held, and Whitelocke was ordered to lead the forlorn hope,
which he undertook to do. Taking a letter with him by
way of credentials, he soon contrived a private interview,
arranged matters, returned, and came in force the next day to
the gentleman's dwelling ; then courteously took leave of him,
after rescuing the fair prisoner, and placing her in the coach.
Being safely consigned to her lover, they were married
without loss of time, and the happiness of the parties secured
as far as friendship and zeal could compass it. Subsequently
in Parliament Mr. Pyne attached himself to the more rigid
party, and became, through political excitement, the strong
and determined enemy of his former friend.

But about this time Bulstrode's own friends and relations
were thinking of a match for him. They proposed to his

father a Miss Willcox, the daughter of a London citizen, who
was able to give her a great portion, and they advised Sir
James Whitelocke to propound the business in a letter to
the citizen, which he did in the following terms :—

"Mr. Willcox,

"I am very sorry to hear of your sickness, and I pray
God send you health. I ask leave to commend unto you the
suit that my son maketh to your daughter ; I should do him
wrong, if I did not give that testimony of his behaviour
which I know to be true, and that is, that he is a sober and
honest young man, dutiful to his parents, a good proficient
at his book, and provident in his expense. I foresee his
likelihood to run on in his profession with the forwardest.
I have 1000*l*. per annum already for him in possession and
reversion, to help him in his course, and I hope in God, if
I live, to increase it. ·I have no more children but himself
and two daughters, the one of which I have married to a
gentleman of 3000*l*. per annum, and the other is not yet
ready for ·a match. I will assure all my land upon their
issue, and yield to such conditions for your daughter's
advancement as shall be thought reasonable, nor do I intend
to be a penny the better for his portion, but to bestow it all
for his good. For myself you shall find me assured to do
you and yours any good, as if I were your own brother,
and to be a stay and friend to you all. Thus I thought
fit to make offer of my good intention to you, and so I
pray God to whose protection I leave you, to bless you with
health and strength. I rest, &c."

Mr. Richard Oakley, a most loving, faithful servant and
friend of the family, endeavoured to compass this match,
but the two fathers could not agree upon the marriage
conditions and settlements, so the treaty was broken off.

Mr. Grymston (or Grimstone), a young gentleman of
Lincoln's Inn, the son and heir of Sir Harbottle Grymston,
of Essex, with a good estate, had better success in his
treaty of a marriage with Judge Croke's daughter. As

Whitelocke was the lady's kinsman and the lover's friend, he was made the instrument of bringing about the match, which turned out a most happy one. On taking the bride home, the bridegroom's father and mother, many friends and Whitelocke himself accompanied the young husband; and for a frolic, Bulstrode, whom his former disaster at charioteering had not dismayed, turned coachman, and drove the bride's coach. Upon the way they stopped at a mansion, where a gentleman of quality and his lady came to the door, bade the newly married couple welcome, and treated them with wine and sweatmeats. The coachman sat mannerly with his hat in his hand upon the box, all powdered over with dust, but the lady looking earnestly and archly at him, advanced to him with a cup of wine in her hand:

"Sir, I do not use to drink to coachmen, but you seem to be an extraordinary one, and therefore I present my service to you."

What could a coachman do when thus greeted? He descended from his post and replied gaily—

"Madam, I believe you do not use to give leave to coachmen to salute you, but let one whom you judge extraordinary have that extraordinary favour from you."

With this he saluted the lady and reascended his box. Decidedly, puritanical starchness was not yet in the ascendant, and with similar passages of mirth the journey was shortened, the old baronet gave them all high entertainment and a hearty welcome, and we may safely conclude that politics were forgotten.

And now, the leave of his father not being expired, he resolved to travel as before " in quest of Crowland." This time he went the western circuit as a traveller, and as this was the part of the country that subsequently rose so sternly in arms, and greatly if not chiefly conduced to the defeat of the King and his adherents, I shall extract a little from the notes Whitelocke took whilst on his journey. He set out

from Fawley Court, which is close to Henley, and rode to
Wargrave, a little town, pleasantly seated like the other on
the Thames, and the rural scenery of which he took pleasure
in contemplating.   Hence on to Wokingham, which was
formerly the seat of his ancestors, the effigies of some of
whom as gigantic crusaders, like those in the Temple church,
at Winchester cathedral, and elsewhere, were still preserved.
But all else was then changed, for at the time he arrived the
inhabitants were knitting silk stockings and weaving cloth.
Hence he proceeded to Odiham in Hampshire, where he was
hospitably entertained by Mr. Robert Doiley and his lady.
Next day he continued his route to Alton, thence to Peters-
field, and leaving that, ascended into Sussex through the
pleasant "champion" downs to Chichester, where the Recorder
Whatman at his house regaled him with a choice variety of
sea-fish, unknown to the inhabitants of inland counties.   In
the roof of the cathedral there, they showed him a curiosity
of workmanship in stone, of six faces that only had six eyes
among them, and yet every face seemed to have the normal
allowance of eyes.   He calls this the workman's conceit, and
never imagined that mythical and traditional lore was
preserved in a cathedral.   But we now know that even irony
was often handed down by those ancient workers in stone,
and that their craft had its secrets, as well as the one that
once employed them as builders.   Then he had pointed out
to him a cross of rare artificer's work, that was built by
some unknown bishop to shelter the people on rainy days.
From thence he rode through Havant on to Portsmouth, and
by the way was shown an acre of land, which yielded its
owner 40l. a year by the profit of "purls," that bred here
so thick as to prevent any one from treading on the ground
without breaking the eggs.   At Portsmouth, by means of the
Recorder, he was shown the fortifications, which he narrowly
inspected.

    There can be little doubt from this visit, and from some
that he made to other fortresses, in the course of this trip,

that his movements were not guided by mere curiosity, or love of adventure. No doubt change of scene had charms for him, as it has for youth in all ages, but deeper motives were also at work. He wished to see with his own eyes, and hear with his own ears, whether all the rumours and accusations respecting the Duke and his royal patron were well founded, or the offspring of malevolence. Too prudent to entrust these thoughts to writing, he gives results alone, and leaves it to the intelligence of his children to divine the rest.

He was now at Portsmouth, the fortifications of which had been raised by Queen Elizabeth. It was a "rampire" of earth with bulwarks and a trench. On each bulwark ordnance was planted, and a sentry-house, together with scouring pieces to defend all the broad trench between them. This work encompassed the town on all sides, but towards the sea the place was defended by a strong stone wall, at the beginning of which, coming from the main sea, was a platform with a dozen pieces mounted, three or four of which were cannon and demy-cannon. Upon two sides of this platform, a blank space being left towards the harbour, there were little rooms for shot, powder, instruments for loading and scouring the ordnance, linstocks, and the like, conveniently placed. This platform commanded the main between the guns and the Isle of Wight, and likewise the harbour. There was a small strong castle near the stone-wall; its own walls were two feet thick, and on its flat roof ordnance might be planted and pointed to any quarter. From this spot he viewed a goodly fleet of nearly 100 sail lying near the Isle of Wight, under the command of the Earl of Denbigh, their admiral, and who was then with them. But his Excellency having no commission to fight, suffered various English vessels to be taken away "by our enemies" in his sight, without rescue by their countrymen. Some foreign ships taken as prizes, being brought before him as admiral, it was wondered at, that almost all of them were adjudged

by him to be no prize, and released.   But one captain pursued a liberated ship, recaptured her, took her round to
London, and there she was adjudged a good prize by the
Admiralty.   If the sea could be brought round Portsea, so
he conceives, it would be the strongest port in Europe, " but
the fortifications are not now in good repair, nor the maga-
zines furnished (though in time of war), and this made the
inhabitants fearful of an enemy's attempts upon it."

Leaving this place he passed through Tichfield, admired
its stately mansions, and conversed with its opulent merchants.   Then on to Winchester, where, it being assize time,
he met the judges, of whom he was ever the welcome guest.
Here, in the time of the Romans, the emperors had their
textrina sacra, or sacred houses for weaving and embroider-
ing stuffs used by themselves alone ; and here too were
manufactories for the garments of their soldiers, the sails
of their ships, for linen, sheeting, and the like ; and in
addition to these a college of monks.   From here he
attended the judges to Salisbury, the cathedral of which
had its first stone laid by Henry III., as appears in the
charter of his grant.   Being so near, he of course paid a
visit to Old Sarum, the ruins of which convinced him of its
former strength ; a few stones of the castle gate upon the
hill were still hanging though seemingly ready to fall.
He saw Ambresbury (Amesbury) and Stonehenge, the stones
of which he attempted in vain to count, and so back to
Salisbury.

The whole of his excursion through Dorsetshire, like the
preceding ramble in Hampshire and Wiltshire, is very dull,
because marked with no personal adventures, so that it
affords but little matter for extract, saving his allusion to
the state of the defences on the coasts.   Thus the castles of
Portland and Sandfoot he found unfurnished.   Having viewed
the Cobbe of Lyme, Whitelocke and some of the barristers
on the circuit were invited to dine at the Mayor's.   One of
the party told the Mayoress, that he really must make an

"apology" for being so troublesome to her; but she not knowing the word, which it seems was recently coined, fired up with indignation, told him that his speech was too high, and unbefitting both the time and place; she wondered at him speaking to her in that way, and to her husband's face, and he must not think them so ignorant down there, but allow that common discourse was one and the same thing with what he called "apology."

At Dartmouth, as at most of the other havens, he took a boat, had himself rowed to the mouth of the harbour off from the town, and gathered whatever local knowledge he could. Here they showed him three castles on the shore,— one of which was the King's,— and places where they fastened a great chain, that was kept in an old tower, to be used as a boom in case of danger. The French had been frequently repulsed here, not always by force, but the natural security of the waters. The dearest commodity was wood, being sold by weight. He was much struck with the pilchard fishery, and on inquiring the price, found that 1000 were sold for 6d.

Visiting Gatcombe in his way, he reached Plymouth, where he met with some friends. They showed him the setting of the watch that night. The guard consisted of about 100 men, armed with muskets, pikes, and halberts; their captain was one of the twelve principal burgesses of the town, an alderman, who had for lieutenants two of the twenty-four secondary burgesses; and, by this arrangement, every one of the number had to keep watch every twelfth night, but only in the summer season. Having inspected the Haw, the fort, and the island, he was regaled with a wondrous variety of fish, which he washed down with cider, and this constituted his breakfast.

At Launceston, while dining with the judges, he formed the acquaintance of a Mr. Arundel of Trerize, who gave him an invitation. They rode together to St. Cullombe, and so along the ridge of Cornwall to his house. Here he was confined within doors for a day by the tempestuous weather, and equally unconscious of wreckers as those Greeks who first called the Black Sea the Euxine, he pronounces the people to be "*humaniores erga hospites.*"   Having proceeded with a guide to Penzance, not quite nine miles from the Land's End, he was received here by the Mayor and the Captain, the Searcher and officers, and they brought him store of wine.   This respect to a stranger and a mere country gentleman was occasioned by a special message from their Recorder, Mr. St. Aubin, as Whitelocke conceived.   Having inspected the entire neighbourhood and all the curiosities, which he describes in his MS. at some length, the *ne plus ultra* being attained, he commenced his return, and was met by Mr. St. Aubin.   They could not, of course, neglect the Careg Clowse en Cowse, or the Grey Rock in the Wood, but no trees were there at that time.   At the foot of the mount they were stopped by the Lieutenant, who made a shift, though extremely drunk, to lead them up into the fort that was on the mount.   At the entrance stood the Warder in a red waistcoat without a doublet. This doughty champion held his warlike hand upon his rusty sword, and looked grim withal.   By his side stood three or four more defenders, but in truth, they were all quite as drunk as the Lieutenant, their commander.   The visitors were charged to render up their weapons before entering the fort, an order that was obeyed, not without surprise at finding some show of dis-cipline where least expected.   All that was to be seen here consisted of a few pikes and an old cross-bow, formerly taken from the Earl of Oxford, who fortified this place against Edward IV.   In the hall there were some pieces, and about the fort a few guns mounted, but everything neglected, a matter of no consequence in a strategical point of view. Hard by is St. Michael's chair, and near it a stone, which causes a remission of sins for any one that shall walk round it without touching it.   Our traveller, in repeating this legend, observes that it may well be doubted, unless the penitent come well prepared, as he would be sure to break his neck by falling down the rock, if he let go his hold of the stone for one instant. In a hole like an oven, on the side of the rock, there is a fresh water spring, called St. Michael's well, but the rock itself is entirely surrounded by the sea.

As at Stonehenge, so here, he does not attempt to give any explanation of what he saw or heard, but we ought not to conclude from this silence, that he had not an inquiring mind, and did not attempt to gain some perception of cosmical and moral phenomena. Newton and Galileo had shed no light as yet, and science had not yet dawned; his reveries, therefore, must have been very vague. That he inquired, at least, is evident from what follows, for when he came to the house of Mr. St. Aubin's brother, they told him of great fishes, called seals, eleven or twelve feet in length, which at high tides lie on the rocks with their calves till the next high tide enables them to depart; when, if pursued with guns or stones, a sport much in vogue about there, they would cast a stone backwards with great strength against those that follow them.

Referring the reader to any work on Cornwall for a more modern description of the curiosities which our traveller then visited, let us sojourn with him for a few moments at Pendennis Castle. Mr. St. Aubin's influence procured them admission, and leave to see the rooms. The castle was the best fortified and kept of any that he had seen in the west of England, and he had visited nearly every one. Here there were fifty good pieces of ordnance mounted, with store of powder, shot, and arms. A competent number of soldiers were constantly on duty; the walls were strong; the mound or wall of earth palisaded with a trench around it; the entrance was by a drawbridge through a gate-house, and within these were some buildings for the soldiers. The castle itself was not large, but that part of the hill, that lay without the wall, had been taken in lately by an outwork, on which ordnance had been planted. On the side of the hill was a

blockhouse similarly armed.   The powder was kept dry on
the castle-leads in a little room, where it was free from fire
and ready for use.   He thought the harbour to be one of the
finest in the world, and where ships could sail out with any
wind except full south.   At Glasseney College he took leave
of his kind friend Mr. St. Aubin.

At Exeter, by the Bishop's special direction, the choir
performed some of their choicest music and best anthems,
and being a good judge, he considered the performers quite
as good as those of the King's chapel.

At Taunton the inhabitants assured him that Somersetshire was the garden of England, and Taunton the garden of
Somersetshire ; and here, as usual, his eloquent silence must
not prevent our receiving the boast *cum grano salis.*   Here
he took leave of the judges, and made for Wales, not forgetting the Holy Thorn at the ruins of Glastonbury.   "It
buddeth every Christmas, and grows out from the broken
end of Joseph of Arimathea's staff—if you believe the
tradition."   Ochie Hole detained him also, and he gazed at
the stones called the Porter and the Witch.   He was silly
enough to go down the hole, *facilis descensus Averni,* but
found it no easy matter to regain the light of day, being
very glad when "well out again."   Leaving Bath he came
to Bristol, where the hot well of St. Vincent's rock had only
been found a short time before, though already famed for the
cure of leprosy and the stone, "if drunk in a large quantity."
At St. Brevills the commoners told him a story of a lady of
that place, who besought her Lord to bestow a parcel of land
upon some poor neighbours distressed for want of ground to
keep their cattle in, but as my readers are doubtless familiar
with the myth of Actæon, and the veritable legend of
Peeping Tom at Coventry, a repetition of this tale may be
omitted.   At Ludlow he found the castle in good repair.

At length with much difficulty of travel, he finds rest at
the house of Mr. Thomas Mostyn, his brother-in-law, and the
place was called Shoc in the township of Kilken in the

county of Flint. All spots had something marvellous in
those days; and here, likewise, at no great distance was
St. Katherine's Well, "into which if any garbage or unclean
thing be cast, the water (as if offended at the filth) will cease
springing, become dry, and so continue till the next St.
Katherine's day, after which it begins to spring and fill the
basin again till the like injury be again offered." Apparently
fond of wells, but slightly sceptical of their miraculous
powers, he repaired, not as a pilgrim, to St. Winifred's at
Holywell, much frequented by Papists "and others." Here
the sick have to go into the water and out again a set
number of times, or else they hold it will do them no good.
From this reverend spot he rode by the coal-hills upon the
sea-sands to Mostyn, the house of Sir Roger Mostyn, his
sister's father-in-law, where he had a kind, outward welcome,
"but I had rather sit at coarser fare myself, than that in a
journey my horses should want provender."

This family of Mostyn was very ancient and worshipful;
their name was Trevor, from their lineal ancestor Tudor
Trevor, a very great man in his time, one of the Welsh
princes, from whom three great houses, those of Edwards,
Mostyn, and Trevor, derive their pedigree. Camden sets
down the occasion, how in the time of Henry VII., Mostyn
left off his many names, and called himself by the name of
his chief residence, Mostyn. The house was large, but not
uniform; it stood upon a coal-hill, under which the sea beat,
and it was opposite the point of Werall in Cheshire, and the
little island of Helbree. Kilken was a small house, built of
stone, upon a mountain, with good corn-land, but little
pasture about it. After describing the country and its
produce, he observed: "that some of their ministers here
are miserably debauched," a stigma that does not apply now,
it is to be hoped, to Welsh parsons. At the base of Giant's
Hill he saw another well, that rose and fell like the tides, but
without regularity, from twenty to thirty times in one hour.
He waited on Baron Trevor, then in the country, who took

him to the house of Sir John Trevor, his brother.   His residence was called Placetege, or "Fair Place," a modern
structure and well designed.   There were five knights of the
Trevors in the district.   He and the Baron went to Trevallen,
the house of Sir Richard Trevor, built near the river Allen,
and in one of the most charming spots of North Wales.

His return lay through Caergusle, where Owen Glendower
was to have met Henry Hotspur and join their forces against
King Henry IV.   It had been agreed that when Hotspur
came to Whitchurch, he was to set it on fire by way of
signal, to which act he was instigated by the Welshman, in
order to avenge an affront offered by the townsmen not long
before to his father-in-law Sir David Hanmer, the Lord
Chief Justice of England, and indeed at his house, called
Hanmer, in the vicinity.   The townsmen by their humble
carriage prevailed on Hotspur to spare their homes, and set
fire to a stack of gorse instead.   The Welsh chieftain, informed by his scouts of the deception, suspecting treachery,
refused to come up, and the ally, thus deserted in his hour
of need, unable to sustain alone the brunt of the battle, was
discomfited.

Whitelocke went to church at Mostyn, when part of the
service was read in Welsh and part in English, and the vicar
got into the pulpit with the laudable design of preaching a
Welsh sermon.   Sir Roger desired him to do it into English,
but as the vicar was unable to perform such an impromptu,
his further services were dispensed with for the nonce, the
baronet being so obliging as to say, that even he himself did
not thoroughly understand Welsh sermons.   Penguerne was
the ancient seat of this illustrious family, its name meaning
the head of an "owlet tree."   At a wake held at Mostyn,
and at which much company was present, a party, including
himself, went on board a barque of Sir Roger's, that was
lying at anchor near the house ; they raised the anchor for
the purpose of having a little yachting, when a terrific storm
came upon them with the suddenness, that is so common in

mountainous countries at particular seasons of the year.
He considered their escape on this occasion quite providential.
Being himself a lawyer, he felt a curiosity about Hanmer,
the house previously alluded to, but he says nothing about
it ; all that he commemorates is the water, which the worthy
Lord Chief Justice had imbibed there before him ; it had a
singular taste, like that of milk.

At Wolverhampton, where there was no river, he went to
see their spring, which gushed out of the side of a hill in the
town ; it was walled about with stone, and from this inclosure
men were constantly conveying " leathern budgets " of the
vital fluid on the backs of horses. Leaving Cotshill he rode
through a dusty country by Astley Park and Castle, once
the property of that Duke of Suffolk who was beheaded by
Queen Mary, quite a distinct personage from the other
unfortunate peer of that title, whose head was taken off by
Mary's bluff father, Henry VIII. A fortunate race, these
Tudors, in one sense, for here was a fine estate, from which
both father and daughter derived " casual revenue !"

At Soley our tourist was entertained by his uncle Bulstrode, and then passing through Coventry, Warwick, and
Banbury, he takes note of the Puritans in this latter place.
There were two sorts of them there, just as in other places,
one being the knave-Puritan or hypocrite, and the other the
knave's Puritan, a really virtuous man, whom knaves reproach
with the title, because he will not do ill as they do. " May
you all be such Puritans !" he exclaims. He revisited Islip,
where in his boyish days he had suffered so acutely, and
thence through Milton came home to Henley at last, after
performing a journey of about 1000 miles, which he called
his *Iter Occidentale.*

I have deemed it right to give a very slight sketch of it in
this place, by way of sample, to show what the other five
journeys were like, from all of which we may infer that he
" discovered Crowland " at last.

CHAPTER IV.

1628—1629.

New Parliament to which Bulstrode is not Elected—He and his Father opposed to the King's Arbitrary Measures—His belief in Astrology—Chosen Master of the Revels by the young Templars—" The Oracle of Apollo"—Presence of Court Ladies at the Revels—Bulstrode and his Companions in Vogue at the Court Balls —Death and costly Funeral of one of the Revellers, and singular Litigation that ensued—Dialogue between Bulstrode and Noy the King's Attorney on this matter—Another futile Negotiation of Marriage—Whitelocke's Disgust at the Conduct of Public Men—Craft of Charles in seducing Wentworth and others.

IN the meantime, and while the posture of affairs continued to be in so unsatisfactory a condition, both at home and abroad, those gentlemen * who had been imprisoned illegally for refusing to contribute the forced loan were released, and orders issued to use moderation in the business of the loan-money.

The King felt his weakness, and vainly attempted to propitiate the people. He was compelled to convoke a new Parliament, when several of the gentlemen he had imprisoned were elected. The Jesuits formed great hopes at this period respecting this particular parliament, but upon what grounds we are not told ; one of the reasons may have been founded on the disgrace of Abbot, the Archbishop of Canterbury, and that of the Bishop of Lincoln, by which the power of Laud seemed more consolidated. It does not appear that Whitelocke was returned to this Parliament, and it would seem, that his independent conduct in the last had deterred not only his father's friends, but even the judge

* Some of these prisoners had consulted Whitelocke on their case. He was a reporter in the King's Bench, when it was argued, and he refers to his papers in Rushworth. The arguments are given at length in the "State Trials."

himself, from procuring his nomination. Sir James, who
had once been himself a member of the Opposition, who was
deeply versed in the politics of the day, and who found his
principles of right so gravely shocked by the late conduct of
Hide, the new Lord Chief Justice, was doubtless fearful of
compromising both himself and his son during the troubles
which he foresaw to be impending. Indeed, what man of
sagacity could fail to divine the issue? Wrangling, recriminations, accusations, were the least evils to be expected.
And they came. Matters reached such a pitch, that on the
King's sending another message to the Commons to know
whether they would rest upon his word, as a monarch,
which he declared he would perform, they actually debated
upon it, and some said that "his royal word was only to be
taken in a parliamentary way." They petition for the rights
of the people, and at a conference with the Lords, the
Commons object to the amendment made by the Upper
House, in which the latter wished to qualify the rights of
the subject by the addition of a phrase, that they should
not "infringe sovereign power." But these scenes belong
more properly to the domain of history, and it is only requisite to insert here one striking feature.

Upon finally presenting the "Petition of Right," about
which so much jealousy had been mutually evinced, the King
gave a different answer from what he had previously given,
and one which the Commons and all good men regarded as
satisfactory, but it was in French : "*Soit droit fait, comme
il est désiré.*" The King could speak English when he liked,
and talked English when he violated the privileges of either
House ; but he knew he was regarded, like his father, as a
foreigner, rather than an Englishman. He would have done
better to have assented to their petition in broad Scotch,
rather than in French, and better still to have kept his
promise in whichever language made. Nor was he gracious
long, for in reply to their remonstrances, he orders the bill
in the Star-chamber against the Duke, and His Grace's

answer, to be taken off the file, because he was "satisfied of
the Duke's innocence." Another remonstrance was drawn
up in behalf of the people's rights, against the unlawful
taking of tonnage and poundage without the grant of Parliament, and which they alleged to be contrary to the
answer he had given to their petition of right; but he
replied that he could not do without tonnage and poundage.
Having obtained the subsidies he required, upon the strength
of that promise, he prorogued Parliament, made Dr. Montague a bishop, and preferred Dr. Mainwaring to a good
living, both having been previously pardoned.

About this period several little facts occurred and were
faithfully recorded, which from the wording of them give
rise to the inference that Whitelocke, like most of his
countrymen, especially those of elevated rank and position,
was a believer in astrology, portents, prodigies and the like.
His early education at Merchant Tailors' and Oxford, the
influence still exercised over his mind by Laud, the seemingly
inexplicable coincidence of phenomena in the heavens, with
events passing around him, will in part explain his credulity.
Thus he was very indignant at the conduct of the rabble,
who, with no fear drawn from astrology before their eyes,
had attacked a pseudo-doctor Lambe in the streets, called
him witch, devil, and conjuror, and beat him till he died.
It was a cruel act, but it was not mere humanity that
induced the Council to take up the affair and desire the
Lord Mayor to find out and punish the chief actors; or to
fine him and the aldermanic body because they were unable
or unwilling to do so. Nor was it from mere humanity that
our historian remembers the occurrence, but rather from a
superstitious mystic dread. In like manner he records the
Earl of Pembroke's death, because it had been predicted to
him by an astrologer; and how upon the 29th of May,
1630, the day when Charles the young prince was born, "a
bright star appeared, shining at noon-day in the east." It
is this secret belief, which he seems half-ashamed to confess,

that induced him subsequently to act in opposition to his
own better judgment—to trust the stars and their interpreters rather than the evidence of his own senses.   The
reader will do well to keep this circumstance in mind, for it
may be again referred to when we come to our analysis of
his conduct about the time of Cromwell's death.

He was now in his 24th year, had returned to London,
and for a season kept close to his studies, but towards
Christmas was interrupted in them.   By the unanimous
consent of all the young gentlemen in the Middle Temple,
he was chosen Master of the Revels, which, after great
importunity he somewhat reluctantly consented to become.
The company was about twenty in number, and they met
nearly every evening at St. Dunstan's tavern, in a large new
room, called the " Oracle of Apollo;" each member brought
friends with him, when he thought fit, provided there was no
secret sitting specially appointed for discussing "ways and
means."   In this hall they held, after their sage consulta-
tions, both solemn dinners and sober suppers, for not one
among them was ever seen to be drunk, and not one of them
was ever guilty of debauchery during that whole winter's
season.   On the contrary, they "generally hated that dirty
and beastly vice, and despised those that were subject to it."
Mine host was the better pleased, when he found that they
spent their money freely, and had often high treatments
without disorder or lasting scuffle.   It was, in short, a kind
of miniature parliament, of which Bulstrode was the speaker,
and when they voted supplies they taxed no man's pockets
save their own.

The weighty business to be transacted there was " to
practise their dancing, to exercise both their wits and
bodies ; not to cloud their reason or parts with excess or
debauchery, but to improve their judgment and knowledge
by good discourse and conversation ; sometimes by putting
of cases, and they did appear together much more like
to grave ancients in a council-chamber than to young

revellers in a house of drinking." The dancing itself was a
very grave ceremony, as the reader will perceive, for on All-
hallows day, which the Templars considered the beginning of
Christmas, the master, as soon as the evening was come,
entered the hall, followed by sixteen revellers. They were
proper, handsome young gentlemen, habited in rich suits,
shoes and stockings, hats and great feathers. The master
led them in his bar-gown, with a white staff in his hand, the
music playing before them. They began with the old
masques; after that they danced the Brautes,* and then
the master took his seat whilst the revellers flaunted through
galliards, corantos, French and country dances, till it grew
very late. As might be expected, the reputation of this
dancing soon brought a store of other gentlemen and ladies,
some of whom were of great quality; and when the ball was
over, the festive party adjourned to Sir Sidney Montague's
chamber, lent for the purpose to our young president. At
length the court-ladies and grandees were allured,—to the
contentment of his vanity it may have been, but entailing on
him serious expense,—and then there was a great striving for
places to see them on the part of the London citizens. A
great many challenges were given on this occasion by a few
silly young men, who imagined their dignity was hurt by
the classification of the guests after the rules of precedence,
but firmness and impartiality restored order and obedience.
To crown the ambition and vanity of all, a great German
lord had a desire to witness the revels, then making such a
sensation at court, and the Templars entertained him at great
cost to themselves, receiving in exchange that which cost the
great noble very little—his avowal that "dere was no such
nople gollege in Ghristendom as deir's."

In the vacation time, as if to be revenged on the boroughs
for not returning him at the last election, our Master of the
Revels got up a private Commons for himself, at the house

---

* Probably the bride's dance, unless I have mistaken the word for branls or brawls.

of one Mr. Percy, in Fleet-street ; the other members were,
Messrs. Palmer, Tichbourne, Hall, Solmes, Challoner, Hyde,
Grymston, Freake, and many more. Most of these were
great wits and scholars as well as lawyers, but their mirth
seems at this day to have been extracted as it were from
parchment and vellum. For they exercised their wits by
instituting a Star-chamber of their own, wherein they tried
any one of their company who offended by swearing and ill-
speaking, or who broke any of their rules. The ingenuity
and learning displayed on these occasions equalled, and I
am afraid resembled, what the public then heard in the
courts of justice, where what was said was no joke, at least
for the suitors. At these meetings, no reporters being
present, they inquired into public affairs, and thereby fitted
themselves for future public services. In one instance, the
speaker being in the chair, our Master of the Revels made a
long speech in vindication of his proceedings, which had
been impugned by the Opposition, and although it would
occupy too much space to reproduce it here, I cannot but
allude to its success. It is one of the most masterly I ever
read, and it instantly secured an overwhelming majority.
Its reputation, indeed, followed him into the Long Parliament, and led to his early if not precocious distinction. His
head was now getting completely turned. The maids of
honour to the Queen, and divers other great ladies, were
constantly inviting him to their balls ; they insisted on his
bringing some of his revellers with him, which he did, and
at this epoch of his life might, had he so willed it, have
easily been received as a young courtier in the train of
royalty. The King smiled upon him, and old wily lawyers
of the day were not blind, as they thought, to the future.
The following little occurrence may serve to show what
time-servers some of these gentry were.

A young gentleman, by the name of Baring, the only
child of his father, a rich man in Dorsetshire, happened to
catch a fever, of which he died. He was one of the comp-

trollers, and his brother revellers, to show their respect for
his memory, empowered their master, who was also their
treasurer, to provide a grand funeral for him.   The order
was obeyed, and the bill of the undertaker came to 50*l.*, no
trifle in those days of tonnage and poundage.   He also in
the name of the society, sent a letter of condolence to the
father, in which the " little" bill was inclosed.   To this no
answer was vouchsafed, but a second letter, rather more
quick than the first, extorted the reply, that they who had
ordered his son's burial might see it paid, for he would not.
No explanation availed to change this resolution, and
accordingly the young lawyers agreed to file a bill against
the churlish father in the Court of Requests.   This was at
that time a court of honour, and it was the fashion then to
canvass the judge.   Accordingly Whitelocke by command
waited on the Lord Privy Seal, who presided in that court,
and begged his leave to prefer a bill.   His Lordship smiled,
bade him in God's name exhibit his bill, and added, gratuitously, upon King James's principle of *not* hearing the other
side, " If Baring does not pay it, I'll make him."   This was
encouragement enough ; the bill was perfected, and even
grave serjeants-at-law subscribed it, for the honour, customs,
and societies of the Inns were admirably expressed in it.
Whitelocke then took it to Noy, the King's attorney.   On
seeing him arrive, and knowing him (better than Bulstrode
imagined), Noy told his man to conduct him into his bed-
chamber, then left his levee of obsequious clients, and came
to his youthful visitor.   The following dialogue ensued :—

WHITELOCKE.—" Sir, I attend you by command of my
masters, the Parliament of the Middle Temple, in Christmas,
to desire your advice in a matter touching that, and all the
rest of the Inns of Court, which this paper can relate better
than I, if your leisure will give you leave to read it.

NOY.—You come to me from a considerable body, whom
I shall be glad to serve, and we will read over the bill
together.

WH.—I pray, Sir, what think you of this passage, or would you have it altered ?

NOY.—I think well of it altogether, and that there were good wits as well as good lawyers in the framing of it. These things I would have expressed thus.

WH.—It wants nothing but your approbation, and these alterations are very material. I pray, Sir, do you think upon the whole matter, that it is proper for a suit in the Court of Requests ?

NOY.—Yes, or else nothing is proper for them to meddle with. Put in your bill as it is now.

WH.—I fear I shall be too troublesome to you in it.

NOY.—Not at all ; come to me when you will, you shall be welcome ; I will advise and assist you the best I can in it.

WH.—Sir, all our Society, especially the young gentlemen, will thankfully acknowledge your favour.

NOY.—As I have given you my advice in your business, so I desire to have your advice in mine, or rather the King's, which I will show you. It is a patent the King commanded me to draw of association between England and Scotland, concerning the business of fishing.

WH.—I have never had such honour as to have my advice asked by such a one as yourself, and in so great a business as I have heard this is, though it be above my capacity.

NOY.—The business is indeed of the greatest consequence to this kingdom, if it were well managed, that any can be ; so I have told the King, and he is sensible of it. Therefore, he commanded me to draw this patent, but I've forgot my Latin, and I know you write Latin well,* so I must have your advice in this patent.

WH.—I was never good at it, but as well as I can, with your permission of freedom, I shall tell you my humble thoughts of it.

---

* Noy took this for granted, because Sir James, the Judge, was renowned as an extemporary orator in the Latin language.

Noy.—That is the end why I ask your advice. Come, let us read it over.

Wh.—Methinks, Sir, with your favour, this clause might be thus expressed.

Noy.—I like it well, and it shall be so amended, What say you to this phrase?

Wh.—I think, Sir, if it please you, it may be thus worded in proper Latin.

Noy.—It pleaseth me very well, and so it shall run, and to let you see that I am pleased with your advice, I will give you a fee for it out of my little purse. Here, take these single pence.

Wh.—Truly, Sir, I did not expect a fee from you, nor did I offer you any.

Noy.—No; if you had, I should have taken it ill from you, but you must learn never to refuse anything from your friends.*

Wh.—I thank you for that profitable rule, and for this fee extraordinary, but I pray, Sir, why have you given me eleven groats more than an attorney's fee, whereas my advice is not worth an attorney's?

Noy.—I give you more, because you will be a better man than an attorney, yea, than an attorney-general.

Wh.—I never doubted your opinion in anything so much as this.

Noy.—You will find this to be true.

Wh.—I doubt you find me troublesome, therefore I shall humbly take my leave.

Noy.—You are not troublesome. I pray come to me, whensoever there is occasion.

Wh.—You make me ashamed by using this compliment of bringing me to your door, which much greater men than I do not expect from you.

---

* Such was the worldly training of an old lawyer; we shall see ere long, what the churchman's worldly counsel was.

Noy. —You are Lord Treasurer of the Temple, therefore I will bring you to the stairs' foot.

Wh.—I must not contradict your pleasure, but humbly take my leave.

Noy.—Farewell, my Lord Treasurer."

After a few more waggish quirks, of which Noy was fond, they parted, and the great man returned to his levee. To make a long story short, the bill was put in, the impartial Lord Privy Seal granted more than was even asked. Noy— merciful and bountiful Noy—moved for an attachment against Baring, because his answer had not come in, and the obstinate man, growing frightened at last, sent up the 50*l.* to the Treasurer, with a letter of excuse for having delayed doing so. The money (I am happy to add) was generously distributed by the Templars among the poor prisoners.

But a most serious change was now again meditated for him, one that does indeed give birth to true joy or true sorrow, one that polarises the heart of youth, and enables it to absorb and radiate the spirit of true humanity, or turns it into throbbing and living steel—that of marriage. But marriage in those days was brought about like a modern treaty by diplomatic negotiations, that were not always successful, since it was not love, but mammon (the Jewish Cupid), that inspired the text of marriage settlements. Thus, a "motion was made" to his father, the judge, for a match between him, the son, and Sir John Garret's daughter, of Hertfordshire, a great beauty, and seemingly of a sweet disposition, but the conditions of settlement were not acceptable to the fathers, and this treaty was also broken off.

About this time some repentance began to be felt at such misspent time, and what with the revels, waiting upon ladies, going to the court, treatments, the Christmas expenditure and the like, he had run himself into debt. Not that it was to any ruinous amount, but yet too much for him with his modest allowance. As for telling his father, that he did not dare to do; and the only means he saw of ever liquidating

it was by diligently attending to his profession. This resolution he acted upon, and his first fee was received from
Michael Bolt, an honest neighbour of Henley. Sir Thomas
Freake, the town of Henley, and other clients succeeded,
and his gains began to be pleasing. A match was propounded for his sister Cecilia with Sir John Tyrrell's son, of
Buckinghamshire, and he was sent to see the estate, but
terms were not accorded, and so this treaty likewise was
broken off.

His political instincts were strongly re-awakened by the
sad scenes of turmoil, confusion, assassination, imprisonments
and nefarious trials, that disfigure our annals of this year
(1629). His eyes were moreover opened to the true character of many men whom he had been accustomed to look
up to with reverence, as the ornaments of his own calling.
Thus he began to perceive that Heath was a fit instrument
of the times, who was now prosecuting in the Star-chamber
some of the men who had most figured in the late parliament for the rights of their countrymen, and he was shocked
by the report, that the King intended to have no more
parliaments at all, but to abolish the institution as Louis XI.
had done in France. A pamphlet that appeared at this time
strongly advocated the measure, and, had the Duke been
living, it would doubtless have been carried into effect. The
King himself, naturally tyrannical and arbitrary, but without self-reliance on his own isolated judgment, preferred
another course, for he loved favourites, and private counsel,
and the mystery of affairs. He thought it better to baffle
than annihilate the mutiny of his commoners, and seems to
have preferred the subtle craft of a politician to the iron will
of the unyielding despot. He rejected therefore this plan,
but adopted another more consonant with his convictions,
and one which he deemed more likely to insure his ultimate
success, acting as he did, solely by the blind instinct of hostility to popular freedom. Accordingly, overtures were made
to Sir Thomas Wentworth, and his countryman, Sir John

Savile, the successful issue of which gave encouragement;
they betrayed their party, and became Privy Councillors.
Sir Dudley Digges was next seduced, and was appointed
Master of the Rolls.   Noy became his Majesty's Attorney,
and Littleton his Solicitor-General.

CHAPTER V.

—————

1630—1632.

Bulstrode goes the Oxford Circuit—A Match on Foot between him and a Daughter of Alderman Bennet—His successful Courtship—Unpropitious Illness of the Bride at the Wedding—Effect of this upon Bulstrode's Mind—His Domestic Life—Death of his Mother—Birth of his Son James—His Comments upon Public Affairs—Pays his Father a Visit in the Country—Betrothal of his Sister Cecilia to Mr. Edward Dixon of Tonbridge—Laud's High Church Zeal favoured by the King—Death of Sir James Whitelocke—Peculiar Nature of his Testamentary Documents—Bulstrode elected Recorder of Abingdon—Determines to serve again in Parliament.

THE Liberal party was now disorganised, and eschewing politics for awhile, our barrister applied himself to his profession, went the Oxford circuit, and realised in this first year the respectable sum of 152*l.* 16*s.* He preferred this independent course of life to playing the courtier against his conscience, and now, a third time, a match was proposed to his father between himself and a daughter of Mrs. Bennet, the widow of Alderman Bennet, and sister-in-law of Sir Thomas Bennet, another alderman of London, then living. She herself was the sister of Sir Humphrey May, a man in close attendance upon the King, a privy councillor, and high in office, who, with his brothers, had maintained through life their friendship for his father, the judge, having all of them been fellow students at Oxford and the Temple.

The treaty was concluded, the portion was 3000*l.*, and the young people, in obedience to parental orders, met for the first time at Mrs. Bennet's house in Cheapside. Here mother and daughter treated him civilly, and he found his bride "comely, proper, handsome, and ingenuous." He gained upon the mother's good opinion, as he thought, and left

F

under the distinct impression that the daughter felt well
affected towards himself.   The courtship having become
thus initiated in a business-like way, he was permitted, on
receiving due notice first, to have meetings with his affianced
fair one, sometimes in that fashionable quarter of the city,
sometimes at Mortlake in Surrey, a spot which he considered,
so blind does love make its votaries, a pleasant one "in
summer." It was a house of good "receipt," with gardens
and a chapel.

At length the wedding-day was fixed, and friends mustered
thick at this village of ominous name.   His father came,
but his mother, being too ill, was absent.   Persons of quality
attended in honour of both sides ; the bridegroom with a
train of his old companions and revellers, all in gallant array,
took a barge at the Temple and came joyously up the river.
The company was met, the hour of marriage was at hand,
but the bride seemed disturbed and ill ; her relatives confessed she had been very ill that morning, as well as the whole
of the previous night, and while they were so explaining,
she fell into a fit, so violent, that it deprived her for the
time of her senses and reason.   "Her understanding left
her, and she was ragingly seized on by her distemper." The
marriage could not proceed, and some said it was a high
fever, others a violent fit of the mother, others maiden fears ;
her mother inclined to the high fever, and whilst some were
for going on with the ceremony, others were for postponing
it, but all wondered.   During this consultation, word was
brought in that the bride had recovered, the alarm passed
off, and affection pleaded too powerfully.   It was a lovely
day in June (1630), and at two o'clock the nuptials commenced.   The wedding feast was great ; mirth and cheerfulness revived ; music, dancing, revels succeeded, and
Sir James left his son full of hope and unconscious of the
future.   The night was far spent, and the company having
escorted him into the nuptial chamber, withdrew.   They
were no sooner departed, than the bride fell into the same

strange fit attended with such appalling convulsions, that he shrieked for aid, and the women came rushing in. Thus she lay for hours, whilst he expected nothing less than her instant death throughout that night of agony and distress.

In his private papers I have found his sad and melancholy reflections, occasioned by this sudden overthrow, so entirely unforeseen, of all his hopes. Religion came to his aid ; and in the true spirit of the English mind, in that phase of its development, he took to reading Epictetus as well, where he soon fell upon a passage that gave him the support he wanted : " All things are fortunate for me, if I so will." The words made such an impression upon his mind, that he took them for his motto, with a little alteration, and never changed it for the rest of his life, " Quodcunque evenerit optimum," "whatever happens is the best." And finding music to be no small refreshment to him in his trouble, and filled with lyric thoughts, he composed verses, and set them to his lute. Were the taste of this age less prosaic, I might be tempted to insert a verse or two, but I forbear. Utterly ignorant of what his wife's malady really was, as soon as she grew better, his spirits rose accordingly, and he put his trust in Providence.

About Michaelmas, some political prisoners, of great note, consulted him, and Sir Miles Hobert, who was one of them, sent him a letter to move in the King's Bench, that greater freedom might be allowed him and his companions. The application, however, failed at that time.

His domestic sorrows had rendered him very attentive to religious duties : he now began to think, indeed, that every man ought to be a priest in his own house, and he formed the resolution of reading prayers daily to his wife and servants—a custom that he never after neglected to observe.

Bulstrode Whitelocke was now in his twenty-sixth year, and for some time past had resided with his wife's mother at Mortlake. Here a great deal of company was kept, and some of the simple amusements of that age were indulged

in, such as bowling and going on the water. His wife,
Rebecca, continued in health and good temper, and although
sometimes he observed her to be a little melancholy by fits,
he found her for the most part cheerful and very good
company.

As soon as the summer had passed away, the mother took
up her quarters, for the winter, at her town house, where her
daughter's health proved also tolerably good. The married
couple took much satisfaction and contentment in each other,
and the "testimonies of conjugal affection did mutually appear."
The husband's parents, who had felt great anxiety, rejoiced in
the happy prospect of seeing their race perpetuated, but
domestic affliction of another kind was impending. After
Easter term the judge went down to Fawley Court, to keep
there his Whitsuntide ; his wife, being ill and taking physic,
unfortunately not of her own making, remained in town a
little after him. On Whitsun-eve the son accompanied his
mother in the coach, and she discoursed much against the
fear of death. On reaching home, at the end of the elm-
row, she alighted, and with her son's assistance walked up
to the house, resolved, she said, to look at the scene around
her for the last time. She supped in the hall, where her
husband and herself were accustomed to take their repasts
in summer on account of its coolness, or rather she feigned
to do so, lest she should alarm her husband ; she was
seemingly cheerful, but drank to them all in a way that made
her son sorrowful. In the night she died, and her hands
were found raised as if in prayer. Whitelocke's narrative
here occupies several pages, and enters into minute details,
that would not interest the world. He dilates upon his
mother's private acts of charity, her uniform gentleness and
kindness, and concludes by saying : " Thus, and not without
some tears, let us leave the memory of this good woman."

He did not go the summer circuit on this occasion, and
stayed at home with his wife. On returning to London,
however, he resumed his professional duties, went the Lent

circuit, and during the four terms of the year, which expired in March, he found his gains to be 187*l.* 17*s.*

On the 13th of July, 1631, his son James was born, who, in after times, was knighted by Oliver Cromwell, and was, if I am not mistaken, the entertainer of William III., when journeying up to London as the deliverer of the nation.* The child saw the light for the first time in Soper Lane, which was in the parish of St. Pancras, and it was baptised there on the 28th of the same month. "The Lord be merciful to thee, my son," was the father's heartfelt prayer nearly forty years later.

On reviewing the political events of the same period, Whitelocke records here another act of Bishop Laud's. When peace was being concluded with Spain in November, the articles were solemnly signed, and sworn to be observed upon a Latin bible, expressly brought by Laud. But the English divine knew very well that the Roman Catholics do not acknowledge the authority of the Greek version as orthodox, and, therefore, this act of his appears to have been regarded with undue asperity.

Bulstrode condemns as erroneous the several accounts published this year about Gustavus Adolphus by the English chroniclers, whose works were, of course, licensed and modified in some underhand way. He declares that those accounts were very different from the real truth of the proceedings, as related to him by the actors themselves, by men such as Oxenstiern, Grave Horn, Bannier, Wrangel, Douglas, and several others. The English people witnessed also at this time with indignation the ascendancy of popery in Ireland.

Hitherto we have seen the various schemes resorted to for increasing the King's "casual revenue," in other words, his private purse for his own particular expenditure. These

---

* Since writing the above I have ascertained this to have been Sir William Whitelocke, Sir Bulstrode's second son, who became afterwards an eminent lawyer and a privy councillor to Queen Anne. He was the owner of Phyllis Court.

schemes had been realised in every reign by forfeitures,
escheats, attainders, fees, bribes ; by sale of titles, honours,
offices, and the like ; by corrupt dealings ; by the sale of
pardons to criminals who had not landed property, and by
the debasement of the coinage.* In addition to every one
of those illicit modes, Charles, like his son in after times,
began to look about him for other additional modes of
acquiring money, and accordingly the feoffees in trust for
the buying in of impropriations, were summoned before the
Exchequer, on a pretended charge of having broken their
trust, by bestowing maintenance on non-conformists. Their
corporation was dissolved, and their money adjudged to the
King.

Having returned from the circuit, Whitelocke posted up
to London to see his wife and new-born son. He sent their
grandfather an account of their health, and of their desire to
pay him a visit in the country, which they did shortly after.
The child was put out to nurse at Woburn, the same place
where he himself had been forced to swallow the "shaffling
broth," and singularly enough, with the daughter of the very
woman who had half-poisoned him. To this spot the old
judge repaired one day for the sake of seeing his grandchild,
and ascertaining by a harmless divinatory process, what his
future disposition would be, and how he would conduct himself hereafter in the management of money concerns. He
accordingly went in state, for he had his children, chaplain,
and servants about him, and brought song-books with him.
When they arrived at the nurse's house, they sang grave and
serious songs, this being the only pastime in which the old
gentleman indulged since his wife's death ; but the people in
the cottages and neighbourhood were not used to such sym-
phony. Such was the first trial ; and it gave him great
delight to see his grandchild "strangely attentive" to his

---

* For instance, the "martyr-king" leased Major Prichard's life, just as a bishop
does land, for seven years. The major, a murderer, who escaped hanging on this new
principle, was obliged to renew the lease septennially by payment of a fine

music, but what special end he had in view was never revealed. The reason may be discoverable perhaps in Aristotle, or some note of the scholiast, or in some psychological work of the day, that had made an impression on his mind. The second trial was one which the nurse at least must have comprehended better. Taking a twenty shilling piece of gold, he put it into the infant's hand to test its natural inclination; the child let it drop presently on the ground, at which he said, "I doubt this boy will throw away too much of his money." *

Shortly after this, a " motion was made " to the judge for a match between his daughter Cecilia and Mr. Edward Dixon, the son of Henry Dixon, of Hilden, near Tonbridge, in Kent. The sum of 1000l. per annum was settled on the son, and a portion of 2500l. demanded. Old friendship prevailed at the interview between the parents, and the treaty was concluded. The judge did not live to see the marriage performed, and it was left for his son to give his sister away, and fulfil the intentions of his father.

After giving a prolix account of the consecration of the chapel in Fawley house by the Bishop of Lincoln, Whitelocke reverts to what is historical ; for about the same time the repairs of Paul's church in London were commenced, chiefly by the zeal of Laud, who caused different images and ornaments to be set up, by which he gave occasion for great discontent. Popular indignation was regarded as something amusing, therefore the King came himself to this church, and made a kind of procession to view it ; in anticipation of which he granted a commission to some bishops and others to raise contributions and see the work done. Nearly 80,000l. was accordingly collected, of which a certain *saint*, Paul Pindar, gave no less than 19,000l. But while all this was

---

* The prediction came true Some years after Sir Bulstrode Whitelocke's death, this child, then become Sir James Whitelocke, thought proper as heir-at-law to allow the mortgaged family estate of Fawley Court, with even the family pictures in the house, to be sold to Colonel Freeman Nor had he the excuse of poverty, having married a very rich widow at Trumpington, near Cambridge, as Cole informs us

being done for Paul's church, a portion of London bridge
that had been burned down, was allowed to continue as it
was without being repaired. Again his Majesty, who had
just recovered from the small pox, gave audience to the
Polish ambassador, a man that was chancellor in his own
country, but who nevertheless came over to England to
request the King's help against the Turks. Charles with
that generosity for which he was already distinguished, when
dealing with the lives and fortunes of his subjects, gave the
Polish chancellor some money and 2000 men.

After alluding to the fate of Gustavus Adolphus, Whitelocke
proceeds to describe the death of his own father, whose
private and public conduct well deserved whatever tribute of
love and respect his son could pay. "And assuredly no
father had more reverence and obedience paid him both in
life and death." * The son was not present when the mourn-
ful event took place (June 22, 1632), but arrived one hour
too late to see his father alive. The servants brought him
the key of the cabinet, in which were papers of consequence.
Some of these were prayers, and two were respectively a
deed of gift, and the will of the deceased judge.

It might be supposed by many that the will would have
been sufficient, but this able judge of the King's Bench did
not think so himself; no man knew better than he the mode
in which administration was conducted in that and the
preceding reign. His MS. contains some curious revelations
of what was then practised by the officers of the Crown.
He had accordingly prepared the Deed of Gift for the
express purpose of preventing his personal estate from
being inventoried and discovered by the harpies of the

---

* One anecdote of him may be introduced here, if only for the purpose of authen-
cating a well-known story, which has been carelessly or intentionally associated with
other names. His ancient servant, Mr. Anthony Bull, who had lived with him nearly
forty years, had so offended him, that he bade him get out of his house, for he should
stay no longer with him, but Mr Bull would not go ; and, being asked the reason,
answered "If you do not know when you have a good servant, I know when I have
a good master, and therefore I will never leave you." The reply pacified the master's
wrath, and Mr. Bull survived him to pass over into the service of the son.

Ecclesiastical Court. The heir found, after deducting his sister Cecilia's portion, there was coming to him £4500 in ready money, plate, household stuff, books, and rare manuscripts collected during a long life of indefatigable industry, horses, and other effects. The house was furnished in a style corresponding with its late owner's rank, and the contents were therefore of no little value, for the judge had been a successful agriculturist, had farmed his own lands for a long number of years, on what was then a most remunerative system, and accumulated his savings. Besides the " *liber familicus*," which contained the short story of his life, and many passages connected with the court of King James, there was a large collection of his notes upon the Hebrew Bible and Greek Testament, together with several works in manuscript upon different branches of the law. The son inherited also the Manor of Fawley, the woods of which were well stocked, and the reversion of the Manor of Fillets * as to one moiety of it, upon the expiration of a lease, that had still about 14 years to run. All this land was left to him free, to dispose of as he pleased, to give it to whom he thought proper, " in case," he adds, " any of his children should be disobedient to him." So gentle and tender a heart as this man possessed would be sure, however, to prevent the evil passions of anger and revenge from inflicting permanent misery upon others, and therefore no cruelty or injustice of the kind happened in his family.†　But he was still so far imbued with the feudal prejudices of his age as to look upon the eldest son as the heir of land. Strong as his mind was, either education or the vanity of name and rank and social position caused him to regard the eldest son as more entitled than the other members of his family to the possession of a particular kind of property.

---

* Commonly called Phyllis Court, and which played no insignificant part in the civil war before the battle of Naseby.

† It is a solemn question, whether a parent has a moral right to disinherit a child on any pretence whatsoever, but the law of this country confers the power.

But this was not all that this fortunate son received from the hands of his sire. For in the cabinet he found his own declaration which he had given his father, at the desire of the latter, under his own hand and seal, that he the son held in trust for the father all the bonds and securities for money belonging to the latter in reality during life, but nominally taken in the son's name, with the same wise and prudent design, that of preventing the Ecclesiastical Court from requiring an inventory. The value of these bonds and securities was probably considerable; but we are left uninformed as to the amount.

Whitelocke was now, if that could be any solace or cause of contentment, his own master. From the piety with which he carried out in spirit even more than in letter his father's bequests and last earthly wish, I cannot believe him to have been one of those vulgar " laughing heirs," that sicken us when we contemplate them. On the contrary, he determined on following up what he knew to have been his father's plans, and never entertained a thought of wasting life in inactivity and luxurious ease. Some months previously he had suffered himself to be elected Recorder of Abingdon, an office involving both trouble and expense, as well as loss of time, with no other compensation than the modest fee of £5 per annum ; and now the town of Henley chose him to be of counsel for their corporation, with the equally liberal annual fee of 40s. He took great pains in his profession, had attended diligently to his practice, and had earned by fees no less than £310 11s., which with his father's liberal allowance of £400 a year had amply sufficed for his maintenance. All his debts had long since been cleared off, and therefore this present accession of wealth might well have tempted him to withdraw from the drudgery of a profession, and taste the sweets of indolent retirement. It was the crisis of his fate, the ordeal of his soul. He had nobler objects in view. His ambition was to serve his country in Parliament, to acquire renown by knowledge and action, to distinguish himself in his calling, and not to vegetate among the rural gentry of that day, with whom intellectual companionship was impossible.

He was now in his 28th year, and having secured the happiness of his sister by uniting her in marriage with Mr. Dixon, he made up his mind to prosecute some evil-disposed persons in Oxfordshire, in Oxford itself indeed, who had slandered his father's memory.

CHAPTER VI.

1633.

Laud's growing Power—His Interview with Whitelocke at Henley—Henry Bulstrode
named High Sheriff of Bucks—Death of Gustavus Adolphus, and of the King of
Bohemia—Whitelocke's Mode of Life at Fawley Court—His Wife's melancholy
Disorder—He inherits his Father's love of Hunting—Is afflicted with Stone in
the Bladder—Curious Question of Precedence on Circuit—Bulstrode's Intimacy
with Littleton, afterwards C. J of Common Pleas—Religious Troubles in Scot
land begin—Charles goes to Edinburgh to be crowned King of the Scots—
Festivities on his Return—Whitelocke's Views on fishing with *Cormorants*—
His Professional Labours become profitable.

ABOUT this period the death of Abbot, the Archbishop of
Canterbury, led to the promotion of Laud, who at that time
filled the see of London.   Rumour stated, somewhat malig-
nantly, that Laud had been offered a cardinal's hat, which
he had refused, knowing he should shortly be as high as
England could make him, that he had no wish to be second
to any man in another kingdom, and preferred substantial
power in this.   At the end of summer, towards Michaelmas,*
the new Archbishop went from London to Oxford.   He had
to be there for the purpose of receiving the King and entertaining him in the University, of which Laud was Chancellor. . On his way the Primate came with his train to
Henley, where he put up at the Inn called the Bell, and
learning that Whitelocke was at Fawley, sent for him.   The
quondam pupil obeyed and met with a courteous reception,
the old man saluting him with more than ordinary respect
and friendship, and with a tone of voice very different from
that which sounded in the ears of the sad victims doomed by

---

* All persons reckoned time formerly by the terms, or, on special occasions, by
Saints' days, just as peasants still do by certain fairs and markets.

him to torments and penalties in the Star-chamber. The following conversation then took place between them :—

ARCHBISHOP.—" Mr. Whitelocke, I am very glad to see you well, and it was my desire, on coming into these parts, to see you and speak with you ; indeed I purposed to have lain at your house, to have graced you in your own country ; but I was told that you were gone from home, and thereupon I took up my lodgings here ; but when I heard that you were at your house, I sent for you, and am very glad to see you.

WH.—My Lord, I was very unhappy in that mistake and misinformation, which was given to your Grace of my being from home at this time, and I return my humble thanks for the honour your Grace intended me, and for your favour in sending for me. I hope it is not too late for your Grace yet to remove but a little distance to my house, where you shall have a most hearty welcome, and I hope somewhat more convenient accommodation for yourself and your retinue, than this place will afford.

ARCHB.—I thank you very kindly for your invitation, but now that I am settled, and my people in our inn, it would be troublesome to remove, and we must take it as we find it.

WH.—Will your Grace then be pleased, on your return from Oxford, to honour me with your presence at my house ?

ARCHB.—I cannot promise that, because I know not how it may please the King to order his return to London; and I am partly engaged, if I do not attend his Majesty, to lie at a kinsman's house of mine at Turvile.

WH.—I am sorry I cannot hope for this honour of seeing your Grace at my poor house.

ARCHB—I may find some other opportunity, and I assure you, Mr. W., that I shall be ready upon all occasions to do you any good for his sake who is gone to God, my old friend your father, and for your own sake too.

WH.—I have a great affliction in the loss of my dear father, but your Grace is pleased to give me much comfort in your expressions of favour to me.

ARCHB.—Let me ask you to what course of life you intend to betake yourself now upon the death of your father, who was an old man, and his time was come to leave this world. God hath taken him to himself to a better world, and we must all submit to the will of God, and go on in our own course whilst we are here. I shall be willing to give you counsel for your direction in your way.

WH.—I shall very readily pursue your Grace's directions in all things concerning myself, and humbly acquaint you with my own thoughts and inclinations, if your Grace shall approve of them.

ARCHB.—Let me freely know what they are, and you shall as freely have my opinion therein.

WH.—Since in my father's lifetime I was brought up in the study of the law, and initiated in the practice of that profession, I have thoughts of continuing in that way.

ARCHB.—I am clearly of that judgment, that it will be best for you to keep on in that course, and still to continue the practice of the law; it will be an advantage to you in all your affairs, and a shield to you in your country against injuries.*

WH.—I expect great discouragement therein, now upon the death of my father.

ARCHB.—Those things you must look for, such is the baseness and ingratitude of many men; but be not discouraged, be diligent in your calling, God will bless you in it, time will work off those discouragements, and new hopes will grow and come to effect.

WH.—It pleased God to bless my father very much in that way of his profession.

* This advice is still applicable.

ARCHB.—Your father was a most industrious man from the first beginning of his studies, when I came acquainted with him at St. John's College [in Oxford], and so he continued all his time ; and I observed when you came a young man to the same college, and your father committed you to my care, who was then president of that college, I had a particular eye over you, and found that you were not negligent in your studies, nor debauched nor idle in your conversation.

WH.—I most thankfully acknowledge your great favour and the care which your Grace was pleased to take of me, and of my education, when I had the happiness to be under your government in Oxford, and I then and always had an inclination to my study.

ARCHB.—I promised your father to take care of you there, and so I did, and will take care of you now* that you have lost a good father ; and I shall be ready to show you countenance and to further you in your profession, what may lie in my way; and as God blessed your father, so doubt not he will bless you, if you serve and love him, and his church.

WH.—I shall endeavour to testify that duty which lies upon me herein.

ARCHB.—I know your father left you a competent estate, and sufficient to maintain you like a gentleman ; but if your estate were much greater, yet to be in a profession will be no disparagement nor diminution to you, but every way an advantage.

WH.—I shall be faithful to my clients, and willing to take pains in my profession.

ARCHB.—For matter of labour and pains, I shall counsel you to be industrious, yet you need not to sweat so much as others at it ; make such progress in your studies and practice as may become you, and enable you to serve the King

* Poor man, he could not take care of himself, and over-estimated his care of Whitelocke at Oxford.

and your country, and I for my part shall not be wanting to further your preferment, when any opportunity shall fall out in my power. It is an unhappy and ungodly life, that too many gentlemen do lead, to spend all their time in hunting, or hawking, or in worse things, and often their greatest care is how to spend their time. You will know how to spend yours in your study and profession, and it will keep you from many inconveniences."

Whitelocke adds : "We had much more discourse of this and other matters, till company coming in did interrupt us, and supper being ready, the Archbishop commanded me to stay and sup with him. He treated me with so much kindness and respect, that all his own company and strangers took great notice of it, and it caused the more respect to me from others. He was pleasant, as he used to be at meals, and after supper I took my leave of him, but waited on him again the next morning, when he and his company set forth early from Henley, and went the direct road to Oxford."

Before leaving his seat for Michaelmas Term in London, Whitelocke gave the charge to the jury at the Quarter Sessions for the borough of Abingdon, as its Recorder. It was the first he ever gave, and had occasioned him, of course, some trouble and anxiety, but practice soon rendered the performance of this duty familiar to him. The preambles of his charges are preserved, and of this particular charge, the entire text. Some idea may be formed of the pedantry of that age, and of the small intellectual powers of persons thought to be well educated, when we reflect how incapable the great majority of men of every rank then were of seeing what was right or wrong upon its own merits. He bolsters up his charge, and was of course obliged to do so, with allusions to heathen writers ; quotes from Plutarch when speaking of perjury, and always bases whatever is asserted upon some authority or another duly quoted. Thus, in the course of his specifications, and towards the end, he desires them to inquire about the present miscreants, heretics, and sorcerers, "who, as appears by Britton, an ancient book of the common law, and by old statutes, were inquirable in leets and eyres, and so are now by you." The reader may safely conclude that the Papists were not forgotten on this occasion ; no speech, no sermon could well be perfect without some allusion to them, and there is accordingly in this charge a denunciation of seminary priests and Jesuits, who at that period spread soul-terror among most classes of society in this country—a feeling strikingly analogous to what is felt at this day respecting the insidious nature of their tenets and doctrines.

As may be expected, political economy was wholly ignored by the lawyers of that and every preceding age. So he desires the jury to find out "Ingrossers," who buy and hoard up great quantities of corn and other fruits, making them dearer and so injurious to all, especially to the poor.

The High Sheriff of Bucks died this year in his shrievalty, and Mr. Henry Bulstrode of Bulstrodes, to the great joy of all his family and friends, was named his successor to serve the residue of the year ; not indeed on account of the honour, but because he escaped serving a whole year, with all the attendant trouble, vexation, charge, and all the imposition of the King's officers of the Exchequer, not forgetting the bullying by the judges at the assizes.

It was not so very long before, about a twelvemonth in fact, that the King granted to the Polish ambassador a sum of money, and 2000 men to serve against the Turks. In this short interval the political wind has veered, and his Majesty for some reasons of state best known to himself, now sends Colonel Saunderson with 2000 English soldiers to the Emperor of Russia " to assist him against the King of Poland." Upon arriving there, Colonel Leslie, a Scotchman, basely murdered Saunderson, and the "Muscoviters" were overthrown by the "Polanders." Nor did Leslie escape the fate he merited, for he was hurled from a tower and dashed

G

to pieces. To the great grief of Protestants, the King of
Sweden was slain at Lutzen, and the whole of this afflicting
and bewildering intelligence seems to have reached this
country by the same post that brought word of the King of
Bohemia's death from the plague. The death of kings was
universally looked upon as portentous, and no less than
three of them perished in this critical year, that swept off so
many illustrious persons of both sexes throughout Europe.
England's condition was so gloomy, and our Recorder's own
mood so overshadowed by her constant humiliations, that he
was led to compose an ode to Death. The personification of
that principle, so inevitable in a finite world subject to
change of seasons and all the laws of development, is so
entirely opposed to the sounder views of modern science,
that I may well dispense with exhibiting this dismal lyric,
representing only the funereal images of a saddened spirit.
Such thoughts, however, were then not inopportune, for he
was setting up a monument to the memory of his parents in
Fawley Church, where he had caused a mausoleum to be
constructed, having previously obtained from the Bishop of
Lincoln, his father's friend, an instrument under his own
hand and seal episcopal to authorise it. With this licence
he set to work and had the satisfaction of completing what
he regarded as a pious and holy duty. A long and minute
description of the monument and vault was duly recorded
by him at the time, and would be inserted here if I thought
any further example necessary to teach men the vanity and
folly of attempting to preserve what Nature has recalled
from the isolation of life to the community of elementary
matter.

His wife passed her time in the country this winter with
the more patience as her child was at Woburn ; she went to
see him frequently, and both mother and child enjoyed good
health. She herself was apt to be melancholy, and it occasioned many fears of a vague nature in the mind of her
husband, who tried to cheer her to the utmost of his power.

He entertained his tenants, friends, and neighbours this Christmas at Fawley Court, taking for his rule the course adopted by his late father as nearly as he could ; and he thanks God that "he was not ill beloved by them." He retained the old chaplain and the old organist, Mr. Ellis, but instead of anthems (what a falling off was there !) they sang the ordinary psalms to the organ. Whenever any of his father's servants, or others, skilful in music came to him, which they often did, then they had good music in memory of their old master and benefactor. Moreover, in conformity with the habits acquired at Oxford, they had prayers constantly twice a day in his chapel. Poor lady, no wonder she was apt to be melancholy, when living in what was nothing better than a secular convent, with dirges and droning wails and other lugubrious sounds for ever ringing in her ears; she who required the cheering tones of a mother's voice to soothe her distracted thoughts, and above all that which alone would have been holy for her,—silence, quiet, serenity, absence of domestic care, the constant supervision of feminine gentleness and watchfulness. Well might he have the saddest forebodings ; but foreknowledge was mercifully withheld in the case of this most gentle being, his first love, but a love pursued by such ceaseless omens !

The charm of gentleness was indeed rare in those days, both in private and public life. Men fed rudely, thought rudely, and acted rudely. Cruelty and sternness, not gentleness, prevailed ; and hence the conduct of Whitelocke to his wife deserves the more commendation. The will was not wanting, at least if he erred in judgment, and in not knowing how to treat this gentle flower. It is his great praise that he was, throughout his life, of a naturally humane, tolerant, and kind nature, ever ready to do good if he did but know how. In this want of unyielding sternness he differed from only too many of his countrymen that distinguished themselves in that ruthless epoch.

After Christmas, our Recorder was again called to

Abingdon, where he kept the Quarter Sessions, and again charged the jury ; in reciting this circumstance he informs his children, for whom these memoranda were especially prepared, that he intended to give all his charges separately, and incidentally observed that the introductions or preparatives were generally of different matter. But, the progress of knowledge has rendered these matters wholly uninteresting at the present day.

In the management of his paternal estate he made no change ; but followed the course adopted by his father. He had the same leaseholders and copyholders, and, to his credit be it said, the same rents. He neither raised nor felt a wish to raise them. Amongst his tenants, a man named William Cook seemed to him a good husbandman, and well versed in rural affairs ; he had gained the esteem and confidence of the previous owner, and was therefore appointed to be the overseer and manager of the property. The demesne was sown by halves ; or, in other words, half the land was alternately suffered every year to lie fallow ; this being judged in that century the most profitable mode of farming. When the young esquire found recreation and exercise necessary, he went a hunting, as had done his father before him. His companion on these occasions was one Mr. Rogers, a kinsman of old Lady Scrope, who lived at Hambleden in what was then called the New House ; but when that ancient dame died, and her place was taken by the Countess of Sutherland, the widow of Lady Scrope's son, having no longer a friend and a pack of hounds within reach, he kept some beagles of his own. True to his resolution, however, of leading a professional and laborious life, he went to town in Hilary Term. Little encouragement awaited him here, unless it were the assurance he received from Judge Jones, that so long as he lived Whitelocke should not want a father. Mr. Charles Jones, the judge's son, a particular and valued friend, rendered him all the good offices in his power. But the young gentleman died, and when the body was

examined after death, the cause of death was found to be
stone, a disease on which he observes :—" I have the more
reason to inquire into it, being myself troubled, with
exceeding violence sometimes, by the like distemper ; and
may, when God shall so order it, look for the like dissolution
to be occasioned by it. I shall only hope and pray that God
will give me patience to undergo the torment, and prepared-
ness whensoever my change shall come."

He was so dispirited by the seeming neglect of his professional services that he thought it a waste of time to go
the whole circuit, which he had previously been accustomed
to ride as a practiser, though strongly advised to do so by
his friends. He went part of the way only, and the following
were the companions of his journey : Mr. Platt, the celebrated evidencer ; Mr. Lenthall, the future Speaker ; Mr.
Glyn ; Mr. Jones, already alluded to ; Mr. Hale, afterwards
the great Sir Matthew Hale ; and others. Above all there
was Mr. Littleton, who became Lord Keeper. Whitelocke
and he had long been on the most intimate terms, for
Littleton had instructed his junior in practice and demeanour
when he first turned circuiter. He only records one
passage on this circuit respecting his friend. It seems that
when the lawyers were invited with the judges and justices
of the peace to a sheriff's entertainment, the justices of the
peace, like kings in their own domains, would take their
seats before the lawyers, and crowd these down to the lower
end of the table, where not unfrequently, for want of room,
the excluded guests could get no dinner at all. This
exclusiveness on the part of the local magistrates was the
more resented, seeing that many of them were not men of
quality ; and Littleton took the matter up with great
warmth. He held it to be an injury to his profession, and
plotted with Whitelocke how best to show these boorish
justices their error. In Whitelocke he found a ready
coadjutor, and accordingly a scheme soon presented itself.
They found by the laws of heraldry that they, as eldest

sons of knights, had precedence of all the esquires who were
not themselves sons of more ancient knights.   Having previously assured their fellow circuiters that no discourtesy
was intended them, they resolved upon bold measures   but
some timidly remonstrated, and argued that as the justices
of the peace were at the assizes in the execution of their
office, they might possess temporary higher local rank in that
particular county.   To this Whitelocke opportunely replied
that their design was to be carried out at dinner, the par-
taking of which was no official act of justiceship, and cited
as a precedent the case of his own father, against whom a
justice of the peace complained once to the Lord Chancellor,
how he, a mere barrister-at-law, and no justice of the peace,
had nevertheless taken place of him, the justice.   In answer
to this complaint, the supposed offender observed merrily,
that if he happened to be entering with an esquire, who should
be a justice of the peace, officially into an alehouse, that then
he would give him the precedence, but if they went together
to that alehouse to play a game at tables, he saw no reason
why he might not walk before the justice as well as behind
him.   He took the difference between *actus indifferens* and
actus administrationis ; in the latter case the justice was to
have priority before other esquires, but not in the former.
The Chancellor approved of the distinction, and the authority
cited in point was Bartolus, the great civilian.   With this
argument—based on authority—the rest of the lawyers
were satisfied, and the experiment was successfully made
at the next sheriff's banquet, not without the knowledge and
approval of the judges themselves.   This Mr. Littleton was
in eminent practice at that time, fully justified by his great
abilities, learning, and spirit ; his generosity was notorious,
and he was one of Selden's best friends, although their
studies did not lie in the same direction.   Passing through
the several grades of preferment, he was made at last a
baron, upon receiving his final promotion to what was the
highest but most troublesome office in England, quitting for

this unstable dignity the best and most profitable office that could be held by a legal dignitary—the Chief Justiceship of the Common Pleas—but he neither left a great estate to his heirs, nor any son to inherit his honours.

On this circuit, when he only visited Oxford, Reading, and Aylesbury, Whitelocke had hardly anything to do, finding out practically how fatal a thing it was for him to have been a judge's favourite.

Treason must have been meditated about this period against the throne, for certain parties in Scotland were spreading the rumour, that the King did not think the crown of Scotland worth coming for, and others went so far as to conspire with the view of setting up there another king. It was the knowledge of these occurrences, that induced the King to proceed to Edinburgh, where he was crowned with all show of affection and duty, but in the Parliament the members stood upon the liberties of the kirk. His Majesty gratified many of them with new honours, which did not prevent several from muttering and even mutinying at a later period, and on returning to London through Dumfries, his person was exposed to danger. Lord Lowden, jealous of the Earl of Traquaire's appointment to the treasurership of Scotland, was showing his intentions in that Parliament, and unequivocally revealing a hostile course of conduct. About this time the Queen gave birth to another son, the future James II., but no star shone at noon in the East to chronicle his future destiny, so that he was far less honoured than his brother had been by the celestial bodies.

These signs and symptoms upon earth of growing dis-affection were not suffered to pass unnoticed, and his superstitious feelings were not roused to action by any singular phænomenon in the heavens ; nature proceeded on her silent and accustomed course, and he in his ordinary duties and callings. Whilst professionally engaged as a circuiter, or recorder, he received letters from home breath-ing affection and describing the well-being of their child.

Even his loyalty was reawakened, supposing it to have ever slumbered for the brief season of his parliamentary career as an oppositionist. Sir Arthur Ingram, having resolved to entertain the King at York and regale him with music worthy of royal ears, wrote to Whitelocke, and requested the loan of his servant Mr. Wensley, whose rare voice had become renowned. Happy at such an opportunity of obliging a friend, and of promoting the King's amusement, he gave his servant the permission required. And now, feeling more sympathy with royalty, and generously ascribing past misgovernment to the pernicious influence of favourites, a new fancy seized him : that of fishing with cormorants by way of variety to the sport of falconry. In the last sport he ever delighted, regarding it nearly as a duty of filial piety to cultivate the venerable science, to the successful practice of which his family in past ages were indebted for their rise and prosperity, as his heraldic studies had (though erroneously) led him to conclude. Such was the explanation he gave at the time, though frankly admitting its folly, and in after times regarding it as one of those vain expenses that young men are but too apt to incur for the gratification of a passing idle whim. It may be thought perhaps by the reader that he had some higher object in view, that of discreetly indicating by these living symbols or types those man-cormorants who at that time filled the Exchequer, and nearly every other office of the state—the Lord Chief Justiceship of the Common Pleas, for instance. To have stated this in words would have been dangerous in the extreme, for it would have subjected the unfortunate speaker of truth to all those pains and penalties, which for many dreary years to come were yet to be inflicted on such traitors and malefactors. To speak, write, or print one's political sentiments entailed as the rule, the death of the speaker, as if guilty of high treason, and under the most favourable circumstances, the offender could expect nothing less than mutilation, public ignominy, and branding. To write truth and explain

one's sentiments fully was not safe, even where no intention
of publishing them existed. Hence the extreme caution of
the liberal lawyer, who assigns to the frolic fancy of youth
what was more probably a mode of disseminating amongst
his neighbours and friends one of those lessons in politics,
which at this period were eagerly desired by nearly all
classes.

Whether for amusement or instruction the sport was
expensive. He procured some cormorants from Mr. Wood,
the master of the King's cormorants, and one of these
birds was held to be the best fisher of his day ; all of them
were manned like hawks, and came to the hand when called.
He then made a pond on his grounds, and had an arch built
upon piles, in which cool recess he kept wine in summer-
time, and a pleasure-boat. Not knowing the Egyptian
proverb of old, that an arch never sleeps, he built a banquet-
ing house upon his, whence the Thames could be seen
winding its way below, and woods looking fresh above it.
Like a true sportsman that always allows "law,"—a very
different law from that which prevailed in our English
courts, since in this case it means time for escape,—he contrived in behalf of the persecuted fish a sanctuary secured
by grating, so that when the cormorant came to the sport
he found his progress arrested, and his destined prey pro-
tected. He compares the motions of these birds beneath
the clear and transparent water, and the efforts of the fish
to escape, with a course in a paddock, and confesses with
a reluctant sigh, "that it was a very pleasant pastime."
Nor was this the only expensive whim he then indulged in,
for being anxious to counteract the prodigality it led to by
thrift, he joined his intimate friend Mr. Bartholomew Hall,
and some merchants of that gentleman's native place, the
well-known town of Pool, in a little adventure at sea,
whereby he learned, that there were other " cormorants "
besides those maintained by the King. He was a loser of
course, gave over that trade, and attained the conviction

that gentlemen do not thrive so well with the merchants, as the merchants themselves do.

On the 11th of July, Thomas Napper, by consent of his father, bound himself apprentice to Whitelocke, and his future career must have been successful, since his master intended to allude to it, and very likely did in some lost document. This, with several matters of seemingly trivial importance, may serve to disclose to us the secret state of his mind; it shows him to have been liberal in his housekeeping, generous in his expenditure, but at the same time fond of making money. The words of Laud had made a deep impression upon him—the effect intended by that virtual prime minister of England; his proffered friendship and well-known influence with the King, had led Whitelocke's friends to anticipate great things, and accordingly Mr. Harbottle Grimstone endeavoured to get the Mastership of the Requests for his kinsman and friend. Sir Sidney Montague, who was then the master, upon being delicately sounded, and asked whether he felt disposed to vacate the post, replied magisterially that he had no intention of selling the King's favour, and of course as he had previously purchased it, his right of holding it could not be disputed. Our barrister's circuitous life recommenced, and Laud, if he ever troubled himself to inquire, would have learned to his satisfaction that his old pupil had made professionally this year no less than ten journeys between Fawley and London, twelve to Abingdon, four to Oxford, four to Aylesbury, besides others in various directions. He pursued his studies with unremitting energy, and yet found, at the end of the year, that the entire profits of his profession had only reached the modest sum of 46*l.* 14*s.* A great falling off from the prosperity and hopes of the last year, when the judge his father was still living. And now for his moral, which most will think superfluous :—

"This gives some show of the baseness and corruption of men's ways, who will retain one that goes under the name

of a favourite for no other end, but because they hope
thereby to have more favour than otherwise they ought to
have, a kind of close intention of bribery. But this, I may
confidently affirm, that no one who retained me ever had
from your grandfather the least advantage for that reason.
Yet, when their glosing and fawning hopes of such advantage
was gone, by the judge's death, then was I wholly neglected
by them."

This neglect, which seems to have mortified him so deeply,
may be more charitably explained by a desire on the part
of the common attorneys and solicitors, who usually retain
counsel, to do the best they could for their clients, and it
was at all events productive of good by rousing him to still
greater exertions. He felt such disdain at their conduct,
he says, and such an emulation to achieve success "by the
blessing of God on his endeavours," that he rejected the
advice of his relatives to renounce the profession and betake
himself to a country life, where he might by good husbandry
create for himself a far better income than any mere practice could yield him. The advice of the Archbishop prevailed, and he armed himself with fresh courage to surmount
the apparent obstacles in his path.*

---

* About this time he set up the monument to his parents in Fawley Church, by
the inscription on which it appears he was connected with the De La Beche family,
and with those of Colt, Mostyn, Dixon, Bennet, Bulstrode, and others. In the course
of his works he alludes to his kinsmanship with the Duke of Buckingham and Lord
Fairfax.

CHAPTER VII.

On returning from Abingdon, where he had delivered his
third charge as Recorder, his wife Rebecca pressed upon him
her dissatisfaction with the lonely life she led in the country
during his absence at London in the terms, and at the
assizes, and wished to take a house in town, where she could
have more the benefit of his company and be nearer to her
friends. He accordingly took a house in Salisbury Court,
which seemed to him a very desirable residence, and removed
to it with his wife and household at Michaelmas term.

Adieu to the calm tranquillity and that glow of health
which green woods, fresh waters. and laughing fields conspire
to produce. Adieu to peace; for he had no sooner arrived
than a contest broke out between the parishioners who
attended public worship in St. Gregory's Church and the
Dean of Paul's, who had interfered, by which his devout wife
must have been alarmingly excited. The Dean had caused
the communion table to be removed to the east end, and
transformed into an altar, as was erroneously thought, by

inclosing it with rails, raising it on a dais, and perhaps also by placing candlesticks upon it. The process, in short, was similar to what has been recently enacted in this country, and the aggrieved parishioners complained ; in answer to which the King in council approved of the Dean's act. The people obtained accordingly quite as little redress as they have on recent similar occasions. The table in every church retains its supposed altar-site to this day ; the innovation was submitted to by the people at the Restoration, and thus slowly but resolutely the priesthood of the Anglican church have introduced stealthily one innovation at a time after long intervals, believing that where form can be set up, the substance will follow inevitably, however slowly.

Not contented with this decision, applicable not merely to St. Gregory's but to every church in this kingdom, the King in council, surrounded by advisers who had presided in the Starchamber, sent a peremptory order to Scotland that prayers and divine service should be celebrated twice a day in the King's chapel after the manner sanctioned in England ; that the communion should be taken monthly by the recipients on their knees ; that the ministers should wear the surplice ; and that other ceremonial innovations should forthwith commence. The Dean of the Royal chapel was afraid to put such orders into execution for fear of displeasing the people. Another act of the King gave great offence to the majority of Englishmen, who, it must be confessed, were on this occasion in the wrong. But Charles showed a lamentable want of tact and political management in these endeavours to set the prejudices, however stolid, of a whole nation at defiance. He revived his father's declaration for tolerating lawful sports on the Lord's day, and offended by this proclamation, not merely the puritans, who regarded it as the Sabbath, but many others usually opposed to puritanical views on every religious question with the exception of this. Nor had Whitelocke at this period any strong taint of puritanism about him. On the contrary, he frequented from time to time the theatre in his neighbourhood, and opposed the extreme opinions of men, who like the author of Histriomastix, were desirous of putting down stage-plays altogether. As the Queen herself had figured in a dramatic piece, the lawyers, who as a body in every age and country vie with an endowed priesthood in their manifestation of loyalty and in the maintenance of constituted order, were now especially anxious to evince their attachment to the Crown. Entirely dependent on court favour and money for advancement to place and honours, exposed as they were to the arbitrary will and caprice of the monarch for a continuance in any office so acquired, this demonstration devised by them may have had some political significance, but assuredly no moral weight with the stern Covenanters of the age. At a hint from the court, not imparted to the young members, but merely to the old successful officials of the bar, to the servants of the King in short, which judges then especially were, and serjeants not merely in name but in humiliating reality, the obsequious Societies of the Four Inns of Court resolved at Allhallowtide to present their service to the King and Queen, to testify to them their affection, to give them the outward and visible testimony of their homage in the form of a Royal Masque. A committee was nominated for this purpose, and for the Middle Temple Whitelocke and Mr. Edward Hyde were chosen. Even Selden did not escape.

The reader who feels any interest in the exact description of this absurd formality must consult " Whitelocke's Memorials," where minute particulars of the ceremonial seem to have been most scrupulously recorded. The design had from the first a political object, and it is amusing at least to perceive the compromise that took place in the course of its elaboration. For the popular and liberal portion of it the spectators were indebted probably to Selden, and the exhibition of this part of the procession may have created passing mirth, not wholly unproductive of more permanent results. It was called the Anti-Masque, and consisted of mounted beggars and cripples, whose "habits and properties were most ingeniously fitted." They were followed by a band of horsemen playing on pipes, whistles and various birdcalls ; the meaning of which was to contrast ironically with the scientific music still faintly heard in the distance. The men-birds followed : there was an owl in an ivy bush, with several sorts of birds clustering round and gazing at him ; but what judge or chancellor he represented was left to the fancy of the spectators. Hideous bagpipes, squeaking hornpipes, and other kinds of "northern music" ensued, preluding the political symbols in their train. A fellow rode upon a little horse with a huge bit in his mouth, and upon his head, whether that of the man or the beast I cannot pretend to say, were fastened another bit with headstall and reins. In those days of monopoly and court protection the greatest dullard must have caught the allusion. It represented a projector who begged a patent, that none throughout the realm should ride their horses with any other bits but his. Then came another fellow with a bunch of carrots on his head and a capon on his fist, who represented that happy projector who claimed a patent of monopoly as being the inventor of the art how to fatten capons with carrots, and that he might enjoy the privilege for fourteen years according to the statute. Strange to say, it was not Selden but Mr. Attorney Noy who got up these latter personifications, in the hope that the King might know what the people thought of such patents and projectors. If this were so, and Noy affirmed it at the committee, he must have little known his master, who valued the opinions and wishes of the people at a straw when contrary to his own.

This vast procession of carriages and horsemen proceeded to Whitehall, where they were honoured by the presence of the King and Queen, who stood at a window that looked down upon the street ; that very window through which the King was conducted fifteen years after to the stage of the scaffold. Their Majesties were so well pleased that they sent a message, desiring that the whole show might take a turn about the tilt-yard, and the command was obeyed. After this, all alighted at Whitehall Gate, and were led to several rooms and places prepared for their accommo-dation.

The masque itself now commenced, when the actors performed their parts. Whitelocke and Hyde were signally honoured on this occasion ; for while the others sate in the gallery reserved for them, these two were placed below among the grandees and near the scene. Whitelocke says it was done in order that they might be ready to give their assistance in case it should be required ; and he admits it to have been an extraordinary favour vouchsafed to them at that time, "and in that presence." He seems not to have perceived any secret motive in such preference, forgetting, probably, his own and Hyde's opposition principles, or rather his own good nature, and a delicacy when alluding to Hyde, who at that time was not yet bought over like Wentworth to the court, made him averse to comments of the kind. In his own case there might have been some reason for the distinction, because he really had contrived with professional assistance the musical portion of the spectacle. As no opera or concert is complete without dancing, there was a ball at the conclusion of the masque, when the Queen danced with some of the masquers herself, and was pleased to declare they danced as well as any she had ever seen. When the morning dawn had put an end to their sports, a stately banquet crowned this "earthly pomp and glory, if not vanity, that was so soon past over and gone, as if it had never been."

The whole account seems given to point a moral, super-fluous indeed for those that came after him, who would be very unlikely to play a part in a masque, a kind of pageant never revived to serve the political emergency arising from a train of peculiar circumstances, when new monarchs and new follies superseded those of an antiquated description. The Queen, who was much delighted with these solemnities, was so taken with both show and masque that she desired to see it all acted over again. An intimation was accordingly given to the Lord Mayor of London, and although this dignitary may well have deemed it as somewhat tending to detract from the glories of his own civic raree-show, he was too dutiful a subject to hesitate an instant in showing dutiful compliance with the royal wish. The forms of his court being hurriedly gone through, that no lack of zeal to the crown or his fellow magnates might be laid to his charge, he invited the king and queen and the masquers to the city, where he entertained them with all state and magnificence in Merchant Tailors' Hall. The same show that had gone to Whitehall now marched through the heart of London, and the same masque was presented. There were the same horsemen, lacqueys, liveries, torches, habits, chariots, music, and all other parts of the former solemnity. The fair sex were especially gratified, and if the Lord Mayor Freeman derived very great honour, it was obtained by reason of his very great expenditure alone, and not from the usual source. As soon as the dream was over, the committee for the masque required an account of all the disbursements, and all claimants were bountifully satisfied. For the music, which had been committed exclusively to Whitelocke's charge, he gave to Mr. Ives and Mr. Lawes £100 a piece, and as for the four French gentlemen who were the queen's servants, he thought he should best gratify their royal mistress by rewarding them not merely liberally but with grace and delicacy. He accordingly invited them one morning to a collation in the great room of St. Dunstan's tavern, already familiar to us as " the Oracle of Apollo," where each of them had a plate and cover laid for him, with the napkin tied. On opening these the foreign guests found in each of them no less than forty pieces of gold for the first dish. The other musicians were rewarded according to their respective

H

merits, determined I am afraid too much by their quality, as in the former case by interest. The whole charge of the music came to £1000, equivalent in value to a much larger sum in the present day. The dresses of the horsemen, the liveries of their pages and lacqueys were at their own particular charge, costing each individual about £100 upon the average, and there were at least one hundred of such suits. The remaining expenses of the masque were found to exceed £20,000, which had to be borne by the societies of the Inns of Court, and by some of the wealthier members individually. Considering the large income of an English lawyer at the zenith of his profession, we can only sympathise with the briefless barristers, who could scarcely have hoped to reap any ultimate benefit from this extravagant parade, the sole object of which, by its originators and promoters, was to throw dust into the eyes of a formidable but deluded people.

The want of a quiet happy home was acting injuriously on our young templar at this time, and even his principles, notwithstanding his association with Selden, and the independent example of his late father who never played the courtier, were inclining to yield too much to court influence, and the only too well remembered advice of Laud. His mind seems to have become unhinged, and turning away from Coke, Littleton, and Bracton, he sought the company of lutists and harpers, consorted with them, and strove to gain their favour. With the assistance of Mr. Ives he composed an air himself, called Whitelocke's Coranto. It was first cried up and played in public by the Blackfriars musicians, considered in those days the best band in all London. Whenever he went to that house to see a play, which he sometimes did, the musicians called for the Coranto, and the spectators would have it repeated again and again. The Queen conveyed to him her Majesty's especial commendation ; the air had such life and spirit in it, she could hardly believe an Englishman was its composer. It spread rapidly from town to the country, and was played publicly every where for above thirty years. Nor did he ever regret in after life this passionate predilection of his for harmony and sweet sounds, but enjoins the culture of music to his descendants, provided they attain perfection in it, and deeply imbued with the religious spirit of the times, quotes texts from Scripture, by way of authority and precedent, to vindicate his attachment to harmonious numbers.

Shortly after the performance of the masque, the committee ordered Sir John Finch, Mr. Gerling, Mr. Hyde and Whitelocke, to attend their Majesties, and return in the name of the four Inns of Court their humble thanks for the gracious acceptance by Royalty of their humble service in the late masque. They were first brought to the King, who gave to each of them, in the exercise of the Royal prerogative, his hand to kiss. Then came the speech, to which the King, " with great affability and pleasingness," vouchsafed an answer presently, in which the fact of its having been a testimony of respect and affection to himself was thankfully acknowledged, with the promise that he should be ready upon all occasions to manifest the good opinion he had of them, and to render not merely to the societies they represented but to themselves in particular any favour. From the King they then repaired to the Queen, and were graciously permitted to kiss her hand also. The address and answer were given, the report to the committee followed, and a vote of thanks for their zeal obtained from the Benchers. " But the black night overtakes the glorious day ; the fairest calms have storms in their bosoms ; the chain of earthly affairs for one link of joy has two of sorrow. And 'tis well that it is so, lest the constant smiles of this world should allure us unto too much love of it, and to forget God. This high pleasure and jollity, this honour and favour, this joy and gallantry was, as to my private concerns, soon plunged into the depth of grief and misery."

Spring was approaching ; a term that implies in London

no zephyr or Favonian breeze, but the rheumatic and agueish
east wind ; no sunny flowers, but wet clammy clay in the
purlieus of Alsatia.   His wife fell desperately ill again of her
former distemper, and was attacked with far greater violence
than at any time before.   " I forbear to relate the manner of
it," he exclaims, "for tears would blot the paper."   The accidental use of the words " any time" sufficiently reveals the
nature of her malady.   Her husband and the world believed
it to be madness.   Insanity it was not, though little less
dreadful, and too often its harbinger ; it was that mysterious
scourge of humanity in every age, that visitation regarded
as divine by the ancients, that Sybilline inspiration—epilepsy.
Far better would it have been for the helpless and hapless
victim, had she lived in those ages when the patients were
either cared for in temples, or suffered to roam at large and
breathe at least the pure free air of heaven.   Her lot was
cast in an age when madness was deemed a crime, a libel on
mankind, to be charged with irons and whipped with cords,
as witchery was to be burned with fire or drowned with
water.   Their cries for help, their moans and screams, and
the rolling lustreless eye-balls glazed with agony, excited no
sympathy, but horror, and dread, and cruel persecution.
Thank God, the man whose life I am now writing, ignorant
of medical knowledge as he was, steeped like all his cotem-
poraries in superstitious notions, was not inhuman ; and if he
sinned in the sequel, which admits of some doubt, he sinned
through ignorance, through want of a stern but manly fixedness of purpose.   He states what does him honour, that never
poor creature had a more dismal sickness than that under
which she laboured, that no man ever had sharper affliction
than he had by it.   "Friends sought out help for her, and
it was advised to place her in the house of a doctor of
physic at Bowe, near London, the man being famous for
cures of such distempers."

The son of Æsculapius was treated with, and his greed
was betrayed in the first interview.   He demanded £200 for

the cure, and 50s. a week (a large sum in that age) for her
accommodation in his house.   The cunning doctor undertook
" by the blessing of God " to cure her perfectly and restore
her to her former health, but refused to meddle with the case
save on one condition—that no acquaintance nor friend of
hers, not even her own mother or her husband, should see
her during that course of her physic.   The doctor went on to
observe, that at the sight of any one she knew or loved,
especially of her mother or husband, her fancy would be so
disturbed, that it would endanger a relapse, and possibly her
life ; and at least retard if not quite hinder her recovery.
Unless this demand of his was complied with, he would
undertake nothing in this business ; but if they would
forbear coming to her for five or six months, he was confident in that time they might see her as well again as ever.
Her own mother and friends consented, and persuaded her
husband to assent also.

And so now, the desolate man says, being banished from
her company whom he most loved, his own thoughts distracted and overwhelmed with gloom, he took a sudden and
rash resolution.   He determined on quitting the spot, on
leaving the kingdom where she was, in order to seek mental
quiet or excitement abroad.   A nurse, well known to his
wife's friends, and strongly recommended, was appointed to
attend her, and the doctor promised to send a bulletin to her
mother from time to time ; their child was left by him under
proper care and vigilance, and his conscience being lulled, he
obtained, by the favour of the Lord Chamberlain, a license
from the privy council to go to France.   Without this license,
so little was the right and liberty of a subject respected in
England, no man could leave his native country of his own
free will.

Whitelocke took with him letters of introduction from
various lords and men of mark, and was strongly recommended to the King's resident then at Paris.   " By advice,"
he says—his own mind being in a sad vacillating condition,

when not rash and headstrong, which showed too plainly
its disordered movements—he went down to Rye, intending
to take shipping for Dieppe, in Normandy, but spring was
setting in with its usual severity, and the weather was tempestuous in the extreme.   When near Tonbridge, he accidentally met with Mr. Dixon, his brother-in-law, who
wondered, he said, that he should pass so near his house and
not call upon his sister.   In an agitated mood he acquainted
Mr. Dixon with recent events, enjoined secrecy towards his
sister, which was kept ; but his own conduct must have
furnished matter of self-reproach, since he durst not venture
to see so near and dear a relative and hear what her
opinion would be.   So he reached Rye, and there, detained
by adverse winds, having put out to sea more than once and
narrowly escaped foundering, he spent ten long miserable
days.   To drown care he went out shooting, studied the
localities, the history of the place, and strove to banish
thought.   On the eleventh day, a fair wind springing up, he
set sail, and towards the evening of the following day gained
the shores of France.   His first encounter here was with
the rude shallopers, who all contended which of them should
carry the traveller on his back from the ship to dry land.

Upon touching the shore, in deference to custom, he
waited upon the governor of the castle and town, who was
a man of high rank.   Every mark of attention was shown
to him and the companion of his journey, Mr. Robert Cole,
an old and valued friend, who had volunteered to accompany
him abroad.   Both of them had never left England before,
and accordingly were both attacked here with what foreigners
call a fit of the spleen, which, in reality, was profound
melancholy in his own case, and sympathy in the other.
Whitelocke and the governor contracted a great mutual
esteem, and kept up a correspondence by letters for many
years after ; it was the Englishman's good fortune to do
great service to some of the Frenchman's friends in England,
and it was most gratefully acknowledged.   From this place

he travelled with his company to Rohan (Rouen), admired
the apple trees fringing the road for leagues together ; was
pleased with the orchards, especially the vines "married to
other trees," and the corn crops planted in rows between
them.   At Rouen he visited, like English tourists ever since
have done, the church of Notre Dame, and was shown the
Duke of Bedford's tomb.   He was accompanied by an
individual calling himself a prior of the order of the
Celestines, and whose house was near Paris.   They conversed together in Latin, and he had to draw upon his whole
stock of scholarship whilst explaining to the other, who
seems to have had a very inquisitive mind, and more
liberality of sentiments than is usual with Celestine priests,
the laws, customs, and government of England, its public
monuments, and remarkable places.

Upon his arrival at Paris he first lodged, as he had done
in Dieppe, at an inn ; in each instance the mistress of the
house endeavoured to divert him from his sadness.   He is
pleased to pay the landladies of France a compliment on
this occasion, for he observes that the mien of those women
was very comely, and superior to that of hostesses in other
countries.   He and his friend soon found it desirable to take
up their quarters in a "pension" where there were no
English, in order that they might learn to speak French
with·greater ease and propriety.

He had no sooner installed himself at a French family's,
than the cold he had caught at sea, gradually increased by
his journey, was now changed into a high burning fever.
The danger was so imminent, that his friend and himself
expected every hour would be his last.   He was given over
by the French doctor and the family with whom he was
staying.   "But it pleased God, who had more service for
him to do, in his great mercy, to bless the means used by
another French doctor," who according to their way ordered
him to be let blood three times in twenty-four hours.   There
were other applications, perhaps hot water, upon the Sangrado

principle ; but whatever they were, the bleeding and fast-
ing saved his life, so at least it was supposed to do, and
he recovered his strength in a few days. The king's agent
now honoured him with a visit, and his recent acquaintance,
the prior, found out also where he was. Cardinal Richelieu
was made acquainted with his presence, and sent various
lords of high quality to do him honour ; for the Queen of
England's French servants, who had served in the masque,
and been so liberally rewarded by him, had written very
favourable accounts to Paris, and enlarged on the eminent
favour he enjoyed at his own court. Such, at least, was
the intimation he received from various French courtiers ;
but Richelieu had probably kept him in sight from the
moment of his landing at Dieppe. In after years, when he
himself became a member of Cromwell's government, and
initiated into the mysteries of a Privy Council, he may have
better comprehended the anxiety of Richelieu respecting
him and his friend. Whatever his personal merits may
have been, that which made the greatest sensation was not
his person or accomplishments, but the dress he wore. It
consisted of the finest English cloth, the colour of which was
cinnamon, and it was lined with suitable plush, without lace.
Having grown intimate with courtiers and men of high
quality, Richelieu, the all-powerful minister, sent word to
him, by one of his creatures, that he should be welcome to
him ; and a dark hint or two was dropped, which led the
Englishmen to attribute sinister motives to his Excellency.
Our countrymen, however, were not in a position, at that
time, to disregard the dictates of prudence, and he therefore
returned his most humble thanks for the intended honour
of presentation, and signified how happy he should be to
pay his respects to the Cardinal in person. By dint of good
management he obtained leave to spend some time with the
French army in Picardy, and a commission having been
offered him to command a troop of horse, he accepted it.

His conduct at this critical time of his life was unquestionably occasioned by his firm belief that his unhappy wife was mad, and that she would never recover. It seems to have been his intention to abandon his native land for ever, and strike out a military career in France, as one of his uncles had done a quarter of a century before. But he kept up a correspondence with many of his friends, such as Hyde, Wall, Walrond, and others, of the Middle Temple, and with Cely and Oakley, the old servants of his father, to whom he had left the care of his affairs and the duty of reporting any intelligence respecting the condition of the unhappy lady at Bowe. Some of Mr. Hyde's letters about this time display great friendship and intimacy, which subsequent events and even rivalry could never wholly efface. It is in his answer to the first of Hyde's letters, that we perceive the profound grief of the wanderer, and his unsettled state of mind, for he says : " I know your goodness will not only give me your pardon, but plead with others on my behalf, and be a friend to my poor wife and child. My disease is above the cure of philosophy, nothing but the divine hand can apply a remedy, and my present indisposition of health is so great, *that I can hardly hope to see England again.*"

Soon after this phrase was penned, his resolution was shaken by a letter from the doctor, in which that gentleman, as well as others, assured him of his wife's recovery, that she was in a very hopeful way, and would shortly get rid of her distemper. The postscript contained intelligence more consonant with his own doubts and fears. The disciple of Galen repeated his assurance, that his fair patient was so nearly recovered, that her mother had come and earnestly desired to see her, and another of her daughters, Mrs. Amcotes, who had been similarly placed with the writer for the cure of the same distemper. By this disclosure the unfortunate husband now comprehended better, why this practitioner had been selected by the mother, and so strongly recommended to him. The mother, so the doctor went on

to observe, would take no denial, would listen to no entreaty,
and on being admitted had, after the first inquiries were
over, retired with her daughter to a distance from the nurse,
and conversed privately with her for about an hour.   The
result was, that the invalid's weak spirits being tired and
oppressed, she had fallen into a relapse, which still continued.
The traveller's design of proceeding to Orleans and joining
the French army was now at an end, and while still irresolute and distracted, fresh letters from his friends brought
tidings more disastrous still. These described the further
result of the mother's interview with her daughter, and how
on the 14th day from that date, after lingering for twelve
days without taking ordinary sustenance, his wife had expired
on the 9th day of May.   He was consoled, he says, by one
thing only, that she had died in the Lord.   It appears, that
shortly before her decease, she had recovered her senses, for
on the day before her death, her brother, Mr. Richard
Bennett, and some other friends, had been with her, when
she had discoursed very sensibly with them, very affection-
ately of him, and most religiously of her own change, which
she both expected and desired.   She had also conversed
piously with the minister, who administered all the solace
in his power.   Other letters by the next post informed him,
how his mother-in-law had given out that he was dead, and
that she would petition the king to have the custody of her
grandchild together with the profits of its father's estate,
until it was ascertained whether he were living or not.   One
of the letters was from Hyde, and ran as follows :

"To my very good friend Mr. Whitelocke, these :—

"My dear friend,—I will hope, that all sad relations
have ere this arrived with you, and that you are as well as
your condition will bear.   The best part of the world per-
forms you justice in professing all your known friendship
to your wife, and just respects to her friends.   Let this and
your own conscience preserve you unconcerned in the
censures of her mother and family for your going out of

England, and know your reputation is much above the reach
of their impotent malice.   If you stand fast upon your own
virtue, you are fully vindicated from any shadow of blame
by that journey, but if you think by any compliance to
prevail with people of such compositions, you but expose
yourself to the mischiefs of insolency.   Whether your
return ought to be speedy or only a little hastened I shall
leave to your own wisdom, which understands best how you
have settled and disposed of your estate, and whether the
air of France be fitter for melancholique than ours. My
little friend at Salisbury Court is lusty, and shall live your
comfort.   If there be any clamours at Court (as your mad
mother threatens) I have taken a sure course for intimation,
and shall easily prevent any mischiefs they can intend.
Among your afflictions suffer not yourself to be so much
confounded, as to forget your fair proportion of blessings too,
among which your fame with all good men will find a chief
place, and let the share we bear of your griefs ease your too
heavy burden.   Whilst others perform you real services,
I am only busy in my resolutions and vows to be, your most
humble and affectionate servant,   EDWARD HYDE."

  " Middle Temple, this 21st of May."

  To this most kind letter he replied in terms of proper
acknowledgment. I find one phrase in it, which in common
justice to his memory I cannot omit. " They," speaking of
his wife's relatives, " must acknowledge, if they will own the
truth, they know it was my affection, not unkindness, that
carried me out of my own country and banished me from
my most beloved wife and worldly comfort." Nor was the
society of his friend Cole unseasonable at this juncture. In
after years, when describing his late partner to his eldest
son, then grown up to man's estate, he tells him that his
mother "was of personage tall and comely, of a tender and
good nature, of ingenuous and rational discourse, when her

parts were not eclipsed by sickness;" that "she was just, faithful, and charitable, and above all affectionate to her husband."

And now having abandoned all idea of riding the tour of France, he passed, as well as he could in his then sad condition, the ceremonies of taking leave ; and quitting Paris at 7 o'clock in the evening of a Wednesday, early in the month of June, he took the road to Boulogne. He and his friend resolved to ride all night, the best time for escaping the straggling soldiers, who infested the roads by day. He found this French mode of riding post a speedy and convenient one, for fresh horses were always ready, which kept up a round pace to the end of each stage, the length of which varied from four to five English miles. They stopped in the day-time at Pontoise and other places, for the sake of refreshment, and he did not fail to perceive that his mourning suit of black, which the people mistook for the garb of a priest, procured them more civility and attention than would have been conceded to the scarlet and richly laced cloak of his companion. To him they first brought the fresh horse, the wine, the dish, and called him "Père." When riding near the quarters of the army in Picardy on Thursday night, several bullets came whistling about their ears, to the great alarm of their guides, who explained to them that small parties of disbanded soldiers were posted in trees to shoot at travellers passing by, and that if any fell the soldiers would rush in, despatch and rifle them ; but that if they missed, and the passengers went on, they would take no further notice, and remain concealed. In this way they ran the gauntlet as far as Amiens, part of which city he found to be built on a chalky soil, and here some soldiers upon duty, who were not enacting the part of marauders, stopped them and politely requested the favour of their company to the officers of the patrol. This civility was so contrary to the usual rudeness of foot soldiers that they could but comply with a good grace, and they were taken to the captain of the citadel, who, finding who they were by his examination, dismissed them with all courtesy. On Friday morning they reached Boulogne, having ridden all the way from Paris in one day and two nights, a distance he computed to be equal to about 200 English miles. A French vessel was prepared for them whilst they visited the upper and lower towns, and they quickly got on board. Leaving Mr. Cole's man, a Frenchman, behind to bring the heavy luggage as soon as it arrived from Paris by the carrier; a fortunate act that seemingly preserved their lives; Mr. Cole himself and his servant were the only passengers. The order to the French servant had been heard and understood by the crew. Wearied to the last degree by the long journey and want of sleep, Mr. Cole and Whitelocke's domestics threw themselves on the bare boards of the cabin and fell into a heavy slumber. He himself was kept awake by a tide of contending thoughts and violent emotions. Externally calm and sunk in deep reflections, the mariners supposed him to be likewise sleeping, and to his horror he overheard some of the ruffians proposing to the rest the murder of the sleeping Englishmen and the division of the spoil afterwards. The scene, described at length in the wanderer's journal, it is scarcely necessary to insert here, as no real danger was actually incurred, since the plan was not adopted by the rest of the crew from prudential motives and the certainty of detection. A favouring breeze soon brought the vessel in safety to Dover, when he took post for London, and reached his house on Sunday morning. He found here his motherless son plump and thriving, and was soon welcomed back by all his friends.

CHAPTER VIII.

—✦—

1634—1636.

Resumes his Professional Pursuits, and cultivates Literature and Music—Returns to
his Seat, Fawley Court, and is made a Justice of the Peace—Progress of Public
Affairs—Laud's Persecution of Prynne and Bastwick—Encroachments of the
Dutch on our Coasts—Selden's Controversy with Grotius on the *Mare Clausum*
—The King tries to levy Ship-money—Public Discontent increases—Establish-
ment of the Thirty-nine Articles in Ireland—Foreign Intrigues—Whitelocke
charged with aiding Nonconformists—His Remarks on the "Annals of his
Life"—His Charge to the Grand Jury at Oxford—Subserviency of the Judges—
More Popish Innovations.

HAVING left France before he could perfect himself in the
language, he took the son of a Parisian goldsmith, one
Piccasta, into his service, chiefly for the sake of hearing him
speak his own tongue and play the lute, on which instrument
he excelled. And now upon resuming his former professional
habits, he found himself sadly forgotten by the judges,
"those wise men of the world." With rare exception, a
judge in those days was an attentive watcher of court
favour and royal smiles. Neglected at Whitehall, where
masquing and mummery, not moping and sadness, were the
passports, he ought not to have wondered at his frigid treatment in the minor courts, where the king's servants dispensed laws only too commonly in due ratio to the bribes
and presents of suitors, or at the orders of their master in
political matters. Corruption ruled in every court, and the
only mode for a barrister to gain the judge's smile was by
achieving success,—in which he had failed as yet. All Whitelocke's practice for the year had only yielded the paltry sum
of 35*l.* 10*s.*, but he was now no longer to be daunted.

Giving up his house in town, which he had only taken, he

says, to please his wife, he resolved to remove his son to Fawley
Court and re-establish his household at that seat. He had
not yet renounced the muses, and he still affected those
eclogues and elegies that schoolboys love. He composed a
dialogue between two shepherds, and Mr. Ives adapted these
verses to the lute. Both the words and the music cheered
him in his solitude, and I cannot allow this opportunity to
pass, when speaking of poetry and song, without expressing
my astonishment, that he who mingled so much in society,
who knew life, and consorted with musicians, should never
once have alluded in the remotest manner to one single play
of Shakespeare! It is the more extraordinary, because the
owners of the inn, that Shakespeare frequented with his
companions, were the friends of his father and himself.
This hankering after poetry at that period discloses the still
undeveloped and unmatured state of his intellectual powers,
and he showed this in other things as well. Resuming his
sport with the cormorants, which were it not for its political
significance would have been purely childish, he played the
boy by pulling down the banquetting house, which he had
built upon the arch near the artificial lake in his park. He
resolved to reconstruct it on higher ground, near his orchard,
which stood in a different county, that of Oxford. In this
new sanctuary he officiated as a Justice of the Peace, and it
is difficult to say of which he was the more proud, his civil
dignity of magistrate, or the classic abode just reared. The
steps, bayboards of the windows, the hearth and pavements
were constructed of Bletchington marble, the blue and white
colours of which he thought most beautiful, and had selected
them from the quarry of Sir Thomas Coghill, his noble friend
and kinsman. The room was only twelve feet square, but
what with the ponds, arch, marble, materials, removal, workmanship, and other charges, he found the whole had cost
him full five hundred pounds. Meanwhile he showed himself
in his gown, during the summer assizes, in Bucks, Berks,
and Oxfordshire—to very little purpose. Having thus so

much learned leisure, he directed his attention once more to what was passing in the public life of the nation, as well as to his abstract professional reading. And, in truth, there was much in public events to astonish even him.

Laud, the Primate, had procured a sharp sentence in the Star Chamber against Prynne. Before the fine was estreated, Laud and the other high commissioners had, by their warrant, caused Prynne's books and papers to be seized, removed from his lodging, perused and sifted for matter to be brought up against him.

On Prynne's complaining of this in the Star-chamber, the Archbishop denied that any such warrant had been given. The bishops about this period, and, indeed, until the execution of Strafford, were nearly all of opinion, that a public and private conscience were two distinct things. Laud favoured undoubtedly this episcopal dogma, peradventure, that good might result.

Flushed with success, and eager for church-militancy, he then cited the author of Elenchus Papismi, poor Dr. Bastwick, who had answered a certain Mr. Short, a Papist, and maintainer of the Pope's supremacy, of the mass and Popery in general. The Doctor in his preface assured the reader, he intended nothing against our English bishops, only those of Rome, but this availed him little. He was fined 10,000*l.*, excommunicated, debarred the practice of his profession, imprisoned, and degraded. On the other hand, a man named Chowney, a fierce Papist, wrote a book in defence of Rome and His Holiness, averring Papacy to be a true church, and it was dedicated *by permission* to Laud. Not only was Chowney not punished, he was not even so much as questioned. Moreover, in that very Star-chamber, and whilst collecting the opinions of the Bench respecting Bastwick, all the bishops then present denied openly, that they had their jurisdiction as bishops from the King, a denial that would have cost them their heads in the time of bluff Harry. Were these priests already beginning to see the moral weakness of their master, and were they the only men that did so? The lawyers seem to have been equally sagacious, for they compared the *regia manus* of the reigning with that of the dead but still dread potentate. Whitelocke was a reporter in the Star-chamber, and witnessed these proceedings, all but that part of them which took place in the High Commission Court, which however he had faithfully conveyed to him by the reporter engaged there. To his horror, he actually heard the Archbishop maintain that Chowney's book was true, that the Romish Church was a true one, that it did not err in fundamentals. He and other bishops took that opportunity of abusing Calvin, and depreciating the Holy Scriptures. It is probable, however, that in making this last declaration, Whitelocke may have misunderstood the sentiments he heard.

With the return of summer, the English coasts were once again infested by pirates, who came all the way from Turkey and Algiers. As for the Dutch, they were then masters by sea, and although Charles did nothing to repel the encroachments of their fishermen on our coasts, his subject Selden replied to Grotius, refuted the idea of his "Mare Liberum," and contended in his own "Mare Clausum" for the maintenance of our coast-rights and sovereignty over our own seas. So great and so notorious had the supineness of the monarch and the consequent national ignominy become, that even Charles himself felt, or feigned to feel, the humiliation. He wanted ship-money, and disdaining to ask the aid of the people, issued a writ for the levying of it, at first to the maritime towns and counties, but later to all the counties. As in the days of Joseph, Pharaoh spared the priesthood, so were the English clergy favoured on this occasion. With the exception of courtiers and official personages, who of course never grumble, the laymen of this nation were loud in their murmurs, not so much at the tax itself, for that was adjusted equitably enough as far as it affected them, but at the illegality of it, at its arbitrary imposition without the

I

consent of Parliament. Sweden too was grievously slighted in the person of its ambassador Grave John, the son of the old Chancellor Oxenstiern. The English court, so lavish of this nation's resources in men and money for Russia and Poland, refused to assist the Prince Elector against the Emperor, and the Grave, who felt very warmly for the honour of his country and the Protestant cause, returned to Sweden in a state of stern displeasure. On the other hand, the Irish Parliament gave some subsidies to Charles, and were so complaisant as to establish in that country the well-known thirty-nine articles of the Anglican Church.

If we turn our eyes to Scotland, we find that the people were murmuring there against their late parliament. Lord Balmerino was questioned about a complimentary letter, that King James had written to Pope Clement. Some worthy persons, too tender of that King's memory, suggested that his Lordship's father, when secretary to the King, had shuffled the letter amongst other papers, and so obtained its royal signature. A most unlikely explanation, but if true, why was that Lord subsequently pardoned, honoured, and preferred ? In part explanation of these tokens of discontent, Whitelocke asserts, that Richelieu was employing incendiary agents in both kingdoms, and that these emissaries met with very combustible materials. Having just returned himself from France, he brought with him, what history has long since confirmed, a very true estimate of that unconscientious statesman's character ; and there can be little doubt that such individuals as he adverts to were at work, in the pay of France. Their presence was hardly needed, unless to inflame the vulgar, for with almost the same stroke of the pen that recorded his suspicion of foreign intrigue, he devoted a few lines to the memory of his father's illustrious friend, Sir Edward Coke, who died this year,* and of whom he says, that he opposed earnestly in Parliament the *illegal* actions of the Court. And as for the covert agents of the

A.D. 1634.

Pope, since Rome had her projects as well as France, one generally suspected, the Lord Treasurer Weston, died also about this time, whose family at least were undisguised Papists. The appointment of Spotiswood, Archbishop of St. Andrews, to a secular post of great eminence, the Chancellorship of Scotland, an appointment without precedent since the earliest dawn of the Reformation in that country, was not calculated to allay the general discontent. Here likewise at home, a complaint was actually lodged with himself officially, as Recorder of Abingdon, against several non-conformists in that town, who during divine service, at which they were compelled by law to be present, did not stand up at the Creed, did not bow *to the altar*, nor at the name of Jesus, nor receive the sacrament on their knees at the high altar. A similar complaint may have been made to every recorder, or mayor and corporation in the kingdom, for it is not likely that only one should have been singled out, and only one borough honoured in this way ; can we therefore, wonder at the indignation of the people ?

The complainants at Abingdon were ostensibly some of his brother magistrates, who, he states, were related to the Ecclesiastical Court ; but, being " much for liberty of conscience," and sympathising with the Mayor, who was somewhat inclined to the opinions of the non-conformists, he refused to interfere in a matter so utterly foreign to his jurisdiction. For this he was cited to appear before the Council Table, the accusation being worded as follows : "That he did comply with and countenance the Nonconformists there, and refused to punish those who did not bow at the name of Jesus, and to the altar, and refused to receive the sacrament kneeling at the high altar, and the like offenders, that he was disaffected to the Church, and the ceremonies thereof enjoined by authority." In his vindication he replied : " That he knew of no common law nor statute in force for the punishment of them, especially by justices of the peace ; that the complainers did not prefer any indictment

against them ; and that the matters, whereof the pretended
offenders were accused, were merely, as the accusers
acknowledged, spiritual matters, proper for the spiritual
judges, and that he might have been censured to encroach
upon the jurisdiction and rights of the Church, if he should
have cognizance of them." This answer appeared to satisfy
the council, and his further attendance at the Board was
dispensed with.

These covert and overt attacks on the small amount of
mental freedom asserted by the people, and on the first
efforts made by a few independent men to disengage the
amplexicaule legs of the priest, were amply sufficient to awaken
a strong tendency, without any suggestions from abroad, to
get rid of the burthen altogether. The yoke was not easy,
and the burthen was not light.

Whitelocke had now completed his twenty-ninth year, and
at this point his unpublished manuscript, forming a thin folio
volume, terminates. It has been most fortunately preserved, and its pages have furnished materials for much that
has long since appeared in both editions of the "Memorials,"
the familiar title of his well-known work, but one that he did
not use himself. The title he gave to his own narrative was,
" The Annals of my Life ;" and he wrote them specially for
the use of his children. At the end of the first volume,
when reviewing his past career, he addresses them in his
usual kind and affectionate language, which need no longer
be withheld from what he himself did not contemplate—
publicity. His reasons for silence no longer exist. The
press of England is now free—practically free, at least, so
long as the Attorney-General allows the unrepealed statutes
to slumber ; but it was not so in his time, when poor
printers or authors were partially hanged, cut down, evisce-
rated, dismembered, and otherwise mutilated, previous to the
distribution of their limbs among the respective quarters of
London. Could he have foreseen, like Milton, the time
when printing should be unlicensed, he might have enjoined

their publication ; but at least he never interdicted it. He proceeds to say in this manuscript :—

"Thus through the blessing of God I have finished the first volume of my labours, which I have remembered in the 'Annals of my Life' to the thirtieth year of my age. If you reflect on the many slight and trivial passages inserted therein, you may answer for them as I told you in the dedication,[*] that this work is intended only for your private, and not for public view. I thought it not amiss for you to know all the vanities, errors, and infirmities of your father, as well as anything that may be styled good, to the end that seeing the unbecomingness of those things, which you find ill, you may avoid the doing of the like ; and it may be a motive to you to order your own actions more seriously and solidly than he hath done many of his of that nature. If you find anything that is good, the example of it in your father may be an incitement to you to imitate those courses. And that you may receive instruction from them for the managing of your own affairs, is one end of this laborious work, which I should have hardly undertaken for any but your sakes."

Then follows a variety of religious and moral reflections, with a retrospective glance of what he accounted heavy afflictions, severe chastisements. Most of these have been faithfully related here, and require no recapitulation ; but I cannot forbear, in justice to his memory, from stating how constantly he breathes out gratitude to Heaven for such prosperity as had been accorded to him. Not that he placed trust in any joy, which he deemed a sure prelude of some counterbalancing grief, *sicut unda supervenit undam.* This grief he thought preparatory and beneficial, a legacy of Christ, and if requiring an antidote, the latter to be obtained by prayer alone. "And therefore come joys, come afflictions, come health, come sickness, come life, come death, let us with patience and cheerfulness submit to the pleasure of our God in all things."

---

[*] This dedication is preserved in the British Museum.

These admonitions were written when he was broken
down with years, and the excruciating anguish of a lingering,
deadly, malady ; he wrote indeed so much of the past, but
thought far more, far better of the future.   The blessed consolation of hope was strong within him, whilst the remembrance of many a good deed may have strengthened his
vision, as he gazed dimly into futurity, into the trackless
space of coming infinity.

Not that he was irreligious in his youth—far from it ; but
like other young men, he was in those early days not wholly
exempt from vanity and pride, as he himself confesses.   His
thirtieth year was ushered in by a passage of this nature.
It was at the Quarter Sessions for Oxford, when owing probably to the absence of the regular chairman, or perhaps by
a little scheme of Laud's to ensnare and catch him in his
net, he was put into the chair when least prepared to accept
such a distinction.   For he was dressed in coloured clothes,
with a sword by his side and a falling band, then quite
unusual for lawyers, and in this garb he gave an extempore
charge to the Grand Jury.   He did not lose the opportunity,
however, of enlarging upon the jurisdiction of temporal
courts in ecclesiastical matters, wishing, he says, with due
caution, and, as naturally as possible, without seeming to
drag the subject in by the head and shoulders, to allude to
it in this way ; because spiritual men were beginning to
swell higher than ordinary, and to take it as an injury to
the Church, that ignorant laymen should meddle with what
did not concern them.   Very few men, I take it, will be
inclined at the present day to abdicate their spiritual rights,
but at that juncture, a broad line was certainly but usurp-
ingly drawn between the priest and the layman, and the
word priest had not a social but professional distinction, not
warranted, it was thought, by any authority in the New
Testament.   His charge was listened to with satisfaction by
the gentlemen and freeholders, a very different race from
the monkish and non-resistant, passively obedient heads of

the colleges ; these laymen felt bold enough to say, that a man might speak as good sense in a falling band as in a ruff, and they treated him not only then, but afterwards, with extraordinary respect and civility.   In this behaviour we see likewise the dawn of that "unorthodox" spirit towards a sister profession—that lucrative profession of the law, which harbingers the day of emancipation from the night of anti-quated formalities, with which law-ceremonial is invested in these islands—a day but little advanced yet towards its meridian light.   May his example be now followed at no distant period, of rejecting and discarding all feudal para-phernalia, ridiculous wigs and the rest of the trumpery, in which our members of at least two professions are still forced by effete custom to appear !

The judges of this country, now happily relieved by a statute from slavish obedience to the Crown, are nevertheless still subject to the slavery of a cramped education, and the etiquette of the bar.   They are moreover not judges in equity ; they have no power, for instance, and clearly no wish to examine into the birth, circumstances, education, hereditary defects, capacity, and natural disposition of a prisoner.   They study not the rights of man, nor right in the abstract as defined by philosophy and science.   They are consequently still mere instruments, who confound the mere laws of this country with the sacred name of justice. Their training, properly considered, has counterbalanced the gift they received of holding their places as freeholds, with-out the constant dread of dismissal.   Even modern judges have rarely counselled clemency, unless in consequence of discovering that a jury will no longer convict.   An improve-ment has taken place, I admit, to a limited extent, as com-pared with what their predecessors were in the days of Charles the First.   If now they remain the instruments of parliamentary legislative incapacity, they were then the tools of regal despotism, and seldom failed to obey the rein, when quickened by the lash.   We find accordingly, that about this

time, the tenth year of Charles Stuart's reign, the Lord
Keeper Coventry, a man of very inferior attainments and
totally unfit for his office, thought proper, by command, to
harangue the judges in the Star-chamber at the end of Mid-
summer Term.   The nature of their novel duty will be best
explained by his own words :—

"You, my Lords, the judges, are commanded in your
charges at the assizes, and at all places opportunely to
acquaint the people with His Majesty's care and zeal to preserve his and the kingdom's honour, in the dominion of the
sea by a powerful fleet.   And you are to let them know
how just it is for His Majesty to require ship-money for the
common defence, and with what alacrity and cheerfulness
they are bound in duty to contribute."

Some of the judges, our reporter states, but the reader
will be more likely to believe *all* of them, obeyed this injunction, and zealously endeavoured to advance the King's
pleasure, without convincing many of the legality of that
business.   Nor were the High Sheriffs forgotten, being likewise directed by the Privy Council to assess and levy the
tax "with more care and equality" than obtained in other
taxes.   This gilding of the pill did not succeed in causing it
to be swallowed by the "knowing gentry."   To complete
the calamities of this year, as if the plague had not sufficed
to render it sufficiently disastrous, the indefatigable Laud at
his visitation enjoined conformity with his orders, of which
the modest regulation subjoined was one :—" That the Communion table should be removed in every church, from the
body of the church or chancel, to the upper east end of the
chancel, and the side of the table to be set against the wall,
altarwise, with a rail or balluster about it."   This innovation
was resisted in words by many, and the Bishop of Lincoln
wrote a book called the "Holy Table," in which he showed
the practice of the primitive times,* and used arguments

---

* The learned author of the "Memorials" was evidently of opinion that the bishop
was correct in his arguments, as based upon the practice of the early Christians.   In

against Laud's injunction.   But if our passively obedient
and non-resisting clergy, submissive to the divine right of the
Oxford Chancellor, did not obey, whence comes it, that we
find in every English cathedral and church the very same
position, condemned by the people as idolatrous, and isolation of that table, as enjoined by Laud ?   By what authority
in the New Testament do our Anglican clergy make that
table "holy," or in other words isolated, which ought to be
common and accessible to all men that seek it, and why at
the east end, where the sun rises ?   Could Laud have worn
the rose upon his pontifical breast, and have possessed certain esoteric secrets of the Pope and his conclave ?   The
prompt obedience of his clergy was in the end most fatal to
himself.   It acted on his nerves as the blast of a trumpet
upon some knight-errant of old, or as the permission to
teach youth on the hearts of modern Jesuits in the Roman
Catholic and Anglican churches ; for in the following year,
that of 1637, he caused what remained of Mr. Prynne's ears
to be removed, and the entire ears of two other culprits,
Burton and Bastwick, to be lopped off.   Nor could mere
forfeiture of ears content him, so the three were further
doomed, one of them to perpetual, and the two others to
indefinite imprisonment.   Poor Prynne had a large S.
branded on either cheek, that being the initial letter of
Schismatic ; but this indignity was not inflicted upon Bastwick, who had used some strong language—not stronger, it
is true, than what vast numbers of his countrymen thought
just.   The following is the passage that cost him his ears :—
" That the prelates are invaders of the king's prerogative
royal, contemners and despisers of the Holy Scriptures,
advancers of popery, superstition, idolatry, and profaneness.
They also abuse the king's authority, to the oppression of
his most loyal subjects, and therein they exercise great
cruelty, tyranny, and injustice.   In execution of these

this point of view I am inclined to think Laud's practice more consistent with the
primæval usage.

impious performances, they show neither wit, honesty, nor temperance. Nor are they either servants of God, nor of the King, but of the devil, being enemies of God and the King, and of every living thing that is good. All which the said Dr. Bastwick is ready to maintain, &c. &c."

That an English bishop was an advancer of profaneness, unless the Doctor used this word in a classical sense, must be in allusion to a vague something connected with popery, superstition, and idolatry, that the Doctor, it may be thought, would not have been capable of explaining.

CHAPTER IX.

— • —

1637.

Whitelocke re-marries: his second Wife a Daughter of Lord Willoughby, of Parham
—Corrupt Conduct of the Bench at this Period—Birth of Whitelocke's second
Son, William—Disastrous Expedition of Prince Rupert and his Brother in West-
phalia—Opposition in Scotland to the new "Service Book," followed by serious
Disturbances—Origination of the Covenant—Episcopacy condemned by the
Covenanters—Their energetic Preparations for Resistance.

BUT long before these scenes of blood and atrocious
cruelty were being enacted, Whitelocke had been tricking
himself out with a falling band and sword at his side for
other purposes, besides giving charges at Quarter Sessions.
We already know that he was no good housekeeper, and
have seen that he had a tender heart. Devotedly attached
to his late unhappy wife ; until successive fits of the falling
sickness and the temporary insanity it produced had caused
his love to subside into pity, he has at length fixed his eyes
upon a new mate. He consulted on this occasion the dictates
of his own feelings,—instead of marrying, in deference to his
father's wishes, the daughter of an old college friend,—and
was not now required to love upon a principle of duty,
without consulting nature in the first instance.

The lady of his choice was the daughter of the late Lord
Willoughby of Parham, whose widow had lately taken a
house in the neighbourhood of Henley. The editors of the
two editions of the "Memorials" have not inserted any details
connected with this event, and indeed I may opportunely
state here, that the mutilations of the original text—portions
of which they either destroyed or secreted—are greatly to
be deplored. We know very well that Whitelocke lived long

enough to complete his Annals, and yet, with the exception
of the first volume, embracing the first twenty-nine years of
his life, and some fragments of transactions that occurred
between his forty-seventh and fiftieth years, no trace exists
of this voluminous production. The "Memorials" are in
truth mere extracts from the work in question, inserted by
him at the end of each year's narrative. All the children
he had by his second marriage with Miss Willoughby were
nine, and yet they all, like the Willoughby of Parham family
itself, became extinct in the course of two generations. Some
of them lived long enough, however, to prevent the publication of this work in its entire state, and there can be little
doubt besides, that a few interpolations have been made at
their suggestion. Such are, indeed, easily selected by their
incongruity, and the critic will be at no loss to distinguish
them from the genuine text.

His marriage, and renewed social intercourse with the
gentry of two or three counties, achieved what his residence
in Salisbury square had been unable to do ; it gained for
him a considerable practice and large emoluments. His being
retained as counsel at the justice in Eyre's seat, appointed to
be held for the forest of Whichwood in Oxfordshire, was
what first gave him the opportunity, so long desired, of
distinguishing himself, and taking a high rank in the estimation of those who furnish barristers with briefs and
fees. He displayed great activity in behalf of his clients,
and felt zeal, because he even wished to appear no friend
to the designs of the Earl of Danby, who as lieutenant of
the forest under the King, was attempting to serve his own
interests at the expense of the gentlemen and freeholders,
whose liberties and privileges any minion of the King was
sure to invade. He wisely commenced his career by
thoroughly mastering his cases, and spared no money, not
merely to procure the transcribing of valuable records for
this business of the forest, but for his private studies as
well. It was about this time that Mr. Falconbridge ab-

stracted for him divers notes out of the records remaining in the Exchequer, notes that are lying before me at this moment, and of a nature to excite much indignation in the breast of any man among the " knowing gentry." The judge before whom he had to plead was the Earl of Holland, a man who became subsequently his friend, and whose hard fate he lamented. This is only one proof among many, that while performing his duty as an advocate, he never forfeited the good opinion of his adversaries by the display of intemperate zeal. The celebrated Hampden had consulted him so early as the spring of 1636 respecting the payment of ship-money, which he had refused to pay as an illegal tax; indeed Whitelocke's advice was frequently required by that so-called patriot, and never withheld. The opinion of the judges was utterly worthless. The Lord Chief Justice Finch had obtained their assent by bribery, corruption, and intimidation. To some he had promised preferment, to others he had held out sharp threats, and more than one of their number confessed as much to Whitelocke himself. His own relative, Judge Croke, had been thus menaced, and had made up his mind to concur with the rest of his brethren on the bench, but his wife, " a very good and pious woman," implored her husband, a few days before he was to argue, to reconsider the matter, to do nothing against his conscience, and not to be apprehensive on her account; for as to her, she would rather suffer want and misery with him, than be the occasion of his doing or saying anything against his judgment and conscience. Her prayer prevailed, and he declared his opinion against the King.

With that watchful eye, which every harpy of the crown seems to have possessed to so remarkable a degree in this reign, the heralds summoned him at this time to enter his pedigree in their office, according to the order of the Earl Marshal, which had not been done since the death of his father. He obeyed their order, and produced to them thirteen descendants on the part of his father, and fourteen

on that of his mother, proved by evidences and other testimony, which were also allowed by them and entered
into the records of their office.

The fluctuating foreign policy of Charles I. induced him
at this time to send the Earl of Arundel as ambassador to
the new emperor Ferdinand III. The mission failed of
course, but the object at least was creditable, for it was no
other than the restitution of the king's nephew, the Prince
Elector. Richelieu might have powerfully served the Protestant cause in Germany on this occasion, but with him the King
had long been at variance, and indeed, at this very period,
the French statesman was plotting his eventual overthrow.
Whitelocke's friendship with Hyde continued unabated. A
letter of his from the Temple to the former at Fawley Court
complains merrily that no judges die of the plague, and " for
your bishops," that there had been no new addition. The
best news was, that good wine had come abundantly over,
the love of which and good cheer, I may here parenthetically
remark, though it enhanced his future dignity as a chancellor
by giving him ponderous proportions, brought with it the
gout, that secret but inflexible reprover of our high dignitaries.

Shortly after the birth of his second son, who eventually
became Sir William Whitelocke, the same friend wrote to
him again : " My dear,—I am glad you prosper so happily
in issue male. God send the good woman well again, which
my wife prays for, as an encouragement for *her* journey,
which she shall shortly be ready for. You may depend on
a doe on Monday, God willing, although this weather forbids
you to look for a fat one. My pen is deep in a Star-chamber
bill, and therefore I have only the leisure and the manners
to tell you, I am very proud that you are a friend to your
most affectionate servant, Edward Hyde." This sending of
a doe, out of season, from London to a gentleman living in a
park well stocked with game, may appear superfluous in our
days. It was then considered a great proof of friendship,

and the most valued present between equals. Such was the tenacity of customs engendered by Norman laws, and especially those which regarded the forest.

This letter was closely followed by news from town, respecting the ill-advised expedition of the Prince Elector, his brother the well known Prince Rupert, and an Englishman, the Lord Craven ; its fate was soon sealed. The small army, upon entering Westphalia, was encountered by the Emperor's general Hatzfeldt, and defeated with the loss of two thousand men slain upon the field. The Prince himself escaped with difficulty, but his brother Rupert and Lord Craven were taken prisoners.

Such an expedition, planned in England, was not calculated to promote the foreign policy of England.

The arrival of Lent in the year 1637, brought down to Whitelocke his old friend Hyde as a guest to Fawley Court, with his "little wench," as he facetiously denominated the future grandmother of two English queens. Hyde was already obliged to resort to physic and change of air. As Lilly was the medical adviser of the one, so was Moore of the other, and both the almanack-maker and the drawer of horoscopes were at this particular period attentive observers of passing events. The explosion, so long apprehended, was now at hand, and dangerously imminent. It did not take place in this country, but in Scotland, which has the honour on this occasion of first shaking off the yoke that despotism, supported by episcopalianism, sought to impose upon both countries. It is well known, that King James had designed to bring the Kirk of Scotland into a state of conformity with the Anglo-Catholic church, by courtesy called Protestant, of England. For this purpose, he appointed some of his Scotch bishops to compile a form of liturgy, "a book of common prayer" to be used there. They obeyed, and sent it him when ready for his approbation, but here King James stopped.

His son, King Charles, in prosecution of his father's design,

directed Archbishop Laud, the Bishop of Ely, and other
bishops to review, and alter as they pleased, that service-
book. They obeyed likewise, and introduced some material
alterations, which do not exist in our common prayer-book,
—that abridgment of the Popish mass-book, as Edward VI.
most truly confessed it to be. By the advice of this pontiff
and others, the new service-book was sent into Scotland,
with his Majesty's command that it should be regularly read
there. Richelieu must have smiled when he heard of it, and
thought how much better the King was plotting embarrass-
ments for himself, than he with all his French emissaries and
astrological appliances.

The first novelty was, that " in the chapel of the King's
house at Edinburgh, the Communion is to be administered
in that form, and taken on their knees, the bishop in his
rochet, the minister in his surplice." The Scotch bishops
liked the matter of the book, but objected to the translation
of certain psalms, epistles, and gospels, and this being not so
paramount in Laud's mind as the imposition of form and
ceremonial, it was amended, not as the modern reader may
suppose with a view to increased accuracy, but to correspond
more with the Scotch text. This concession made, it was
ordered to be read in all churches, which the Dean of Edinburgh did on that ever memorable day, Sunday, the 23rd of
July. Not passive submissive sheep,—no ; rather a tumultuous and incensed multitude filled up every nook on the
ground-floor of the church, and commenced their wild uproar.
In vain did the bishop ascend the pulpit and attempt to calm
them. They threw stools and cudgels at his head, and his
life was in danger. The Chancellor called down from the
gallery, and bade the provost, baillies, and magistrates of the
city, for these were all present, thrust out the rabble, as he
called them, and make fast the doors. This was effected,
but while the service proceeded, the people outside became
more and more violent, and assaulted the bishop as soon as
he came out. In the afternoon, the prelate was rudely

treated again. Nor was the storm of short endurance, for by the time the harvest was got in, an organised resistance was effected. Fearing the consequences, the Council issued three proclamations, one dissolving the meeting in relation to church matters, another removing the session from Edinburgh to Linlithgow, and the third decreeing (what all parties then thought a good mode of refuting error), that a seditious book called "A Dispute against the English Popish ceremonies, obtruded upon the Kirk of Scotland," should be called in and publicly burned. These proclamations increased the flame. The City Council was forced to sign a paper, in which that body promised to oppose the service-book, and to restore three silenced ministers, Ramsey, Rollock, and Henderson. The Lords of the Council-house, of whom the Lord Treasurer was one, were on one occasion compelled to beg some disaffected noblemen and gentlemen to come to their aid, which they kindly did, and escorted them in safety to their respective homes.

And now, noblemen, ministers, burgesses, and commons all joined in a petition against the liturgy and canons. Upon the receipt of it, the infatuated monarch, blinded by destiny, gave instructions for the adjournment of the term to Stirling, and published a proclamation,* prohibiting, upon the highest penalties, tumultuous resorts of a like nature in future. It was instantly met by a protest from the Earl of Hume, the Lord Lindsay, and others. These erected four tables, of the nobility, of the gentry, of the boroughs, and of the ministers. They were to prepare what was to be propounded at the General Table, consisting of several commissioners chosen from the rest. The first act of this General Table was to renew the ancient confession of faith, and enter into a general covenant to preserve the religion there professed, —and the King's person. The Council, upon this combination,

* When plundering the English knights, Charles had alleged triumphantly, that his proclamation was not law, that they should have obeyed the law and not that proclamation. We now see him caught in his own trap.

sent off an express by Sir John Hamilton to the King, who on reading it, observed : " That in this covenant, contrary to what was formerly, neither his own nor his delegated authority was implored : and whereas preceding bands, annexed to confessions, were formed in defence of himself, his authority and person, this new edition hath a combination against all persons whatsoever, himself not excepted." Upon second thoughts, however, and on learning how serious the defection was, he stifled his resentment, and sent the Marquis of Hamilton to Scotland as his high commissioner, for the preservation of peace. The diplomatic ability of Charles may be easily seen by the instructions he gave the Marquis. This nobleman on reaching Edinburgh, a place he did not venture to enter until he had received due assurance of safety, propounded those instructions in the shape of two questions :

What did they expect from the King in satisfaction of their grievances ?

What assurance would they give of their returning to due obedience, and renunciation of the covenant ?

The incongruity of these two questions is so startling, that we can hardly conceive the head to have been quite sane that framed them. They met the reception they deserved. The answer to the first was peremptory and emphatic : " Nothing but a general assembly and a parliament could give them satisfaction ; " to the second, the other reply, less brief, was not less to the point : " Disavowing any retreat from their loyalty, they needed no return towards it ; " and as for the covenant, " they would sooner renounce their baptism than it, and would not endure to hear this proposition a second time." Upon the delivery of these answers, the Covenanters doubled their guards at the castle and in the city. The Marquis, alarmed for his safety, retired to Dalkeith, and sent to the King for new instructions. These came, and were made known in the form of a proclamation, in which he, the King, assured that kingdom of his constancy

in the Protestant religion,* that he would not further urge
the practice of the canons and service-book, save in a fair
and legal way, and that he had given order for the discharge
of all acts of council concerning them.   He had taken into
consideration, he said, the indicting of a general assembly
and parliament, in which they might discuss what best
should promote the peace and welfare both of the Kirk and
the kingdom.   In return for which, he expected that his
subjects, sensible of his gracious favour, would give testimonial
of their future loyalty, and no further provoke him to make
use of that power, which God had given him, for the
reclaiming of disobedient people.

As soon as this proclamation, in nearly the same language,
was read, the Covenanters were ready with a protest, in
which they resentfully declared how ill they took it, " to have
their actions branded with the notion of disobedience." They
declared that they would never abandon their covenant upon
such suggestions ; that they would not wait the King's con-
venience for convoking an assembly, but would call one
themselves, if he did not approve of their proceedings.

In reply to this bold defiance, the Marquis informed them
that the stock of his instructions was spent, and that he
must have recourse to England for a fresh supply.   He was
apprised, in consequence, that they, the Covenanters, expected
his return with his Majesty's answer by the 5th of August
next at the latest, promising to remain quiet until that date.
The fatal day arrived, and brought with it the reappearance
of the Marquis.   Every one coupled this compliance with the
royal approbation of the Covenant, but the general rumour
was mistaken.   Having called in the Lords of the Council
and others of the nobility to bear witness that he had not
authorised that rumour, he proceeded to confer with the
Covenanters about the convocation of the assembly, and had
the coolness to ask them of what members it should consist,

---

* But his Scotch subjects did not regard the Anglo-Catholic religion as Protestant,
having already declared it to be Anglo-Popish.

and what matters it should discuss. Astonished and indignant, they replied, that such proposals were destructive of
their liberties, and a prelimitation of that assembly, who
ought to be free, and to judge both of their own members
and the matters of their cognisance. This caused the Commissioner to declare that he had instructions to indict an
assembly upon the concession of ten articles. To this the
Covenanters refused their assent, and appealed to the General
Assembly, where they said "those matters were properly to
be decided." Upon this refusal, his Lordship resolved on
going back to England, and the rumour arose, that he had
neither power from the King, nor inclination to satisfy the
people. He grew so angry at the insinuation, that he reduced
his former proposals to two. One of these was, that no
layman, but only presbyterian ministers, should vote for
returning members to the General Assembly; and the other,
that ecclesiastical matters should be left to the determination
of that assembly, and to the parliament such things as were
settled by acts of parliament. Let them grant these, he
urged, and he would presently indict an assembly, and he
further promised, *upon his honour*, to call a parliament
immediately after.

Further negotiations led to a prolongation of the term to
the 21st of September following, until which time they
would yet forbear convoking the assembly. On that day
the high commissioner re-appeared with fresh instructions,
and ignoring what must have been notorious, that the
assembly were actually to meet on the following day, he
nevertheless desired the King's declaration to be read. In
this document the King abolished the service-book, the book
of canons, the high commission; insisted no longer on the
five articles of Perth; ordered that all persons whatsoever,
ecclesiastical or civil, should be liable to censure of parliament and the General Assembly; that no other oath should
be administered to ministers (or members) at their entry,
but what was contained in the act of parliament; that the

ancient confession of faith, and band thereunto annexed, should be subscribed and renewed, as it was in his father's time ; lastly that a General Assembly should be holden at Glasgow on the 21st of November, and a parliament at Edinburgh on the 15th of May ; that he pardoned all bygone offences, and concluded by indicting a general fast. This declaration being published, the profession of faith was read, to which the Marquis and the members of the council severally affixed their names. It was followed by one proclamation convoking the assembly, and another the parliament. Then came an act of the council requiring a general subscription to the confession of faith, and a commission was appointed to carry out the measure by obtaining the signatures. But in the homely phraseology of that day, the Covenanters "brought up the rear" with a protest, in which they moved the people to consider with whom they had to deal, decried the new subscription to the article of faith, and excepted against the archbishops and bishops, as not entitled to have any votes in the assembly.

They then elected commissioners for the assembly, and ordered at their table, that every parish should send to the presbytery one layman, whom they styled a ruling elder, and whose vote was to be on a par with that of the minister, Having attempted in vain to procure from the high commissioner a citation against the archbishops and bishops to appear at the assembly as delinquents, they framed themselves a bill against them for sundry misdemeanours. This bill was preferred by the presbytery at Edinburgh, and they warned them to "compeer" in the General Assembly at Glasgow. The admission of the lay elders was not passed without a severe contest, when the assembly met. The prelates protested against the validity of the meeting altogether, but their protest was refused a hearing, upon which the high commissioner protested in his turn. The King had nominated six lords of his privy council to be assessors to his commissioner in that assembly. They were not allowed to enter ; their right of suffrage was denied, and the members affirmed, that if the King himself were present, he should have but one vote, and *that no negative one.* Such dogged resolution induced the commissioner to call in question the lawfulness of the assembly, and, assembling the council they drew up a proclamation for dissolving the former body. All subscribed to it save one, the Earl of Argyle, a name at that time of paramount weight. Emboldened by his adhesion to their cause, the Covenanters refused to be dissolved, declared six former general assemblies null and void, cashiered all the bishops, excommunicated some of them, and shortly after abolished episcopacy itself, as inconsistent with the laws of that church. The commissioner retreated to England, and as matters had gone so far, the Covenanters threw down the gauntlet at once, not by idle challenges and the bandying of hard words, but by the raising of fortifications, the blockading of others, the seizing of the king's castles, and preparing in earnest for the war.

.

CHAPTER X.

1638—1640.

Causes of the Civil War—Arrival of the Queen Mother of France—Military Prepara-
tions of the King—His Proclamation against the Covenanters—Their Counter-
Declaration favoured in England—The King meets his Army at York—
Humiliating Results of this Movement—Abolition of Episcopacy by the General
Assembly at Edinburgh—Disputes between the King and the Scotch Parliament
—Charles attempts to relieve his Financial Difficulties—Growth of Republican
Ideas in England—Parliament Convened in April, 1640—Subsidies demanded
on the part of the King refused—Parliament abruptly dissolved—Laud's Inter-
ference in Temporal Matters—Convocation of the Clergy—Illegal Attempt to
extend its Powers—Public Indignation and Riots in London—The Convocation
breaks up—Preparations for War against the Scotch—Forced Loans—Royal
Proclamation against the Scotch "Rebels"—Disaffection in the Royal Army,
which is defeated, and retreats to York—Negotiations with the Rebels.

SUCH was the origin of the civil wars between Charles and
his subjects—wars provoked by the aggressive spirit of
himself and his evil councillors, and which inflicted such
unnumbered calamities upon the state. The law of Nemesis
had been slow of operation as usual, but as sure, for it was
in 1598 that King James had restored to the bishops their
votes in the parliament of Scotland, and evinced no great
love of the Consistorian government by his writings. On his
accession to the crown of England, in 1603, he had been
urged by one thousand ministers against episcopacy, in a
petition which he contemned ; nay, he caused every act in
the Scotch parliament against bishops to be rescinded ; and
as the presbyters kept silent, both he and his successor mistook their silence for tame acquiescence.

In the month of October the queen-mother of France paid
England a visit. The people regarded her presence with
intuitive dislike, and believed instinctively that her followers

were the sword and pestilence ; for who could be well ignorant that confusion and discord had hitherto been her
attendants. She came by the invitation of her daughter, the
Queen of England.

And now, an episcopal war being threatened, the King,
with the advice of Laud and others, conceived in his wisdom
the desirability of forestalling the insurgents. He accordingly hastened his levies, while the two English primates
assembled the clergy of each diocese, and invited aid for the
preservation of their own hierarchy. Some weak-minded
nobles and gentry contributed also to this iniquitous act, so
that a large army was collected, the command of which was
entrusted to the Earl of Arundel. In conformity with the
whole tenor of his conduct, so oblivious of the past and
blind to the present, his Majesty, who was fond of proclamations, thought proper to issue one to his English subjects, in which he informed them that certain seditious
persons in Scotland were seeking the overthrow of regal
power, under the false pretext of religion ; that this was
discovered by the multitude of their pamphlets and libels
against regal authority, and by their letters to private
persons, inciting them against the King; by the private
meetings of Covenanters in London and other places of this
kingdom ; by their contempts and protests against his
commands ; by their rejecting his covenant and taking up
one of their own ; by their conspiracy against him and their
hostile preparations of arms. · He then enters into a description of what the Covenanters had done, in return for all his
grace, clemency, and indulgence towards them on previous
occasions ; how they, undutiful and insolent, had erected a
printing office,* raised taxes, blocked-up and besieged his
castles, treated his councillors with contempt, and set up
their tables. Then, as was usual with some of his predecessors, he takes God to witness that he is constrained by

---

* This was the first grievance, and shows how tyrants dreaded the liberty of speech,
and consequently of the press, the danger of which was foreseen by Wolsey.

these their treasons to appeal to arms for the safety of either kingdom. He finally declares his intention to preserve episcopacy in Scotland, and alludes to a more ample declaration as being shortly to appear. In this document there are two statements that prevented all possibility of reconciliation. Charles should have reflected, that if he failed to conquer, no course was open to himself but one of abject submission and virtual abdication. In the first place, if he had the right, he had not real power to wage war without the consent of parliament; he ·might declare it if he pleased. He had declared the insurrection of the Scotch nation to be under pretext of religion, and thereby accused a whole people of hypocrisy, as well as half, or at least one-third of his English subjects, who he knew were non-conformists and dissenters in their hearts. Were his conjecture correct, it was nevertheless hopelessly impolitic to declare it, since how could he expect to see harmony restored unless by conquest and permanent subjugation, for which the subsidies of his English clergy would prove wholly inadequate? Did he entertain a vague hope that the war would become popular with the English, from their well-known antipathy to their Scotch neighbours? If so, his judgment was again at fault, by forgetting that he himself was scarcely regarded as an Englishman, and that his own father spoke broad Scotch. And supposing this to have been his secret hope, what conscience could he himself have had to encourage and foment a deadly war of religion between two nations, hitherto existing in peace upon the same island for the space of at least two reigns? As a king, having access to our records, and acquainted with state-secrets, he knew that religion had been indeed the pretext with Henry the Eighth, for the carrying out of his ambitious and dynastic projects; with Edward and Elizabeth for securing their thrones; with his own father for the preservation of despotic and usurped power; with himself for the same object, quite as much, at least, as from any conviction in the potency of bishops to confer

essential vitality on Christianity ; but to accuse an unini-
tiated and credulous people of using religion as a pretext,
he knew, as every king must know, to be absolutely false.

Well may the politicians of the time have regarded this
proclamation as fatal, in whichever way they viewed it. The
event did more than justify their prescience. Whitelocke
was only one among many who foresaw the result. From
this hour his line of conduct was marked out, and he became
identified to a limited extent with the party of Hampden,
and of all Englishmen who understood the paramount necessity of constitutional law as a check upon the encroachments
of arbitrary power.* The answer of the Covenanters gives
a calm refutation of the calumny attempted to be fastened
on them by their king. One passage made a deep impression on this side the Tweed. It was this :—" And for doing
any harm to England, cursed be their breasts if they harbour
any such thought ; they rather implore the good opinion of
their well-affected brethren in England."

As might be expected, their remonstrances, declarations,
and pamphlets, were dispersed throughout most English
cities and towns ; they had their emissaries and agents
incessantly at work, and the eyes of the Covenanters were
more especially directed towards those gentlemen who had
been imprisoned for not contributing to the loan, or had
been distrained for the ship-money. If presbyterianism had
not as yet many adherents, the majority of Englishmen felt
nevertheless some sympathy for its cause, being only too
fatally predisposed thereto by the acts of their own government at home. The nomination of the Marquis of Hamilton
to the chief command of the fleet was another of those
extraordinary deeds that baffle all attempts at logical explanation, for his mother was a rigid covenanter. His
countrymen conjectured that the son of such a mother
would do them no harm.

---

* He admits this in words, and confessed in a passage most cautiously written, that
he himself had been solicited by the Covenanters, but that he had persuaded his

As the royal forces advanced towards York, their progress was marked by every species of licentiousness and atrocity, inclusive of murder. As soon as the King reached this, his second English capital, with his council, he revoked a great number of his unlawful grants and projects, thereby admitting their injustice ; but his revocation only applied to those in which the Marquis and the Scotch were concerned. The feeling which prompted the King was not that of justice to Englishmen. At Berwick the two armies gazed at each other, without fighting, and a pacification was set on foot. I must refer the reader to history for a full description of this humiliating affair, which ended in the return of the King to England by the end of July—an act so portentous, that Whitelocke actually thought it was doomed and foreboded by the great and strange eruption of fire with a horrible noise "near the Ferrara islands," giving birth to a new island continually burning.

The pacification was little relished at London, reflecting as it did no small disgrace on English prowess. And after all his high threats, the General Assembly at Edinburgh, convoked by himself, abolished episcopacy, the five articles of Perth, the high commission, the liturgy, and the book of canons, to which decree the Earl of Traquair gave the King's assent. The Scotch parliament met, and so revived the King's displeasure, that he ordered his commission to prorogue it. But they declared, as the Long Parliament did subsequently, that this prorogation was of no force in law, *being without consent of the parliament.* They added, that although they did not intend on this occasion to continue their session out of regard to his Majesty, they would take, nevertheless, such course as might best secure the kirk and kingdom from the extremity of confusion and misery, in case their enemies should prevail by false suggestions.

friends not to foment these growing public differences, from which he feared great and evil consequences. But acts speak better than words, and he was returned to the Long Parliament as a popular member.

About this unhappy and critical period, a Spanish armada of
seventy sail appeared off the English coast, the destination
of which was thought mysterious by many in this country.
Whether intended for the invasion of England, with the connivance and previous invitation of Charles, or not, most
people thought that such was its object. It was attacked
and greatly crippled by the Dutch fleet then lying off Dunkirk, under the command of Van Tromp, and afterwards
destroyed by that renowned Dutch admiral while vainly
claiming Charles's protection in Dover roads. Nor was this
the only ambiguous act in which the King's name was mixed
up. The report had been industriously circulated, that
Charles's junto of three—Laud, Strafford, and Hamilton—
who met on the 5th of December to devise some remedy for
the growing evils, as the King himself described them during
that sitting, had advised his Majesty to convoke a parliament at Westminster. Another was to be called in Ireland,
to which country Strafford, as its lieutenant, would have to
repair, but to return by the 15th of April, the day on which
the English parliament would meet. Now if this report,
officially circulated, were true, how came the King to tell his
lords at this very juncture, " that it would be long ere the
parliament meet, and the subsidies granted by them would
be long in levying. In the interim his affairs will suffer,
without some speedy course for supplies ?" Strafford set the
example by subscribing 20,000l. ; Richmond gave the like
sum ; but Hamilton alleged poverty, and some few refused.
The judges and judicial officers, both ecclesiastical and temporal, were assessed by the council and compelled to pay,
whether they liked it or not. The Roman Catholics contributed most, so much so, that the forces raised by means
of this subsidy were nicknamed the " Popish Army."
Great intrigues were now at work, and republicanism raised
its head. A formidable conspiracy was set on foot, in which
the Earls of Essex, Bedford, Holland, Lord Say, Hampden,
Pym, with many other noblemen and gentlemen, were

deeply engaged. Foreign aid was solicited by the Scotch, from Holland and France, and one letter of this nature to Richelieu, intercepted in its passage, was laid before the King. Two of the cardinal's retainers, one being Chamberlain, the chaplain of his eminence, and the other Hepburn, his page, became known as his agents. The Scotch seized upon the castles of Edinburgh, Stirling, and Dumbarton, and were trying to form foreign alliances. At home the disaffection was spreading, and had even extended to the Middle Temple—that *sanctum sanctorum*—that hallowed spot, so loyal, so devoted, but a short time before.

On the 13th of April, 1640, the parliament did meet, as rumour had given out in the previous month of December. Whitelocke watched its proceedings with great interest. Secretary Vane demanded twelve subsidies, and was accused subsequently of having purposely doubled what the King really did demand. The charge was not substantiated, nor did it much matter, for the Commons would not even have granted six, no "lean gift," without a preliminary redress of grievances, which the King had no wish to grant. By the advice of his junto he ordered the dissolution of this parliament on the 5th of May, in less than a month from its first meeting. Laud came in for a much larger share of odium from this measure, than his two co-adjutors, because he, a spiritual functionary, was interfering in the temporal affairs of the state to an extent unprecedented since the administration of Wolsey. His character had been defined, although far too much in his favour, by Judge Whitelocke, his cotemporary at St. John's, in Oxford, and prophetic indeed it was! "Laud," he would say, "is too full of fire, though a just and good man; his want of experience in state-matters, his too great zeal for the church, and his heat, if he proceeds in the way he is now in, will set this nation on fire."

Notwithstanding the dissolution, Laud persuaded the King to continue the sitting of the convocation of the clergy, by granting to them a new commission "for the conclusion of such matters as were then in treaty among them." Five judges delivered their opinion, that the convocation might sit until dissolved by the King's writ, upon the summons of which they had met. But so little was a judicial opinion considered to be worth, so little reliance did the government place upon it, that a new commission was deemed advisable. On the 9th of May a paper was posted up at the Royal Exchange, exhorting the apprentices to rise and sack the archbishop's house at Lambeth on the following Monday, which they attempted to do. Unacquainted with the law, they took a drum with them, and this caused their act to come within the pale of treason, and to be construed by the judges as an act against the life of the sovereign, for which one of the insurgent captains, a cobbler, was hanged, drawn, and quartered, and his limbs set on London Bridge. In reality, there had been merely a breach of the peace, a few panes of glass broken, and some prisoners released. Treason may have been at work; but the simple and excitable creatures that made the riot were not the really guilty parties. The disturbance, by way of a beginning, had probably been planned by the secret agents of the Covenanters, who thought they might have their junto there, as the King had his. Nor was his Majesty kept ignorant of its existence; and when it came to his knowledge he caused a guard to be set about Westminster Abbey, where the convocation sat. The members were thrown into great agitation by this imprudent measure, that secured them, it is true, from any sudden irruption, but exposed them to the rage and fury of the people, rendered them unpopular in the highest degree, and obnoxious to the next parliament, that must meet sooner or later.

In the mean time the subject of episcopacy, abolished in Scotland, was now taken up in England by the masses, and the discontent increased by the canon this synod made respecting the communion table, in confirmation of Laud's ordinance. They granted the King an ample benevolence from the clergy, of four shillings in the pound for six years, towards his intended expedition against the Scotch, and broke up on the 29th of May, amidst the all but universal censures of their lay fellow-countrymen.   The preparations for war were now actively carried on, and a junto of select counsellors convoked, of whom Sir Henry Vane was one.   At one of their meetings he took short notes of the debate, which fell, unfortunately for Strafford, into the hands of the son, and were revealed at the trial of the earl.   The title of them was : " No danger in a war with Scotland, if offensive, not defensive."   Then followed the opinions of the parties deliberating.

KING CHARLES. " How can we undertake offensive war, if we have no more money ?

STRAFFORD. Borrow of the city 100,000*l.*; go on vigorously to levy ship-money.   Your Majesty having tried the affection of your people, you are absolved and loose from all rule of government, and to do what power will admit.   Your Majesty having tried all ways, and being refused, shall be acquitted before God and man.   And you have an army in Ireland, that you may employ to reduce this kingdom to obedience ; for I am confident the Scots cannot hold out five months.

LAUD. You have tried all ways, and have always been denied.   It is now lawful to take it by force.

LORD COTTENHAM. Leagues abroad there may be made for the defence of the kingdom.   The Lower House are weary of the King and Church.   All ways shall be just to raise money by, in this inevitable necessity, and are to be used, being lawful.

LAUD. For an offensive, not any defensive war.

STRAF. The town is full of lords : put the commission of array on foot, and if any of them stir, we will make them smart."

On the breaking up of this council, all the wheels of prerogative were put in motion to raise money.   Knighthood money was set on foot.   All knights and gentlemen that held lands *in capite* of the King were forthwith summoned

to send men, horses and arms, agreeably to their tenures and
qualities.   The City of London was invited to raise a loan,
which the citizens refused.   They were displeased, not
merely with the general conduct of affairs, but at having
been pillaged by the Star Chamber of property belonging to
them at Londonderry, in Ireland.   The military officers,
however, and many of the gentry came forward, and the
royal army was completed.

On the 20th of August the King left London to join his
forces in the north; and on the 22nd appeared his proclamation, in which he declared the Scots rebels, repeated his
previous accusations, and promised pardon to all that should
acknowledge their crimes and crave it.   A prayer was put
up in all our churches for the King, in his expedition against
the rebels of Scotland.   But disaffection prevailed in the
ranks of the royal army, and even officers were heard to
declare, "that they would not fight to maintain the pride
and power of the bishops."   After sustaining defeats, the
English forces retreated to York, where the King was, who
received here the petition of the rebels "for satisfaction of
their full demands, and the repair of their wrongs and losses,
with the advice of the Parliament of England to be con-
vented."   These demands were sent in three days later, at
the King's request, and they were followed by two other
petitions, one from twelve English peers, and the other from
the citizens of London.   Whitelocke admits that the English
nation at this juncture generally favoured the proceedings of
the so-called rebels, but does not affect to deny the painful
humiliation that was produced by the King's temporary
treaty with them.   But his Majesty saw how unwilling his
private soldiers were to fight against the Scotch in what they
considered an unrighteous cause, and therefore peace became
doubly desirable.   One of the stipulations was, to allow the
Scotch army a contribution of 850l. a day from Northumberland, Westmoreland, Durham, and Newcastle,—without
the consent of the inhabitants, it may well be conjectured.

Previous to the ratification of this disgraceful treaty, the Scotch commissioners had refused to enter York, as not a safe place for them, so long as the Lieutenant of Ireland commanded there in chief, who had proclaimed them traitors in Ireland before the King had done so in England, and had there threatened to destroy their memory. Against him they, the Scots, had high matters of complaint. The resolution of calling a Parliament set many at work to canvass for seats. The court laboured to bring in their friends, but these had lost all respect in the country. It was not a little strange, observes Whitelocke, to see what a spirit of opposition to the court proceedings there was in the hearts and actions of most of the people, so that very few of that party had the favour to be chosen members.

CHAPTER XI.

THE 3rd of November, 1640, was the day appointed for
this, the ever memorable Long Parliament, to meet; but
some persuaded Laud to get it adjourned for two or three
days, because this 3rd of November was an ominous day,
that on which Wolsey fell, and when acts commenced that
ended in the dissolution of the abbeys. Superstitious as he
was, he nevertheless took little heed of this variety of the
omen, which the physicians I before spoke of, Lilly and his
mates, were not likely to neglect as the basis of their predictions.

The King insisted on Strafford's taking his seat in the
Upper House, as soon as it met, having, he said, much confidence in his faithfulness and abilities. Conscious of what
was impending over him, the Earl remonstrated, and his
objections for once were overruled. His master laid his

commands upon him, and declared to him "that as he was King of England, he was able to secure him from any danger; and that the Parliament should not touch one hair of his head." He repeated, that he could not do without his minister's advice in the great transactions likely to ensue. The scapegoat went, and, to his honour be it said, prepared to suffer mortification and disgrace, without anticipating the dread fate that awaited him. His faith in princes was unbounded; and as Laud disregarded black days, so did Strafford despise proverbs.

Whitelocke was a candidate for Great Marlow, but was not returned, through the conduct of the mayor, who sent for some of the burgesses, and made a false return. The election, upon his petition, was quashed, and a new one ordered for both members. To this new writ Whitelocke was returned, with Mr. Hoby for his colleague. He took his seat in the House, and from this time became an actor in events that must ever be justly regarded as the most signal in this country's annals. The very first week of the meeting of this Parliament was conspicuous, for bands of horsemen came flocking in from the country as the bearers of petitions demanding redress of grievances, both in church and state. The use of the word "rebels" in the speech from the throne was excepted against; Prynne, Burton, Bastwick, and others, Laud's victims, were ordered to be released. A formidable array of grievances was soon drawn up; and Lord Cottington's special and sudden appointment to be constable of the Tower, with a garrison of 400 men, suspected, seen through, and protested against. The King submitted, and revoked the nomination. Then the House purified itself, by ordering that all projectors and unlawful monopolists should be "disabled to sit in it." The Lords were equally zealous, and the first act of theirs was to commit Sir William Becher to the Fleet, for having, as one of the clerks of the council, by order of the Secretaries of State, searched the pockets, cabinets, and studies of the Earl

of Warwick and Lord Brooke, directly after the dissolution
of the last Parliament. Then came Strafford's impeachment,
and that of his confederate, Sir George Ratcliffe, for whom
they sent a serjeant-at-arms. The Bishop of Lincoln was
released. The City came forward with a loan of £100,000
to pay the Scotch army and relieve the counties where their
troops were quartered. And now the debate came on in
the Lower House respecting the writs of habeas corpus, and
that celebrated case in which, years before, Selden and the
rest of his fellow prisoners had demanded to be bailed, but
had been refused, contrary to law, by the judges, who
required of them sureties for their good behaviour. The
case being taken up most warmly by some of the speakers,
they moved, that the prisoners might have reparation out of
the estates of those judges who then sat in the King's
Bench when they were remanded to prison. These judges
they named to be, Hide, Jones, and our new member's own
father; Judge Croke they excused, because his opinion
differed from the rest. Seeing their mistake as to the true
facts of the case, his son rose to deliver his maiden speech
in defence of his father's memory, in which he asserted
" That it was not unknown to divers worthy members of the
House, that Judge Whitelocke had been a faithful, able, and
stout asserter of the rights and liberties of the freeborn subjects of this kingdom, for which he had been many ways a
sufferer, and particularly by a straight and close imprisonment, for what he said and did, as a member of this honourable House, in a former Parliament.* And he appeals to
those honourable gentlemen, who cannot but remember those
passages, and some who were then sufferers with him; and
for his opinion and carriage in the case of *habeas corpus*, it
is affirmed to have been the same with that of Judge Croke.
He appeals for this to the honourable gentlemen who were
concerned in it, and to others who were present then in
court." Hampden and several others, Selden himself per-

* He was committed to the Fleet in the time of James I.

haps, bore out this statement, and absolved Whitelocke as well as Croke.

At that identical sitting, or closely upon it, the Secretary of State, Sir Francis Windebank, escaped to France to avoid trial. He was the intimate friend of Laud; and although in this country only a concealed and suspected papist, he openly professed it on reaching the continent, where he remained to his death. And on the day after this sitting, the House ordered the other judges, amongst whom was the Lord Keeper Finch, to be impeached on account of Hampden's business. On this same day our member for Marlow was appointed one of the select committee to prepare articles of impeachment against Strafford, and it fell to his lot to manage the evidence. Their proceedings were to be secret, so great was the affair considered, so important its nature. Pym, Hampden, Hollis, Lord Digby, Stroud, Sir Walter Earle, Selden, St. John, Maynard, Palmer, and Glynne, were the others, so as to form the number twelve; but one of these, Lord Digby, was a traitor, who revealed what passed to the King, and by the latter Strafford learned their proceedings also. Whitelocke was made the chairman; the papers were all committed to his custody, and a voluntary oath was taken by all of them to maintain secrecy. They sat nearly every day to get up the articles of the charge. On the 15th of December the House resolved: "That the clergy in a synod or convocation hath no power to make laws, canons, or constitutions, to bind either laity or clergy, without the Parliament; and that the canons made by the late convocation are against the fundamental laws of this realm, the King's prerogative, the propriety of the subject, the rights of Parliament, and do tend to faction and sedition." They then voted, that a bill should be brought in to fine those clergymen who sat in the late convocation, and were actors in making those canons.

Now this bill was retrospective, and consequently unjust.

They then sent up one of the committee, Mr. Hollis, to the

Lords with an impeachment against the Archbishop of Canterbury, Laud, whom, as well as Strafford, the Scots denounced as "incendiaries in the national differences." The Scotch commissioners concluded their accusation against him by saying, " that if the Pope had been in his place, he could not have been more zealous against the reformed churches, to reduce them to the heresies, doctrines, superstitions, and idolatries of Rome." As for the Lord Keeper Finch, like a wise man, he escaped in time to Holland ; but Strafford and Laud were secured. The Commons began now to direct their attention to the subject of triennial parliaments, for the due consideration of which they named a committee, who had to bring in a bill to that effect. This bill was reluctantly assented to by the King about the end of February. On the 10th of March the Commons voted : " That no bishop shall have any vote in Parliament, nor any judicial power in the Star Chamber, nor bear any authority in temporal matters ; and that no clergyman shall be in the commission of the peace."

All this time the proceedings against Strafford were actively carried on. The whole House even wished to attend his trial in a body ; but as the Lords would not consent to this, a compromise was effected, and the committee of the whole House was to attend instead. An intrigue was set on foot, which goes far to deprive this celebrated trial of the solemnity that ought to have invested it. A proposal was made to the leading members of the opposition of the Lower House, and apparently approved of by them, to restore the Earl to his former favour and honour, provided the King would prefer some of those notable persons to offices at court, whereby Strafford's enemies should become his friends, and the King's desires be promoted. It was that —— (and here the name is left in blank*) should be made lord treasurer ;

---

* Why in blank? Was it merely because the annalist, at the moment of writing, forgot the name and intended to supply the omission, which was subsequently neglected, until the defect had escaped his memory? Two or three similar omissions occur in Whitelocke's writings.

Lord Say, master of the wards ; Mr. Pym, chancellor of the exchequer ; Mr. Hollis, secretary of state ; Mr. Hampden, tutor to the Prince ; and others to have other places.   To effect this arrangement, the Bishop of London resigned his treasurer's staff, Lord Cottington his mastership of the wards, and the rest could easily be voided.   Whitelocke became acquainted with this attempt, which, had it been carried out, must have altered the whole ensuing phase of history ; but it failed, from some cause of which he remained ignorant ; and he never knew whether the King or others had prevented this scheme from coming to pass.   Certain it is, that the great men were baffled, and more bitterly incensed than ever against the Earl ; and that they joined, from motives neither pure nor patriotic, the Scotch commissioners, who were implacable against the illustrious prisoner.

The trial of Strafford came on in Westminster Hall, and the bishops were excluded by the canons of the Church, which forbid their being assistant in cases of blood or death. For this reason they absented themselves, and therefore it is fair to presume, that the vote of the Lower House on the tenth of March, that no bishop should vote at all in the Upper House, had been summarily or provisionally rejected by the latter, as an interference with their privileges.

Into all the details of this trial it is not my province to enter ; they may be read in the State Trials, and I shall confine myself to that portion of it, in which our chairman of the committee was more immediately concerned.   The articles that fell to his share were matters of a very high nature, especially the twenty-fourth article, that related to the design of bringing over the army from Ireland into Scotland, and thence to England, for the purpose of reducing this kingdom.   Now Whitelocke spoke with Sir Henry Vane the elder (whose notes of secret debate I gave some pages back), and also with the other witnesses, respecting the twenty-fourth article, and finding that their testimony would not substantiate it, he thought it "not honourable for the

House of Commons to proceed upon an article whereof they could not make a clear proof ; " and he consequently proposed to the committee to omit it.   The committee were of the same opinion, but upon Sir Walter Earle's undertaking to manage it, they left it to him, and when the chairman had enforced the evidence upon the twenty-third article, he sat down.   Sir Walter, with much gravity and confidence, began to aggravate the matters in the twenty-fourth article, the dangerous consequences and high crime in it, and then called in the witnesses to prove what he had alleged.   Some of these, when called, were not in England, and others could or would answer but little to the purpose, at which the knight became very blank and out of countenance.   The Earl of Strafford took instant advantage of his dilemma, and addressing his peers, said, *inter alia verba :* " The learned gentleman who urged the matters of the last article against me, when he came to this twenty-fourth article, sat down and seemed to decline it, and yet he left nothing material, which was not urged home by him."   After the earl had sat down, Lord Digby stood up, and in a witty, rhetorical speech took off Sir Walter, desired their Lordships to pass over a mistake,—that this article was not intended for prosecution, as might appear by the gentleman's declining it, who managed the former,—and begged them to regard what the noble knight had said as a " superfœtation."

After the Lord Digby had spoken—and his speaking at all, under the circumstances, was a flippant impertinence, if not pregnant with latent meaning—Whitelocke rose again, and as soon as the Lords had done smiling, proceeded with the twenty-fifth article.   The Queen, who was present at the trial, inquired who that knight was, whom the Lord Digby relieved ; and on being told that his name was Sir Walter Earle, she said, " That water-dog did bark, but not bite, but the rest did bite close."

The Earl of Strafford, speaking of the committee who managed the evidence against him, and particularly of the lawyers, said to a private friend, "that Glynne and Maynard used him like advocates, but Palmer and Whitelocke used him like gentlemen, and yet left out nothing material to be urged against him." The Lieutenant of the Tower acquainted both Houses on the following day, that the Earl had been extremely ill during the night from a violent fit of the stone, that he was not able to come abroad that day, and humbly desired their Lordships to excuse him. The Houses adjourned to the 10th of April, and on the 12th Mr. Pym produced in the Commons a paper of some notes taken by Secretary Vane, already inserted in these pages. The document was said to have been discovered in this way. The Secretary being out of town sent a letter to his son, Henry Vane the younger, then in London, and a Member of Parliament, with the key of his study, for his son to look in his cabinet and send certain papers to him. On looking through many of these papers, the son fell accidentally on these notes, which he saw at once were of the highest importance, and felt urged by conscience* to make known to the public prosecutor of the Earl, Mr. Pym. This gentleman obtained leave from the younger Vane to make use of them, and having produced them in the Commons, the notes were read in the presence of both Houses and of the accused. Having been published in this manner, the subsequent loss of the paper does not seem to have been so serious as Whitelocke supposed. To himself, who had as chairman the custody of all the papers, it was a source of great annoyance, when he found it missing. The House viewed it very properly as a most suspicious circumstance, and ordered, "that every one of the committee should make a solemn protestation in the House, that they did not convey it away, nor know what was become of it." All did as required ; the Lord Digby with deeper impreca-

* There are different accounts of the way in which the younger Vane got possession of these notes. His real motive in making use of them was surmised to be revenge, because the Earl had assumed a title, which the Vanes regarded as exclusively belonging to them. This surmise throws strong doubt on the authenticity of the notes.

tions, and more earnestness than any of the rest ; but afterwards at the battle of Naseby, where the King's cabinet was
taken, a copy of these notes in Lord Digby's hand was discovered.   Then, but not till then, was Whitelocke fully
cleared from the suspicion of having conveyed the paper by
stealth to some party interested for the Earl.   It is clear
from one or two passages, that our chairman, as a lawyer,
considered the Earl not guilty, and that he greatly admired
his defence.   He even calls him a great and excellent
person (supposing this expression to have been really written
by him in his annals), which possibly might have found some
echo with posterity, were we not now more fully capable of
appreciating the dictatorial and imperious spirit of this man,
who conspired with his master to crush what small remnant
of liberty the people of this country yet enjoyed upon the
death of James.   But when he affirms, that the Earl moved
the hearts of his auditors, some few excepted, to remorse
and pity, he erred by supposing his own clement and for-
giving nature to have been common to all.   So far from
feeling pity, the House abandoned the form of proceeding
against the Earl by prosecution, merely because they saw
the victim might escape through technicalities, and introducing a Bill of Attainder, they voted him guilty of high
treason.   During the debate Lord Digby openly espoused
the Earl's cause, and formed one of the minority of ninety-
nine.   This partiality, no longer disguised on the part of a
committee-man, seems to have taken off the keen edge of
suspicion, that down to that moment must have attached to
the chairman, though his position required for many months
to come the greatest circumspection.   The fate of the
attainted Strafford, in whose ultimate liberation he for one
evidently believed,—and, indeed, what moderate Englishman
could at that time have deemed the King capable of such
criminal weakness and treachery as to suffer his minister's
execution?—left a profound impression on Whitelocke's mind.
His conscience seared him here : he admits that he felt

remorse, and from this hour he meddled no longer with deeds
of blood, nor would he have anything to do with prosecutions
on capital charges for the future. I, for one, have ever
lamented the unrelenting cruelty observed towards Strafford,
not from any conviction of his innocence, but because I see
in so impolitic as well as inhuman an act the commencement of that long series of crimes and errors, which
counterbalanced those of the King's party, and ultimately led to a yet more disastrous reaction. Where
cruelty and bloodshed obtain, no cause however holy in itself
can thrive. We, as a people, still suffer from those violent
deeds.

Such was the sanguinary and vindictive temper of the
House, that numbers of its members were more or less constrained to go along with the torrent, or consent to be sub-
merged. Neutrality at such a crisis was out of the question,
and as no reliance could be placed on the King, whose own
friends could not depend upon him, we must not wonder to
find Whitelocke yielding on some points, where his superior
sagacity prevented him from approving. Thus the House
had taken into debate the subject of Ways and Means, how
they should find the money for the payment of those great
armies that lay like a nightmare on this country, when a
Lancashire knight offered to procure his Majesty 650,000*l.*
till the subsidies should be raised, provided he would pass a
bill, " Not to prorogue, adjourn, or dissolve this Parliament,
without consent of both Houses, which was to endure till
the grievances were redressed, and to give the Parliament
credit to take up monies." They were already falling into
temptation. Such a bill, if passed, would be tantamount to
the King's abdication, and, in fact, when he did sanction it,
he virtually lost his throne. It was suicidal, in so far as the
House itself was concerned, by compelling them to rebellion
and revolution ; by making the sword the only means of
adjustment ; by creating and not redressing grievances ; by
imposing the tyranny of many in lieu of that of one. Up

to this moment the King had probably few supporters, and although he himself, by his sacrifice of Strafford, committed an irreparable error, or still worse, a great crime, he nevertheless, as a personification of regal power, derived strength from this usurpation of the Commons, until finally by his death he secured the throne and paved the way for the overthrow of Anglican republicanism. Whitelocke, as a lawyer and historian, must have seen the impolicy of this bill, but the "heat of the House," as he gently calls the fury that now animated it, overpowered all thought of remonstrance. He himself was ordered to draw the bill, and to have it ready by the next morning, when being prepared, it was passed the same day. It belongs to the historian, and not the biographer, to state the reasons why Charles gave his consent to this disastrous measure, and the other bill, hardly less disastrous, by which Strafford's life was forfeited. The reader is aware, that the execution of this eminent man induced even Juxon to resign his office, Juxon,* by far the wisest and best counsellor, perhaps the only wise and consistent man, that had access to his Majesty. For some time these concessions of the King seemed to have allayed the national discontent; matters went on more smoothly, and the various armies in England were disbanded at one and the same instant; the Parliament adjourned to the 20th of October, 1641, and the Commons left a Committee of fifty to sit during the recess, with ample powers. In Ireland also, the army was disbanded.

A deceitful calm prevailed to the end of this month, October, when a hideous storm, that had long been collecting, broke loose, and convulsed society to its deepest foundations. As the first troubles commenced from Scotland, so now they began from Ireland; and as in the one country, so likewise in the other, the cause was religion. If Presbyterian

---

* I call Juxon wise, because, unlike the other bishops, he made no distinction between public and private conscience, and strenuously exhorted Charles to act uprightly, let the consequences be what they might.

and Anglican clergymen fomented discord in the former,
popish priests were no less influential in the latter ; and the
ready coadjutors of the clergy in all countries, the lawyers,
were equally mixed up with almost every passage in both.
They rule the world between them.   In Ireland they pro-
mulgated such maxims of law as the following : " That any
one being slain in rebellion, though found by record, gave
the King no forfeiture.   That though many thousands were
in arms, and exercising the violences of war, yet if they professed not to rise against the King, it was no rebellion.   That
if any one were outlawed for treason, his heir might reverse
the outlawry, and be restored."   Tenets of this kind, supposed on this side of the water to be wrong, were uttered in
their parliament ; and having been encouraged by the successes of the Scottish army, they proceeded to raise forces,
and indulged in the strong hope of shaking off the English
yoke.   One of their proclamations was, " that the King and
Queen were curbed by the Puritans, and their prerogatives
abolished ; that the Catholic religion was suppressed in
England, and the Catholics in that country persecuted with
rigour."   I cannot agree with Whitelocke, that these, and
many statements of a like nature, were "manifest untruths;"
but true or false, they produced the same result.   On the
20th of November, 1641, the lords justices and council in
Ireland, greatly alarmed at the progress of Phelim O'Neale,
the Irish rebel general, sent over a full statement of affairs
to the Lord Lieutenant, the Earl of Leicester, who was sojourning in this country.   He replied, "that he had acquainted
the King at Edinburgh with all their despatches ; and that
his Majesty had referred the Irish business and management
of the war there to his Parliament of England."   Such an
answer from a king betokens great mental discontent ; and
indeed it became soon evident how alienated he was from a
body of men that had so thoroughly humiliated and degraded
him.   Mutual confidence, it was clear, could not be restored,
since the executive was lodged in the hands of a body whose

functions were, and ought never to have been other than, purely administrative and legislative.

All idea of working in harmony and concert, if it existed in the minds of the inexperienced members of the House, so new to power, had found no entrance into the mind of the Sovereign. Indignant with himself at his own weakness and submission, there is too much reason to believe that he was not altogether innocent with respect to this Irish rebellion, the plan of which had been laid, if not hatched, in England. The Commons were of this opinion; for they had promptly voted, upon receipt of the sad intelligence, six resolutions, one of which was to secure every papist of quality in England. In virtue of this decree, the Lords Ditton and Taff were arrested on their journey to England, and their papers seized. Both these lords were afterwards great with the King. His own absence from his capital was inauspicious; and when he did come, his conduct soon re-awakened the partially lulled spirit of jealousy and discontent. His return was towards the end of November : he was sumptuously regaled by the citizens of London, and he banqueted them in turn at Hampton Court, dubbing many of the aldermen knights. On the 2nd of December he made to the House a speech, and to the country a proclamation, that were regarded as unseasonable. It offended many. He also issued another proclamation for all the members of Parliament "to repair to the Houses by a day," as if they required his invitation or permission—they whom he had constituted sovereigns, and to whom he had abdicated his functions, if not nominally, at all events essentially. On the 14th of December he spoke again to both Houses, and elicited from the Commons for so doing a petition, in which we may find both sharp language and renascent distrust. They told him, the privilege of Parliament was their birthright, and declared, with all duty, that the King ought not to take notice of any matter under debate in that House or the other, save by their information ; that he ought not to propound any condition, provision, or limitation to any bill or act in debate or preparation, or to manifest or declare his consent or dissent, approbation or dislike, before it be presented in course, nor ought to be displeased with any debate of Parliament, they being judges of their own errors and offences, in debating matters depending." They then told him, that these privileges had been broken of late in the speech of his Majesty on the 14th, wherein he had specially mentioned the bill of Impress, and had offered a provisional clause by a *salvo jure*, before the bill was presented. Then noticing the expression of displeasure used by the King, they desire to know the names of such persons as seduced his Majesty to that item, that they may be punished as his great council shall advise his Majesty. This language, whether strictly constitutional or not, stung to the quick a monarch who could not comprehend, any more than his immediate successors, the doctrine of mutual concession and forbearance, that rigid adhesion to form and precedent, that eternal compromise of extreme opinions, that mixture of abstract truth with practical error and fiction, on which constitutional government ever has been and ever must be based. The King dissembled his resentment at first, and withdrew to Hampton Court, hoping that his absence would shield him from such rude and stern lectures ; but it merely served to increase the displeasure of the House.

About this time Whitelocke, with Hyde, Palmer, and Maynard, espoused the cause of parties seeking redress from the magisterial and illegal exercise of the royal power by the Earl-Marshal ; and, at the motion of Mr. Hyde, who subsequently held, but did not adorn, the post of Chancellor, the House voted, that the Marshal's court and its proceedings were illegal, and a grievance. It was followed up by a remonstrance respecting the state of the nation, in which they mentioned all the mistakes, misfortunes, illegalities, and defaults in government, since the King's coming to the crown, the evil counsels and counsellors, the existence of a malignant party, and that they had no hopes of settling the distractions of this kingdom, for want of a concurrence with the Lords. The debate lasted from three o'clock in the afternoon to ten o'clock the next morning ; and the long vigil caused many from sheer exhaustion to leave the House, so that the resolution was compared to a verdict from a starved jury. Palmer, with two or three others, protested against the vote, but were sent to the Tower next day for daring to do so, and from which they were not released till they had asked pardon. The House printed this remonstrance, and shortly after the King published his declaration in answer. Such were the distractions now prevalent in the state and its capital, whilst Ireland lay miserably bleeding !

Another crisis was at hand, and, as usual, the King's impatience and petulance led him to strike the first blow; whereas his true policy was to have temporised and gained strength by the reaction of public opinion. Having been informed that some members of Parliament held meetings and kept up a correspondence with the Scotch, that they had also countenanced the late tumults in the City, he issued a warrant for a search to be made in the chambers of six members,* and for their persons to be arrested. This act was highly resented as a breach of privilege. The King's next step was to cause articles of high treason, and other misdemeanors, to be prepared against them ; and in the morning of the next day he knocked hastily at the door of the House, entered it alone, stepped up into the Speaker's chair, and after looking in vain for the men he sought, sat down and made a speech to his amazed lieges. Upon his leaving, the cry was raised by some of "Privilege, Privilege;" others exclaimed, "that there never was so unparalleled an act by any king, to the breach of all freedom, not only in

---

* Lord Kimbolton, Denzil Hollis, Sir Arthur Hazlerig, John Pym, John Hampden, and William Strode. None of the courtiers, it would seem, had courage to move the arrest of the peer as a traitor. The five members of the Lower House, making sure that the Commons would take the affair upon themselves, took care, on being warned of the King's design, to be absent from their places.

the accusation of their members, ransacking and searching their studies and papers, and seeking to apprehend their persons, but now in a hostile way he threatened the whole body of the House." The votes they passed were in this spirit; and not long after they impeached the whole bench of bishops. These humbled men were all brought on their knees to the Lords' bar, and although two, from their age and infirmities, were confided to the Black Rod, the other ten were committed to the Tower. After much plotting and counterplotting, the refusal by the King of a guard to the House, or to part with his command of the militia and the Tower, he was accused openly at length by Pym, at a conference with the Lords, of complicity in the Irish rebellion, where it was affirmed that many of the chief commanders then at the head of the rebels, and great Papists, had been licensed to pass thither by the King, after the Lieutenant had put a stop at the ports to prevent their ingress. The King demanded his vindication, but failed to obtain it. A motion came on respecting the militia, and, in the course of that debate, some maintained that the power over that body was vested solely in the King, that it ought to be left to him, and that the Parliament never did nor ought to meddle with it. Others were of opinion, that the King did not possess this power, but that it was solely vested in the Parliament ; and that, if the King refused to order the same according to the advice of Parliament, they then by law might do it without him. Upon this debate, and in conformity with what formed ever after the rule and guide of his conduct with that which forms now, not theoretically but practically, the constitutional law of this country, Whitelocke spoke to this effect :

"Mr. Speaker,—I have often heard it said in former debates on other matters in this House, that such and such a thing was of as great concernment as ever came within these walls. I am sure it may be said so on the matter of

your present debate ; it is truly of the greatest concernment that ever came within these walls.

"It highly concerns us all, and our posterity after us,
where the power of this militia shall be placed.   This great
power, which indeed commands all men and all things,
cannot be too warily lodged nor too seriously considered ;
and I do heartily wish that this great word, this new word,
the militia, this hard word, might never have come within
these walls, but that this House may be as the temple of
Janus, and for ever shut against it.   I take the meaning of
those gentlemen who introduced this word to be, the power
of the sword, *potestas gladii*, which is a great and necessary
power, and properly belonging to the magistrate ; *potestas
gladii in facinorosos*, without which our peace and property
cannot be maintained.

"But *potestas gladii in manibus facinorosorum*, in the
hands of soldiers, is that whereof you now debate, and it is
best out of their hands.   I hope it will never come there.
Some worthy gentlemen have declared their opinions, that
this power of the militia is by right and law in the King
only.   I crave pardon to differ from both those opinions.   I
humbly apprehend that this power of the militia is neither in
the King only, nor only in the Parliament ; and if the law
hath placed it anywhere, it is both in the King and Parliament, when they join together.   And it is a wise institution
of our law, not to settle this power anywhere, but rather to
leave it *in dubio*, or *in nubibus*, that the people might be
kept in ignorance thereof, as a thing not fit to be known, not
to be pried into.   It is the great *arcanum imperii*, and the
less it is meddled with, the less acquaintance we have with
it, the better it will be for all sorts of persons, both for King
and people.

"That this power of the militia is not in the King
only appears in this, that the power of money is not in
the King, but, as will be granted here, is solely in this
House ;   and without the power of money to pay the

soldiers, the power of the militia to do so will be of little force.

"But if the power of the militia should be in the King, yet the power of money being in the Parliament, they must both agree, or else keep the sword in the scabbard, which is the best place for it.

"It is true, that the King by his tenures may require the service in war of those that hold of him, but if they stay above forty days with him, unless he give them pay, they will stay no longer. And it is also true, as hath been observed, that our law looks upon the King as the Jewish law did on theirs, that by his kingly office he is to go in and out before the people, and to lead them in battle against their enemies. But by the laws of the Jews, their King could not undertake a war abroad without the consent of the great Sanhedrim."

This speech might have made a profounder impression, but unfortunately it was already known to every one, that the Queen on leaving this country for Holland had taken with her not merely her own and her husband's jewels, but those also of the Crown, in order that the money they would fetch, together with the assistance expected from the Prince of Orange, might raise forces for the King. Self-preservation therefore compelled the House to act with violence; and when we reflect that the safety of the people is the grand law, the fundamental law of all others,—we may add—with justice. Not that they decided in haste. The King's answer to their petition concerning the militia was not received before the 15th of February, by which time he had returned from Dover to Greenwich, in which he mildly alleged the inconvenience of complying with it, and he would be clearly exonerated by the impartial historian, if he had not plotted against this Parliament. They sent two of his subjects whom he had once honoured with his intimacy, the Earls of Pembroke and Holland, with a declaration, in which they plainly told him, that he had attempted to

incense the late army of the North against them, and how he
had fostered underhand the Irish rebellion, and a few more
homely truths, all of which he denied of course.   To one
accusation he briefly replied, " That is false," and to another,
" That's a lie."

The breach was not to be repaired, and the King took up
his residence at York.   That the suspicions of the Parliament were correct was soon proved.   Foreseeing what his
Majesty was scheming, they had committed the town and
magazine of Hull to one of their members, Sir John Hotham,
and this place the King attempted to secure by surprise.

CHAPTER XII.

—◆—

1642—1644.

Commencement of the Civil War—Secession of Hyde and other Lawyers—Contrast
between Hyde and Whitelocke—Whitelocke deputed to prevent the Execution
of a Royal Array in Oxfordshire—Is joined by Hampden with Troops, and
Captures the King's Commissioners—Enters Oxford with more Forces · holds
a Council of War, and proposes to fortify that City—Receives many Offers of
Support—Battle of Edgehill—Essex's Want of Energy—The King's partial
Successes—Prince Rupert defeated by one of the Bulstrode family at Aylesbury—Fawley Court pillaged by the King's Troops—Whitelocke serves with
Hampden's Regiment on the eve of an expected Battle at Acton —Is appointed
a Member of two successive Commissions to treat with the King at Oxford—
Interview with Charles—Insincerity of the King—The Commission recalled—
The King bestows Fawley Court on Sir C. Blunt—League and Covenant with
the Scotch—Whitelocke exculpated from a Charge of Plotting—He and Selden
appointed to meet the Assembly of Divines convened for the Settlement of the
Protestant Religion—Trial of Laud—Whitelocke refuses to take part in the
Impeachment — Reflections on Laud's conduct (*Note*) — Dispute between the
Houses of Parliament on the subject of Proposals for Peace — Whitelocke's
Speech on the occasion.

By about the beginning of May, 1642, the civil war may
be said to have commenced, but all men had been long
prepared for its arrival. This struggle for the power of
militia, or in other words of commanding the army and
declaring war, lost the Parliament the services of Hyde,
Palmer, Bridgeman, of many other eminent lawyers, and of
nearly all those gentlemen, it is to be presumed, who had
spoken positively against the bill. The loss of Hyde to their
cause was eventually the source of great calamity to this
nation, for, both as the lawyer and the historian, he retarded
national progress and checked the development of the
human intellect in this realm more perhaps than any
other individual the land has ever produced. It was he
that restored the dog-latin and Normanism of the law, and

made it subservient to the cause of despotism, religious intolerance, corruption in equity and misrepresentation of motives, when daring to impeach with his pen the actions and principles of others. But, on the other hand, Lord Littleton thought the claim of Parliament lawful under the circumstances.

That Hyde, or as I may hereafter call him, Clarendon, could suddenly assume with sincerity the spirit of blind loyalty upon deserting his former party, is not to be supposed. To explain so desperate a step we must look around, and endeavour to find for our analysis some other potent considerations. In making his calculations therefore as to the eventual issue of the coming contest, he may have reflected that all the strongholds were already, with few exceptions, in the hands of the King, and that the principal gentry of the land in the majority of the English counties would eventually rally round the throne. He did not, and I think could not, believe that the party he now left would ultimately triumph, and his prognosis was very nearly correct. The cause of the Commons to a military eye, to any eye accustomed to scan minute appearances and arrive rapidly at a decision, seemed hopeless in the long run. Whence were they to obtain men and money, if the great landowners should by degrees return in masses to their allegiance ? The time soon came that seemed to justify his prescience. No sooner had Essex fallen into the snare and lost his army in Cornwall, than the most sanguine despaired,—all but Cromwell and Fairfax in the field, and a knot of veteran stern spirits in the council. If Whitelocke reasoned analytically like Clarendon, and as a rational being he must have done so, he arrived at a different conclusion. But in truth their principles differed. Whitelocke, the monarchist, was a reformer ; Clarendon, the royalist, was not. Whitelocke wished to see the Augæan stable cleansed ; and above all contended for the liberty of private conscience, the native rights of the people : Clarendon looked to the divine right of kings, and thought the people possessed no rights, not even that of being well governed. At least he learned to think so as soon as he grasped office and power. Before Clarendon left his ancient friends, he knew in common with them, that the chief gentry of Yorkshire, England's largest county, had already declared for the King and joined his banner. These friends had voted that what was done at York for a guard to the King was a preparation for war against the Parliament, and that all such persons were traitors. These and similar considerations must have been at work, for even Littleton went over to the King not long afterwards, and after the King's rejection of the propositions for peace presented to him about the 2nd of July. By the 10th of the same month, the names of Royalists and Parliamentarians, of Cavaliers and Roundheads, were in the mouths of men. Whitelocke's own brother-in-law, the Lord Willoughby of Parham, who was the Lieutenant of Lincolnshire, and was there raising the militia, received a letter from the King commanding him to desist, but the noble replied, " that this was not in his power to do without breach of that trust, which he had undertaken to the Parliament, and to which he was encouraged by the opinion of some of his Majesty's great officers, eminent in the knowledge of the laws, wherein he was not learned."

The Parliament now thought it high time to provide for their own defence, a debate ensued, and Whitelocke made a long speech. It shows that he clearly foresaw the consequences of the struggle, and yet he unflinchingly stood forward as the champion of peace. His exhortations were useless, and the House voted "that an army should be raised for the defence of King and Parliament, that the Earl of Essex should be Captain-General of this army, and the Earl of Bedford General of the Horse." They found money by means of loans on the public faith and by private subscriptions. Some poor women brought in their wedding rings and silver bodkins. On the other hand the King was furnished with money upon the pawned jewels,* or by the Cavaliers, and also by a loan from the University of Oxford.

Whitelocke was commanded to prevent the execution of a royal commission of array in Oxfordshire, in opposition to the Earl of Berkshire and the chief gentry of the former county. He had orders to arrest any or all of the commissioners, and they gave him some troopers of Colonel Goodwyn's regiment of horse with some men of Colonel Hampden's regiment of foot, at the head of which force he set out, and was joined by Hampden himself. They hastened to Wattleton, where learning that the commissioners had retreated to Sir Robert Dormer's house, his company hurried on in pursuit. They soon surrounded the building, and summoned the party inside to surrender. A few shots were fired, the storming was prepared, when the besieged lost heart and yielded upon promise of quarter. There were only the Earl and two or three more of note who were thus captured, and sent up as prisoners to town.

Forces were soon raised in sufficient numbers. Whitelocke himself had a gallant company of horse, the men being neighbours under his command. The day before he marched out, Mr. Russell, son of Sir William Russell, the ex-treasurer of the navy, joined him at Henley. He was a brother-member, and was on his march towards the head-quarters at St. Albans, but finding what service Whitelocke was engaged upon, accompanied him instead. His servants, twelve in number, wore scarlet cloaks, and like their master were well horsed and armed. When they came near Oxford, Whitelocke's scouts brought word that the Lords Say and St. John were likewise on their march to the place of rendezvous. Then rapidly combining with these their united forces, more than

---

* Whitelocke penned a remonstrance by order of Parliament, and it was taken over by Mr. Strickland, their future resident in the Netherlands, to the States. One of the arguments used was, that as they had formerly received assistance from the English to recover their liberties, so it was not expected now that they should assist those, whose design it was to deprive the English nation of its rights and liberties.

3000 strong, they made their entrance into Oxford without meeting the least resistance, and were welcomed by the citizens. From the scholars, unaccustomed yet to wear the mask of riper life, their reception was very frigid, but the Mayor and Aldermen, the Vice-Chancellor, Heads of houses, and Proctors, in their official visit to Lord Say, protested all of them, with grave faces and an air of sincerity, their desire of peace, their duty to the Parliament, and engaged not to act in any way against it.

A council of war was held at Oxford, at which they discussed the importance of the place, the strength of its situation, the plentiful resources of the country, its nearness to London, and the disaffection of the University to the Parliamentary cause. It was held, that should the King, who was then at Shrewsbury, come here, he would probably make it a principal quarter for his forces, fortify the city, and seriously prejudice his opponents. To prevent this, Whitelocke, who was no novice in strategy, propounded to the Lord-Lieutenant to fortify the city for themselves, and place a good governor there. He himself was actually recommended shortly after to be the governor, being well known there, and a member of the University, but Lord Say would not hearken to the suggestions, and opposed the entire proceedings. This was the first great blunder committed in the war, and one which more furthered the King's cause in the field than any other, always excepting the expedition of Essex into Cornwall, where he marched into a trap with his eyes wide open. But for these two pernicious mistakes the contest would not have been prolonged as it was, and might have ended with perhaps half the sacrifices on either side. Lord Say did not explain the true motives of his conduct, and yet no less than 1000 men were offered by Whitelocke's neighbours, at a day's notice, to be under the new governor's command, provided he were chosen; and the townsmen joined in the request. Say's excuse for his refusal was, that the King's settling there was too unlikely; but, on the other hand, he allowed the plate to remain in the colleges ; not appearing to doubt the solemn promises made by the several Heads, that their plate should be forthcoming, and should not be made use of by the King against Parliament. Lord Say affected to believe this promise from political conviction, little justified by events. Many were dissatisfied with this unwonted lemency at the time, and foretold the consequences,—" but his lordship had the sole power in himself, and thus carried all this business, for which he had no thanks from either party."

The first great battle was fought at Edgehill, where Essex gained a small victory on the 23rd of October, 1642, and lost its fruits by neglecting to pursue the enemy in his retreat. On the other hand the town and castle of Banbury having yielded to the King without a blow, the garrison, which consisted of two regiments of foot and a troop of horse, enlisted in his service, and so strong did he feel himself, that he soon turned round and came on towards London. The first person who suffered for his folly was Lord Say. Prince Rupert seized his house at Broughton, and made such formidable excursions near London by way of diversion, that the Parliament was forced to recall Essex for their own defence. And now members of one and the same family were seen fighting on different sides, brother against brother, cousin against cousin. One near relative of Whitelocke's, Richard Bulstrode, was dangerously wounded on the head at Edgehill, while fighting on the side of the Cavaliers. He was afterwards knighted, made a general of horse, and at length died at Brussels in his one hundred and seventh year. Another Bulstrode defeated Prince Rupert at Aylesbury, and preserved that town, of which he was governor, to the popular party.

It was now that Prince Rupert set the fatal example of pillage, waste, and wanton destruction ; and one of his horse-regiments was quartered at Fawley Court at that juncture when the King was marching in all haste to town, expecting succour there through the treachery of some powerful party. Sir John Byron and his brothers commanded the regiment of horse that occupied Whitelocke's house and grounds. Sir John gave orders to the soldiers to commit no plunder, to which they paid no attention, but, on the contrary, omitted no kind of insolence and destruction. They consumed one hundred loads of corn and hay; littered their horses with sheaves of good wheat, and gave them all sorts of corn in the straw. There were various writings of consequence and books in the study, and in fact it was one of the noblest libraries in England. Some of these inestimable manuscripts they tore up, others they made wisps of to light their pipes with, and others they took away with them, including the title-deeds of the estate, with some learned manuscripts by his father, and some written by himself. They broke down his park-palings, killed most of his deer, though rascal and carrion, let loose the rest, all but a young pet stag, which they gave to Prince Rupert. The Prince had conferred upon him, through the same bountiful channel, Whitelocke's pack of hounds, the pride of the county. After eating and drinking up whatever they could find, the soldiers began to break open the trunks, chests, and coffers. The linen and household stuff they took, and the ticks of the beds, after strewing the feathers about. His four carriages and all his saddle-horses went the same way, and into the coach they stowed articles of antiquity, gems and ancient plate, collected by his father and himself throughout a long number of years. All these things were lost to the owner for ever. So seriously was the house injured, that it could never be used as a comfortable residence again. Forty years later it was pulled down, when Sir Christopher Wren erected a new seat for the new proprietor, Colonel Freeman. Whitelocke bore his loss without a thought of retaliation. He says :— "All this is remembered only to raise a constant hatred of anything that may in the least tend to the fomenting of such unhappiness and misery." In another place a further liberty which the King himself took with the estate will be remembered also, and which Whitelocke would have passed over in silence, but for his Majesty's breach of promise of his word plighted as a Christian king and a gentleman, by which the life of the man who tried to save him was placed in imminent peril.

Essex, although a favourite with the soldiers, who would toss up their caps and shout "Hey for old Robin!" at the sight of him, committed a series of military blunders about this time. Whitelocke was serving in Hampden's regiment, which, with other troops, had been ordered by the commander to march round Acton Green, get beyond the King's army, and commence the attack on that side, when at a given preconcerted signal Essex and his forces were to attack on the opposite side. Just before the charge Sir John Meyricke, the major-general of Essex, rode galloping after them, recalled them, told them that the general had changed his mind, and expressly desired them to rejoin the rest of the army. A fine opportunity was thus lost of striking a severe blow. They retreated to Turnham Green, where the two armies stood drawn up for several hours, and looked at each other with mutual irresolution. Sometimes one side appeared to take heart, sometimes the other— advancing and shouting—but before Essex could make up his mind to strike a blow, the Royalists withdrew, and another favourable moment was lost. Many of the latter confessed afterwards, that had they been then attacked, they must have been beaten for want of ammunition, not having bullets enough to maintain the fight for a quarter of an hour. In justice to Essex it is to be said, that the King's presence here was a breach of treaty. So perfidious was it considered, that the Parliament, in their first impulse of resentment, voted "they would have no accommodation with him."

In all the great transactions of this time, Whitelocke refused to identify himself with any faction or party, but followed the dictates of his own reason and conscience, and on all occasions when overtures for peace were made, laboured industriously to promote them. He was accordingly named one of the commissioners to present the propositions of peace to the King at Oxford. His colleagues were the Earl of Northumberland, with five other lords, and five more commoners. The very number shows the sincerity of the mission, as great virtue was then believed to be inherent in twelve and its multiples. Two lords and two untitled gentlemen sat in each coach drawn by six horses, with a great number of servants on horseback to attend them. As they passed through the streets of Oxford some of the soldiers and the vulgar crowd reviled them with the names of traitors and rebels. No notice was taken of them, but some of the King's officers, on learning this, affected to be very angry at it. The commissioners had their first access to the King in the garden of Christ Church, where he was walking with the young Prince, and several lords attending him. The new comers all kissed his hand, not as they were ranked in the safe conduct, but according to their several degrees—Mr. Pierpoint before the knights, he being an earl's son, and Mr. Winwood before Whitelocke, he being the eldest knight's son, and Mr. Waller was the last. The King said to the latter—the well-known poet—"Though you are the last, yet you are not the worst, nor the least in my favour." These words were a secret allusion to the plot that was then in hand, and in which Waller was engaged. After kissing the King's hand, the Prince gave them his hand to kiss. The Earl of Northumberland read the propositions, and, on being interrupted by the King, said smartly, "Your Majesty will give me leave to proceed?" The King answered "Aye, aye!" with that tendency to stammer that was hereditary, and the Earl read the propositions all through. The proposals on both sides were moderate under the circumstances; they paved the way for a treaty, but nothing was done in it till the 4th of March. Meanwhile hostilities continued, the issue of which was on the whole favourable to the Parlia-

mentarians.   On the other hand, the Queen had landed with
officers, money, and ammunition in the north, advanced to
York, and by her active exertions greatly strengthened the
Royalist party, which, in the course of a few months, had
succeeded in forming an army, besides sending arms and
ammunition to the King at Oxford, then much in need of
such aid.   Hitherto pillage and spoil, but without great
violence, had obtained, to which calamity scenes of barbarous
cruelty were, however, now to be added ; and the first spectacle of this nature was exhibited at Oxford.

The nineteenth year of King Charles, 1643, which did not
begin till the spring quarter, opened with futile negotiations
for a treaty of peace between him and the Parliament.   The
commissioners on this occasion were fewer in number, only
one lord and four commoners, of which last Whitelocke was
one.   The Earl of Northumberland carried with him his own
furniture and accommodations, and provided sumptuously
for the entertainment of himself and his colleagues.   The
King used them with great favour and civility, and came in
for his share of the good things, which he did not disdain to
accept.   Whitelocke had the drawing up of all the papers to
the King, and they were then transcribed by the secretaries.
Their instructions were very strict : they were only permitted
to treat with the King himself, to whose lodgings in Christ
Church they often repaired ; they were never refused admit-
tance when they desired it, and when in debate were allowed
full liberty of speech by the monarch.   Prince Rupert, the
Lord Keeper Littleton, the Earl of Southampton, the Lord
Chief Justice Banks, and several lords of his council, were
invariably present at these audiences, but never spoke with
the commissioners, or indeed at all, unless in answer to a
question from the King, or to remind him of something
when requisite.

In these negotiations, Charles, in the opinion of the commissioners, manifested his great parts and abilities, his
strength of reason and quickness of apprehension, with great

patience in listening to what formed the grounds of complaint against him. He would himself sum up all the arguments and give a clear judgment of them at the end. But his unhappiness was, says the narrator, who invariably pitied his fate, that he had a better opinion of the judgments formed by others than of his own, the stronger and better of the two when different. Of this strange partiality the commissioners had too soon experience, to their own great trouble. Thus, on one occasion, and there seem to have been many such, they pressed his Majesty on one of the most material points, and used the best reasons and arguments they could for inducing him to grant what they desired. He said he was fully satisfied, and promised to give them his answer in writing, as they desired, but it was past midnight, and too late then to reduce it to writing. He therefore said it should be done in the morning, desired them to wait on him again the next day, when they should have this answer in writing, and, as it was already verbally agreed upon, they returned to their lodgings in strong hopes that all was arranged, that a happy issue was secured for the treaty. The hour approached, and a paper was presented to them. It contained not the answer promised and expected, but one the very reverse, and tending to the breach of the treaty. They expostulated humbly with his Majesty, and pressed him now upon his royal word, not omitting to state the evil consequences that might result from the new paper he had given them. He merely replied "that he had altered his mind, and that this paper which he now gave them was his answer—the one he had now resolved to give upon their last debate." They were no longer able to subvert this last determination.

Whitelocke made inquiries to ascertain what could have occasioned so abrupt a change, and learned that as soon as the King was left alone, he retired to his own apartments, where the Queen, or Mr. Murray, for some personage of the bedchamber was alluded to, had persuaded him to undo all

that he had done.   The treaty now went slowly on, and the
King wished to see their private instructions, which they of
course were not at liberty to show.   Upon this he thought
fit to interrupt its course by sending a message and inviting
the Parliament to adjourn to some place twenty miles away
from London, a most suspicious move on his part, especially
with the remembrance of the passage at Brentford so fresh
in the minds of men, and with the settled conviction of
nearly the entire country, that he had promoted and fostered
the Irish rebellion.   It is true he communicated his intention
of doing so to the commissioners, who tried in vain to dissuade him from taking a step so injurious to the treaty.
The message was answered not by its acceptance, the trap
being too visible, but by the instant recall of the commissioners from Oxford.   On the 15th of April Whitelocke left
that city with a heavy heart and the most poignant regret at
finding all their efforts had been fruitless.

Although Whitelocke refrains from indulging in any
reproach, he must have felt, in common with the rest, that
the civil, benign treatment they had received was part of a
scheme to lull the Parliament into false security, and inveigle
them into the King's hands.   As for the commissioners, the
advocates of peace, Charles thoroughly despised them as
simple-minded dupes, whom he had not thought it worth
while to proclaim traitors, like the Lord Say and others.
But Whitelocke's estate at Fawley Court he had seized, and
bestowed on one of his adherents, Sir Charles Blunt, a
stretch of prerogative, in which Charles indulged, and which
he may have fancied lawful.   The commissioners thought
his Majesty a man of talent, but in reality Charles was
perversely stolid in all matters connected with the rights of
his subjects, and not immediately touching his own divine
pretensions.   The commissioners were well chosen, and
Mr. Pierpoint is expressly stated to have acted his part with
deep foresight and prudence ; but how they could have
seriously entertained a belief that his Majesty would sur-

render that which he alone prized, his prerogative and the supreme command of the army into the hands of men, whom rightly or wrongly he deemed his enemies, is inconceivable. They may have thought the King irresolute and destitute of a strong will, because he had sacrificed Strafford ; but this sacrifice showed a want of heart, a defect of judgment far more than any lack of will.

The rejection of this treaty humiliated his adversaries in a way the King little supposed ; and as he drew over to his cause the Irish, specially encouraged thereto by the Pope's fatherly benediction and plenary absolution, so the Parliament were compelled to bring in the Scotch, to whom they swore the "Solemn League and Covenant," for the preservation and reformation of the Protestant religion, for the extirpation of Popery and Prelacy, with all superstitions, heresies, and profaneness. It required a long debate in the House to cause this bitter pill to be swallowed ; but the measure passed. There was no help for it. In a second debate, quite as long and gloomy as the other, all other persons in town and country were ordered to take the oath, and whoever refused was branded with the mark of malignancy. Of a naturally grave and religious temperament, Whitelocke must have sighed at thus being made a Presbyterian against his will, and converted by the dire exigencies of party. But there was no means of eluding the dilemma, no going back possibly for him or any other man that had put his feet into the stirrups, and "forwards" was the cry.

All this broke Pym's heart, the man who first and spontaneously contributed to secure for Whitelocke the great moral influence the latter subsequently obtained in the councils of the revolutionary chiefs. At present, a shade rested upon Whitelocke on account of Waller, the man that was last in heraldic rank, but not the least in royal favour, before the King extended his hand to him in Christchurch Walk. When Waller was examined about the plot and the conspirators, he was asked whether Selden, Pierpoint,

Whitelocke, and others, their names being given, were privy
to it.   He answered, that they were not; that he had gone
one evening to Selden's study, where Pierpoint and Whitelocke happened to be, and intended to divulge it to them,
but on alluding to the subject in a general way, those gentlemen so inveighed against such a thing as treachery and
baseness, and as sure to occasion bloodshed, "that he durst
not, for the awe and respect he had for Selden and the rest,
communicate any of the particulars to them, and was almost
disheartened himself from proceeding in it."

On the 28th of August (1643) both Houses passed an
ordinance, for demolishing and removing all monuments of
idolatry and superstition from all churches or chapels in
England and Wales.   Several members also of both Houses
belonged by this time to the Assembly of Divines; both
Whitelocke and Selden, being Hebraic scholars, had seats
there, and debated and voted with the rest.   On any
important subject Selden spoke admirably, and confuted the
Divines repeatedly with their own weapons.   For when they
would quote a text from Scripture, in proof of their assertion,
he used to say, " Perhaps in your little pocket Bibles with
gilt leaves," which they were in the habit of pulling out and
consulting, " the translation may be thus, but the Greek or
the Hebrew signifies thus and thus," and so would totally
silence them.   This assertion of Selden has never been
impeached; moreover, since his day the construction of both
languages has been far more profoundly investigated, and
some thousand manuscripts collated, digested, and classified,
but these same gilt-leaved pocket-Bibles remain, because the
people of England are satisfied with them, regarding them
as an honest, truthful, and faithful translation.   Whitelocke
merely held it to be the best that the country then had; but
in his own religious studies and meditations he invariably
used either the Hebrew or the Greek version for the Old
Testament, and contented himself with the then Greek text
of the New.   No man of that day knew better than he to

what extent reliance ought to be placed on our English authorised version.

The object of this Assembly was, nevertheless, a laudable one, and far more likely to be attained by this course than any other,—the settlement of the Protestant religion. The wags,—for there were wags even in those days,—did not give Selden any support, but confined themselves to satiric and jocular effusions. One of the best of their sayings has an historic value, and it was made nearly on the eve of Laud's trial. "The Queen's army of French and Walloon Papists," they said, "and the King's army of English Papists, together with the Irish rebels, are to *settle* the Protestant religion, and the liberties of England."

Whitelocke was appointed to be one of the committee for drawing up the charge against the fallen Primate, but he declined the office, and gave his reasons to Mr. Miles Corbet, the chairman, why it was not fit for him to appear in the case, against one to whom he had been beholden for his education. But this would not satisfy Mr. Corbet, who still pressed and urged, and at last sent him a kind of summons to attend, when he absolutely refused to do so. This so displeased the chairman, that he acquainted the House with the refusal, and moved for a peremptory order to enforce the attendance of the refractory party. This motion brought Whitelocke on his legs, who made his apology by stating "That the Archbishop had done him the favour to take special care of his breeding at St. John's College in Oxford, and that it would be disingenuous and ungrateful in him, the pupil, to be personally the instrument in taking away the life of a man, who had been so instrumental for the bettering of his." Upon this explanation, the House, to Mr. Corbet's annoyance, discharged him from the objectionable employment.*

---

* There seem to me two modes of explaining the conduct of Laud, an uncharitable and a charitable one. In the text of this work I have faithfully represented what his fellow-countrymen thought of him at the time, especially those who had smarted from his intolerant and cruel persecution. They could make no allowance for deep conscientious convictions opposed to their own; they thought their own opinions infallibly

Whitelocke's moral courage on this occasion deserves great
credit, for the reign of terror and the right of brute force
might break out within those walls at an hour's notice, so
great at that juncture was the feverish irritability of the
whole body, at the desertion and flight of more than one
hundred of their own members ; and a man's private feelings
were never less likely to be soothed or respected. Even
gallantry to the fair sex was seemingly disappearing, how
much less then could a man venture on showing sympathy
with one of his own sex, and that man too the detested

right, those of their adversaries infallibly wrong. But in this more tolerant age we
can afford to be just even towards Laud, who expiated his cruelty on the block, though
put to death not for cruelty, but for those same conscientious convictions. Political,
but still more, religious animosity formed the strong incentive in the breasts of his
accusers and judges.

In the first place, then, let us suppose uncharitably, that Laud had by his exalted
position at Court and his intimacy with Royalty acquired the knowledge, that the
Queen was more or less secretly, but nevertheless obstinately, bent upon rearing her
children in the same faith as her own ; that the wily churchman contemplated as a
certainty the presumptive eventuality of a Roman Catholic king upon the throne of
England, possibly at no distant period, and believed that the bulk of the people would
conform, as history told him they had ever conformed, but more especially under the
sway of Henry VIII., Edward VI., Mary, and Elizabeth ; that the ancient faith of
the land would be preferable to the new doctrines and the existence of new sects, if
not heretical, at all events unorthodox. This mode of inquiry might be carried out
more into detail ; and it is certain that most of the members of Parliament in that
day so reasoned about him, and found their justification in many imprudent acts of
his, that countenanced their belief in his papistical tendencies. But Sir James Whitelocke, who had known Laud from his youth, considered him a just man, meaning a
conscientious man, and it appears from a circumstance recorded at some length by
Wood in his " Annals," that Laud had, long before his accession to high dignities and
whilst a simple clergyman, preached at St. Mary's, in Oxford, a doctrine that created
much animadversion at the time, and caused him to be shunned. Moreover, the publication of Laud's Diary shows him to have had a mind naturally prone to venerate
the supernatural even in the most trivial phenomena, to have been weak minded and
credulous to excess.

Charitably, then, we are led to presume that his Oxonian studies presented to him
views analogous to those entertained by the Puseyites of more recent times. This
mode of inquiry also might be carried out more into detail, and it induces me to
believe that Judge Whitelocke formed the more correct estimate of Laud's character,
with respect to its conscientiousness and over-zealous imprudence. The Judge's prediction also appears to be the true solution of the English so-called revolution. It
was the misgovernment of Charles that partly collected the combustible materials,
but it was Laud who really by his fanaticism raised the pile and set it on fire. But
for him, it is difficult to believe that any mere political misconduct of the Crown
would have given rise in that monarchical age to such extensive defection and to so
great a rebellion, as Clarendon calls it, a rebellion less universal after all than that
which caused the downfall of James II. : both so different in their social results
from those which subsequently overthrew the dynasty of the Bourbons in France,
both being antithetical to our two in their religious aspect.

Laud, the abhorred tyrant of the Star-chamber! It was not
so very long after Whitelocke's apology, that the Lords sent
down to the Commons to hasten their impeachment of the
Queen. What chance had Laud with such a jury, what
chance would Whitelocke himself have had, if he had striven
to save him? But, in truth, he was powerless; he knew too
well what fate was in store for his father's friend before such
a Rhadamanthine tribunal; and he knew also in his secret
conscience that Laud had not only worked his own destruction, but to some extent deserved it.* Indeed, he was
compelled to be exceedingly circumspect in his conduct, and
accordingly his correspondence with Hyde and Palmer now
ceased; they being deeply engaged with the King, and he
no less so with the Parliament. So strict were the regulations
of the Lower House, that they were carried into the most
minute details of conduct; if a member absented himself
from morning prayers, or entered after they were over, he
had to pay a fine of one shilling to the poor, and five
shillings for every motion made after twelve o'clock. Desertion
from their ranks entailed fines equivalent to ruin, and
neutrality was tantamount to hostility, because a text of
Scripture was thought to warrant such an inference.

Shortly before the end of this year, which expired in
March, a difference of opinion broke out between the two
Houses on the subject of peace. The Lords wished a new
committee to be named, and the Commons desired it to be
referred to the Committee of both kingdoms. In the debate
that ensued, several members of the Lower House seemed
averse to any proposals at all, and Whitelocke, with a view
to keep that party in check, delivered a speech, which is
here reproduced :—

* In the course of his trial one article was urged against him, and several witnesses
produced, that he had assumed the title of Pope; that in letters from the University
of Oxford he had been styled *Optimus, Maximus*, and *Sanctitas Vestra* (Your Sacred
Holiness), *Æternum reverendissime Cancellari*, and *Maxime Pontifex*. It was a day
or two after this evidence, that the candlesticks, crucifixes, and plate in Paul's Church
were ordered to be sold.

"MR. SPEAKER,—It would be no wonder to see a unanimous concurrence of the whole House in furthering propositions for a good peace. The calamities of our distractions have brought us to it, and who is there amongst us that has not in some measure felt the strokes of them ? I am sure, sir, I have smarted by them. We may say here, but I hope never with the like application, what Tacitus said of the Romans : 'All things are weary of the civil discords.' * The land is weary of our discords, being thereby polluted with our blood. God has given you great successes in many places against our enemies, and sometimes he is pleased to give our enemies successes against us. In all of them, whether of the one or the other party, the poor English are still the sufferers. Whose goods, I pray sir, are plundered ? Whose houses are burnt ? Whose limbs are cut or shot off ? Whose persons are thrown into loathsome dungeons ? Whose blood stains the walls of our towns, and defiles our land ? Is it not all English ? And is it not then time for us, who are all Englishmen, to be weary of these discords, and to use our utmost endeavours to put an end to them ? I know, sir, you are all here of the same opinion with me on this point, and that it was an unhappy mistake of those who told us, in the beginning of our warfare, 'that it would be only to show ourselves in the field with a few forces, and then all would be presently ended.' We have found it otherwise ; let us now again seek to recover these blessings of peace, whereof we are told that 'nothing is so popular as peace,' † that nothing is more gracious to be heard of, more pleasing to be desired, and more profitable to be enjoyed. I am sorry we have so much and such sad experience, as well as other arguments, to convince us of this truth. You think best to refer it to the committee of both kingdoms, and you cannot find more able and faithful men to trust in this business. The Lords think fit that another committee be named, to

---

* *Omnia discordiis civilibus fessa.*
† *Nihil tam populare quam pax.*

whom this may be referred.   Whilst we differ on the committee, we lose the business, and do not pursue peace.   I
am persuaded, sir, you can hardly name any committee,
either within or without these walls, but would be ready to
take pains to effect this good work,—unless it were those
who. have said, 'that if this war be well managed, it may
last twenty years.'   But those were not Englishmen.   And
although we have Irish, French, Dutch, and Walloons, as
well as other Papists, engaged for the settlement of the
Protestant religion and the laws of England, yet I am persuaded that his Majesty and you mutually endeavouring
as it is both your interests, none can hinder it.   It is true,
that those foreigners help to open the veins wider ; but
a peace will rid us of them, and stop the issue of blood.
For if it bleed on still, we must faint, and perhaps become
a prey to foreigners.   Sir, I humbly move that we may
endeavour without more loss of time to satisfy the Lords
with reasons, that it is fittest to have this matter referred to
the committee of both kingdoms.   Yet if their Lordships
shall not be satisfied herein, let us consent to name another
committee, rather than to suffer so desirable a business to be
protracted.   Let us consent to anything that is just, reasonable, and honourable, rather than in the least neglect to seek
peace, and to insure it."

The Commons complied with his motion and appointed
the committee.

CHAPTER XIII.

In the month of May, 1644, such strong jealousies had
shown themselves among the leaders of the House respecting
Lord Fairfax, that Whitelocke found himself bound in common
prudence to decline the chief command of the forces that
could be drawn together from Oxfordshire, Berkshire, and
Buckinghamshire. He would have had to serve under a
brigade to be sent out of London under Major-General Browne,
"a creature* of the Lord-General." He foresaw that this
would lead to a breach of friendship between himself and
Fairfax, extremely wilful and captious at this time, having
been deeply offended by the refusal of the Commons to allow
the Earl of Holland to accompany him, the Lord-General.
Nor was Whitelocke mistaken in his foresight, for the parliamentary committee was injudiciously interfering with the
strategical movements of their chief commander, who fancied
himself undervalued. " Nor were there wanting pickthanks

---

* The expression is not mine, who find much to admire in the conduct both of
Browne and Fairfax. The word was written under political excitement.

to blow those coals of jealousy," that injured the national cause so deeply in the sequel.

A committee of lawyers was appointed for the sequestration and sale of those chambers in the Inns of Court that belonged to malignant lawyers. Whitelocke saved these from being ransacked, and prevented the removal of most valuable documents. He particularly rendered great service to his friend and relative, Mr. Palmer.

In this same year, 1644, the Houses received from their generals a letter, in which they stated, "that now, if it pleased the Parliament, they believed the King would be more inclinable to peace than formerly." In this dispatch was enclosed —"A gracious message to the Lords and Commons in Parliament assembled at Westminster," in which there were proposals for a treaty to that effect, and the French agent was mixed up in the matter. There was an air of sincerity about it, and the generals were justified in their belief, for the battle of Marston Moor had then been fought, and York captured ; nor was this the sole defeat of the Royalists. The war party in the House gave it their decided opposition, but Whitelocke and his side being the stronger, a day was set apart for the consideration of the business. He had the Lords with him, and they made no secret of their anxiety to have the day hastened. It came on, and the propositions were taken into debate, but the proceedings advanced slowly, because the Scotch commissioners had to be consulted upon each proposal.

Events soon showed how thoroughly they had all been duped. For, even before the first opening of the debate their General, the Earl of Essex, deceived by advice and induced not only by the arguments of Lord Roberts, but also by reasons that have never been clearly explained, was trepanned into the narrow noose of Cornwall. The enemy retired before him ; most of the garrisons near Plymouth and on the borders were withdrawn at his approach. Mount Stamford with four pieces of ordnance, Plimpton with eight,

Saltash, and yet many more forts were evacuated, Launceston and other small garrisons yielded. The General was enchanted at his good fortune. At Newbridge, Sir Richard Grenville disputed the pass into Cornwall, but Essex was not to be kept out, and he stormed the bridge with a loss of only forty men, being five times less than that of his opponent. He soon got as far as Launceston, and was reinforced here by 2500 of the Plymouth troops. In the meantime the King reached Exeter, and being there joined with some of the forces of Lord Hopton and Prince Maurice, he instantly proceeded in pursuit of the unsuspecting victor. All the cattle were seized and all the provisions ; but the King was still all smiles and meekness. He even wrote to his intended prey, whom he was surrounding with his toils. He invited him to join with himself in that which was the aim of both, the happiness of the kingdom, and should any oppose them, to make them happy against their wills. Others in the King's confidence wrote letters also to the General, entreating him to come to them, where he should be as safe as in his own tent, and that a committee of both parties might be nominated to discuss the matter *seriatim*. But the blunt reply of Essex was, that he was trusted by the Parliament to fight, not treat, and that he would not break the trust reposed in him, to treat without their consent. Whilst he was thus dallying, the King had crept on as far as Liskeard, eight miles from Lostwithiel, where Essex then was ; and then he and Prince Maurice strengthened themselves at Boconnock, Sir Richard Grenville at Bodmin, and Sir Jacob Ashley at Hule.

By the end of August the eyes of Essex were opened, for he escaped what he palpably saw was a base incendiary plot to destroy him and the whole of his army by means of sixty barrels of gunpowder placed for that purpose in two waggons. The enemy were drawn out in battle array, awaiting the explosion as a signal to make their attack, when the design was perceived just before the intended work of destruction was to take place. There was an apparatus discovered in

each of the waggons, with lighted matches at the ends, and
the flame was within an inch of the wild-fire, when first seen
and then promptly extinguished in one of the waggons ; the
match had gone out spontaneously in the other.   This deliverance was followed by another discovery ; the General saw
he was hemmed in and could not escape.   In his letter to
Parliament, he concluded by saying :

"If succour come not speedily, we shall be put to great
extremity : if we were in a country where we could force
the enemy to fight, it would be some comfort, but this country
consists so much upon passes, that he who can subsist longest
must have the better of it, which is a great grief to me, who
have the command of so many gallant men.   My Lords, I
am sorry I have no discourse more pleasing ; resting your
faithful servant, Essex."

The petty jealousies of the generals made Sir William
Waller and Middleton slow in marching to his relief, and no
succour reached the Earl.   Desperate at length, he cut his
way through the enemy with the greater part of his horse;
but his infantry under the brave Major Skippon had to submit
to the terms imposed on the vanquished.   He was suffered
to march away with a safe conduct for 6000 men to Dor-
chester.   Such at least was the account of the disaster as
published in London ; the King's account gave a very different version.   The Royalists stated that Essex with most
of his commanders, deserting their whole army, had fled by
sea. It admitted the escape of the horse, who by a manœuvre,
as if preparing to skirmish, had obtained a clear space and
made a clean run of it.   These, however, were under the
command, not of Essex, but of Sir William Balfour.   Neither
had the foot tamely surrendered, nor laid down their arms,
until they saw the utter folly of further resistance.

This signal defeat retrieved the King's affairs ; he who so
recently saw himself pursued by two great armies, those of
Essex and Waller, and hardly knew how to avoid them ; who
saw the power of Parliament to be outshadowing his own ;

who had seen his own armies routed,—was now victorious in
his turn, and again in possession of great military resources.
His stratagem to lead Essex into a snare, by whomsoever devised, had met with complete success ; and so far from desiring
peace, Charles turned his thoughts to new schemes of victory
and revenge.   And indeed the popular forces were in sorry
plight in more than one direction, as the following letter to
Whitelocke from Major-General Browne will satisfactorily
demonstrate :

"HONOURED SIR,—I received your letter, do well approve
of the completing of my regiment, and of the Windsor, but
shall advise it may be forborne, unless there can be a more
certain way of paying them, else you will (as we do daily)
lose both men and arms. I have been constrained from want
of money to send for victuals into the country for the poor
hungry soldiers, and am now forbidden that, both by the
comptroller at Ailesbury and Reading. Truly, sir, we cannot,
must not starve. Sir, I pray, suffer me from the civility I
have always found from you, and shall acknowledge, to assure
you that as I have endeavoured to my utmost the service of
these counties, so I shall be as willing, might I receive any
encouragement. But these things, and many others, make
me request that I may rather be discharged from the employment, than thus labour under so many wearing griefs.
Sir, I thank you for your letter and respects ; shall never
forget those formerly received and still preserved in the
memory of your thankful friend and servant,

"RICHARD BROWNE."

"ABINGDON, *September* 16, 1644."

By this time the King had probably devised a fresh stratagem, and therefore he sent in another letter to the Parliament, declaring his affections for peace, said God had given
him a late victory, and begged them to consider of his long-
rejected message from Evesham. The King whilst penning
this letter summoned Plymouth, and said "that God had

given him a late victory over the rebels." The Commons appointed a day to take this letter into consideration, although the friends of tranquillity, still in the majority, were losing their hopes. A correct decision was adopted. They laid the letter by, as not being a sufficient acknowledgment of their power, but went on with the propositions of peace, notwithstanding their reluctant convictions.

The second victory of Newbury, on the 27th of October, 1644—although less decisive than that gained in September, 1643—restored the drooping spirits of the Parliamentarians. Whitelocke was named Lieutenant-Governor of the garrison at Windsor under the Earl of Pembroke, who was Constable of the castle and forest. Not long after, he, Lord Wenman, Mr. Pierpoint and Mr. Hollis were appointed, with two more lords and some of the Scotch commissioners, to carry the propositions of peace to the King, but they had to wait for a safe conduct before they could proceed.

In the meantime an insidious attempt was made, during a very thin attendance, by a few members of the House, in concert with the Assembly of Divines, to settle the Presbyterian government, and declare that it was *jure divino*. Glynne and Whitelocke were in the House, however, and contrived to defeat the manœuvre. Both of them resolved to speak against time; the former rose and occupied a whole hour in the delivery of his speech, when he was relieved by the other, who enlarged his discourse beyond all ordinary bounds, till perceiving the House to be full, he made an end. The great question of *jus divinum* was decided against the Presbyterian clergy, and numbers thanked the orator for the good service he had rendered the House by preventing its surprisal.

The safe-conduct was brought at last by a trumpeter of Prince Rupert's. It was under the King's hand and seal, for the lords and gentlemen appointed to bring him the propositions of peace, but took no notice of them as members of Parliament, only as private individuals. The affront was

passed over in silence, and they set out upon their journey.
Supposing the King to be at Marlborough, they first went to
Reading, and there they received information of his having
gone to Wallingford. It was very late, the weather and the
roads equally bad, yet they hasted away in the evening
across the country, were benighted, and not without many
mishaps reached Nettlebed, which being but a small country
town, proved a sorry quarter for so many great persons.
They made the best of it, however, and were very merry
over their poor fare and still worse lodging.

The next morning they went on to Wallingford, and stayed
at Cromash, about a mile from the town, whilst they sent on
a letter to Colonel Blake its governor, stating their destination and desiring free passage. He sent back for their pass,
but they would not part with the original, and only for-
warded a copy. After waiting about two hours, a troop of
horse came to escort them. They repaired at once to the
governor's quarters, who ordered in wine for his guests, and
told them the King had returned to Oxford, where they most
likely would find him. Unluckily the Earl of Denbigh and
the Governor broached the subject of war, and spoke of a
passage at arms, where they had both been present. They
soon came to high words, and Blake looking very big grew
insolent and threatening. Glad to escape from the clutches
of so unscrupulous a person they continued their route, but
Whitelocke forgot to state where they passed the night. They
may have bivouacked by the blaze of a wood fire in some
sequestered spot, unless they reached Abingdon, which was
garrisoned by troops of their own party. Early the next
morning they halted in a field upon a hill, distant half a mile
from the city, whilst waiting for the return of their messenger, whom they sent to Sir Jacob Ashley, the governor
of the place. The message brought back was to the effect,
that Sir Jacob would acquaint his Majesty with their coming,
and having learned his pleasure about it, would then send to
them accordingly. After staying three or four hours in the

wet and cold open field, an officer rode up with a troop of horse to convey them through the streets. As they passed along, the rude multitude, the people, part of that body for whom they were undergoing so much hazard to their lives and fortunes, to preserve them in their rights and liberties, " and from slavery and popery," which some about the King* " as was believed," endeavoured to bring upon them,—part of this people of England, as they passed along the streets, reviled them with the names of traitors, rogues, rebels, and sundry other appellations of an equally flattering description, threw stones and dirt into their coaches, and Whitelocke found it no very great encouragement or reward for his service in their cause. However, they went on their way without taking any notice of affronts and invectives, and were brought to a mean inn, called the " Catherine Wheel," near his own college of St. John's. It was little more than an alehouse, and yet no better accommodation could be had. The officer made a slight excuse for the delay they had experienced before gaining admission into the garrison, and took his leave.

As soon as they were settled in their quarters, many of the King's great officers and lords came to visit them, and each met with some particular friend. Whitelocke and Sir Edward Hyde forgot their recent estrangement for a season, and both desired earnestly a successful issue to the mission. The Earl of Lindsay, confined to his bed by his wounds, sent a message of regret that he was too ill to visit them. On the following day they had access to the King. He used them civilly, and gave them his hand to kiss as usual. The Earl of Denbigh read to him the propositions, which he heard with much patience, and when they were all read, told the commissioners he would consider of the answer to be given them.

Hollis and Whitelocke were now about to commit a great

* This expression is intended classically for the King himself, as the phrase, " Those about Priam" means Priam.

indiscretion, to say the least of it, but both were moved
in so doing with secret pity at the sight of fallen Majesty,
fallen from his high estate,—doomed to fall yet lower. The
termination of the contest could be no longer doubtful to
him, who had been scanning the political horizon so long,
and who knew that the meridian of regal power had long
been past. The very insolence of the rabble and the defe-
rential politeness of the nobles were a sure sign of weakness.
They might still struggle, might yet contend in battle and
lay waste many a fair field, destroy many a homestead, but
the brunt of the shock had been borne, and the waves were
now receding slowly. Whitelocke's object was to save the
King, to save monarchy, to save the throne, to prevent the
irruption of anarchy, and the government of the sword ; but
at the same time, to guard that throne with constitutional
laws. I have always been given to understand that Hyde
and he understood each other in this—that the King was to
be saved if possible.

The following is the way in which the editor of the " Memorials " has suffered this incident to appear. Whitelocke and
Hollis thought themselves obliged in civility to return Lord
Lindsay's visit. Now the commissioners had all agreed not to
pay any visit singly to any royalist, nor even in company
with another of their own body, without previously informing
the rest of their intention. Fortunately for Whitelocke and
his companion they observed the rules on this occasion.
Their call was made between eight and nine o'clock in the
evening, and they found Lord Lindsay in bed, with several
lords in the room—amongst whom the Earl of Sussex, better
known as the Lord Savile, was one. This worthy was even
more gracious in his reception of them than the rest, if that
were possible, for nothing could exceed Lord Lindsay's
courtesy. This room formed one of the King's suite of
apartments, was part indeed of the court, and therefore we
may conjecture it to have been at Christchurch. They had
hardly been there above a quarter of an hour, when the King

with Prince Rupert and many great lords came in. White-locke says he did not know whether this was accidental or designed, but his good sense must have shown him, that accidents of this nature rarely happen. The King fell into discourse with them, and the conversation was as follows :

KING. " I am sorry, gentlemen, that you could bring to me no better propositions for peace, nor more reasonable than these are.

HOLLIS. They are such, sir, as the Parliament thought fit to agree upon, and I hope a good issue may be had out of them.

WHITELOCKE. We are but their servants to present them to your Majesty, and very willing to be messengers of peace.

KING. I know you could bring no other than what they would send. But I confess I do not a little wonder at some of them, and particularly at the qualifications.

HOLLIS. Your Majesty will be pleased to consider of them as a foundation for peace.

KING. Surely you yourselves cannot think them to be reasonable or honourable for me to grant.

HOLLIS. Truly, sir, I could have wished that some of them had been otherwise than they are, but your Majesty knows that those things are all carried by the major vote.

KING. I know they are, and am confident that you who are here and your friends (I must not say your party) in the House endeavoured to have had them otherwise, for I know you are well-willers to peace.

WHITELOCKE. I have had the honour to attend your Ma-jesty often heretofore on this errand, and am sorry it was not to better effect.

KING. I wish, Mr. Whitelocke, that others had been of your judgment, and of Mr. Hollis's judgment, and then I believe we had had a happy end of our differences before now.

HOLLIS. We are bound to your Majesty for your gracious

and true opinion of us, and wish we had been, or may be capable of doing your Majesty better service.

KING. Your service, Mr. Hollis, and the rest of those gentlemen, whose desire hath been for peace, hath been very acceptable to me, who do earnestly desire it myself, and in order to it, and out of the confidence I have in you two that are here with me, I ask your opinion and advice what answer will be best for me to give at this time to your propositions, which may probably further such a peace as all good men desire.

HOLLIS. Your Majesty will pardon us if we are not capable in our present condition of advising your Majesty.

WHITELOCKE. We now by accident have the honour to be in your Majesty's presence, but our present employment disables us from advising your Majesty, if we were otherwise worthy to do it in this particular.

KING. For your abilities I am able to judge, and I now look not on you in your employments from the Parliament, but as friends and my private subjects I require your advice.

HOLLIS. Sir, to speak in a private capacity, your Majesty sees that we have been very free, and touching your answer, I shall say further, that I think the best answer would be your coming amongst us.

WHITELOCKE. Truly, sir, I do believe that your Majesty's personal presence at your Parliament, would sooner put an end to our unhappy distractions than any treaty.

KING. How can I come thither with safety?

HOLLIS. I am confident there would be no danger to your person to come away directly to your Parliament.

KING. That may be a question, but I suppose your principals, who sent you hither, will expect a present answer to your message.

WHITELOCKE. The best present and most satisfactory answer, I humbly believe, would be your Majesty's presence with your Parliament, and which I hope might be without any danger to you.

HOLLIS. We should be far from advising anything which might be of the least danger to your Majesty's person ; and I believe your coming to your Parliament would be none ; but we must humbly submit that to your Majesty's own pleasure and great wisdom.

KING. Let us pass by that, and let me desire you two, Mr. Hollis and Mr. Whitelocke, to go into the next room and a little to confer together, and to set down somewhat in writing, which you apprehend may be fit for me to return in answer to your message, and that in your judgments may facilitate and promote this good work of peace.

HOLLIS. We shall obey your Majesty's command and withdraw."

They went together into another room, where they were private, and upon discourse together agreed in opinion, that it would be no breach of trust on their part to do what the King wished, because it would facilitate the solution of what was desired by all, and that was, peace. At the entreaty of Mr. Hollis, and according to the tenor of their mutual opinion, Whitelocke wrote down what he conceived ought to be the substance of the King's answer, taking care, however, to disguise his hand. And here I may observe that this was not difficult, for his writing was very peculiar, and such as would be instantly recognised. I have reason to think it was forged more than once in his life, to which fraud the singular form of the letters offered great temptation in an age when literary forgery was not uncommon. This precaution eventually saved their lives, and warned by his previous experience of the King's sentiments, Whitelocke prudently affixed no signature to what he had written, nor did the King admit of any others to hear the discourse which passed between them and himself.

The nature of that very brief but additional conversation does not appear verbally in the "Memorials." I have reason to think Whitelocke never wrote it down at all in his Annals, nor even stated in writing what it was. All that family tradition

ever knew was, that the King pledged inviolable secrecy to
him, both as to the memorandum and the oral advice,
upon his word as crowned king and his honour as a gentleman. It is also known that he broke it deliberately before
half an hour was past, and showed the paper itself to Lord
Savile. The account states, that when the paper was written,
they left it lying on the table, that the king entered, took it,
and bade them farewell with much civility and favour. He
was in prodigious haste to betray his dupes, apparently ;
he fancied he had them now in his power, and could sow
distrust in their councils ! And in truth he was nearly right
in his conjecture, but his scheme was baffled by a fact he had
utterly overlooked,—the paper was written in a feigned
hand and unsigned, and he did not know Whitelocke's usual
handwriting. The dupes, for such indeed they were, after a
few mutual compliments, took leave of the general company,
and returned to their lodgings at the inn. And now for
Whitelocke's plea in defence of this transaction.

" This being the truth of those secret and private passages
for which Hollis and I were afterwards accused in Parliament by the Lord Savile, no indifferent person can justly
censure us for any unfaithfulness, or the least breach of our
trust to the Parliament, whose servants we then were. And
this may be answered for us, that what we did herein was
in compassion to our bleeding distressed country, and for
the effecting of that which was universally longed for, the
settlement of a just and happy peace. But this was not
imparted by us to our fellow commissioners, nor could all
the examinations at committees and in the House of Commons get it out of us."

The King soon threw off the mask, as the following report
by the commissioners, whilst still at Oxford, will best prove.
They stated—"that on the Lord's day they presented the
propositions for peace to the King, which were read by the
Earl of Denbigh," and then the King asked them if they had
power to treat, and on their saying they had not, but only

to receive his written answer, he told them : " Why then
a letter-carrier would have done as well as you." Whitelocke
admits this hasty speech displeased them all.   At last the
answer came, not open, as it should have been, but sealed
up ; at which they remonstrated ; when the King told them,
" What's that to you, who are but to carry what I send ?
and if I will send the song of ' Robin Hood and Little John,'
you must carry it."   To another objection they made, that
the letter had no address, the King said, " that it was delivered to the Parliament's Commissioners, which was sufficient :" nor could any of his own lords about his person
prevail on him to write the superscription and acknowledge
the Parliament.   They said so, at least ; for they urgently
entreated the commissioners to receive it as it was, and not
endanger their common hopes by persisting in their demand.
The answer was read in Parliament on the 29th of November,
before a conference of both Houses, and they found the pre-
amble satisfactory.   His Majesty expressed his pacific desires,
and requested a safe conduct for the Duke of Lennox and the
Earl of Southampton, who would bring his answer to the
propositions.   Whitelocke and the rest were severally thanked
by the Speaker for their discreet conduct in the business,
and the King's request was complied with, provided he
would send to the Parliament of England assembled at
Westminster, and to the Commissioners of the Parliament of
the kingdom of Scotland.

    This affair being concluded, so far as the commissioners
were concerned, another subject of grave import arose, to
which some future phases of Whitelocke's public life may
unquestionably be traced.   Colonel Cromwell, not long since
made lieutenant-general of the Earl of Manchester's army,
had given great satisfaction to the Commons in the affair
connected with Donnington Castle, after the last battle of
Newbury.   With great caution, for this quality is ever visible
in all great men, he had seemingly censured the officers of
the Lord General's army.   Such a letter gave rise to jealousy

in the breast of the Earl, and efforts were made to get rid of Cromwell, who had likewise used some terms which the Scotch Commissioners conceived to be derogatory to their countrymen in general.   One evening, at a late hour, Whitelocke and Maynard were sent for by the Lord General to Essex House, the message stating the urgency but not the nature of the summons.   They went accordingly, and found a conclave already assembled, consisting of the Scotch Commissioners, Whitelocke's own associate and friend, Hollis, Sir Philip Stapleton, Sir John Meyrick, and many other friends besides.   After the usual compliments were over they took their seats at the council board, and the conference commenced.

LORD GENERAL. " Mr. Maynard and Mr. Whitelocke, I have sent for you on a special occasion, to have your advice and counsel; and that in a matter of very great importance concerning both kingdoms, in which my Lords the Commissioners of Scotland are concerned for their state, and we for ours.   And they, as well as we, knowing your abilities and integrity, are very desirous of your counsel in this great business.

MAYNARD. We are come to obey your Excellency's commands, and shall be ready to give our faithful advice in what shall be required of us.

WHITELOCKE. Your Excellency, I am assured, is fully satisfied of our affections and duty to yourself, and to that cause in which we are all engaged ; and my Lords the Commissioners of Scotland will likewise, I hope, entertain no ill thoughts of us.

LORD GENERAL. My Lord Chancellor of Scotland, and the rest of the commissioners of that kingdom, desired that you two by name might be consulted with upon this occasion ; and I shall desire my Lord Chancellor, who is a much better orator than I am, to acquaint you with what the business is. .

LORD CHANCELLOR OF SCOTLAND. Master Maynard and

Master Whitelocke, I can assure you of the great opinion both my brethren and myself have of your worth and abilities; else we should not have desired this meeting with you; and since it is his Excellency's pleasure that I should acquaint you with the matter upon whilke your counsel is desired, I shall obey his commands, and briefly recite the business to you.

Ye ken vara weel that Lieutenant-General Cromwell is nae freend of oors; and since the advance of our army into England, he hath used all underhand and cunning means to take off from our honour and merit of this kingdom. An evil requital for all our hazards and services; but sae it is, and we are nevertheless fully satisfied of the affections and gratitude of the gude people of this nation in the general. It is thought requisite for us, and for the carrying on of the cause of the twa kingdoms, that this obstacle or remora may be removed out of the way, whom we foresee will otherwise be no small impediment to us, and the gude design we have undertaken. He not only is no freend to us, and to the government of our church, but he is also no well-willer to his Excellency, whom you and we all have cause to love and honour. And if he be permitted to go on in his ways, it may, I fear, endanger the whole business. Therefore we are to advise of some coorse to be taken for prevention of that mischief. Ye ken vara weel the accord 'twixt the twa kingdoms, and the union by the solemn league and covenant, and if any be an incendiary 'twixt the twa nations, how is he to be proceeded against? Now the matter is, wherein we desire yoor opinions, what ye tak the meaning of this word 'incendiary' to be, as is meant thereby, and whilk way wud be best to tak to proceed against him, if he be proved to be sik an incendiary, and that will clepe his wings from soaring to the prejudice of our cause. Noo ye may ken that by our law in Scotland we call him an incendiary wha kindleth coals of contention, and raiseth differences in the state to the pooblic damage, and he is *tamquam publicus hostis patriæ.*

Whether yoor law be the same or not, ye ken best who are mickle learned therein; and therefore, with the favour of his Excellency, we desire your judgments in these points.

LORD GENERAL. My Lord Chancellor hath opened the business fully to you, and we all desire your opinions therein.

WHITELOCKE. I see none of this honourable company is pleased to discourse further on these points, perhaps expecting something to be said by us, and therefore not to detain you longer, I shall, with submission to your Excellency, and to these honourable Commissioners of Scotland, declare humbly and freely my opinion on those particulars, which have been so clearly proposed and opened by my Lord Chancellor.

The sense of the word "incendiary" is the same with us, as his lordship has expressed it to be by the law of Scotland —one that raiseth the fire of contention in a state, that kindles the burning hot flames of contention, and so it is taken in the accord of the two kingdoms.

Whether Lieutenant-General Cromwell be such an incendiary between these two kingdoms, as is meant by this word, cannot be known but by proofs of his particular words or actions, tending to the kindling of this fire of contention betwixt the two nations, and raising of differences between us. If it do not appear by proofs that he has done this, then he is not an incendiary, but if it can be made out by proofs that he has, then he is an incendiary, and to be proceeded against for it by the Parliament, upon his being there accused of those things. This I take for a ground, that my Lord General and my Lords the Commissioners of Scotland, being persons of such great honour and authority as you are, may not appear in any business, especially of an accusation, but such as you shall see beforehand will be clearly made out, and be brought to the effect intended. Otherwise for such persons as you are, to begin a business of this weight, and not to have it so prepared beforehand as to be certain of carrying it, but to put it to a doubtful trial—in case it should not succeed as you expect, but that you should be foiled in it, this would reflect upon your great honour and wisdom. Next, as to the person of him who is to be accused as an incendiary, it will be fit in my humble opinion to consider his present condition, parts, and interest, wherein Mr. Maynard and myself, by our constant attendance in the House of Commons, are the more capable of giving an account to your Lordships ; and for his interest in the army, some honourable persons here present, his Excellency's officers, are best able to inform your Lordships. I take Lieut.-General Cromwell to be a gentleman of quick and subtle parts, and one who has, especially of late, gained no small interest in the House of Commons, nor is he wanting of friends in the House of Peers, nor of abilities in himself to manage his own part of defence to the best advantage. If this be so, my Lords, it will be the more requisite to be well prepared against him before he be brought upon the stage, lest the issue of the business be not answerable to your expectations.

I have not yet heard any particulars mentioned by his Excellency, nor by my Lord Chancellor, or any other, nor do I know any in my private observations, which will amount to a clear proof of such matters, as will satisfy the House of Commons in the case of Lieutenant-General Cromwell, and according to our law, to the course of proceedings in our Parliament, that he is an incendiary, and to be punished accordingly. However, I apprehend it to be doubtful, and therefore cannot advise that at this time he should be accused of being an incendiary, but rather that direction may be given to collect such particular passages relating to him, by which your Lordships may judge whether they will amount to prove him an incendiary or not. And this being done, that we may again wait upon your Excellency, if you please, and upon view of those proofs we shall be the better able to advise, and your Lordships to judge what will be fit to be done in this matter."

Maynard followed and confirmed what his colleague had

just advised; but added that Cromwell was a person of
great favour and interest with the House of Commons.   Mr.
Hollis and Sir Philip Stapleton thought differently ; the rest
of the meeting adopted the wise counsel they had heard,
and the two English lawyers were dismissed about two
o'clock in the morning.   There was reason to suppose that
some person present at this debate revealed what passed to
Cromwell ; in all probability one of his brother officers.
Although the General, whom the Scotch Commissioners and
a jealous Commander-in-Chief desired to crush, was studiously silent at the time respecting the incident, both Whitelocke and Maynard perceived a cordiality in his manner
towards them, that served to convince them of his private
acquaintance with their sentiments.   Notwithstanding all
overt attacks against him were dropped, the House was
induced to pass the Self-denying Ordinance, a measure
from which the republicans expected great results.   It
broke down utterly, as Whitelocke predicted at the time.
Indeed, so little inconvenience did he expect from it, that
he offered no opposition to it, while passing through its three
stages.

Shortly after this, the ambassadors from the States of
Holland were received by both Houses with great ceremony,
and thanked for their kind offers of mediation between the
English King and his subjects.   They replied in French,
and the Speaker, whose knowledge of the language was sadly
defective, as may well be imagined, requested Whitelocke to
act as interpreter, and this incident served as a commencement for his future and frequent management of foreign
affairs.

During the whole of this dark fluctuating period the King
was incessantly plotting for the treacherous surrender of the
Parliamentary garrisons, and it soon became evident that the
two lords whom he had sent to negotiate a treaty, were
labouring and plotting, during the whole time they remained
at Somerset House, against the interest of the Parliament.

These tamperings and intrigues were fully revealed by a petition from the Common Council of the City.

Although Whitelocke had suffered the Self-denying Ordinance to pass without voting against it, yet when the bill was returned from the Lords with an exceptional clause, he thought the opportunity a good one for proposing a remedy to what was felt to be an evil, and which may be best explained in his own words :—

" Mr. Speaker, I am one of that number of your servants, who have no office or employment, but such as you are now about to except out of this ordinance, nor have ambition for any. I therefore may the more freely and indifferently, yet with all submission, humbly offer my reasons against it, concerning that which I apprehend may prove prejudicial to your service. It has been objected, that your House, as that of the Lords, is thin and empty, and you the less esteemed, having so few members here, many of them being employed in offices, so that they cannot attend the Houses, but that by this ordinance they will be at leisure and liberty to attend the service of the Parliament here, and the Houses be much fuller than they now are. I confess, Sir, this is fit to be remedied, but I apprehend you have a fitter way, than by this ordinance, to do it ; that is, by issuing new writs for electing new members in the places of those who are dead or expelled, and this will satisfy the objection, and engage divers of interest and quality the more immediately in your service. Whereas this ordinance will discontent many, and the Houses will be but little the fuller by the passing of it. Another objection is, that if this ordinance do not pass, the treaty for peace will not so well proceed, and the particular interests of members of Parliament may retard the same, but will be all taken away by this ordinance, I am to seek how this can be materially objected, when I suppose whether this ordinance pass, or not yet you intend members of Parliament only to be your commissioners for that treaty, and in case some of them be officers, they will the better understand your business, on which the treaty will be grounded. Another objection is, that unless this ordinance pass, the great work intended of new modelling your armies will not so well be carried on, for that by putting all out, there will remain no exception. I should rather have argued, that by putting all members out of their employments, the exception and discontent would be the more general; and by leaving them still in their employments, there would be the less competition and solicitation for new officers in their room. Another objection or argument is, that the members of Parliament, who are officers, being of equal power in Parliament, will not be so obedient to your commands, as others who have smaller interests, and would not so much dispute one with another. Surely, Sir, those whose interest is the same with yours, have the more reason to obey your commands than others, and have more to hazard by disobedience than others can have. And in your commands, all your members are involved, and it were strange if they should be backward to obey their own orders. Nor will the contests be so frequent and high between them and other officers, as it will be between those who will be of a more equal condition.

But, Mr. Speaker, as you consider the inconveniences if this ordinance do not pass, so you will be pleased to consider the inconveniences if it do pass. You will lay aside, as brave men, and who have served you with as much courage, wisdom, faithfulness, and success, as ever men served their country. Our noble General,* and the Earls of Denbigh, Warwick, Manchester; the Lords Roberts, Willoughby,† and other lords in your armies, besides those in civil offices not excepted; and of your own members, the Lord Grey, Lord Fairfax, Sir Wm. Waller, Lieutenant-General Cromwell, Mr. Hollis, Sir Philip Stapleton, Sir Wm. Brereton, Sir John Meyrick, with many others must be laid aside, if you pass this ordinance. And I am to seek, and I doubt so will they be to whom you shall refer the now modelling of your armies,

---

* The Earl of Essex.   † Of Parham, his own brother-in-law.

where to find officers that shall excel, if equal these. If your judgments are, that for the public service it will be expedient to remove any of them from their commands, let the same, if you please, be plainly made known to them from you. Let them have what they deserve, your thanks for their former good services, and they will not be offended that you, having no more work for them, do lay them aside with honour. But to do a business of this nature, as has been well said, by a side wind, is in my humble opinion not so becoming your honour and wisdom, as plainness and gravity, which are ornaments to your actions. I shall conclude with the example of the Grecians and Romans, amongst whom, Sir, you know, that the greatest offices, both of war and peace, were conferred upon their senators ; and their reasons were, because they, having greater interests than others, were the more capable of doing them the greatest service. Having the same interest with the Senate, and present at their debates, they understood their business the better, and were less apt to break that trust, which so nearly concerned their private interests, involved as these were with those of the public. The better they understood their business, the better service might be expected from them. Sir, I humbly submit the application to your judgment ; your ancestors did the same ; they thought the members of Parliament fittest to be employed in the greatest offices. I hope you will be of the same judgment, and not at this time proceed to pass this ordinance, and thereby to discourage your faithful servants."

CHAPTER XIV.

—•—

1645.

Repeated instances of the King's Plotting—Condemnation and Execution of Laud—
Whitelocke keeps aloof—Rejection by the Lords of the Self-denying Ordinance—
Schism between the Two Houses—A Renewed Attempt to negotiate for Peace at
Uxbridge : Whitelocke again a Commissioner—The issue abortive—Rising of
Club Men against the Cavaliers—Reverses of the King—Lord Savile deserts him
—Lord Essex deprived of his Command—Whitelocke a Commissioner of the
Admiralty—Naseby Fight—Lilly's Prediction—Whitelocke somewhat imbued
with the Puritanical tone of the day—Seizure of the King's Papers at Naseby
fatal to his Cause—Futile Attempt of Lord Savile to criminate Whitelocke—
Whitelocke's impoverished State—He and Selden oppose further Presbyterian
Innovations—Whitelocke succeeds in saving the Royal Library and other valuable
objects—Is seized with severe Illness—Convivialities on his Recovery—His
various Associates of opposite Parties at this time.

THERE are some battles that change the destinies of the
world, and so there are some speeches.   That of Whitelocke's
against the Self-denying Ordinance was one of them, and
although it gave rise to a fierce debate that lasted to a late
hour of the night, and although envy and self-ends prevailed
for the moment, the measure received a blow from which it
never recovered.   Had it really been acted on impartially
we should have had no Naseby, no Protector, no Bill of
Rights, and the people of this country might possibly be
living to this day under a triumphant despotic and autocratic
form of government.   The very passing of the measure by
the House of Commons prepared the downfall of that
Assembly, for Cromwell never forgot nor forgave this
impotent attempt to ruin and degrade him.

Shortly after this Whitelocke attended the Committee, who
received in audience the agent from Christina, Queen

of Sweden, to whom he subsequently was sent as an ambassador.

Fresh instances of royal treachery transpired about this time, though negotiations for a treaty of peace were still pending. Thus Lord Digby was urging Browne to surrender Abingdon, and the King had sent three commissions into Kent, one for the betrayal of Dover Castle, another for Chatham, and some ships to be given up, and a third for levying troops in the west of that county. All were discovered, and these pertinacious efforts may in some degree lessen, though they cannot excuse, the sanguinary cruelty of the Commons, who chopped off the heads of their opponents without pity or scruple. The Lords were more merciful, probably because their power in the state was ebbing so rapidly away ; they might condemn if they chose, they could not save. In vain they attempted to reprieve Hotham ; in vain they pleaded indirectly, and as far as they durst, for Laud. The gentlemen of England proved stern, unyielding, and implacable. All they would do for the Archbishop was to let him suffer on the block, and they forbore in their magnanimity the gratification of seeing him hanged. Their victims in nearly every instance died heroically and with calm submission, not to their sentence, but to irresistible power. It requires ages for martyrdom to work ; the eternal infamy of these judicial murders remains, and we blush whilst we read the atrocities that succeeded each other, that polluted every British tribunal for generations. I am proud to say, the man whose life I am writing refused to dip his hands in blood, and although a lawyer, would take no part in any such prosecution, attainder, and sentence. The remorse he felt at the small share he had had in the prosecution of Strafford, though his intent was guiltless, clung to him through life. It was his first act of the kind, and also his last. Such was the temper of that age, however, that although he shunned cruelty upon principle, he believed Laud truly guilty. But guilty of what ? Of cruelty himself ? It was not for this

they condemned him, but because he was ambitious. They
might have suffered the old man to live peaceably on in the
Tower. His death was not necessary ; they had destroyed
his trinkets and prelatical trumpery ; by putting him to death
they hallowed his cause, and prepared a final triumph for the
very Church they strove to suppress. Our ancestors had yet
to learn, that persecution is the surest way to raise anything,
whether a sect or a party, from the contempt into which it
otherwise might speedily have fallen, and the very best
engine for bringing any extreme measures into collision with
the common sense and milder views of humanity at large.
That Laud strove to exalt his order ; to constitute an Anglo-
Catholic papacy ; to make himself and his successors high
priests ; that he was a thorough priest in his heart was
clear ; but had he not in equity quite as much a right to do
and be all this, as they to enforce their puritanical doctrines, and their mode of explaining the Scriptures, those
Scriptures which in their blind ignorance they conceived
no one could rightly understand or apply but themselves ? Oh, when will men learn to see, that cruelty
perverts and nullifies the attempts of those who labour
for the advancement and mental progress of their fellow-
creatures ?

Although weak and over-complying with the extravagant
demands of the Lower House, the Lords showed some resolution at length, by rejecting the Self-denying Ordinance.
It served to increase the difference between the two bodies,
and ultimately led to the suppression of the Upper House,
thereby raising the Lords in the estimation of the wise, and
tending to increase their social influence. The people of
this country are often angry with them, when they oppose
the strong passions of the multitude, but in time the
inevitable reaction sets in, and the institution rises with
fresh strength, like Antæus, from its fall. The immediate
consequence of their independent act was an attempt to
reject those few lords, whom the Upper House had nomi-

nated as commissioners of the treaty. The Commons appointed eighty of their own body, of whom Whitelocke was one.

Another safe conduct arrived from the King and the place of meeting was settled to be Uxbridge by mutual consent. Sir Edward Hyde and Sir Richard Lane were among those on the King's side, and if calm rational argument, on pure legal premises, could have decided the matters at issue, no better man than the latter could possibly have been chosen. He had displayed his supereminent abilities in defending Strafford. But what could reason do on either side, when the common soldiery, imitating the brutal indifference of their masters to human sufferings, were ravaging the whole country with ruthless pillage and every act of licentiousness,—all but the true, the brave, the invincible soldiers of Cromwell?

Both Houses agreed, that the three first days of the treaty (such superstitious power was still believed to sleep in mere abstract number) should be for religion, the three next for the militia, and another three days for Ireland, and so *alternis vicibus.* The Scotch desired some ' leetle ' alterations in this arrangement, which led to a long and furious debate, that entrenched upon the fast day, nay, consumed it utterly ; the Scots finally yielded, but their yoke was now beginning to gall, and it was thought they listened less to reason than their own will. On the 29th of January both parties met at Uxbridge, where their respective quarters were allotted to them. Whitelocke and his side were domiciled on the north, Hyde and his upon the south, and the separation was rigidly enforced. The two best inns of the town were used reciprocally by the congress for social purposes. On the first evening of their arrival several visits were exchanged, and a great deal of private persuasion was at work. Hyde visited Hollis and Whitelocke as before ; and in his turn Whitelocke visited Hyde, Palmer, Lane, and others. The town was so filled with company, that strangers

P

could hardly find accommodation at all; some of the commissioners even were forced to lie in double-bedded rooms, and
others had to bring their field-beds with them, and many
lay on the bare floor with nothing but a quilt to cover them,
in that cold weather.   Sir John Bennet's house at the
further end of the town was fitted up for the congress to
meet in council; the front entrance was hospitably set apart
for the Royalist Commissioners, while their rivals modestly
contented themselves with the back entrance, and they
met in the middle of the house, where a room existed
large enough for their reception.   They had a table placed
here, the exact counterpart of the one formerly used in
the Star Chamber; it was almost square, but had neither
an upper nor a lower end.   One end with one side was
reserved for the King's party, the other side for the Parliament's, and the Scotch Commissioners had the remaining end
to themselves.   Some of the Parliament's Commissioners, by
this arrangement, were shut out from want of room.   They
sat accordingly together with the divines and secretaries
behind the chairs of those who had the honour of the table.
At each end of this saloon there was a handsome drawing-
room, with its own adjacent smaller apartment, to which
members might retire for private conference and deliberation.
At the very first outset the Scotch Lord Chancellor set up
his claim for precedence, which made the Earl of Northumberland smile, but he was quietly informed that Uxbridge
was not in Scotland, and that his rank here was that of the
Earl of Loudon; nor did the Scotch appear to recognise the
heraldic laws of precedence with a good grace; so, in order
to humour them, the Earl of Northumberland moved and
carried that the Scotch Chancellor and one more of that
body might sit if they chose at the upper end of the table,
which was not taken for the chief, but for the women's place.
The nation paid for the entertainment and diet of all, to
which the Scotch Commissioners offered no impediment.
One of the ministers prayed before every meal, and a very

full table was kept, so that there was no lack of grace or
hospitality.

On the 1st of February something like order was introduced, and certain resolutions adopted. All overtures of the
treaty were to be set down in writing; whatsoever was
agreed to on both sides upon any one or more of the propositions was to be null and of no force, in case the treaty
should ultimately break off upon any of the propositions.
The popular party tendered a paper for the settlement of
religion in a presbyterian way, and this subject was to occupy
the first three days of debate. To this paper the Royalist
party returned certain queries:—What was meant by the
presbyterian government, thus sought to be established?
what was meant by classes? what was meant by provincial
and synodical assemblies? also what was meant by the
bounds of parishes? and some more of the like nature.
Shortly after the queries, and before there was time to
answer them, Dr. Steward spoke very learnedly against
presbyterian government in the Church of England, and
contended for episcopacy as existing *jure divino*. He was
answered, of course, not by one, but by two; and there is no
telling how long this scene of contention might have lasted,
had not the Marquis of Hertford seasonably interposed, who
contended that neither the one church government nor the
other was *jure divino*. He was supported by the Earl of
Pembroke and some others, but Dr. Steward insisted on dis-
puting syllogistically, which challenge was accepted by Mr.
Henderson. The arguments used on this occasion have not
been preserved, nor the sermon preached by one Love at
Uxbridge, who had used disloyal language, it seems, a short
time previously in the pulpit. As the Parliamentary Commissioners were willing to conciliate, they sent for Love, and
handed him over for further examination. And now the
queries being answered, the popular party requested the
others to declare their resolutions respecting it, positively or
negatively; but this was declined for the present.

On the 4th came on the subject of the militia, when Sir
Edward Hyde would have it, that the power of the militia,
by the law of England, was vested in the King alone.
Whitelocke denied this to be so very clear, and undertook
to make it out, that our law does not positively affirm where
that great power is lodged, and doubted not but to satisfy
the commissioners fully on that point. This debate also,
like the previous one on religion, was laid aside for the
immediate present, and the commissioners proceeded in the
treaty upon the particulars of the propositions respecting the
militia. His own party thanked Whitelocke afterwards in
private, for vindicating the honour of Parliament so ably.
It is not improbable that Hyde was congratulated in private by his friends, for vindicating successfully the King's
prerogative.

This vexed question has received in happier times its true
solution, in conformity with the speech Whitelocke had previously delivered in Parliament. The Crown is left nominally
in possession of the power, and the Commons keep the purse,
without which no army can exist. Nor was the King's claim
so very dangerous at this time, whatever it may formerly have
been. He had pawned or sold all his jewels and plate; he
would be incapable for the future of acquiring the lands of
his subjects by judicial spoliation; and would henceforth be
incapable of levying armies without the consent of the
national representatives. Whenever a great perplexity arose,
the only way of meeting it in those days was by abstaining
from beef and pudding; and the commissioners, who seem
already to have been at their wits' ends, appointed a solemn
fast, to which the Cavaliers submitted, and it was so far
useful, that they put off the debate upon excommunication.
The answer of the Royalists about the militia turned out as
might have been foreseen. They agreed to settle the militia
for three years, and to be in the hands of twenty persons,
ten of whom were to be chosen by the King, and ten by the
Parliament, and that it should be high treason for any to

continue such power in the militia after three years. As for the militia in Scotland, they gave no answer at all, though the papers given in to them were for the settlement in both kingdoms. Such an answer created great disappointment, and every effort was made in private to produce a modification, but in vain. Some of the Royal party hinted that they were tied down by the King's instructions, and could go no further. They would send to Oxford, they said, and see if they could prevail there for a further concession from his Majesty in this particular, but nothing came of it. Only further success by arms could cut the Gordian knot, and the Commons took the correct mode. They voted the remodelling of the army, and that Sir Thomas Fairfax should nominate all the commanders in his army, to be taken out of any of the other armies, and to receive the approbation of both Houses.

What further transpired at Uxbridge is of small moment, in so far as harmony was concerned. The King's Commissioners even went the length of solemnly vindicating their master's conduct in Ireland—that he had done right in making a "cessation" with the rebels there; and that he was in honour bound to maintain it. And they would by no means consent "to prosecute the war against the Irish rebels." In another debate they equally insisted on episcopacy, in the very teeth of nearly all that the Commons had recently voted and decreed. They would have nothing to do with the Directory for Worship, and the National Covenant they positively denied. The first triads of days being spent, and the second series having already commenced, Whitelocke was sent to town to report progress, which he did, and the House voted that the term of sitting should be prolonged by three days, so as to make it twenty-four days in all, and that the treaty should either be concluded or rejected by the 22nd of February. The Commons yielded too upon the point concerning the *jus gladii*, for they limited their demand to three years after the declaration of peace by the Parliament, or to seven years from the time of granting the militia, when his Majesty was to take the advice of both Houses for the final settlement of the question. A paper to this effect was delivered accordingly. On the 22nd no compromise had been attained, and thus, not without recriminations and mutual accusations, the negotiations were closed. On the 25th the Houses received a detailed report of all that had been done, and declared that the commissioners had discharged their duty with singular judgment and fidelity. The labour of drawing up the declaration of the proceedings, for the satisfaction of the Common Hall in the City, devolved on Whitelocke and Pierpoint, and gradually the distraction caused by these abortive efforts to come to an understanding ceased.

And now a new phenomenon is added to the general chaos. Clubmen rise in several counties and cry vengeance on the Cavaliers. The tide of battle turns, and one misfortune after another afflicts in quick succession the cause of Charles. Lord Savile deserted him, and on coming in to his new party was committed to the custody of the Black Rod. On the last day of March, in 1645, they were so dissatisfied with his presence, and so suspicious of his intentions, that they ordered him to quit the city without delay, and indeed all quarters and garrisons belonging to the Parliament. They gave him a week to return to the King, or go wherever he pleased, at the end of which time, if caught, he should be dealt with as a public enemy; but he contrived to pacify them, and took the oath prescribed in his case. And before two days more were over, the first scene of the tragic civil war was brought to a close by the exit of the gallant but unsuccessful Essex, who, with several more generals, was set aside by virtue of the Self-denying Ordinance, which seems to have passed in a mutilated shape. A new army was formed with new officers upon the new model, and so great was the contempt the Cavaliers felt at this new order of things, that they called it the "New Noddle." It proved too hard for them to crack, and the second scene of the drama has begun.

On the 15th of April Whitelocke was appointed one of a committee, consisting of six Lords and twelve Commoners, to manage the affairs of the Admiralty : and on the 10th of May, both Houses ordered that Cromwell need not attend the House personally, but might continue his service and command in the army for forty days longer, notwithstanding the Self-denying Ordinance—a measure now shown to have been carried by self-denying pretences. On the 12th a similar indulgence was granted to three other members of the House, and from this time the ordinance may be looked upon as effete, at which consummation Whitelocke had no right to complain, whatever regret he might feel at the disparagement of Essex.

Whoever reads the "Memorials" will admit that the author had access to the very best sources of information. He was even more fortunate—perhaps I should say, unfortunate—in this respect. On the 9th of June Mr. William Lilly, the well-known astrologer and soothsayer, met him accidentally in the street, and asked him if it was true the two armies were near each other ; Whitelocke told him the fact was so, and that they were very likely to engage, at which Lilly observed—"That if they did not engage before the 11th of this month, the Parliament would have the greatest victory that they had ever had as yet." "And it proved accordingly, as you will see by what follows." The writer alludes to the celebrated and decisive battle of Naseby, fought on the 14th of June, 1645, but why it should not have turned out quite as successful on the 10th, had the armies been near enough, the worthy successor of the ancient seers and soothsayers did not disclose. It is certain that this prediction, with one or two more, produced the effect intended, and inclined Whitelocke to follow his advice at a later period on more than one momentous subject, wherein Lilly's predictions were partly falsified. In truth it required no great skill in the stars to predict victory; for the merits of Cromwell were already so conspicuous, and the indomitable character of his troops so notorious, that no enemy could sustain the shock of their encounter.

On the 18th of June, in honour of this news, Whitelocke in common with the members of both Houses, was magnificently feasted at Grocers' Hall, and they did not separate after dinner till they had sung the 46th Psalm. On the 22nd all the pulpits round and about, far and near, resounded with the thunders of the preachers, and with that peculiar hum of thanksgiving that accompanied the "drum ecclesiastic." Whitelocke was fast acquiring a taste for this new creed, and although he never became a fanatic like Laud, or a blind enthusiast like a puritanic parson, he consorted too much about this time with the ultra-religious portion of his countrymen. The Lords and the grandees had long set him the example. Their abject compliance with the party, whose habits and views were little consonant with wisdom, had been boundless, their degradation universal and profound. It is only justice to Whitelocke to say, that he threw off the yoke as soon as he possibly could, and would play a rubber of whist, or go out hunting and fishing for the sake of recreation like any other country-gentleman, as soon as circumstances permitted the indulgence. It is all very well for the dominant party, who alone had permission to express their sentiments, from the end of the seventeenth to the beginning of this nineteenth century, to decry individuals that lived in the midst of violence and blood, but men had then in reality their sole choice between two evils. Whitelocke made his from the first, when stung with court outrage and ecclesiastical aggression. If not actually disgusted with the ultra-religious tendencies of his own party, he could not sanction them in his heart; so neither could he openly thwart and oppose them. Not even Cromwell himself was strong enough to dare this; a man of the most enlarged capacity, of the most liberal and enlightened views at that time, and yet

hardly bold enough to play a game of bowls, till he had
Hampton Court to himself in peace and isolation.

The loss of the battle of Naseby was not perhaps so
pernicious to the King as the seizure of his cabinet and the
publication of the letters it contained.   One of these to the
Queen stated his intention of making peace with the Irish,
and bringing 40,000 of them over to England.   Another
complained, that he could not prevail on his mongrel parliament at Oxford to declare the one at Westminster unlawful ;
and a third stated, that upon the treaty at Uxbridge, he did
not positively own the Parliament, it being otherwise to be
construed, though they were so simple as not to find it out,
and that it was recorded in the notes of the King's Council,
that he did not acknowledge them to be a Parliament.

Whitelocke's reflections on the perusal of these passages
must have been humiliating indeed ; for what more lowers a
man in his own conceit than to discover what a dupe and a
tool he has been ?   Another document was found, by which
Whitelocke was completely cleared of a suspicion that had
long been entertained respecting the abstraction of Vane's
paper about Strafford, and which now was clearly traced
home to Digby.   But the Presbyterian party had another
humiliation in store for him.   They had borne him a grudge
ever since his avowed resistance to their claims of the *jus
divinum*, and the right of excommunicating whom they
pleased.   They learned from Savile something of what had
transpired at Oxford, when he and Hollis held council with
the King, and the party accordingly resolved to crush them.
Mr. Gordon, a member of the House, commenced the attack
by moving that a letter from the Lord Savile, with a letter
enclosed, might both be read, and he carried his motion.
The letter expressed his great affection to the Parliament, to
whom he had come from the King and submitted himself,
and had taken the oath enjoined ; that his sense of duty
urged him to discover to them what he knew concerning two
of their members, who had violated their trust, and to the

prejudice of the Parliament in the matters which the enclosed
paper would explain.   The document revealed nothing more
than what the reader already knows, with the exception of
one additional charge at the end, which accused both Whitelocke and Hollis of holding intelligence and correspondence
with the King and his party at Oxford.

This charge was utterly untrue, whereas the rest of the
accusation was well founded, and amounted to nothing less
than a charge of high treason.   They were not committed,
for which boon Whitelocke was indebted to the chivalrous
conduct of Sir William Lewis, the ancestor I presume of the
author, Matthew Lewis.   He was seconded by Sir Philip
Stapleton, and on the following day Whitelocke made a
speech of very great length, the perusal of which has lost all
interest now.   It gave a lucid statement of what had passed
up to a certain point, but it contained no denial of Savile's
charge respecting the paper.   The *onus probandi* was left to
his Lordship.

This the accuser found to be not quite so easy as he had
anticipated, and it was asked, not unnaturally, why he had
suffered six months to expire, that being about the time
since he had deserted his old friends and come over to his
new quarters, without broaching this charge before.   By his
replies it was soon demonstrated, that the motives of his conduct proceeded from rancour and pique.   A sort of sub-
committee was now appointed to investigate the matter more
closely, and they selected for its chairman, one Brown, known
to be a special enemy of both the accused.   At a fresh examination, Lord Savile protested the truth of his accusation
upon his soul and his life, but could bring no proof to corro-
borate his statement.   He really had spoken much that was
true, but having served so long such a master, they judged
the King's man to be equally unconscientious, where truth
was concerned.   Amongst other things, he was asked, how
he, the Lord Savile, being in those secret councils at Oxford,
should become so well affected all at once to the Parliament,

as he now pretended to be.   He answered, that he was impeached at Oxford for something that he had uttered at those
meetings with Mr. Hollis and Mr. Whitelocke, and that they
had met more than once in the Earl of Lindsay's chamber.
This answer proved fatal to his charge, since it was clear,
that he could not have been impeached as plotting for, but
against the King.   By mixing up truth with falsehood, Savile
had overshot the mark, and destroyed what little credibility
he might have till then possessed.   A few more searching
questions, and the confession was wrung from him, that he
himself had often played the spy, and had carried letters to
and fro.   Whitelocke partly knew this to be the case, for he
was aware that Hollis had received such communications ;
and the chairman of the grand committee, Mr. Gordon,
made no scruple to admit that he likewise had received
letters from the hands of Lady Temple, one of Lord Savile's
agents.

After this, the accused were directed to explain the affair
in the way of narrative,—a very unfair, inquisitorial mode
of proceeding, according to English notions of the present
day, but not unusual then, as any person may ascertain
that will take the trouble of referring to almost any trial for
high treason, when the prisoners had to defend themselves,
explain, and refute the arguments of the prosecutor.   Upon
the adjournment of the case, Whitelocke was privately
informed that they had no wish to ruin him, only Hollis ;
he was entreated to leave his friend to his fate, and think only
of his own safety, which they, the committee, were empowered
to guarantee.   He rejected so base a proposal with the scorn
it deserved, and assured them that he and Hollis would rise
or fall together.   On the following day the Earl of Denbigh,
Lord Wenman, and the other commissioners gave their
evidence, and it completed the discomfiture of the hostile
party, amongst whom the Solicitor-General was one, and, by
his acumen, the most dangerous.   Some letters intercepted
by the Scotch, men whom Whitelocke did not like, but who

acted most generously and nobly towards him on this occasion, from Savile to his old friends at Oxford, were most opportunely presented, which the accuser on his cross-examination confessed were in his handwriting, but added that he had been encouraged and authorised by Lord Say to take that step.

Baffled and confounded, the committee reluctantly made their report, and the accused had now to appear and defend themselves before the whole House. The solemnity of the transaction was enhanced, the real danger, however, not increased, and since honour, fortune, life, were all at stake, they fought their fight manfully and single-handed at what appeared such tremendous odds. Both parties put forth their whole strength—the one to crush, the other to save. If convicted, and should attainder not follow, the least Whitelocke could expect was expulsion, disgrace, and ruin. The House voted, that the business was ripe for judgment, not until they had made the culprits stand the severest cross-fire of interrogatories, that elicited nothing. The major vote declared, that neither Mr. Whitelocke nor Mr. Hollis was guilty; that both were at liberty to prosecute for damages the Lord Savile, now in the Tower. This, of course, they never did, knowing themselves technically guilty, even morally guilty, if party spirit were capable of deciding what moral guilt is. As for the Lord Savile in the Tower, they left him to the stings of his own conscience, if such a pitiful wretch possessed any ; and they had one gratification, that of seeing all the members of high rank and quality strenuously befriending them. Notwithstanding their support, it severed Whitelocke from the ties of all party, and the scene led him to anticipate the breaking up of the House into fresh elements, at no very distant period. Doubtless he felt grateful to his friends, and devoutly thanked heaven for his escape; yet his feelings had been cruelly outraged by the violence of faction. He saw it was no longer safe to risk his own life in future for a monarch that had so heartlessly betrayed him, who had been doing his best to serve the throne.

Well might he be grateful, he who really deserved in this instance the same punishment that befell so many of the King's friends, and who, comparatively, was quite as guilty as they in this instance. He himself thought it no crime to serve the King and effect a peace if possible; but temperance, moderation, charity, pity, cease to be virtues in the opinion of men when battling for life. How strange a thing is humanity in some phases of its development! At the very moment he and his colleague were declared not guilty, about twenty innocent creatures, convicted of being witches, were executed in Norfolk without one pitying eye on earth—without one glance of sympathy—amidst the execrations of the people and the anathema of the clergyman.

On the 6th of August, we find Whitelocke again taking part in a debate for sending propositions of peace to his Majesty, which he furthered all he could. The House would have nothing more to do with a treaty. On the 20th, a book was brought into the House, that had been taken at Naseby; and in this book were the names of various members of the House, with sums of money supposed to have been contributed by them to the King, whose hand was in many places of it. The Speaker said he had perused the book, and did not find there his own, nor Mr. Dunch's, nor Mr. Whitelocke's names; and he believed the reason to be from the fact that the King had taken all from them. This was perfectly true; and so Lord Clarendon's accusation in his partial history, that his old friend had sided with the Parliament because his estate lay in their quarters, is amply disproved. It was the King who ravaged and laid waste his subject's demesne; and so completely were Whitelocke's resources destroyed for a short time, his practice so entirely put an end to, that he was one of those who was obliged to subsist for a while on a weekly stipend of four pounds allowed him by the House. A garrison had been stationed for some time at Phyllis Court,

adjoining Fawley Court, and the burthen of supporting it
fell chiefly, if not exclusively, on the farms adjoining. These
farms were his; and although not confiscated, I question
whether he derived a greater revenue from them than
Clarendon from his.

On the 3rd of September his opposition to the Presbyterians became more marked. A debate came off that day
on the points of excommunication and suspension from the
sacrament, a power they earnestly contended for. Selden
declared his opinion; and after him Whitelocke gave utterance to some strong sentiments in a long and energetic
address. The second period in this speech is unmistakable,
and a dawning sign that he himself was slowly passing over
to the Independent* body: for he says—"By pastors, I suppose they mean themselves, and others who are or may be
preachers in the several congregations, and would be ἐπίσκοποι,
bishops or overseers of them." Another passage runs
thus: "Surely it is not proper for pastors, for feeders of
flocks, to deny food to any of their flock who shall desire
it." In another passage, in something like the spirit of
Socrates, he confesses abruptly—"I am sure that I am a
very ignorant person. . . . The most learned, I doubt,
may be called in the large sense, ignorant." And again,
with great truth: "I have heard here many complaints of
the jurisdiction formerly exercised by the prelates, who were
but a few. There will be by the passing of this now desired
measure a great multiplication of spiritual men in government." He omitted some things in his argument which he
thought might give most offence, and yet not further his
opinion. He said enough, however, to incur the censure of
the more rigid Presbyterians, against whose design he was
held to be one. They were pleased to term him a disciple
of Selden, and honour him with the title of Erastian.

* I use this word here not in its sectarian but proper sense, and mean that Whitelocke studied and judged for himself. Cromwell's sentiments were equally liberal
and tolerant.

On the 10th he represented in warm terms the miserable condition of Oxfordshire, which was now paying contribution to the soldiers of no less than eighteen distinct garrisons; and on the following day, at the request of the Earl of Northumberland, he procured some business to be settled to that nobleman's satisfaction, respecting those children of the King that had been confided to his guardianship.

The multiplicity of labours, vigils, incessant distractions, and the worst forebodings with respect to the Commonwealth, began to impair, if not undermine, Whitelocke's health. On the 25th he was seriously ill, when his humble dwelling was honoured by visits from Lady Willoughby, the Dowager Lady Thornhill, and the Countess of Holland. He preserved the memory of this little incident by jotting it down in his diary, to show his children how sure men are to be caressed and visited when thought capable of doing any favours. But, by the 2nd of October, he was so far recovered as to celebrate that day of thanksgiving by entertaining Mr. Maynard, Mr. Lane, and some others, at dinner. He little foresaw that this same Lane, or rather a relative of his, would utter a shameful calumny against him to that industrious collector and retailer of gossip, Mr. Anthony à Wood, the well known author of the *Athenæ Oxonienses*, a man who seems to have completely ignored the signal benefits conferred by Whitelocke upon the University of Oxford, and the various colleges throughout the kingdom; the cause of learning generally, by saving the King's library from destruction or dispersion; and the College of Heralds from extinction; together with many more acts of a similar nature, which the careful reader of the "Memorials" will find recorded or adverted to.

On the 3rd of October he found himself so convalescent as to venture on accepting an invitation from Major-General Browne, not long before the commandant of Abingdon, but now living quietly as a citizen at Fish Street, in the City of London. Here he met Sir John Danvers, the Earl of Clare,

Lord Fairfax, Mr. Martin, and many other Parliament men. On the 20th he dined with Sir Henry Vane, Mr. Solicitor, Mr. Browne, and other grandees of that party, and was now treated quite as kindly by them as he had been by the other party. There must have been a rupture then of some sort between him and the latter, since these new friends, whom he mentions by name, had only recently shown themselves animated by no very friendly spirit towards himself. Could anger and pride have had any share in leading him to accept their invitation? He knew in his heart how far he had been led astray by Hollis, and the secret supporters of the Sovereign; how cruelly he had been betrayed by royalty itself; and we now see the fruits.

From this day we may trace his gradual conversion from royal to monarchical predilections. A republican he never became. A kingly government he ever preferred; but his attachment to the dynasty of the Stuarts had been weakened. Besides, he half believed Lilly's positive assurance, that the family of that race was doomed: and, as we have already seen, he was no disbeliever in destiny. Milton himself, though declining to reason on it, had faith in its invisible operations, as any admirer of the poet may see, who reads with its true key that beautiful poem, the Samson Agonistes. Whitelocke, with a mind incensed against the wilful and intemperate course of England's rulers, may have clutched, in a moment of despondency, at the faint image of power, now dimly assuming an indistinct outline; or he may have seen some sign of superior energy in the half-developed Independent party, and deemed their rise inevitable. Whatever his motives,—and they were doubtless strong, when he could thus dally with violent men like Vane, violent though sincere and honest,—one fact remains to plead in extenuation. He had a large family, and had little time left him to make provision for their future settlement in the world; he had, moreover, lost the prime of life through the internecine contentions that hitherto had blighted his prospects, and was

partly convinced that the cause of monarchy was lost for
many a year to come. He looked around him, and saw no
King to rule ; he would hear, at least, what plan republicans
and Fifth-Monarchy men—or by whatever name fanatics of
Vane's stamp were then called—had to propose. Again,
for the sake of others, of those nearest and dearest to him,
he found it expedient, after the danger he had just parried, to
stand well with all the world, as far as this lay in his power.
Acting as he did, not exclusively as a Parliamentarian, but
as the father of a family and whose wife's health gave no
promise of long life, or even survivorship, what moderate
man of the present day would throw the first stone at him ?
Is there any liberal thinker that does not coincide with a
declaration he often made, that the first and most sacred
duty of a man is to take care of his own family ? To this
duty patriotism, under certain circumstances, must yield.
There are times and phases of national development, when
every man, if he pleases, has the right of turning his back
upon his country for ever, of fleeing it as a charnel-house, of
emigrating to another land, and adopting a fresh hearth ;
but no time, no phase of life, can justify a man's neglect or
desertion of his offspring. To him, at least, his children
were the first objects of his solicitude. "What will a father
not do for them ?" he exclaims in a manuscript book I have
been lately perusing. Now England's condition at that
moment, and for many years then to come, was so sad, so
distracted, so confused, that any man might conscientiously
withdraw from it. But how was he to do this, and whither
could he go ?

Although he dallied with these new men, it must not be
supposed that he ever refused good offices and acts of kindness for any friend. Nor did he quarrel outright with the
old men, whose private friendship he still cultivated and
preserved, even when slowly receding from their purely
political circle of attraction and repulsion to a more independent sphere of his own choosing ; to another luminary,

Q

that central mass of gleaming steel, which he as historian
and politician could not but foresee would ultimately decide
everything.

His diary teems at this period with social recollections,
and the titularly great were unusually attentive and obsequious to him.   They too perceived the approaching changes,
and were striving like himself to shut out the phantom by
the forced gaiety of converse, the excitement of daily intercourse.   And now his professional duties, too long abandoned,
were suddenly and abruptly re-engaging his attention, so
much so, that on one day he attended as counsel in the
King's Bench, the Chancery, the Court of Wards, and the
House of Lords ; and in the afternoon entertained twelve
guests at dinner.   As he simply pens it, " he had often store
of company with him."   Before a week had elapsed he
writes again with Cicero's fondness for the redundancy of
the conjunction : " I attended the Chancery, and the House,
and after dinner with the Earl of Clare I attended the
Committee of Privileges, and the Committee of Petitions,
and came late and weary home."

Mindful of the faithful services they had formerly received
from Sir James Whitelocke, the Committee of Westminster
College appointed the son on the 16th of December to be
steward likewise of the lands of that college.   Like his
father too, he was now gaining influence in the City, for
after attending the House, he dined by invitation with the
Sheriff of London, Kenricke, who had requested him to
bring his friends with him.   This he did, and chose the Earl
of Winchelsea with his lady, the Lord Wenman with his
lady and daughter, the Lord Willoughby and his lady, Sir
Christopher Wray, Sir Edward Ascugh, Mr. Maynard,
Mr. Hall and his wife, "and my wife." Strange doings, when
peers could be taken in tow by commoners, but the " order "
then thought the earth was about to turn topsy-turvy, as
Diogenes had predicted ! The House sat on Christmas-day
to debate on the question of making the members of both

Houses liable to arrest, which portentous measure however was not passed. On the last day of the month and year, a note is inserted that shows the little satisfaction Whitelocke derived from this bravery and feasting and junketing, when the times were so out of joint: "I doubt I have spent too much time in mentioning such trivial things as my private and particular labours, some attendances, treatments, and company, with the particular applications, caresses, and courtships, visits, &c., used to me, which also continued long after." Now why was he thus courted? The future alone can solve the enigma. It could not surely be owing to the corrupt state into which the Long Parliament was falling, which while voting against any further personal treaty with the King—a resolution that gave rise to much gloomy discontent—was bestowing largesses of one hundred up to five hundred pounds on knights and esquires, though suffering the wives and widows of soldiers and other national creditors to starve. Was he considered one of the few props left to the aristocracy? The peers of England were themselves fast striking these away. I shall insert the answer they gave to a petition from the Lord Mayor, Aldermen, and Common Council of London, in which this sapient body desired the speedy settlement of church government according to the covenant, and that no toleration be granted to popery, prelacy, superstition, heresy, schism, profaneness, or anything contrary to sound doctrine; and that all private meetings contrary to the covenant may be restrained. To which the humble peers were forced by expediency to return this answer :

"They complimented and. thanked the City for their care and zeal for God's worship, and assured them as they had been, so should they continue ready to advance so good a work, whereto they held themselves obliged by the covenant, and they recommend it to the City to suppress such unlawful courses, as are by them mentioned in their petition."

In other words, they recommended Master Mayor and his

worthy coadjutors to take the law into their own hands—and
what a law! It was time for the Lords to dissolve, and
recover purity in the uncontaminated atmosphere of their
parks and fields. Whitelocke was right when he eventually
drew up the ordinance for their dissolution, though he did it
with a sigh and ill-dissembled repugnance. Nor did these
peers represent their order. A goodly portion were at
Oxford, and they themselves at heart all ill-affected at last,
through the tyranny of the mob, to the cause of the
people.

On the 24th of February, which was still in the year 1645,*
the successful arguments of Selden, Whitelocke, and others
induced the House to pass a bill for the total suppression
of the Court of Wards, the second grand step in the path
of legal reform.

---

* I need hardly remind the historical reader, that the legal year, and the one
universally adopted by English lawyers of the period referred to, commenced at the
spring-quarter, and not on the 1st of January.

CHAPTER XV.

1646—1648.

Progress of the Siege of Oxford—Whitelocke in the Confidence of both Fairfax and Cromwell—Takes Command at Phyllis Court, then fortified—Opposes a Puritanical Ordinance touching the Liturgy—Monk employed in Ireland by the Parliament—Whitelocke's constant Efforts to resist the Progress of Religious Fanaticism—Is actively engaged in Public Matters as well as in his Professional Pursuits—Dr Morley's Letter to him—Growing Disputes between the Parliament and the Army—Parliament in Disrepute—Its Selfish Conduct on Religious Questions—Whitelocke Resumes his Seat, and is the rumoured Successor of Lenthall on the Illness of the Speaker—Declines the Recordership of London—Appointed one of the Commissioners of the Great Seal, through the influence of Fairfax and Cromwell—His Emoluments therefrom—Revolt of his Friend the Earl of Holland, and of the Duke of Buckingham—Whitelocke's Pluralities—Fulfilment of Lilly's Prophecy.

THE Royal cause was now at its lowest ebb.   Sir Ralph Hopton had been obliged to capitulate and disband his forces, Sir Jacob Ashley also sustained a total defeat in a desperate endeavour to cut his way to Oxford, and was made prisoner, when he addressed the Parliament's officers in these memorable words : " Now you have done your work, my masters, and may go play, unless you choose to fall out among yourselves." So utterly prostrated was the Royal power, that the Archbishop of York, Dr. Williams, put a garrison into his house at Purin near Conway, fortified it, protested against the King's party, and persuaded the country in his neighbourhood not to send any further contribution to Conway. The rats were deserting the ship, and the King himself, by the 6th of May, 1646, was dreaming of succour and safety in the midst of the Scotch army near Southam.

By the 12th of May the siege of Oxford was so far advanced, that its surrender became inevitable, and merely a question of time.　Whitelocke asked leave of the House to go into the country, and when he had reached his own residence, he rode over to the General's camp.　Sir Thomas Fairfax he found to be a man of few words in discourse or council, to be unalterable when once his judgment and reason were satisfied, but he met at his hands the greatest kindness and respect.　In fact, the visit had been prearranged by an invitation from the General in a letter to the Speaker, for he wanted his kinsman's company and advice, he said, as well as the advantage of his local knowledge ; the possibility that commissioners might be found necessary to treat with those of Sir Thomas Glenham was held out as a further motive for his presence.　On entering the "leaguer," he was greeted most cordially by Cromwell, and cheerfully admitted into their councils of war.　Here Whitelocke found the second in command to be naturally taciturn, and that he trusted his own judgment alone.　It is not a little singular that Cromwell assumed not merely the greatest mildness, but softened his voice, whenever he transacted business on this as well as on every future occasion with the civilian, who was now present to procure the most favourable terms for the Colleges of Oxford.　The articles of the treaty, twenty-six in number, are preserved in the Memorials, and must be regarded as more than usually considerate ; and as soon as this business was concluded, the General commanded a select council, composed of Cromwell, Ireton, Lambert, Fleetwood, and Whitelocke, to consult about disposing portions of the army to take post at several places and sieges where there was need of them, and also as to the reduction of Wallingford. He drew up, as secretary, the articles for this latter place, and when the commissioners of both Houses repaired to the King at Newcastle with the propositions for peace, his Majesty, if he had a memory and a conscience, must have observed that the man he had so wantonly and superfluously betrayed, did not form one of the number.

The next intimation we have of his whereabouts was on the 28th of July, when we find him receiving Serjeant Wilde, a member of the House, who was passing through Henley on his way to Worcester, to which place he had been sent as a commissioner of Oyer and Terminer, and this seems to be the first symptom of restored tranquillity. Hearing that his friend was in his garrison at Phyllis Court, the Serjeant paid him a stately visit, and greeted him as Colonel. The fort was very strong, and Whitelocke was really in command there of three hundred foot-soldiers, besides a troop of horse. He could do no less than convey the judge with his cavalry, a protection the judge was not sorry to have, and for which he had probably paid his visit. They must have been great children in some things, these grave men of the law, delighting in noise and meaningless ceremonial, like a modern grandee on an official mission. Upon the entrance of the judge, our Colonel presented to him the linstock, the symbol of command, and thereupon he gave a sign, when the soldiers bellowed forth a loud shout, and fired off five great guns. As the escort rode past Wallingford, the Royalists in the castle fired some great guns off too, and the shot came whistling near them, fortunately doing no harm.

As soon as this latter fortress was reduced, the owner and commander of Phyllis Court, most heartily weary of the war, thought the proper time had arrived for obtaining an order to " slight " his own garrison.* On the 15th of August he came down from London to carry it personally into effect, sent round warrants to all the neighbourhood, and soon col-

---

* There is a letter of Whitelocke's, preserved in the British Museum, to Mr. John Rushworth, the secretary of Sir Thomas Fairfax, dated June 9, 1646, which shows his anxiety for a return to order : " Sir, I am very glad that yᵉ Genˡ hath given order for yᵉ sliting of my house at Fillis Court, but some of yᵉ Committee of Oxfᵈ have been so unkind to me, as to appoint yᵉ doᵉ of it at this time in yᵉ middle of yᵉ Term, when they know I cannot be there myself (which is very necessʸ I shᵈ be) when thᵗ work is to be done. I entreat you therefore to procure an order from yᵉ Genˡ to stay yᵉ sliting of yᵉ house until I may be there present, &c. &c." His request was complied with.

lected carts and workmen with mattocks and shovels. He armed every one of the soldiers with a pickaxe, allowed every one of them sixpence a day besides their pay, but the common workmen were paid by the towns and villages that had sent them. In a few days they threw in the breast-works on two sides, made two even mount-works, one being on the side next the Thames, the other on the north. On the remaining two sides, he had the bulwarks and the lines levelled, the drawbridge removed, and the "grafts" or ditches filled up. He sent away the armament, and persuaded most of his men to enlist for Ireland. Up to this period it is possible that he continued, like many other members, in the receipt of the allowance that each of them received, four pounds a week. If so, it ceased on the 20th by an order of the House ; and if his estate should prove overburthened for a time, he must look to professional emoluments alone in future, to compensate him for the enormous sacrifices the late war had specially entailed upon him. On the 25th of September he used all his influence to have the Castle of Wallingford demolished, and on the 29th was very active in contriving ways and means for getting rid of the Scotch army in the north and in Lancashire, where their presence was a cruel scourge.

On the 26th of October some members complained of an indictment in Buckinghamshire, for not reading prayers from the Common Prayer Book, when the House directed that an ordinance should be brought in to annul the statute that enjoins it, and to disable malignant ministers from preaching. Whitelocke and others made a desperate but ineffectual opposition to this proposed measure, as contrary to that principle of liberty of conscience, which the Parliament had avowed, and as being identical with that very conduct they had formerly complained of in the bishops, when those dig-nitaries silenced ministers in the same despotic manner. He might as well have not spoken at all, for the country did not understand the principles of liberty, nor of toleration, nor of allowing the free utterance of a man's private opinions, nor the duty incumbent on our rulers to leave a man's religious convictions alone ; and although they were now through their representatives about to suppress one established religion, it was solely for the purpose of setting up another, quite as intolerant, in its stead. Of such labour is it to found rational freedom, and to free religion itself from an abject subserviency to state-policy ! So far from desiring religious liberty and toleration, the Commons on the 4th of November passed an ordinance for compelling the payment of church-rates.

Their deserved punishment was even then being prepared by Providence, for on the 13th, which was little more than a week later, in compliance with a message from the Lords, the Commons gave Monk—who had already taken the covenant, and was ready to do the same with the Negative Oath, or any oath whatsoever—a commission, and employed him on their service in Ireland. On the 16th Whitelocke laboured hard to save the Duke of Buckingham's property from entire sequestration, and took pains in this business in respect of the near relationship that existed between the two families. Here too, as in nearly every other instance, it was his fate to experience no kind return when his own hour of adversity arrived, but on the contrary, as we shall see by-and-by, was suffered to linger out the last remnant of his life in neglected solitude, a victim to the rapacity of the second Charles, and perhaps of this very profligate minion, who now owed to his benefactor the safety of a portion of his property, and his life or liberty on subsequent occasions.

On the 7th of December, chiefly through Whitelocke's exertions, an order was made to free the libraries, and other things in Oxford useful for learning, from sequestration. On the 11th, in a sub-committee, he laboured equally hard " to take away all coercive powers of committees," and " to take away all arbitrary power from the Houses, singly or united, or from any of their committees in any matter between party

and party." This was indeed a signal triumph in the cause
of justice.

But what had become of the King, whilst all these religious commotions and mutilations of innocent "herses," or
effigies, or recumbent statues in cathedrals, and these
ejections of village clergymen, and other persecutions were
taking place every hour of each miserable day? I say miserable, for while the Royalists in Church and State were
paying dear penalties, humanity was gaining nothing, posterity was gaining nothing, but one more example of mis-
directed national enthusiasm; of sincere deeds prompted
by gross ignorance, by the bigotry and mental slavery it
engenders. The King was on the 15th still at Newcastle,
where a Scotch minister preached "boldly" before him, and
after his sermon called for the 52nd Psalm, which begins
with these words, "Why dost thou Tyrant boast thyself, thy
wicked works to praise." Upon this the King rose, and
called for the 56th, which opens with others of a more
appropriate nature, "Have mercy, Lord, on me I pray, for
men would me devour." The people sang the latter, but if
the unhappy and virtually dethroned monarch really thought
this, why did he not abdicate, why had he not rather
abdicated long before, when time was still left him? His
reflections at this time, when he saw the total ruin of his
cause, and his whole country laid waste, must have been
infinitely worse than the violent death itself that was so soon
to overtake him. Whitelocke, who knew of this particular
passage at the time, could do nothing more in that quarter
than he had done. On the contrary, without neglecting the
service of the Parliament and his duty to his constituents,
he applied himself closely to his practice, and met with the
very best encouragement in it. He attended every committee concerning foreign affairs, and if abstinence from
beef, veal, and lamb for eight weeks, contributed to the
adoption of a true foreign policy, we ought to be doubly
grateful to the Lords, who initiated and sent down to the

Lower House an ordinance to that end.   On the last day of May, 1647, the following letter was received from Dr. Morley, the contents of which were very gratifying.

"For my honoured friend, Mr. Whitelocke.

" Sir,—I understand by Mr. J. Palmer and divers others of my friends in London, how much the whole University in general, and I myself in particular, are obliged to you, for which, in mine own and the University's name, I do return you most humble and hearty thanks, which together with our hearty prayers unto God for you, is the best and only acknowledgment which the condition we are now in will suffer us to make to you or any of our friends, and this we are afraid may be too much too,—any address from so odious a name as we are carrying something of scandal, if not of danger, to him to whom it is made along with it. Otherwise I do assure you, you had received public thanks in a public way before this time.   But we are advised by some of your friends and ours to abstain from such expressions till there be a more seasonable time for them, which yet, notwithstanding, shall not hinder me from telling you, that I am as sensible as any man can be of the obligation which I in particular have to you, and that there is nothing I would not willingly either do or suffer to make you know I am so.   For the loss of my place here, though it was all I had for my subsistence, yet seeing I could not keep it with a good conscience, I thank God it doth not trouble me at all.   Pray God that he, whosoever he be, that succeeds me in it may part with it at his death as cheerfully as I do now, and that my judges may not have cause to be more sorry for their sentence than I am.   It is glory enough for me that Mr. Selden and Mr. Whitelocke were of another opinion, for, being absolved by you two and mine own conscience, I shall still think myself in a capacity for a better condition, and in the mean time not altogether unworthy to subscribe myself,

"Your most obliged friend and humble servant,

"G. MORLEY."

On the 16th of June the servants, as Whitelocke had foreseen, commenced their revolt against their masters in the
shape of a charge sent in by Sir Thomas Fairfax, the officers
and soldiers of the army against some of the members.
The *fetish* number of twelve had been selected, yet at the
eleventh hour Whitelocke's name was omitted; the remaining eleven were those friends of his with whom he had once
acted cordially on nearly all occasions down to a comparatively recent period. The fated eleven were Denzil Hollis,
Sir Philip Stapleton, Sir Wm. Lewis, Sir John Clotworthy,
Sir Wm. Waller, Sir John Maynard, Major-General Massey,
Mr. Recorder Glynn, Colonel Walter Long, Colonel Edward
Harley, and Mr. Anthony Nicholls. Such was the prelude
of "Pride's purge!"

Notwithstanding this omission, he could have derived little
satisfaction from the escape, and to complete the stunning
nature of this strategical blow, a petition was sent in from
the principal inhabitants of Buckinghamshire, his own county,
to the General and his army. More than a thousand names
conjointly extolled the merits and achievements of the
General, of Cromwell, of his victorious troops, and expressed
their readiness to concur, to the best of their ability, in
bringing to condign censure any persons that should attempt
to bring him or them into odium. This example was soon
followed by several counties, and even the citizens of London
began to pay their court, not to the Parliament, but to Fairfax
and the army.

Not ignorant of the immediate future,—too prescient of
impending calamities,—Whitelocke turned his thoughts at
this time away from the surging storm to what he conceived
would be a great boon of peace and calm to humanity. He
had in his custody a famous ancient copy of the Septuagint
Bible, called the " Tecta," and which he sometimes fancied
might be the original manuscript; he encouraged Mr. Patrick
Young, who had formerly been the keeper of the King's
library at St. James's, in his wish to publish this translation,

and devoted himself, in common with Selden, to a task that promised, in his eyes, to be of such benefit to the cause of theology. His attendance at the House became less frequent, and by the 10th of July we find him leading a retired life at Phyllis Court, where he was visited by Sir John Holland, one of the commissioners with the King, and who came from Corsham, where his Majesty then was, for the express purpose of visiting him. Of course, he could do little now to serve a man whose fate depended rather on the stern resolves of a military council than on the efforts of peacemakers, and he expected himself nothing less than utter ruin for all that he had previously done; but Mr. Chute and Mr. Newdigate told him on the 19th, that being of counsel with Mr. Hollis and the rest of the eleven accused members, they had caused his name to be struck out of their answer; and on the same day leave was given the lawyers to go the circuits, by which concession he would have a decent excuse for a yet longer absenteeism.

On the 23rd he was invited by the Countess of Kent to meet Mr. Pierpoint, and here before supper Selden told him, in the stately language then in vogue, how he meant to be beholden to him after his death, and showed him a place in his study where his friend would find papers declaring his "intent and will."

The events that now followed in such rapid succession were of so humiliating a character, that even Lenthall, the Speaker, felt himself constrained to publish a declaration of the reasons why he absented himself from the House; several peers and commoners quitted the Parliament, and took refuge in the General's quarters, and the conviction was gaining ground among the people that their members "were strong in wine but weak in wisdom." Whitelocke was happily remote from the shifting scenes of this drama; he was busy with the causes of his clients, found great encouragement in his practice, and on the 2nd of August was retained in thirty-nine cases at Abingdon, where thirty-four records

were put in.   On the 4th the trials at Oxford ended in the
forenoon.   The records entered had been fifty-one, and he
himself retained in fifty causes.   The judges hastened out of
the town, and after dinner the lawyer went to Burford, a
distance of twelve miles, where they spent the night.   Being
the "most ancient" on the circuit, he was called their general;
he appointed their quarters, and his opinion swayed in their
private affairs.   On the 14th the judges sat at Hereford, but
the people would not come in ; the whole court had little or
nothing to do, not from any dearth of causes, of which our
"ancient" had his hands full, but apparently from the
universal distrust and contempt with which the people were
animated, against what they thought a court of misjustice.
It must have been a singular scene, and the querulous lamen-
tations of the clerk may have moved some of the godless
spectators to the most irreverent mirth.   For once in the
history of England the lawyers had the laugh against them.

On the 20th Whitelocke's powers at Shrewsbury were
highly taxed, being retained in thirty-eight causes out of
seventy-five records put in ; and at Worcester, on the 31st,
he conducted thirty-six causes out of forty-two records.
Eight days later, his brother-in-law, Lord Willoughby, of
Parham, was impeached of high treason by the new faction,
and he expresses his own mortification at such a reward
for that gallant officer's past services, by inserting in his
private journal the only comment that it was prudent to
commit to writing in such a dangerous period : "This is
no great encouragement to engage in public affairs ;" and
practically evinced his secret disapproval of our criminal
law, by refusing the Recordership of London.   Towards the
end of September he went on a visit to a Mr. Libbes, at
Hardwick, where he found a vineyard, and made the pleasing
discovery that part of the estate was called "Whitelockes,"
and that his ancestors had once possessed that seat.   This
simple visit made a deep impression on his mind ; it recalled
to him the death of his grandfather in a foreign land, at

Bordeaux, and where, from his being a heretic, his remains had been refused burial by the priests in consecrated ground. Upon which the English merchants had taken up arms, had carried by force the dead body of their brother-merchant to a vineyard in the suburbs, and had there deposited it beneath the vines. If my readers like to see how remote causes produce results in after ages, I may mention, that a lineal descendant of the man once pensively musing at Hardwick, in remembrance of the two scenes just alluded to, planted vines near the fortress of Chitteldroog, in India, on the road to Seringapatam, shortly after the downfall of Tippoo Sahib. The fort became a ruin soon after its abandonment by the Company, but the vines remain, where one weary traveller at least enjoyed its grateful fruit, and the comfort of its shade, some few years back, and found the name of the planter still preserved by the inhabitants that peopled the secluded spot.

On the 3rd of October Whitelocke resumed his attendance in the House, and must have been highly edified by the votes passed on the 13th, 14th, and 16th of this month. On the first of these days they decreed that the Presbyterian government should be established till the end of their next session, until which period no clergyman, unless he could make it convenient to conform, was to have any power and right of receiving tithes, or even a stipend ; and that liberty of conscience was not to extend to the preaching, printing, or publication of anything contrary to the first fifteen of the Thirty-nine Articles, the eighth alone excepted ; and that no popish recusant was to be allowed any freedom of conscience at all. On the following day they voted liberty to tender consciences, by way of indulgence ; and, on the last day named, they stipulated that their indulgence, allowed two days previously, should not imply any tolera-tion of the Common Prayer. The Parliament were now preparing for themselves the punishment they deserved, for in the pride of their success they had forgotten to reform

abuses, contrary to their previous professions; the majority
of the members were actuated by the most undisguised
selfishness, and the people of this country benefited little by
their rule.   They might have decreed a national education,
the formation of a simple code, the creation of a legislative
body, in which no professional legist should sit (for how can
a hireling make just laws?); they might have declared
absolute freedom of conscience from all religious persecution,
and they could not plead ignorance of the popular rights
and wants.   These had been made known to them by
numerous petitions, to which they turned a deaf ear, as other
Parliaments have since done.   Therefore, I say again, posterity may owe this Parliament one debt of gratitude, for their
having destroyed the old autocratic encroachments; but
what debt do we owe to them for their substituting an autocratic power of their own, for their conniving at the perpetu-
ation of nearly every feudal abuse, and for their utter neglect
of the humbler classes to the undue glorification of the
wealthy and the great?

Whitelocke, himself a member, and therefore predisposed
to view their acts with lenity, was compelled, by the numerous passages of disaffection and hostility he was daily
recording, to notice the perplexed condition the Parliament
was in at that time, and how the army, which they had
raised, paid, and commissioned, now held the sword over
their heads.   The City too, their old friends, their constant
assistants, and who had held life and fortune ready for the
disposal of the House, was now become full of sedition and
aversion to the members, questioned their integrity, re-
proached them, and sought to cast them off.   On the 4th of
December he went to the House, and after learning that the
Speaker was ill, he heard it whispered about, that in case
the illness of Lenthall continued, they should call Whitelocke
to the chair.   As an offer of knighthood released George the
Fourth, when Prince Regent, from the presence of old Coke,
of Norfolk, by terrifying this proud country gentleman to a

hasty retreat, so the whisper he had overheard drove Whitelocke home to his study in dismay, a feeling partly engendered by the predictions, or manifesto, of the High-German
prophet, which the seer had previously imparted, not merely
to the General, but to the King as well.   The Speaker
rapidly recovered, and Whitelocke joyfully attended the
Chancery upon demurrer, then supped at a tavern in a consultation of lawyers, of which Glyn, the late recorder, was
one, though still a prisoner.   Thus matters went on, without
the least sign of improvement, it is true, in so far as the distant future was concerned, but sometimes with delusive
appearances of recovery.   The House, in short, was in a
phthisis, a kind of political consumption, for which no medicine, but only dissolution is the true remedy.

On the 18th of January, 1647, he procured an order for
the removal to St. James's of the manuscripts and books
from Whitehall, by which provision the public derive inestimable benefit to this day, since those rare monuments of
learning and antiquity, instead of being destroyed by the
soldiers, who thought no books worth saving but the Bible,
are now preserved, as national treasures, in the British
Museum.   On the 29th he was again offered the recordership of London, and again he declined, not merely because
the place was full of trouble and clamour, and the City itself
so distracted and tumultuous, but because his conscience
condemned some of the points of our law in capital cases.
Although he omits to mention them, they are not difficult to
divine.   He would have had, for instance, to sentence to
death men guilty of stealing a horse or a sheep, or a yard of
lace from a shopkeeper's counter, or a watch valued at two
pounds sterling ; and he was not willing to be turned into a
judicial murderer, like the twelve judges of England down to
a few years ago, for the sake of a handsome salary.

On the 2nd of March, the Earl of Kent, Sir Thomas Widdrington, and himself, were created Commissioners for the
Great Seal of England.   It was thought at the time, by

R

others as well as by himself, that the selection of the commissioners had been determined on previously by the private
junto of Cromwell's party ; but if so, of which there seems
no reason to doubt, they were not nominated by the House
till several individuals had been proposed and successively
rejected.   Speaking of himself, in a retrospect of his career
written for his children and not addressed to the public, he
says, concerning this promotion :—"I was less considerable
than the other" (meaning Sir Thomas) "in all respects, yet
was well known and understood in the House by my long
attendance there, and by them not judged incapable of
this employment ; besides, the General" (meaning Fairfax)
"had an affection for me ; he had a good interest in the
House, and Cromwell with his party were willing to engage
me as far as they could with them.   I can truly say I
never heard of this business beforehand, nor was in the
least privy to it or acquainted with it, but God was pleased so
to order it ; it was not my ambition that sought or contrived
it, for I may be believed on much experience, that such
employments are not desirable by a quiet and prudent
spirit.   They seldom afford quiet, never safety.   I had at
this time in the circuit a great practice, wherein none of my
profession had a greater share than myself, and I received
at Gloucester this unexpected news.   The counsellors, officers,
and attorneys, with great respect and much civility, wished
me joy of that honourable employment.   I sent to my
friends of the House to know if my present attendance was
expected there, for without a special summons I did not
intend returning to London till after the circuit should be
ended.   This resolution I grounded the rather on the letters
I received, wherein it was said, that when it was moved in
the House I should be immediately sent for to attend the
service of the Seal, others did not think fit to call me out
of the circuit, where I was engaged in the affairs of many
men, and the House made no order for it."   This may well
be imagined, by the following significant entries in his

diary :—"The records entered at Oxford were thirty-five ; the causes wherein I was retained were forty-four." And on the 7th :—"The records entered at Gloucester were ninety-nine ; the causes wherein I was retained there, were fifty." And again on the 9th :—"The records put in at Monmouth were ten ; the causes wherein I was of counsel were thirteen." And so on in more instances.

On the 17th of April, 1648, both Houses passed an ordinance for bestowing on Whitelocke, as on each of the other commissioners, a salary of £1000 per annum, and on this day he resigned an inferior situation, with some regret—the Attorneyship of the Duchy. He had the gratification of appointing his old and well-tried friend, Mr. Hall, to the post he had just vacated, and which he knew by experience would afford content, by reason of "its privacy and credit."

On the 2nd of June I find an entry of his relating to his new office : "This day the box-money in Chancery came to £27." I am no legal antiquarian myself, and therefore I cannot say what box this was.' Money in a Chancery-box could hardly have been intended for the suitors, however greatly they would be sure to stand in need of it. But whatever may have come to him in the way of fees or even presents from suitors, in those days of "the glorious uncertainty of the law," no moral turpitude attached to such practices. And, be it remembered, there was then no retiring pension of £6000 a-year. Corruption had not reached that acme. Parliament has granted that pension since, and so the modern lawyer concludes he has a right to it. I, a plain layman, have the misfortune to think differently, and, therefore, it is with some feeling of satisfaction I record, that Whitelocke never received a pension from the State, but merely his salary when virtually in office.

Some time after this, on the 5th of July, his intimate friend, the Earl of Holland, and his frivolous and licentious kinsman, the Duke of Buckingham, with his brother, Lord Francis, and the Earl of Peterborough, raised the standard

of revolt against the Parliament, to his great grief, and regret
that the first lord named had not paid heed to his advice.
The Earl had called on him not long before, and in the
course of conversation had inveighed against the Parliament,
especially for their reluctance to conclude a personal treaty
with the King. The discontented noble stated his belief to
be, that if a considerable party should take up arms in behalf
of such a treaty, they would soon become a formidable body,
and be enabled to bring the Parliament to reason. His legal
friend remonstrated with him, and pointed out to him the
true character of the victorious veteran army—how mad any
attempt would be to make head against it ; and he further
urged the Earl not to put his trust in popular support, for
that most people would wait and see which was the stronger
side before they declared for either. He used many more
arguments with a view to dissuade him from joining in
any rash project, to the existence of which he referred
hypothetically, little dreaming how soon his friend was about
so to commit himself, and expiate the error by a premature
death upon the scaffold. This continued misconduct of his
friends was pernicious in every sense, and though it did not
cause, it may have accelerated the great catastrophe.

I am not writing history, and therefore pretend not to
trace the fluctuations, the tides and ebbs of Parliamentary
progress. Suffice it to say, that the Lords were endeavouring
to retrace their steps, and had long since discovered they
had ventured beyond their depth; not so the Commons, who
with the officers saw no safety behind, but only in advancing.
It was one of those eras when circumstances were no longer
under the control of man—when hopes and fears had gained
the mastery—and when the voice, not of wisdom, but of
passion, led men on to the goal, which Providence was
planting even then in mercy to distant races yet unborn.

Shortly after Whitelocke's elevation to the joint-keepership,
the Earl of Pembroke, having been himself created Constable
of Windsor Castle, and Keeper of the Great Park and Forest,

made the former his lieutenant.   This novel appointment
made him look into the nature of the place and office, but he
does not communicate any particulars.   By reference to
Peak's *Desiderata Curiosa,* the Constable's yearly fee in the
reign of Elizabeth is found to have been £20, and the lieutenant's £10—no very large perquisite wherewith to gild so
grand a title; but a constant supply of venison and the
pleasures of the chace no doubt outweighed all meaner considerations.   During his absence in the country a motion was
made to make the Earl of Suffolk Steward of Greenwich, but
the House refused to do it without Whitelocke's consent, and
voluntary resignation of the office.   If inclined to censure him
for this plurality of offices, I am restrained by the remembrance on the one hand of the cruel pillage, devastation, and
temporary forfeiture to which his paternal estate had been
subjected by the King's party—nay, by the King himself;
and on the other hand by reflecting on the morals of all great
men at that time, when right seems to have been blended
with wrong in such graduated hues, that the line of discrimination was purely imaginary.   Imagine the case of the Lord
Willoughby, who was thought guilty of revolting to the King
from his allegiance to the Parliament, and who seized afterwards, at sea, a ship that had on board some £20,000 in
gold, belonging not to the state, but to private merchants by
the name of Wilson.   So far from thinking this a piratical
act, he deemed it praiseworthy and justifiable,—a proof of
zeal and loyalty,—and kept the money.   The invading army
of the Scotch too, not a man of whom perhaps did not praise
in his soul the manly virtues of cattle-lifting and the levying
of black-mail, were at that same hour doing much the same
thing in the northern parts of England, where they played
sweepstakes with chattels of all sorts—cows, sheep, furniture,
down to the very pot-hooks and flesh-pots of the sufferers;
took children for the sake of ransom, and revelled in their
deeds.   If I use no comments, it is because I conceive that
men must be judged by their own consciences; nor can I

plead more than this in extenuation of the pluralist, who committed no sin in the eyes of the world nor, it may be, in his own.

On the 16th of September, 1648, Whitelocke's last tinge of scepticism was fairly washed out of him by the fulfilment of one of Lilly's predictions; he himself says they all were fulfilled, and more especially the one respecting danger to the King's person by a fall from his horse. In fact, Whitelocke's secret attachment to the dynasty of the Stuarts was hanging by one or two slender filaments, the only ones yet left unbroken of that bond that once united his family so strongly to the royal race. His sentiments in behalf of limited monarchy survived to the last hour of his life. Recognising the people as the source of power, avowing this to be his doctrine, even when speaking with a Queen, he felt himself more and more alienated from the establishment of any tyranny, whether exercised by one or by a multitude. He was one of the 150 members who paid no attention to a call of the House, so that a new call had to be ordered. He surely had nothing to do with the order made on the 29th for 5000*l.* out of delinquents' estates, to be handed over as pay to the Horse Guards then attending the Parliament, and guarding them indeed, as tyrants love to be, from popular fury or the knives of fanatics. It was dangerous then for any member of the House, or of the army itself, so short-lived had been its fleeting popularity, to walk abroad without company, for fear of assassination; and they affected to consider the King's party as the sole assassins to be dreaded. The Royalists, I regret to say, only tended by their conduct to justify the aspersion.

CHAPTER XVI.

—◆—

1648—1649.

Whitelocke is made a Serjeant-at-Law—Formal Difficulties—His Speech at the Chancery Bar, and Instalment of the Commissioners of the Great Seal—"Pride's Purge"—Conference of Cromwell with the Commissioners and the Speaker on the "Settlement of the Nation"—Angry Demands of the Army for the Punishment of "Great Delinquents"—Whitelocke refuses to act as a Commissioner on the King's Impeachment and retires into the Country—On the removal of their Names, he and his colleague, Widdrington, return and take their Seats on the Woolsack pending the Trial—Execution of Charles—Whitelocke compelled to join in a Declaration against the King's Conduct in the Negotiations—Abolition of the Upper House voted by the Commons, followed by a similar Vote as to the Monarchy—These Measures opposed by Whitelocke—Widdrington resigns; L'Isle and Keeble chosen as new Commissioners of the Seal—Whitelocke visited by Cromwell and Ireton—Anecdotes related by them—Death of his second Wife—Takes up his Abode at Chelsea—Unsettled State of the Country—Monk makes Peace with O'Neal the Rebel—Whitelocke's Speech on a Motion to exclude Lawyers from the House—Cromwell's Ineffectual Attempts to get Fairfax to invade Scotland.

On the 12th of October Whitelocke was raised with thirteen others to the dignity of a Serjeant-at-Law, was appointed at the same time to be Attorney-General of the Duchy, and one of the King's Serjeants. He earnestly desired to be excused from accepting the last-named dignity, but the major vote and some strong flattery compelled him to accept it with the best grace he could. There is no resisting an appointment by acclamation, for human nature has its infirmities, and there is a limit to resistance as well as to obedience. The vote of the Lords was all that was wanting to stamp the process with validity, and he made application to them to leave out his name, for he wished neither to be King's Serjeant, nor to be made Attorney of the Duchy over again ; but his prayer had merely the effect of causing them to advise about it. The Lords consented in short to the wish of the Commons, and the Speaker, Lenthal, moved that he might be suspended from being a serjeant at present, inasmuch as he would probably be required to swear the rest. This too was opposed, until he himself rose and showed them the necessity that either he or his colleague, Sir Thomas Widdrington, must make the speech to the rest of the serjeants and swear them, which they could not do if both of themselves were to be sworn. Then he stated, how he, by mutual agreement, had taken the trouble of delivering the speech upon himself, and trusted on this statement they would kindly suspend him. To this they assented, and voted that he should not be sworn a serjeant until further order. At this distance of time it may be difficult to comprehend the reasons of state that led to such manœuvering; and now it is merely satisfactory to know that one serjeant cannot swear another. Was it, perchance, for that reason why one augur in ancient Rome could not look another seriously in the face without laughing, as Cicero informs us? Was the farce too strong for the facial nerves of a new-fledged serjeant? Your true reasons of state policy are generally reducible to simple axioms of the kind I have been supposing.

In the evening of November the 3rd, all these serjeants, both old and new, met at Lincoln's Inn, where the new invited the old to supper, and Whitelocke joined them by invitation. They consulted about their dignity, dividing their attention between it and venison-pasty; and all the new dignitaries resolved, that Mr. Solicitor St. John should have the place and antiquity before them all, Sir Thomas Widdrington the second, Whitelocke the third, and the rest in their order. With this decision the second and third were not over-well pleased, as they were the Commissioners of the Seal, but as the new serjeants had "done it" to gratify Mr. Solicitor, who had great interest in the House, they deemed it best to let the affair pass off unquestioned on that occasion. In ten days' time, computing from the supper, no little intrigue

having been at work in the House during the interim to give
Mr. Browne the seniority of Serjeant Jermyn, because the
one had been a commissioner and the other not, the serjeants
appeared before our new Commissioners of the Great Seal in
the Queen's Court, but were not called in till Mr. Browne's
precedency had been confirmed, at which (meaning I presume
either the precedency or the delay, or both) most of the
serjeants "did grumble." On the following day, the same
keepers repaired to the King's Bench and took their seats in
the middle, with the judges on each flank, and here Sir
Thomas Widdrington made a very learned speech to Rolles,
the new Lord Chief Justice, previously to the swearing
ceremony, which all officials at that time, if they had any
conscience at all, could hardly have swallowed with becoming
gravity when the word "allegiance," or any similar expression
of fealty, had to be pronounced. From this court they went
to the Exchequer, and took their seats with the Barons on
either side as in the former case. Here lawyers thronged to
hear his speech to Serjeant Wilde, the new Chief Baron.
Should any of my readers feel interested in the antiquity of
this institution, him I advise to consult that speech as given
at full length in the "Memorials." Here it would be too
tedious. The authorities whom he quotes and enlarges
upon, such as Coke, Lambert, Gervasius Tilbariensis, Pasquier,
Haillan, and others, may interest lawyers, but assuredly not
the general reader. In glancing down its learned contents I
see two or three assertions from which some linguists might
claim to differ, until shown that they are wrong. He says
for instance, that "Baron" is a Saxon word, whereas I have
always conceived that neither baron nor bacon belonged
originally to the Teutonic languages ; and then he traces
"Exchequer" through the Latin *scaccarium* up to the Saxon
or German *Schatz*, a treasure (and *Zecherie*, an office). The
last word, although spelt wrong, is certainly Teutonic, but
the former is much more likely to have been derived from
the Latin. What treasury could the ancient Germans have

had? They would have robbed one, probably, but never could themselves have invented a chamber to keep it in. He thinks too the word was fetched out of England and carried over to Normandy, so great was his predilection for the Saxon origin of our common laws, customs, and names. In thinking thus, he overlooked the utter contempt with which the Normans regarded everything that was Saxon.

I doubt the existence of escheats, tenures, reliefs, and sheriffs, in England, before the Conquest; but admitting that they existed in the time of Edward the Confessor, it should be remembered that this King was no true Saxon at heart, but a Norman in his predilections and conduct, and trained as an enemy to his country by education and habits. If these customs could be traced back to him, it would be a mere quibble to call them Saxon, because the robber William had not yet seized the throne and reduced the inhabitants to serfdom and feudalism. Moderns deny that the honour of his profession or of the law depends on its antiquity. Myriads of years can never sanction wrong nor ennoble right. Whitelocke quoted his own father, who it must be admitted was as good and honest a judge, as those melancholy times of the polluted first James would allow. That judge once said to the Lord Keeper of the day : "The life of a judge is *militia quædam*, if not *martyrium quoddam*, in both which courage is requisite against the assault of friends, of family, of servants, and the many importunities and temptations he shall meet withal. A martyr he must be in bearing the provocations, scandals, and reproaches which will be cast upon every judge, one party being always displeased, and not sparing, especially in these times, to censure the judgment, be it never so upright. He must want no courage to resist even the highest and greatest powers."

That the Revolution, followed by the death of Charles upon the scaffold, was in the main a failure, a cruel disappointment, may be gathered from the speech that Whitelocke delivered on the 18th, three days after the speech to which

I have been alluding, at the Chancery bar, and from which I shall give merely a few extracts :

"Mr. Serjeant St. John, and the rest of you gentlemen, who have received writs to be serjeants-at-law !

"It has pleased the Parliament, in commanding these writs to issue forth, to manifest their constant resolutions to continue and maintain the old settled form of government and laws of the kingdom, and to provide for the supply of the high courts of justice with the usual number of judges, and to manifest their respects to our profession,—and likewise to bestow a particular mark of favour upon you as eminent members of it. The good affections of the public, and the abilities of most of you, they know by experience among themselves, and of the rest by good information."

It will be only justice to our Commissioner's memory to let him speak a little longer for himself; take, for instance, his fourth and last reason, why he did not wish "to see the solemnity of this general call diminished."

"And lastly, out of my own affections to the degree, being myself the son of a serjeant, and having the honour to be one of your number in this call, and I do acknowledge that both in my descent and fortune I am a great debtor to the law."

As usual with my countrymen of that pedantic period, he enters at great length into the question relative to the antiquity of the serjeant, whom Chaucer describes as " wary and wise,"—how he was addressed reverentially as "vos,"— how this title of honour or address of the plural pronoun was used in the Jewish nation,—how he kept his pillar at Paul's, where his clients might find him, which Whitelocke says is a libellous accusation, since he went to the pillar to offer and not to beg. I am sorry to say he quotes the Latin saying—*nec enim virtutem amplectimur ipsam, præmia si tollas*—to show that degrees in general, but more particularly we may conclude as applied to serjeants, are the rewards of study and learning. Virtue, in English law, and at English

universities, is therefore not its own reward. This naïve
admission is followed by another and far happier quotation :—" *senesco discens,*"—and further on he reminds them
of the woe denounced by the prophet on all those who
destroy a good cause by unlawful subtlety and deceit,—on
those men "that call good evil and evil good, that put darkness for light and light for darkness ; " in other words, on
pleaders that attempt to make black white, and white black.
A string of sentiments ensues, which, had they been observed
from age to age, would have robbed our proverbs of their
sting, and made the justice of this country a blessing to the
poor.

On the 21st, while sitting in Chancery, his colleague, Sir
Thomas Widdrington, not being present, and after hearing
many motions, till past two o'clock, the new serjeants entered
in "their party-coloured robes," with their servants, and the
gentlemen of the Inns of Court. Thereupon the Judges of
the King's Bench and the Commissioners of the Seal repaired
to the Court of Common Pleas, where the latter, as supreme
officials, took their seats in the middle of the bench. Here
the serjeants "counted," and, when they had done, a friend
delivered for them their rings, as presents to each commissioner and judge. The next day was also consumed in
ceremonies, but the several speeches are not preserved.

"Pride's purge" came at length upon the 6th of December,
but Whitelocke passed into the House without being seized
at the door, and on receiving a strong injunction from the
Speaker and others to continue by all means the exercise of
his functions in Chancery as before, complied therewith. He
took his seat with his colleagues for the sake of form, put off
the causes, and returned home. On the 9th they sat in the
Parliament Chamber of the Middle Temple, where they heard
forty demurrers. On the 18th Whitelocke and Widdrington
met Cromwell, Colonel Dean, and the Speaker, and held a
conference respecting what the General was pleased to call
the settlement of the nation. On the following day White-

locke paid an early visit to him, and found him lying in one of the King's rich beds at Whitehall; then on the succeeding day the same council, minus Colonel Dean, met again to discuss the actions of the army, and the old story about the settlement. The result of these conferences was, that Whitelocke and his colleague agreed to draw up a document, with a view to bring the army into a fitter temper, and frame something in vindication of the House, that would satisfy the council of the army. " This was a work of no small difficulty and danger," he remarks, " yet at this time not to be declined by us, for both the members of the House and the chief officers of the army had trusted us alone in this matter. We prayed to God to direct us in it, and that neither of us might receive any prejudice, but that the kingdom might receive good by this our employment, and that the courses of the army might be moderated (as it was in some measure at this time, though it broke out again into violence afterwards)."

This " afterwards" broke out in less than twenty-four hours, when they mooted in a debate the bringing of great delinquents to speedy punishment, and did not hesitate to style the King himself the greatest delinquent. Some endeavoured on that ever memorable occasion " to have put the business on the army ; that if they would have the thing done, they should do it themselves, as most proper for such an irregular and unheard-of business, as to bring a sovereign prince to a public trial by his own subjects, to be done in an irregular way and by such irregular men. But they were subtle enough to see and avoid that, and to make those whom they left sitting in the Parliament to be their *Stales*, and to do their most dirty work for them,—many of whom they found, and persuaded to be strangely forward to engage in it." The major vote named a committee of thirty-eight persons to draw up the charge, or prepare for it by examining witnesses, and receiving informations, not solely against the King, but every other delinquent, on whom the House might think fit to inflict condign punishment. White-

locke was named one of this committee, but he never attended
it. On the contrary, he went that very day with his colleague,
by appointment, to the Speaker's house, where several members met them ; they consulted on the means of settling the
kingdom by the Parliament, so as not to leave everything to
the sword. They both spoke their minds freely, but might
just as well have not uttered a syllable, for some were wholly
against having any King at all ; others proposed his eldest,
some the second son, and lastly, a few, distrusting this *par
nobile fratrum*, boldly advocated the election of the third
son, the Duke of Gloucester, who was among them under
their care, whom they could educate after their own fashion,
and in other words train up to be a constitutional King.
This last proposition, had it only been accepted, might have
ultimately been attended with good, but the meeting could
come to no agreement whatever, and adjourned to the
following Monday.

Such procrastination was tantamount to an adjournment
sine die, and, indeed, three days later, at an early hour in the
morning, the committee appointed to draw up heads for the
trial of the King, sent their clerk, one Mr. Smith, with a
message desiring the attendance of the two Commissioners
that day, their advice and assistance being required, and they
were expressly enjoined not to fail in their coming.

Whitelocke knew what the message meant, and told Sir
Thomas, who was then with him, he was resolved not to
meddle in that business about the trial of the King, that it
was contrary to his judgment, and he had declared so in the
House. His coadjutor said he was of the same judgment,
and would take no part in the matter, but did not know
where to go, so as to be out of the way, and where the
committee would not be able to send for him. Whitelocke
replied, that his coach was ready, that he was that morning
going purposely out of town to avoid being mixed up in the
concern, that if his friend would accompany him, they could
both go to Whitelocke's house in the country, and there wait

till the catastrophe was over. Sir Thomas willingly complied, soon made his preparatives, and they both set off.

This passage is by far the brightest in the whole of their mutual career; it has been a great source of consolation to Whitelocke's descendants; the remembrance of it was a cause of thankfulness to himself in his old age, and when he joined his feeble hands in prayer, unseen by his fellow-men, he could truly say, in communing with his conscience and his God, "I have shunned deeds of blood, I have been merciful, I have felt pity, I have forgiven those who offended me, I implore mercy and forgiveness in my turn."

On the 1st of January, 1648, the names of the commissioners for the trial of the King were published. Whitelocke's name was not introduced, for he had avowed his disapproval of their proceedings in the House; he had moreover absented himself from the committee the whole time it sat, and they all knew his mind. He was at that time holding high office by their authority, but he resolved to hazard or lay down everything, no matter how beneficial or advantageous, rather than do an act so revolting to his judgment and conscience.

By the 9th of the month the two Commissioners, Whitelocke and Widdrington, had returned from their sojourn in the country, and agreed to show themselves in the House, notwithstanding the trial now pending, for with that they had nothing to do. They did so, and found a welcome from some, though others looked very shy upon them.

A dreary period, so foreign to the old revels of that season, had now to be passed through; they stood in a doubtful and even false position; at first the House sent for their mace, and there were thoughts of ousting them from their places, but this intention was abandoned; then Whitelocke had to inform the House that a *habeas corpus* could not be denied, as claimed by Prynne, who had been recently arrested; then again they were summoned to attend a committee about settling the course of justice. On

hearing demurrers in the forenoon of the 12th, the very
barristers engaged in the cases used strong and peremptory
language, showed discontent and mutiny by their tones and
gestures, as if they too were infected with the spirit of the
times.   As for the poor Speaker, whom they visited on
Sunday evening, he did nothing but lament, and exclaim
that the army meant to put him out of his place, and claim
all by right of conquest.   How clear-sighted self-interest
makes us!   By the 19th the two commoners, himself, and
Sir Thomas, had the Chancery woolsack all to themselves,
for the two lords had by this time retired in common with
the whole body of the Upper House, from all share in the
administration.   Even Whitelocke's colleague, the only one
that was left, began to feel scruples about signing warrants
for the adjournment of the term in the absence of the
Lords, but at length consented to do so, provided the latter
would attend ; they did so to oblige him, but took no part
in business of any description.

The King is dead ; it is the last day but one of the
month.   There is no cry raised of "Long live the King!"

" I went not to the House, but stayed all day at home
in my study and at my prayers, that this day's work might
not so displease God as to bring prejudice to this poor
afflicted nation."

It did bring prejudice, for whether right or wrong in the
abstract, it was merciless ; it made a martyr of the sufferer
and invested him with a sanctity for which his repeated acts
of tyranny and bad faith in his kingly career, although
originating in mistaken convictions, had disqualified him.

On the 1st of February Whitelocke was deeply humiliated
by the compulsion put upon him.   In common with many
members he had to declare, in a circuitous way, that the late
King's concessions respecting the proposed treaty of peace
had been inadequate and unsatisfactory.   Had he refused he
would have been instantly expelled.   Such is my inference
from a passage in his journal ; but he does not say that he

himself personally was so required to acquiesce, so that if he was not, it is clear that he had originally voted to that effect. Whether he did so in the first or the second instance, his inducement may have been the deep conviction of the King's insincerity, too fatally proved by his entire conduct, but still more irrefutably by the discovery of that remarkable letter to his Queen in the messenger's saddle, in which he revealed his true intentions,—to dissemble, to gain time, and at last have Cromwell's head. On this humiliating day, Whitelocke kept his seat from morning till night, and there declared his disapprobation of the vote that had been passed on the 5th of December last. In this dignified way he made his peace with the "powers that be;" but in sorrow let it be confessed, that he humbled himself and censured the past, because it was past, because it had failed, and because what was done could not now be undone. Nor was this the only act of submission; for although on the 5th he made a long speech in favour of the Lords' House, and argued in behalf of the constitution, his pleadings failed to convince. They voted by a large majority, on the 6th, that the House of Commons should not take the advice of the Lords in the exercise of the legislative power of the kingdom, and then followed up the blow by a second vote, that the House of Peers in Parliament was useless, dangerous, ought to be abolished, and that an act should be brought in for that purpose. It appears he had retired before the passing of this second vote, and urged not merely his absence, but his adverse opinion when they desired him to draw up the Act of Abolition. He urged in vain, and could not get excused. On the following day the House abolished kingship, as unnecessary, burthensome, dangerous to the liberty, safety, and public interest of the people, and ordered an act to be drawn up in that sense. On the 8th Sir Thomas Widdrington resigned, upon the breaking up of the old Seal; and after a long debate the House excused him, gave him a quarter's "wages" more than his due, and allowed him to practise within the bar.

s

"My name was next in the Act," says Whitelocke, "and I was to declare myself whether I would accept of this employment or not; this point I had considered with as much seriousness as I could, such as the matter required; and I had often advised with my friends about it, having known beforehand that I should be named one of the commissioners.

"The most considerable particulars were, that I was already very deeply engaged with this party, that the business to be undertaken by me was the execution of law and justice, without which men could not live one by another. Yet many objections were made against my acceptance of this place."

In short, he made a long speech, that contains some very fair periods, in which he distinctly admitted that he should submit to the pleasure and judgment of the House. Some of the confessions show in what condition the Chancery has been. He says that in this office, as in war, *non licet bis peccare;* that some chancellors have laboured to conceal or obscure the truth, as much as learning, eloquence and subtlety can invent; that a keeper of the seals has nothing but his own conscience to direct him, a guide that is sometimes deceitful; that what is right in one man's eyes is wrong in another's. It was wound up with a request to be excused, which was not granted, and then it was voted, *nemine contradicente,* that he should be one of the Commissioners of the Great Seal, having for his two colleagues, Mr. John L'Isle and Mr. Serjeant Keeble. They were also to be styled Lords Commissioners, because the word Lord would reflect more credit upon the authority of the House who conferred the employment. As the French republicans changed the name of Royal Tiger into National Tiger, so the Commons changed the King's Bench into the Upper Bench; and a few days later they named their favourite, for such Whitelocke seems to have been, one of the thirty-eight to form the Council of State.

On the 19th the councillors of state were all required to

subscribe the test, for approving all that the Parliament had done with respect to the King, his execution, and the abolition of the House of Peers.   Whitelocke deliberately refused to sign this paper, and declined giving his approbation to any acts performed by the High Court of Justice, a court of which Bradshaw was the president ; but on the 22nd he assented to a new proposal, that he should subscribe a test for approving what the Commons in Parliament might do in future by virtue of their supreme authority over the nation.   This act was a sort of return to them for the leave given him and the council generally to see to the preservation of the library, medals, and statues in the palace of St. James.

Two days later, Cromwell and his son-in-law, Ireton, went home with him to supper.   They were very cheerful and seemed extremely well pleased.   They discoursed together till midnight, related to him some instances of the special intervention of Providence in connection with the late wars, and the coming up of the army to town, and described the miraculous passages that occurred at the time of seizing the members of the House.   On returning home in their coach, the guard stopped and examined them ; pretended not to believe them when they said their names were Cromwell and Ireton, and threatened to carry them off to the court of guard.   The younger of these two officers lost his temper, but the veteran general took it all in good part, gave the soldiers twenty shillings, and commended them as well as the captain for doing their duty.   The soldiers acknowledged afterwards they had only been acting a part, to let those great men see how punctual and careful they were to obey orders.   This trivial anecdote is not however without significancy, as it serves to show that martial law was enforced in London and its suburbs.

A short time after this scene Whitelocke resigned his high stewardship of the park of Greenwich to the Earl of Pembroke, and received in exchange the manor, walk, and lodge in the great park of Windsor.

On the 14th he received an order to bring in a declaration, such as would satisfy the people, touching the proceedings of Parliament.

Nothing remarkable occurred till the 15th of May, when a heavy loss befell him. It was the saddest day he had ever known as yet, for his brother-in-law, William Willoughby, brought him the news that his wife was dead. She had borne him nine children, three of whom were sons; and the whole of these, as well as his only son by his first wife, became gradually extinct as to themselves and their issue at the end of the third generation, reckoning in the two mothers as the first. "When we first met it was upon terms of affection only, without consideration of portion or estate or settlement. She was of a very honourable and ancient family; her father was the Lord Willoughby of Parham, whose ancestors were barons near 400 years together, and who had matched into many great and noble families; her mother was daughter to the Earl of Rutland, and he was lineally descended from a sister of King Edward IV., and so from King Edward III., and that great name and line of the Plantagenets."

What he did, or what was done upon the 16th of May, it is now impossible to know; he omitted to make any entry into his journal—too heavily smitten to think of anything—too careworn and depressed to attend to the wants of the republic.

The cares of life resumed their influence insensibly, and the old, dull routine of duties returned. In three weeks he had to dine at my Lord Mayor's, where only drums and trumpets were used for the flourishes, no healths drunk, no fool to jump into the huge custard and tickle himself to excite infectious laughter. All was solemn down to the funeral baked meats; grave as his own prolix speech to the judges two days later; grave as his own aspect: for I question whether he smiled again for many a long and weary year, unless when officially or diplomatically engaged. Men only ventured to laugh in those days in the groves, and the forests, and the fresh fields, and the humble cottages in secluded nooks; but

in London nothing was to be heard but the rumble of some
ponderous wheels, the clank of steel, the nasal twang of new-
born psalmody.   In Scotland they were burning witches by
the score with the help of tar-barrels ; in England they were
whipping actors at the cart's-tail.

There was a house at Chelsea that had once belonged to
the Duke of Buckingham before his recent attempt at revolt;
it had been seriously injured by the quartering of soldiers in
it, and would require a large outlay to put it in order.   The
Attorney-General, at the instigation of L'Isle, moved the
House to bestow it as an official residence on the two First
Commissioners, with a lease of twenty-one years from
Haberdashers' Hall, at the moderate rent of 40l. per annum.
It was instantly granted, and here our first keeper resided
till the Restoration.   There was a design about this time of
removing to the continent, for the purpose of selling them,
the invaluable books, the collection of medals, and the rich
jewels already removed from Whitehall to St. James's.
The plan was discovered, and at the request of Selden—who
feared that all these rare monuments of antiquity, these
choice books and manuscripts would be lost, and to which
none were comparable in Europe, save those in the Vatican
—Whitelocke consented to be the librarian-in-chief, with
apartments for his own use in the palace.   Into these he
placed a German, Duery by name, as his deputy, having
chosen him on account of his scholastic attainments and
knowledge acquired by extensive travel.   He had an exact
inventory made, and although he did not create, was instrumental in preserving an invaluable treasure for the nation.

There had been a report of his own death, as well as that
of his wife, spread about at this time in foreign countries
among the English exiles, who were numerous.   He received
an affectionate letter from Sir John Holland, who wrote to
him from beyond seas, now that he knew him to be still living,
condoling with him on his recent loss, and assuring him of his
unaltered friendship.   But what was this one false rumour

compared to those that were invented and dispersed at every breath ; to those forged works and deeds attributed to him or to other leaders by deep conspirators and practised fabricators ; to those organised libels and false statements systematically coined abroad, then smuggled into England, and distributed by hundreds throughout the length and breadth of the land? The hangman might uselessly burn some of the most dangerous or offensive, but they poured in like locusts, and served for food to restless agitators, plotters, and wild schemers.

It had been a year, as the now desolate man describes it, of great perplexity and danger to the Commonwealth. Had the Parliament lost but one battle, all who were engaged with them would have been in danger of ruin, not merely as to their fortunes but their lives. And though their party gained many battles, yet their enemies still possessed the power of raising up fresh parties and fomenting new troubles.

When these were all subdued, so that not one man remained in arms for the King, there appeared many against the Parliament ; their own friends were converted into foes ; those who fought against the King's party joined with the Parliament, and they fought together against the Cavaliers.

When these were subdued, then the same soldiers fought against their own masters and fellow-soldiers,—as witness the agitators, levellers, and mutineers.

The leaders of the army conspired to overthrow the very power from which they had received their own commissions, and bent their arms against those who had placed those arms in their hands. The conquered were ruined ; but the conquerors, by their own distempers and insurrections, pre-pared new scenes of riot, rout, and confusion. Success made many haughty, set loose the wildest imaginations, and hardly one could be found that did not dream of high command and great distinction. Men's wits were all at work ; and while some were bent on one thing, others were striving to attain or accomplish another thing, with equal violence and all the fury of faction.

The army was divided into levellers and disciplined soldiers; the Parliament into monarchists and republicans ; the whole nation into Cavaliers and Parliamentarians.   These Parliamentarians, or " Roundheads " as their enemies called them, were split into presbyterians, independents, anabaptists, fifth-monarchy men, and nearly all those sects that still subsist entire or fragmentary ; and the only bond of union was the sword, for the olive branch, the bay, the laurel were alike despised ; these had no virtues to compete with pike and musket.

The work of resistance had grown insensibly until they found themselves plunged into a sea of difficulties, that appalled the boldest,   They had all ventured beyond their depth, and knew not how to escape.   The miseries and calamities had been innumerable and unspeakable, and no man could tell what the morrow would bring forth.   One omen was given, but there was no soothsayer to expound it, no prophet to trace it in his mind's eye or obscurely shadow out the issue ; and it was this—Monk formed a peace "with the grand and bloody Irish rebel Owen Rowe O'Neal," and so thoroughly were England's rulers demented, that they extenuated the deed and continued to employ the traitor.

But at last we have a glimpse of something like a continuation of reform, for the House being adjourned, the Speaker, Whitelocke, Keeble, Chute, and two others met on the 18th of June at the Attorney-General's, where they conferred together on the reformation of chancery proceedings, and agreed upon some general points.   After dinner, as a journey to Chelsea was formidable at that late hour, he slept at Sion House, which the Earl of Northumberland had long since placed at his free disposal ; and I trust his reveries were not those of exultation, but fixed on brighter prospects in after times for the entire body of his countrymen, be their present classifications and discords what they

might.   And what if the times were licentious ? and what if
men did take strange license to calumniate all in authority,
or to clamour if they had not themselves what they thought
best for their own or the public interests ?   It was not for
him, who had started on his public career in the belief
that all things were *for* the best, to doubt the eventual issue.
Time has justified that faith, and though nearly every thing
remains to be done, the delay has been advantageous for
the world at large, for the cause of universal progress and
man's real ennoblement in all quarters of the world.

As he had made another great step in the path of reform,
so likewise did the Parliament attempt something of a like
nature, by taking into consideration a few of the late petitions, and debating upon them.   The chief topic was his own
profession, and one argument used was : "that it was not fit
for lawyers, when members of the House, to plead or practise
in the courts of law, so long as they retained their seats."

Now, under all these circumstances, I cannot blame his
advocacy of his own professional predilections on this and
other occasions.   For who were there at that time in the
nation, that could be called learned and yet be independent
of all professional vocation ?   The universities did not
teach philosophy then, did not send out sage men, who had
studied and learned wisdom for its own sake alone.   There
was no body of men, perhaps no one individual then living,
that had the faintest notion of psychology, metaphysics as
now comprehended, ethics or any other qualification essential
to a great lawgiver.   The legislator must belong to a civilised
nation, or if not so belonging, must borrow from its laws and
jurisprudence, so as to incorporate them as a digest with
the scanty and rude morsels already valid in his own
country.   Science was not yet conceived, and therefore the
lawyers still had what jurisprudential knowledge existed to
themselves.   In these days they may not be the best legislators England could have, for their virile education seems
to be behind the acquirements and positive wants of the age ;

their minds may be narrowed, relatively speaking, and their time wasted by the task of finding their way out of the chaos of a law library, through which they have to wade, and creep, and sink, and buffet, like the fiend on his errand to man's paradise. But in those days they were the best legislators to be found, and their minds were relatively expanded; for what were ordinary gentlemen, then, but well-dressed boors? and what were medical men but orthodox quacks? and what were the etablished clergy, but pious, devout married monks, who, if they had been permitted, were still ready to exorcise foul spirits, baptise bells and anathematise witches? Many can still recollect their purification of haunted houses.

Whitelocke's speech accordingly was felt to be a refutation of those instinctive attacks that were made by men who could not explain for lack of proof the justifiableness of them, and who were equally unable to propound the fitting remedy. It is here subjoined.

"MR. SPEAKER,—I was unwilling again to have troubled you upon this argument, had I not been again called up by the mistakes of the worthy gentleman that spoke last, to give you a true account of those matters, and to vindicate the honour of that profession, whereof I am an unworthy member.

"The gentleman was pleased to intimate, that lawyers were heretofore excluded from being members of Parliament; but I suppose he had not much studied the records of that matter, and therefore related the discourses of others by hearsay only.

"But for his conviction and the satisfaction of others, I shall acquaint you with the clear passages of what he aimed at, as I suppose, and as I find them upon record, which are much more authentic than some (perhaps) table-talk, or discourses at random.

"The statute of 23 Ed. III. calls the members of Parliament the learned men, whereof many were learned in the laws, and therefore supposed to have had that title. But shortly after this, the great men degenerating in the old age of the same King into several factions, and being much offended with those who were learned in the laws, because they hindered their oppressions by pleading the right of law on behalf of their clients, 46 Ed. III. petitioned, that *Nul homme de ley, pursuont besoignes en le Court de Roi, ne viscount pour le temps que il est viscount, soient retournez ni acceptez chivaliers des countees;* no man of the law, following business in the King's courts, nor sheriff, be returned or accepted knights of shires.

" To this the King answers :

" *Voet le Roy que chivaliers et serjeants des meaux vaues du païs soient retournees desormais chivaliers en parlements, et qu'ils soient esleus en plein counte;* the King wills, that knights and serjeants (that is, esquires) of the best rank in the country be from henceforth returned to be knights in Parliament, and that they be chosen in full county.

" After this ordinance, and pursuant to it, a clause was inserted into the writ for choosing members of the House of Commons, 5 Hen. IV., to this effect :

" *Nolumus autem quod tu seu aliquis alius vicecomes regni nostri, sive aliquis alius homo ad legem, aliqualiter sit electus;* we will not that you, or any other sheriff of our kingdom, or any other man of law, by any means be chosen.

" According to this ordinance and clause of *Nolumus,* the sheriffs have been since excluded from sitting in Parliament as members during the time of their shrievalty; the debate on which point was held, and full of learning, in a former Parliament, in the case of a very learned and worthy person, Sir Edward Coke, whom most of us knew. He being made sheriff of Bucks, was chosen knight of that shire, and sat in Parliament, and I had the honour then to be a young parliament-man, in the second year of the late King. The objections against him were, the constant usage not to permit sheriffs to sit as parliament-men, on account of their oath to reside in their counties, the custody whereof was committed to them; and that their office was but annual, and so the disability was but for that time only.

"But for a man to be disabled from being a parliament-man in regard of his being a lawyer, is to disable him during his life, or his continuance in his profession, by which he gains his livelihood; and they are not public officers, obliged to another attendance on the public affairs, as the sheriffs are. Yet it is true, that in this Parliament, which was held in 6 Hen. IV., all lawyers were excluded, and none of them returned to serve in this Parliament; and perhaps, from some general discourse hereof by others, the worthy gentleman is pleased, with confidence, to vent his doctrine and motion. But in case he did read and understand the records of this ordinance, and of the clause of *Nolumus*, yet I suppose he never looked into the ground of this business, nor into that which followed thereupon; wherein I shall hope to satisfy him, and so as to alter his opinion.

"King Henry the Fourth, being in great want of money, summoned that Parliament, and caused to be inserted in the writ this clause of *Nolumus*, to exclude the lawyers, because he doubted that they would oppose the excessive demands which he was to make to the Parliament. Thomas Walsingham says: That all the lawyers being excluded, the demands of the King were by this means obtained, and by this Parliament was granted an unusual tax, and to the people *tricabilis et valdè gravis*, a tax full of trouble and very grievous; whereof the historian says, he would have set down the manner, had not the granters and authors of the same desired it to be concealed for ever from posterity by causing the papers and records thereof to be burned.

"Mr. Speaker, this is the precedent intimated by the worthy gentleman, and this was the occasion and issue of that precedent, the like whereof, I presume, is not wished by him. Walsingham styles that Parliament in the margin, *Parliamentum indoctorum*, the Parliament of unlearned men.

SPEED, in his history, says, that this Parliament was called the lack-learning Parliament; either for the unlearnedness of the persons, or for their malice unto learning. But God has blessed this nation with such an age of learned men at this present, that former times knew not; and we must acknowledge, that though the House should lack all their members who are lawyers, yet the rest are of such great abilities that there would be no lack of learning.* Yet, sir, I am sure that the addition of those many learned gentlemen of our profession has been and will be some help in your affairs, and will not be despised by any prudent man.

"The worthy gentleman was pleased lightly to call them gownmen, who had not undergone the dangers and hardships that martial men had done. And truly it might less become the gentleman that said it than others to make that observation, if it had been so.

"The ancient Romans were soldiers though gownmen; nor does that gown abate either a man's courage or his wisdom, or render him less capable of using a sword, when the laws are silent, or you command it.

"You all know this to be true, from the great services performed by Lieutenant-General Jones and Commissary-General Ireton, and many of the members, with other lawyers who, putting off their gowns when you required it, have served you stoutly and successfully as soldiers, having undergone almost as many and as great hardships and dangers as the gentleman who so much undervalues all of them.

"But we are now speaking of their right to be chosen, and to sit as members of the Parliament, which doubtless is as much and the same with all other the commoners of England.

"The historian last mentioned says, that the Commons of

* _The argumentum ad hominem,_ which lawyers fall into from their habit of address ing juries. If all the rest were learned, why did he translate his French and Latin quotations?

England, who have liberty in the choice of their knights and burgesses, would not be debarred therefrom by the ordinance of Ed. III., nor by the clause of *Nolumus*, inserted in the writ of Hen. IV. But notwithstanding the same, knowing the lawyers to be equally interested with them in the public rights and liberties of the nation, they have made a constant choice of some of them to serve in all Parliaments."

The orator then makes a lengthy quotation from "Coke's Institutes," and shows why the objection was raised against their presence in the Commons, because being courtiers, and the servants of the King, they voted in the House more to subserve the monarch than their country ; but then such an objection no longer applied at the present time. By which allusion he reminded them of the King's recent death, superfluously enough, since no man there could ever forget what the most distant posterity can never consign to oblivion, even if it would. I am afraid that many of my readers will find this technical speech tedious enough ; but as it terminates with a confession that may have saved the life of many an innocent prisoner at the bar, a due regard for the memory of Whitelocke demands that I should proceed.

"The like passage with this we are now debating is related in the Roman story, when the law Cincia was made, whereby it was provided, that for pleading of causes, no man should take either money or gift, and this law was endeavoured, upon the like grounds, to be set on foot presently after the death of Tiberius Cæsar. But when some alleged that this would cause the want of counsellors and advocates, whereby the poor would be oppressed by the rich and mighty ; * that eloquence did not come by chance, or gratuitously, without study and labour ; that the care of a man's own family was neglected, whilst he attended to other men's affairs ; that some maintained their life by war, some by tilling the earth,

---

* This is precisely the reason why legal reform is so imperatively required in England. The exorbitant expense of our courts renders justice too dear for the poor ; they cannot buy it.

yet no man laboured in those callings or to attain knowledge, but for the commodity arising thèrefrom,—that the meanest of the people endeavoured what they could to better their estates, and that if the reward of studies be taken away, studies also would decay, as having neither glory nor honour: upon these reasons the Senate thought it not just (and I hope this Senate will be of the same judgment,) to take away the *honorarium* of advocates, but limited the same to 1000 sesterces, which some compute to be about 78*l*. of our money. Neither, says Tacitus, did that law continue or gain compliance with it. Neither do I think that such a law amongst us would be to any effect, or gain compliance with it. But I hope this honourable English Senate, and that worthy gentleman, a member of it, will be satisfied with the reasons given in the Roman Senate, who were very wise men, and not trouble themselves about such new laws, which will be ineffectual, prejudicial to many, and good for none. But the gentleman objected, and it is much argued in these times against the profession of the law and the professors of it, that they are the occasion of multiplicity of suits, and of delays in them, and therefore, after the example of some foreign countries, not to be permitted.

" I have observed to you before, that those in power have most reason to be displeased with this profession, as a bridle to their power. But that the profession occasions multiplicity of suits is as improbable as any of his reasons or his arguments.

" Mr. Speaker, the reason of the multiplicity of suits and law causes amongst us is the greatness of our trade, which causes a multitude of contracts, and those occasion a multitude of law-suits. In those countries mentioned by that worthy gentleman, there is not one of his profession, one merchant, nor one contract for a hundred in England,—that is the cause why they have so few law-suits and we so many. And give me leave, Sir, to tell him, that in the Netherlands and countries where there is much trade, there are proportionably as many law-suits as there are in England. Another ground of what I affirm is, that in foreign countries, every man's estate is disposed of by their law, after a certain rule and proportion, which the possessor cannot, either by conveyance or by his testament, alter afterwards : as when one dies, his estate is thus divided by the law,—his wife has a part set out for her, the eldest son has a double portion, and all the other sons have equal portions, and every two daughters have as much as one son of their father's entire estate, thus divided by the law. Whereas, with us every possessor of an estate has power to dispose of it by his deed, or by his will, as he pleases, which must necessarily occasion the more differences, and suits of law, upon constructions of those deeds and wills, and parties claiming, than where the known law gives a certain rule and distribution of estates, which none can alter.

"Another ground of what I say is the freedom of our nation, where every one has equal right or title to his estate, and there is as full a property to the meanest as to the greatest person, which causes our countrymen to insist upon their right and privileges, and to contest for them with the greatest men, or the prince himself, if right of law be on their side. This occasions many more law-suits than those which arise in countries where the boors and peasants are wholly dependent on the will of their lord, to whom they are slaves, and dare not dispute any matter of right with him, but tamely submit to his good or bad pleasure."

The orator has been imitating the example of Fortescue, and striving to prove the superiority of English over continental law. When will English legists see, that law should be tried as to its excellency on its own intrinsic merits, by educated reason, and not through comparison with that of another country ?

The orator then goes on to say :

"And though in some of those northern countries they have no counsellors at law, as a public profession, because the smallness of their law business will not maintain them, and the great lords are ofttimes their parties and judges themselves, yet in Germany, France, Spain, and other countries, the doctors and professors of the laws are in great numbers and credit, and gain vast estates, though by small fees, yet often taken and long continuing. Whereof, particularly in France, there are many precedents.

" And if we look so far as the times of the ancient Romans and Grecians, their lawyers will be found numerous and in esteem among them ; and when their commonwealth enjoyed the greatest freedom, this profession was in the highest reputation.

" Sir, the worthy gentleman was pleased to mention one thing with some weight, that lawyers were permitted to counsel, and to plead for men in matters touching their estates and liberties, but in the greatest matter of all others, concerning a man's life and posterity, lawyers were not permitted to plead for their clients.

" I confess, I cannot answer this objection, that for a trespass of sixpence value, a man may have a counsellor-at-law to plead for him, but where his life and property are concerned, he is not admitted this privilege and the help of lawyers.

" A law to reform this, I think, would be just, and give right to people.

" What is said in defence or excuse of this custom is, that the judges are of counsel for the prisoners, and are to see that they shall have no wrong. And are they not to take the same care of all causes that shall be tried before them ?

" To that part of the gentleman's motion, that lawyers being members of the House shall during that time forbear their practice and pleading, I shall only give this answer : That in the Act which he may be pleased to bring in for this purpose, it may likewise be inserted, that merchants shall forbear their trading, physicians from visiting their patients, and country gentlemen from selling their corn and wool, while they sit as members of this House, which has the same reason as to debar lawyers from their practice.

"But, I doubt, sir, I have held you too long. My profession and the subject-matter of the debate will plead in my excuse, and I hope, sir, that by your prudence such notions as these will be less frequent amongst us."

The senate, as it was courteously but unconstitutionally termed, accustomed to sermons of three hours' duration, was not jaded by this lengthy speech, and agreed with the sentiments it conveyed. Nor did it forget the new appellation, for on the 2nd of February, for instance, upon the hearing of Sir Jacob Garret's business, it sentenced three of his false accusers to stand in the pillory, a sentence which Whitelocke deemed a gross usurpation of judicial functions. He and some others of his cloth were bold enough to declaim against this and many other acts of jurisdiction exercised by the House, showed them the illegality and breach of liberty in such arbitrary proceedings, and advised them to refer such cases to the ordinary courts of justice ; "but dominion and power was sweet to some of them, and they were very unwilling to part with it."

It is exceedingly difficult to say whether the Parliament of the Commonwealth of England, as they now officially styled themselves, were justified in continuing their existence as a body in the State. The object for which they had first resolved on sitting permanently had surely been more than attained by the most sanguinary vengeance, the most ample retaliation. On the death of the King, but for the apprehended invasion of the Scotch, their clear duty might seem to be to have called together a constituent assembly, and have then surrendered their usurped power into the hands of the country, declared by themselves to be the only source of power. But was the State sufficiently tranquil to enable them to do this with safety to themselves and the country ? A glance at the condition of the three kingdoms will supply the answer. The English were still at variance with the

Scotch and Irish, the Scotch at variance with the English and Irish, while the latter hated both. These last differed also among themselves, rebels from rebels, rebels from the English Cavaliers, while rebels and Cavaliers had formed an alliance against the victorious party in England. In Scotland, the State and the Kirk were at feud, and while both were jealous of the King's party, all were plotting against England. In the latter country the Cavaliers might rise in arms at any moment, for the Presbyterians in the West were desirous of seeing Prince Charles return to his country and ascend the throne; many prayed in pulpits for his restoration. The monarchists and republicans in the House, and out of it, were on terms of enmity, and· discord raged between the Presbyterians and Independents. How was the Gordian knot to be untied? No dependence could be placed upon the military; the lawyers regarded them with that distrust and instinctive aversion that men of the *toga* have invariably felt, and which the well-known verse records: *Nulla fides pietasque viris qui castra sequuntur.*

Fairfax was still the general in chief, but nourished scruples against the invading of Scotland, which the Council of State considered expedient about the end of June in 1650. Cromwell, Lambert, Harrison, St. John, and Whitelocke, were appointed as a committee to wait upon him and remove those scruples. How they fulfilled their task, and with what success, will be seen by the conversation that ensued in a private room at Whitehall, as soon as the preliminary prayers, which Cromwell led, were brought to a close.

CROMWELL.—"My Lord General, we are commanded by the Council of State to confer with your Excellency touching the present design (whereof you have heard some debate in the Council) of marching the army under your command into Scotland, and because there seemed to be some hesitation in yourself as to that journey, this committee has been appointed to endeavour to give your Excellency satisfaction in any doubts of yours which may arise concerning that affair, and the grounds of that resolution of the council for the journey into Scotland.

LORD GENERAL.—I am very glad at the opportunity of conferring with the committee, where I find so many of my particular friends, as well as of the Commonwealth, about this great business of our march into Scotland. I do acknowledge myself not fully satisfied with the grounds and justice of our invasion upon our brethren of Scotland, and I shall be glad to receive satisfaction therein by you.

LAMBERT.—Will your Excellency be pleased to favour us with the particular causes of your dissatisfaction?

LORD GENERAL.—I shall very freely do it, and I think I need not make to you or to any that know me, any protestation as to the continuance of my duty and affection to the Parliament, and my readiness to serve them in anything, wherein my conscience will give me leave.

HARRISON.—There cannot be more desired nor expected from your Excellency.

WHITELOCKE.—No man can doubt the fidelity and affection of your Excellency to the service of the Commonwealth; you have given ample testimony of it, and it will be much for the advantage of their affairs, if we may be able to give you satisfaction, as I hope we shall, touching the particular points on which your doubts arise.

ST. JOHN.—I pray, my Lord, be pleased to acquaint us with your particular objections against this journey.

LORD GENERAL.—My Lords, you will give me leave then with all freeness to say to you, that I think it doubtful whether we have a just cause to make an invasion into Scotland. We are joined with them in the national league and covenant, and now for us contrary thereunto, and without sufficient cause given us by them, to enter into their country with an army and to make war upon them, is what I cannot see the justice of, nor how we shall be able to justify the lawfulness of it before God or man.

CROMWELL.—I confess, my Lord, that if they have given us

no cause to invade them, it will not be justifiable for us to
do it, and to make war upon them without a sufficient ground
for it will be contrary to that which in conscience we ought
to do, and displeasing both to God and good men.   But, my
Lord, if they have invaded us, as your Lordship knows they
have done, since the national covenant, and contrary to it, in
that action of Duke Hamilton, which was by order and
authority from the parliament of that kingdom, it became
the act of the whole nation by their representatives.   And if
they now give us too much cause of suspicion, that they
intend another invasion upon us, joining with their King,
with whom they have made a full agreement, without the
assent or privity of this Commonwealth, and are very busy
at this present in raising forces and money to carry on their
design,—if these things are not a sufficient ground and cause
for us to endeavour to provide for the safety of our own
country, and to prevent the miseries which an invasion of
the Scots would bring upon us, I humbly submit it to your
Excellency's judgment.   That they have formerly invaded
us, and brought a war into the bowels of our country, is
known to all, wherein God was pleased to bless us with
success against them; and that they now intend a new
invasion of us I do as really believe, and have as good
intelligence of it, as we can have of anything that is not yet
acted.   Therefore I say, my Lord, that upon these grounds
I think we have a most just cause to begin, or rather to
return and requite their hostility first begun upon us and
thereby to free our country, if God shall be pleased to assist
us, as I doubt not but he will, from the great misery and
calamity of having an army of Scots within our country.
That there will be war between us, is I fear unavoidable.
Your Excellency will soon determine whether it be better to
have this war in the bowels of another country or of our
own, and that it will be in one of them, I think it without
scruple.

LORD GENERAL.—It is probable there will be war between

us, but whether we should begin this war and be on the offensive part, or only stand upon our own defence, is that which I scruple. Although they invaded us under Duke Hamilton, who pretended the authority of the parliament then sitting for it, yet their succeeding parliament disowned that engagement, and punished some of the promoters.

WHITELOCKE.—Some of the principal men in that engagement of Duke Hamilton's are now in great favour and employment with them, especially in their army since raised, and now almost ready to advance into England. I believe your Excellency will judge it more prudent in us, who have an army under your command ready-formed and experienced soldiers whom God has wondrously prospered under your conduct, to prevent their coming into England, by visiting them in their own country.

LORD GENERAL.—If we were assured of their coming with their army into England, I confess it were prudent in us to prevent them, and we are ready to advance into Scotland before they can march into England; but what warrant have we to fall upon them, unless we can be assured of their purpose to fall on us ?

HARRISON.—I think, under favour, there cannot be greater assurance or human probability of the intentions of any state, than we have of theirs to invade our country. Else what mean their present levies of men and money, and their quartering of soldiers on our borders ? It is not long since they did the like to us, and we can hardly imagine what other design they can have to employ their forces on.

LORD GENERAL.—Human probabilities are not sufficient grounds to make war upon a neighbour nation, especially our brethren of Scotland, to whom we are engaged in a solemn league and covenant.

ST. JOHN.—But, my Lord, that league and covenant was first broken by themselves, and so dissolved as to us ; and the disowning of Duke Hamilton's action by their latter parliament cannot acquit the injury done to us before.

CROMWELL.—I suppose your Excellency will be convinced of this clear truth, that we are no longer obliged by the league and covenant which they themselves did first break.

LORD GENERAL.—I am to answer only for my own conscience, and what that yields unto as just and lawful, I shall follow ; but what seems to me, or what I doubt to be otherwise, I must not do.

WHITELOCKE.—Your Excellency is upon a very right ground, and our business is to endeavour to yield you satisfaction in those doubts you make. If we shall stay till they first invade us, we shall suffer much misery to come amongst us, which probably we may prevent by sending first to them. And surely, by the law of nations, if an ally enter in a hostile manner into his neighbour nation, contrary to the alliance, and be beaten out again, that nation thus invaded may lawfully invade afterwards the other, to requite the former wrongs done unto them.

But, besides this, we cannot but see their present preparations to be against us, for they are in amity with all others ; and their conjunction now with the King's party may plainly enough discover their designs against this Commonwealth.

LORD GENERAL.—I can but say, as I said before, that every one must stand or fall by his own conscience. Those who are satisfied with the justice of this war may cheerfully proceed in it ; those who scruple it, as I confess I do, cannot undertake any service in it. I acknowledge that what has been said carries much weight and reason with it, and none can have more power upon me than this committee ; none can be more ready to serve the Parliament than myself in anything wherein my conscience shall be satisfied. In this it is not, and therefore, that I may be no hindrance to the Parliament's designs, I shall willingly lay down my commission, that it may be in their hands to choose some worthier person than myself: one who may upon clear satisfaction of his conscience undertake this business, wherein I desire to be excused.

CROMWELL.—I am very sorry that your Lordship should have thoughts of laying down your commission, by which God has blest you in the performance of so many eminent services for the Parliament. I pray, my Lord, consider all your faithful servants, us who are officers, who have served under you, and desire to serve under no other General. It would be a great discouragement to all of us, and a great discouragement to the affairs of the Parliament for our noble General to entertain any thoughts of laying down his commission. I hope your Lordship will never give so great an advantage to the public enemy, nor so much dishearten your friends as to think of laying down your commission.

LAMBERT.—If your Excellency should not receive so much satisfaction as to continue your command in the Parliament's service, I am very fearful of the mischiefs which might ensue, and the distraction in the public affairs, by your laying down your commission. But I hope that what has been offered to you by this committee to your serious consideration, will so far prevail with your noble and pious disposition, and with your affection to this cause wherein we are so deeply engaged, as that you will not, especially at this time, leave your old servants and officers, and the conclusion of the most glorious cause that ever men were engaged in.

HARRISON.—It is indeed, my Lord, the most righteous and most glorious cause that ever any of this nation appeared in, and now when we hope that the Lord will give a gracious issue and conclusion to it, for your Excellency then to give it over will sadden the hearts of many of God's people.

LORD GENERAL.—What would you have me do ? As far as my conscience will give way, I am willing to join with you still in the service of the Parliament, but where the conscience is not satisfied, none of you, I am sure, will engage in any service. That is my condition in this, and therefore I must desire to be excused."

The conference lasted some time longer, but neither Cromwell nor any of the rest could shake his resolution in the least. Fairfax kept his word, and resigned the chief command.

CHAPTER XVII.

—✦—

1650—1653

Anomalous State of Religion—Its hazardous bearing on the Legality of Marriages—
Whitelocke takes for his third Wife the Widow of Alderman Wilson—Recent
Recovery of an Autobiographical Fragment left by her—Whitelocke's successful
Efforts to Introduce English as the Language of Law Proceedings—His Linguistic
Disquisitions—Whitelocke and others deputed to congratulate Cromwell after
his Victory at Worcester—Attempt made by Parliament to extend its term of
Existence—Important Conference between Cromwell and Whitelocke—He is
regarded as an Obstacle to Cromwell's ambitious Designs—Conference at White-
hall, when Cromwell points to the Expediency of dissolving the House—
Approaching Crisis—Whitelocke's Caution—Cromwell dissolves the Rump—
Meeting of the Little Parliament—Whitelocke solicited by Cromwell to act as
his Ambassador at the Court of Queen Christina—Preparations for his Departure
—Rumours afloat of his intended Assassination by the King's Emissaries.

NOTHING singular and of a public nature occurred in which
Whitelocke was engaged from this period to the great victory
gained by Cromwell at Dunbar.   I find him entertaining the
Speaker and other eminent persons, and living at Chelsea in
his usual manner.   Whether he was yet married to his third
wife or not it is difficult to ascertain, for by a regrettable
oversight or decision, the fact itself, and the dates connected
with the event, have been omitted or suppressed in the
printed work, though most assuredly preserved faithfully in
the unpublished " Annals."   At the time of its appearance,
the feeling of this country was strongly monarchical and anti-
puritanical.   The Established Church was intolerant, and
neither permitted Dissenters to solemnise marriage, nor
recognised the validity of any marriage performed in England
by any other rites than their own.   Now, when Whitelocke
married for the third time, the prayer-book was not suffered
to be used by law, no minister of the overthrown Anglo-

Catholic Church officiated legally; and hence it becomes probable that Whitelocke, who as a great law-functionary was bound to yield obedience to the law, may have been married by some Presbyterian, or, more probably, Independent clergyman—whether at Chelsea or elsewhere, I cannot say, but no doubt exists as to the fact, and no moral doubt ought now to exist as to its validity. But for 160 years the laws of this country would unquestionably have regarded it as no marriage at all, if solemnised in the way supposed; nothing, indeed, that took place officially from the death of Charles I to the Restoration, was subsequently recognised by the Government. All the descendants now living of the man whose life we are now narrating have sprung from this third marriage, and like the entire series of acts consummated under the Commonwealth, may be assumed to be of illegitimate origin, Parliament having made no provision to the contrary. The law of sense and nature pronounces a *de facto* government, and everything done under the sanction of its authority, to be legal; the monarchical parliaments of this country since 1660 have been of a contrary opinion: let increasing civilisation and posterity decide the question.

The laws of marriage and divorce have been a bitter curse to this country, and all acts of flagrant injustice are apt to entail retribution in the long run. The future enemies of England that will exist hereafter, in America or various parts of the globe, may be the sons and grandsons of persons once grievously outraged and humiliated by the self-styled wisdom of Parliament, and its one-sided class legislation.

About a year before the period to which we have now arrived, when Cromwell was victorious over the Scotch army at Dunbar (31st August, 1650), an Alderman of London died, whose name was Rowland Wilson. He was a member of the House of Commons, of the Council of State, and of the army, in which he held the rank of colonel. He had died of a deep decline, and had been honoured with what was tantamount to a public funeral. So much, and no more, do

we learn from the "Memorials," but they have kept profound
silence as to the fact that he left a widow, young, handsome,
and very opulent.   She was a rigid puritan by birth, education, and conviction.   What she did was invariably done
from religious motives ; and, although the remark may be
premature, as a wife, mother, and stepmother, in her new
connection with a man whom she deliberately chose for her
second husband, her conduct was exemplary and self-denying
in the extreme.   She cheered her husband in his solitude and
disgrace, was faithfully devoted to him, tended him with
affection in his excruciating and last lingering illness, became
the prop of his house, and bequeathed alone the remains of
her private fortune to her own children : for the whole of
Whitelocke's paternal and acquired property had been settled
on his ten children by his two first marriages, on a distinct
understanding with the noble-hearted woman with whom he
was about to contract his third matrimonial engagement.
Not one of her children derived a penny from their father,
and this is said in no disparagement of him, for his means
were limited, and his losses had been very great.   Charles
the Second required a heavy penalty before he bade his
victim go in peace, with his royal pardon.

Some few years ago, at a public auction of books and
manuscripts of an eminent and lately deceased publisher in
Piccadilly, a small duodecimo manuscript, bound in cloth
resembling the worked samplers of girls at charity schools,
was offered for sale, and fortunately purchased by an individual who restored it to the true owners.   It appears by
this work, abstracted from the family about 200 years ago,
unquestionably genuine, and signed with the name of Mary
Whitelocke, his third wife, that while her husband was engaged at his retreat of Chilton Park in composing his various
works on law and religion, wherewith to beguile his time, she
on her part was similarly engaged, by writing a work for the
use and guidance of her eldest son Samuel, the heir of that
estate which had been purchased with her money.   This

work is divided into two parts. The first describes her
wedded life with her first husband, his melancholy death, her
widowhood, her solitary state, the absence of her mother,
Mrs. Carleton, in Holland, the cruel treatment and neglect
she experienced from the parents of her late husband—for
they survived their son—and how, because she had been
childless, they took no account of her. But let us permit
the lady to speak for herself.

" About a fortnight before my dear and precious husband
died, he spoke to me concerning his intention for to make a
will. I desired him to take no other care of me, but to leave
me so, as I might live like his widow ; nay, I did desire him
for to leave me nothing but during my widowhood For
thereby I thought I should not be troubled with any motions
for to alter my condition, if God should ever lay that sad
affliction upon me. My husband told me I was young, and
it was fit that I should marry, and he left that to me to do
as God should direct me, and he would very often say, he
hoped I should live and see many happy days when he was
dead and gone ; that I thought was impossible, but with God
all things are possible.

" I must confess, God was so good to me in that night in
which my husband died, to move the hearts of his father and
mother for to pity me, and indeed at that time I was a sad
object to move pity in the hardest hearts. But the next
day, when his parents did understand he had made his will
and left me full [blank in the manuscript], and had left all
his estate unto me, they did foam and rage both against me
and him, so that I think the like was never seen. His father
came to my bedside the very next day after his son, his only
son, died, and told me I should not have one penny more
than the extremity of the law would give me, but God turned
his cruelty into good for me. For if it had not been for
his hard usage, I think I should have sunk under my sharp
affliction and unspeakable loss. God can bring good out of
evil, so he did for me, for by that means I was forced out

of my bed and chamber. The first time I went out of my chamber was to ask counsel of some lawyers. My cause was so just, that my father-in-law's own lawyers gave their judgment for me, but my father would be ruled by none.

"My husband died a Member of Parliament and one of the Council of State ; he was so good a man, that all who knew him did show love and pity to me for his sake. Some of the chief members of the Parliament House, knowing what a hard-hearted man my father-in-law was, sent to me, and told me if need were, there should come forty or fifty of their fellow-members to speak with him, and to tell him that they would take care of me, so that he should not wrong me, for they said the memory of my dear husband was very precious unto them. I returned them very many thanks, and told them I hoped God would order all things for my good in the end, for I could not endure to go to law with my dear husband's father, notwithstanding his hard usage of me. At last he was persuaded to make an end, and I did compound for a sum of money for quietness' sake. I thought it was a good thing to have peace with all men, and I was so sad for my loss."

A great way further on the lady writes : "I had very many matches offered me, but I could not bring my heart to like any, so that out of very many offers which were persons both rich and honourable, I could not fix my heart upon any one. I would often wish to go to the grave to my dead husband, rather than to be married to the best husband in the world, and when I did not know what to do nor how to be quiet, then I was in great straits. My own father was dead many years before, and my mother was then in Holland, and had been there for many years, so that she was altogether a stranger to those gentlemen, who were well-wished to me, which made her incapable of giving me her advice. Besides, I had very few other friends to advise with, so that I was in a great strait, some telling me I did sin if I did not marry, because I should decay my natural life with my overmuch sorrow, and whom to chuse I knew not, for all were alike to me. At last I went to God by prayer, and did lay my condition before the Lord, and did beg of Him, that if it were His good pleasure to have me alter my condition, that He would chuse out a fitting match for me, as for my own part I did slight riches and honors.

"When I was in this sweet frame of spirit, amongst many others, there came a grave gentleman, that had ten children, which at the first motion did startle me, and did cause all my friends to be against it. But after I had spent very much time in seeking God to direct me, at last I was brought to consider that children were a blessing—'happy is the man that hath his quiver full of them, they shall not be ashamed, but they shall speak with the enemies in the gate.' And seeing they were a blessing and the gift of God, as you may see in Psalm 128, the 3rd and 4th verses, there the Lord saith, 'Thy wife shall be as a fruitful vine by the sides of thine house, thy children like olive plants round about thy table, behold, thus shall the man be blessed that feareth the Lord,'—so that I durst not refuse a man for having ten blessings. Nay, though he told me, he would settle all his estate upon his other children, I durst not refuse him for that neither, for I knew if God would give me any children, that he was able to provide for them. And in marrying him, I thought I might be in a capacity to do some good amongst those children. It is true he was at that time in a very honorable place of trust in the nation, being one of the Lords Commissioners of the Great Seal, but his great office was no motive to move me, for I had before refused both riches and very great honors. But I did consider he was in a place, wherein he might do much good to the people of God, and I thought by marrying of him, I might be an instrument in God's hand to move him to do more for God, and for the good of his people. As for estate, I did not need to stand upon that, for I knew that if God should give me any children by him, I should bring something for to maintain them, and

if God should not give me any, I had rather he, that was to
be my husband, and his children should enjoy my estate,
than any other.   If ever a marriage was a fruit of prayer, I
think ours was, for I found that after I had laid my condition
before God, and did beg of Him to chuse such a man that
might be for His honor and glory and my good, then I went
away from the house I then did live in, to a friend's house
forty miles from my own house, to see if I could be quiet
from all such motions.   But God sent him that should be my
husband quickly after me, though at that time I had no
mind to marry him, yet I was willing to do or to suffer
anything whatever was the will of God to have me to do.   I
must needs say all that knew the gentleman did give a very
good report of him for a very honest, gallant, gentle man.
When all my friends did see I would have him for my husband,
they were much discontented, thinking thereby I should lose
much of earthly contentment, but those who wait upon God,
they shall not wait in vain.   Nay, He hath proclaimed himself
to be a God hearing prayers, and He has commanded us to
pray unto *Him*.

" And God did hear my prayers, and did bless our marriage,
for he did give me a great mercy in my husband, and God
did bless me and gave me strength to conceive with child in
a very short time after our marriage.

" And I did beg of God very much in the time I was so long
without any child, that if ever he would give me a child, He
would be pleased to make it His child, and I did promise to
God, that if ever He should give me a child, I would do what
lay in my power to bring him up in the fear of the Lord,
and to dedicate him to His service.   So God at last, after
sixteen years waiting and praying, did give me hope of a
child, and did wonderfully preserve the child in my womb,
for when I was young with child, I had a very great and
dangerous fall from off my horse, so that all who were then
present did think my life was in danger.   I was so very ill with
the bruise I got in my fall, that none could think I should

escape miscarrying, but what God will have saved, nothing can hurt or destroy. This I set down, that you, my dear son, may see what God did for you before you were born, so that it may be the stronger engagement upon your heart to love and serve that God, who did keep you from harm even in your mother's womb.

"And I called your name Samuel, because I had begged you of the Lord. The Lord make you a true Samuel indeed, and I have great hopes that the Lord will make you so."

So far for the present. The date and place of the marriage are unfortunately not given, but time, the revealer of secrets, may disclose it yet. I cannot say whether it was shortly before or shortly after his celebrated speech in the House, to further the passing of an Act "for putting all the books of law, the process and proceedings in courts of justice into the English tongue," a measure he happily carried by appealing not to common sense, not to right reason, but to precedent in times of yore and to the example of Moses, whom Whitelocke, in common with every other Englishman of that period, scholars included, supposed to have originally indited his laws in the vernacular language, as preserved in what is called the "Hebrew" Bible. The fact of what we now possess as the Hebrew Bible being itself a translation and partly a compilation from an older and consequently still more sacred tongue, the letters of which are preserved to us at least, was not suspected by any, for if it had, this glorious measure might still have been defeated. The speech that he delivered in vindication of the novel course, then first proposed in this country, will be found by any one that refers to the "Memorials" to occupy no less than eleven columns in folio. Here it would be a grievous infliction upon the modern reader to transcribe its voluminous contents, and I shall best consult his patience by confining myself to a few extracts.

Speaking of William the Conqueror, whom he is very unwilling to admit either as conqueror or introducer of Norman laws, he says, what indeed we all know, that this

monarch claimed to be king, as successor and adopted heir
of Edward the Confessor by his will ; in additional proof of
which, not relying solely on historical authorities, such as
Volaterus or others, not forgetting the consecrated banner
sent to William before his expedition by Pope Alexander II.,
he quotes the ancient deeds of Westminster Abbey, that had
been sometimes in his own custody.   In his first charter to
the monks, King William sets forth his own title to the
Crown thus : " Beneficio concessionis et cognati mei gloriosi
regis Edwardi," by the benefit of the grant from the glorious
King Edward, my kinsman.   This seeming proof he bolsters
up by citing from a second charter, in the 15th year of that
king's reign, and yet another, dated 1088, for bestowing
privileges on the Abbey of St. Martin's the Great.   And in
support of his theory, that the laws of England were derived
from Saxon legislation, he contends, in opposition to Matthew
Paris, that a kingdom in the days of the Confessor might be
transferred by will, with or without the consent of the
Barons.   But what do these imaginary proofs, based on
mere words in Latin documents, that high policy may have
dictated, or that the monks may have antedated, avail in
contradistinction to the glaring facts that French was introduced by Normans into the country, that the Grand Cus-
tomary was written in that language, that the Saxon tongue
was superseded at Court, that Saxon proprietors were deprived by force of their possessions, that the people had
been conquered in battle by invaders and reduced to serfdom,
that feudal tenures were established ?   To argue about the
testamentary validity of a king's title is a mere waste of time,
when we find that king acting like a conqueror, and reaping
the fruits of conquest.   And really it is of little consequence
whether Norman laws were grafted on a Saxon stock, or
introduced tree and all from France in the first instance.
The fruit was the same in either case.

His linguistic speculations respecting the affinity between
High Dutch and French may have served the occasion, and

conduced in part to the success of his cause, but are utterly valueless now ; so likewise his exaggerated views, derived from the circumstance that English was much used at Bordeaux, and in other parts of France where Englishmen were resident and conversant. But the following observations may still, I think, be read with interest :

" And though Duke William, or any other of our kings before and after his time, did bring in the French tongue amongst us, yet that is no argument that he or they did change or introduce our laws, which undoubtedly were here long before those times. And some of them, when the French tongue was so much in use here, were translated, written, pleaded and recorded in the French tongue, yet remained the same laws still.

" And from that great use of the French tongue here, it was, that the reporters of our law cases and judgments, which were in those times, did write their reports in French, the pure French of that time, though mixed with some words of art.

" Those terms of art were taken, many of them, from the Saxon tongue, as may be seen by those yet used.* The reporters of later times, and our students to this day, use to take their notes in French, following the old reports which they had studied, and the old French, which, as in other languages, by time came to be varied.

" I shall not deny, that some monks in elder times, that some clerks and officers might have a cunning, for their private honour and profit, to keep up a mystery, to have as much as they could of our laws to be in a kind of mystery to the vulgar, to be the less understood by them."

Having made this last and most important admission, which every student in history would do well to ponder on, and make applicable to all countries that profess to have a primitive history, how Whitelocke could place such

---

* Wamba in " Ivanhoe " first explains properly to Gurth how certain terms came to be retained.

reliance on the credibility and authority of our monkish historians is, I confess, to me incomprehensible. Many may regret the views he adopted. His professional education blinded him, and the only opportunity this country has ever possessed of totally eradicating Norman law, or Saxon law, if the reader pleases, by the substitution of new organic laws, based on man's natural rights as a free-born organization from the hands of God, was totally lost. Time will never, I am afraid, repeat the opportunity, and if conferred by revolution once more, it may rather be deprecated than desired. Some remedies are more dangerous than the diseases, for which they are represented to be the specifics. He found he had made an oversight by his frank admission, and extricates himself as follows :

"But the counsellors at law and judges can have no advantage by it. And perhaps it would be found, that the law being in English, and generally more understood, yet not sufficiently, would occasion the more suits."

But let us hasten to the true purport of his discourse :

"As to the debate and matter of the act now before you, I have delivered no opinion against it, nor do I think it reasonable, that the generality of the people of England should, by an implicit faith, depend upon the knowledge of others in that which concerns them most of all.

"It was the Romish policy [he might have said English with equal truth] to keep them in ignorance of matters pertaining to the health of their souls ; let them not be in ignorance of matters pertaining to their bodies, estates, and all their worldly comfort.*

"It is not unreasonable that the law should be in that language which may best be understood by those whose lives and fortunes are subject to it, and are to be governed by it."

Then glancing around, we will suppose by the context,

---

* An irresistible appeal, one would have imagined ; but Clarendon thought differently when he came to power, and the language of mystery was restored, a language still retained by the physicians alone.

and reading in the faces of the listeners, that some still stronger appeal was requisite, that the claims of humanity were not omnipotent in that assembly where sentence of death had been frequent of late, and mercy obtained by fines and compositions, he clinches the nail by the only arguments likely to overwhelm opposition.

" Moses read all the law openly before the people in their mother-tongue ; God directed him to write it, and to expound it to the people in their own native language,—that what concerned their lives, liberties, and estates, might be made known unto them in the most perspicuous way.

" The laws of the Eastern nations were in their proper tongue.

" The laws at Constantinople were in Greek, at Rome in Latin ; in France, Spain, Germany, Sweden, Denmark, and other nations, their laws are published in their native idiom.

" For your own country, there is no man that can read the Saxon character but may find the laws of your ancestors yet extant in the English tongue.

" Duke William himself commanded the laws to be proclaimed in English, that none might pretend ignorance of them.

" It was the judgment of the Parliament in the 36th year of Edward III. that pleadings should be in English. In the reigns of those kings, when our statutes were enrolled in French and English, the sheriffs in their several counties had yet to proclaim them in English.

" I shall conclude with a complaint of what I have met with abroad from some military persons, nothing but scoffs and invectives against our law, and threats to take it away. But the law is above the reach of those weapons, which at one time or another will return upon those that use them."

If he is here at all alluding to France, the prediction was verified at the end of a century and a half.

" Nor is it ingenious or prudent for Englishmen to deprave their birthright, the laws of their own country."

An exclamatory comment, which modern patriots now trust will never more find credence or respect. When laws are bad—so people now begin to argue out of doors—the sooner they are changed the better, rather than retain them by that implicit faith which the orator had himself condemned only a few instants before. The struggle between scepticism and the traditions of the Temple must excuse those outbursts. It is hard to despise what we have been taught in early youth to venerate and believe.   ·

It was one of the most triumphant speeches on record, quite as much so as a money bill before the days of Joseph Hume. On the question being put, it was unanimously carried that the Act should pass for turning the law-books, the process, and the proceedings in courts of justice into English, and they were done into English accordingly. The principle was one of the greatest boons ever conferred on a long-suffering and law-ridden people. The heaviest and most galling yoke of our bondage was removed for a brief season, and the new-born gift, being once tested, compelled the final and irrevocable abolition of one foreign language in a happier age, when the dynasty of the Stuarts had long ceased to blight by their presence the buds and blossoms of regenerated independence.

The retention of the other language in such phrases as "Le Roi le veult," "Le Roi veult que la justice soit faite," has yet to be explained. From no mere attachment to old forms, we may feel well assured, do these words still jar on our ears, but rather from the esoteric hope, that where forms and ceremonies remain, the substantial reality may at some future date be either restored or introduced. It is for this reason, too, peradventure, that successive administrations are loath to expunge old statutes, and prefer seeing them sink into the arms of sleep to those of death. The old law of England, it may with some truth be said, is not dead but

sleepeth.   Will my readers laugh me to scorn for this assertion ?   Do they forget the revivification in recent times, and
on more than one occasion, by magistrates and others ?

It was many months after the above speech was delivered,
on the 4th of September, 1651, that our Cromwellian forefathers gained the battle of Worcester, in which they used
the same "word" as at Dunbar exactly a twelvemonth
before, the "Lord of Hosts."   On the 9th the Parliament
appointed four of their members, one of whom was Whitelocke, to go out of town and meet Cromwell on his way
from Worcester to London, and to congratulate him on the
great successes that God had given him.   The four members
reached Aylesbury on the following day, and on the 11th
were able to perform their mission.   The General received
them with all kindness and respect, and after a bout at
hawking, they all reached the town just named in time for
supper.   Cromwell conversed with the Lord Chief Justice
St. John more than with the others, and the favour seems to
have engendered a shade of jealousy or envy or suspicion
in Whitelocke's breast, for otherwise he would scarcely
have deemed it worth while recording.   The General gave
to each of the party a horse and two "Scots" prisoners,
as a token of respect; and the nag which fell to Whitelocke's
share was a very handsome and gallant specimen of Sir
John Fenwick's breed.   One of his Scots seemed to be a
gentleman of good quality, and he was of very good parts.
"I freely gave him his liberty, and to the other likewise,
with their passes to go to their own homes in Scotland," but
he omits to state whether his example was followed by the
other three members.   He at least had no wish or intention
to deal in man-flesh, to send them off to foreign plantations
and slavery for life.

On the 27th of the same month the Parliament ordered a
bill to be brought in for eventually defining the term of their
own existence, and for constituting a "New Representative."
They were now in a new path and the right one, could they

only have kept to it. It was their going astray that led to their expulsion, and to the indelible disgrace that has ever since clung to the "Bauble."

Nor was this Cromwell's sole, although best, excuse, since strong petitions had been presented to him, and they show that the House, in proposing its own dissolution, was not altogether impelled by the consciousness of its propriety, but necessity as well. The time they chose for their exit was the 3rd day of November, 1654, thus granting to themselves a fresh lease of life, a respite of three mortal years. Human nature could not endure the infliction, so that this new delay, coupled with the weariness that the nation at large, and not merely Cromwell with his army, had long feverishly endured, provoked the explosion of the tempest, of which we may see the first gathering clouds in the scene reproduced below. It took place at the Speaker's house upon the 10th of December, leaving an interval during which Cromwell had had ample time for meditation and preparation.

SPEAKER.—"My Lord, this company was very ready to attend your Excellency, and the business you are pleased to propound to us is very necessary to be considered. God has given marvellous success to our forces under your command, and if we do not improve these mercies to some settlement, such as may be to God's honour and the good of this commonwealth, we shall be very much blameworthy.

HARRISON.—I think that which my Lord General has propounded is to advise, as to a settlement both of our civil and spiritual liberties, and so that the mercies which the Lord has given in to us, may not be cast away. How this may be done is the great question.

WHITELOCKE.—It is a great question indeed, and not suddenly to be resolved, yet it were pity that a meeting of so many able and worthy persons as I see here should be fruitless. I should humbly offer in the first place, whether it be not requisite to be understood in what way this settlement is desired, whether of an absolute republic or with any mixture of monarchy.

CROMWELL.—My Lord Commissioner Whitelocke has put us upon the right point, and indeed it is my meaning that we should consider whether a republic ·or a mixed monarchical government will be best to be settled, and if anything monarchical, then in whom that power shall be placed.

SIR T. WIDDRINGTON.—I think a mixed monarchical government will be most suitable to the laws and people of this nation, and if any monarchical, I suppose we shall hold it most just to place that power in one of the sons of the late king.

FLEETWOOD.—I think that the question, whether an absolute government or a mixed monarchy be best to be settled in this nation, will not be very easy to be determined.

ST. JOHN.—It will be found that the government of this nation, without something of monarchical power, will be very difficult to be so settled, as not to shake the foundation of our laws and the liberties of the people [it is a Chief Justice that is speaking].

SPEAKER [Another lawyer].—It will breed a strange confusion to settle a government of this nation without something of monarchy.

DESBOROUGH [An officer in the army like Fleetwood].— I beseech you, my Lord, why may not this as well as other nations be governed in the way of a republic ?

WHITELOCKE [coming to the Speaker's rescue].—The laws of England are so interwoven with the power and practice of monarchy, that to settle a government without something of monarchy in it, would make so great an alteration in the proceedings of our law, that you have scarce time to rectify, nor can we well foresee the inconveniences which will arise thereby.

WHALEY [An officer].—I do not well understand matters of law, but it seems to me the best way not to have anything

of monarchical power in the settlement of our government ;
and if we should resolve upon any, whom have we to pitch
upon ?   The King's eldest son has been in arms against us,
and his second son likewise is our enemy.

WIDDRINGTON.—But the late king's third son, the Duke of
Gloucester, is still amongst us, and too young to have been
in arms against us, or to be infected with the principles of
our enemies.

WHITELOCKE.—There may be a day given for the king's
eldest son, or for the Duke of York, his brother, to come
in to the Parliament, and upon such terms as shall be thought
fit and agreeable both to our civil and spiritual liberties, a
settlement may be made with them.

CROMWELL.—That will be a business of more than ordinary
difficulty, but really, I think if it may be done with safety
and preservation of our rights, both as Englishmen and
Christians, that a settlement of somewhat with monarchical
power in it would be very effectual."

Many other points were mooted at this small meeting, but
no record of them preserved.   The lawyers supported
monarchical views, and the soldiers were generally opposed
to them.   Whitelocke perceived by the result, that Cromwell
had been sounding the inclinations of the several speakers,
and his sagacity must have led him to divine that the
victorious man of the sword had some project in his mind,
but whether matured or not, surpassed the powers of his
penetration at that time.   He could hardly suppose Cromwell would ever consent to a restoration of the Royal family,
to the placing upon the throne of a son, whose father he had
decapitated.   The effect it produced, on him, the civilian,
was that of "increased watchfulness," and Cromwell's extraordinary patience in this posture of affairs is best shown by
the fact that another year rolled on without dispelling his
reserve.   Whitelocke spent this period in doing as much
good as his powers enabled him, and has preserved one
grateful letter from Sir William Davenant, for whom he had

granted the liberty of the Tower. On the 7th of November, he wrote down in his journal : "The business of the Chancery was full of trouble this Michaelmas term, and no man's cause came to a determination how just soever, without the clamour of the party against whom judgment was given ; they being stark blind in their own causes, and resolved not to be convinced by reason or law." The reader will mark the distinction caused by the use of the little " or ;" but as it happened to be a fair evening, after one of these unsatisfactory scenes in court, he took a walk in St. James's Park to refresh and invigorate himself with pure air and exercise. Here Cromwell met him, saluted him with more than usual courtesy, and begged him to walk aside with him, that they might have a little private discourse together, which he himself began :

CROMWELL.—" My Lord Whitelocke, I know your faithfulness and engagement in the same good cause with myself and the rest of our friends. I know your ability in judgment, and your particular friendship and affection for me.*

WHITELOCKE.—Your Excellency has known me long, and I think will say, that you never knew any unfaithfulness or breach of trust by me, and for my particular affection to your person, your favours to me, and your public services have deserved more than I can manifest. Only there is (with your favour) a mistake in this one thing, touching my weak judgment, which is incapable of doing any considerable service to yourself or this commonwealth. Yet to the utmost of my power I shall be ready to serve you, and that with all diligence and faithfulness.

CROMWELL.—I have cause to be, and am without the least scruple of your faithfulness, and I know your kindness to me your old friend, your abilities to serve the commonwealth. There are enough besides me that can testify it. I believe

---

* Cromwell was here alluding to the long-standing friendship between Whitelocke's father, the judge, and the family of Williams, of which Cromwell was one, quite as much as to any recent proof of friendship. He took the friendship to be a thing of course.

our engagements for this commonwealth have been and are as deep as most men's, and there never was more need of advice, of solid hearty counsel, than the present state of our affairs doth require.

WHITELOCKE.—I suppose no man will mention his particular engagement in this cause, at the same time when your Excellency's engagement is remembered ; yet to my capacity, and in my station, few men have engaged further than I have done, and that (besides the goodness of your own nature and personal knowledge of me) will keep you from any jealousy of my faithfulness.

CROMWELL.—I wish there were no more ground for suspicion of others, than of you ; I can trust you with my life, and the most secret matters relating to our business. To that end I have now desired a little private discourse with you, and really, my Lord, there is very great cause for us to consider the dangerous condition we are all in, and how to make good our station, to improve the mercies and successes which God has given us, and not to be fooled out of them again, nor to be broken in pieces by our particular jarrings and animosities one against another, but to unite our councils, our hands and hearts, to make good what we have so dearly bought, with so much hazard, blood and treasure, and that the Lord, having given us an entire conquest over our enemies, we should not now hazard all again by our private janglings, and bring those mischiefs upon ourselves, which our enemies could never do.

WHITELOCKE.—My Lord, I look upon our present danger as greater than ever it was in the field, and as your Excellency truly observes our proneness to destroy ourselves, when our enemies could not do it. It is no strange thing for a gallant army, as yours is, after full conquest of their enemies, to grow into factious and ambitious designs, and it is a wonder to me, that they are not in high mutinies, their spirits being active, and few thinking their services to be duly rewarded, and the emulation of the officers breaking out more and more, in this time of their vacancy from their employment. Besides, the private soldiers, it may be feared, will in this time of their idleness grow into disorder, and it is your excellent conduct which, under God, has kept them so long in discipline and free from mutinies.

CROMWELL.—I have used and shall use the utmost of my poor endeavours to keep them all in order and obedience.

WHITELOCKE.—Your Excellency has done it hitherto even to admiration.

CROMWELL.—Truly God has blessed me in it exceedingly, and I hope will do so still.

Your Lordship has observed most truly the inclinations of the officers of the army to particular factions, and to murmurings, that they are not rewarded according to their deserts, that others who have adventured least have gained most, and they have neither profit, nor preferment, nor place in government, which others hold, who have undergone no hardships nor hazards for the commonwealth. And herein they have too much of truth, yet their insolence is very great, and their influence upon the private soldiers works them to the like discontents and murmurings.

Then as for the members of parliament, the army begins to have a strange distaste against them, and I wish there were not too much cause for it. Really, their pride, ambition, and self-seeking, engrossing all places of honour and profit to themselves or their friends, and their daily breaking forth into new and violent parties and factions—their delays of business, their design to perpetuate themselves and continue the power in their own hands, their meddling in private matters between party and party, contrary to the institution of Parliament—their injustice and partiality in those matters ; the scandalous lives of some of the chief of them— these things, my Lord, do give too much ground for people to open their mouths against them, and to dislike them.

Nor can they be kept within the bounds of justice, and law or reason, they themselves being the supreme power of the nation, liable to no account to any, nor to be controlled or regulated by any other power, there being none superior or co-ordinate with them. So that unless there be some authority and power so full and so high, as to restrain and keep things in better order, that may be a check to these exorbitances, it will be impossible in human reason to prevent our ruin.

WHITELOCKE.—I confess the danger we are in by these extravagances and inordinate powers is more than, I doubt, is generally apprehended. Yet as to that part of it which concerns the soldiery, your Excellency's power and commission are sufficient already to restrain and keep them in their due obedience. Blessed be God, you have done it hitherto, and I doubt not but by your wisdom you will be able still to do it. As to the members of parliament, I confess the greatest difficulty lies there, your commission being from them, and they being acknowledged the supreme power of the nation, subject to no controls, nor allowing any appeal from them. Yet I am sure your Excellency will not look upon them as generally depraved. Too many of them are much to blame in those things you have mentioned, and many unfit things have passed among them, but I hope well of the major part of them, when great matters come to a decision.

CROMWELL.—My Lord, there is little hope of a good settlement to be made by them, really there is not, but a great deal of fear, that they will destroy again what the Lord has done graciously for them and us. We all forget God, and God will forget us, and give us up to confusion. These men will help it on, if they be suffered to proceed in their ways ; some course must be thought on to curb and restrain them, or we shall be ruined by them.

WHITELOCKE.—We ourselves have acknowledged them the supreme power, have taken our commissions and authority in the highest concernments from them, and now to restrain and curb them after this, it will be hard to find out a way.

CROMWELL.—What, if a man should take upon him to be king ?

WHITELOCKE.—I think that remedy would be worse than the disease.

CROMWELL.—Why do you think so ?

WHITELOCKE.—As to your own person the title of king would be of no advantage, because you have the full kingly power in you already, concerning the militia, as you are General. As to the nomination of civil officers, those whom you think fittest are seldom refused, and although you have no negative vote in the passing of laws, yet what you dislike will not easily be carried ; the taxes are already settled, and in your power to dispose of the money raised. And as to foreign affairs, though the ceremonial application be made to the Parliament, yet the expectation of good or bad success in it is from your Excellency, and particular solicitations of foreign ministers are made to you only. So that I apprehend indeed less envy, danger and pomp, but not less power and real opportunities of doing good in your being General, than would be if you had assumed the title of king.

CROMWELL.—I have heard some of your profession observe, that he who is actually king, whether by election or descent, yet being once king, all acts done by him as king are lawful and justifiable as by any king who has the crown by inheritance from his forefathers, and that by an act of parliament in Henry the Seventh's time, it is safer for those who act under a king, be his title what it will, than for those who act under any other power. And surely the power of a king is so great and high, so universally understood and reverenced by this nation, that the title of it might not only indemnify in a great measure those that act under it, but likewise be of great use and advantage in such times as these, to curb the insolences and extravagances of those, whom the present powers cannot control, or at least are the persons themselves who are thus insolent.

WHITELOCKE.—I agree in the general with what you are

pleased to observe as to this title of king, but whether for your Excellency to take this title upon you, as things now are, will be for the good and advantage of yourself and friends, or of the commonwealth, I do very much doubt, notwithstanding that act of parliament in the 11th year of Henry the Seventh, which will be little regarded or observed to us by our enemies, if they should come to get the upper hand of us.

CROMWELL.—What do you apprehend would be the danger of taking this title?

WHITELOCKE.—The danger, I think, would be this: one of the main points of controversy betwixt us and our adversaries is whether the government of this nation shall be established in monarchy, or in a free state and commonwealth. Most of our friends have engaged with us upon the hopes of having the government settled in a free state. And to effect that, they have undergone all their hazards and difficulties, they being persuaded, though I think most mistakenly, that under the government of a commonwealth they shall enjoy more liberty and right, both as to their spiritual and civil concernments, than they shall under monarchy, the pressures and dislike whereof are so fresh in their memories and sufferings. Now if your Excellency shall take upon you the title of king, this state of our cause will be thereby wholly determined, and monarchy established in your person; the question will be no more whether our government shall be by a monarch or by a free state, but whether Cromwell or Stuart shall be our king and monarch. And that question, whereinbefore such great parties of the nation were engaged, and which was universal, will by this means become in effect a private controversy only. Before it was national, what kind of government we should have; now it will become particular, who shall be our governor, whether of the family of the Stuarts or of the family of the Cromwells. Thus the state of our controversy being totally changed, all those who were for a commonwealth—and they are a very great and considerable party—having their hopes therein frustrated, will desert you, your hands will be weakened, your interest straitened, and your cause in apparent danger of being ruined.

CROMWELL.—I confess you speak reason in this, but what other thing can you propound, that may obviate the present dangers and difficulties, wherein we are all engaged ?

WHITELOCKE.—It will be the greatest difficulty to find out such an expedient ; I have had many things in my private thoughts upon this business, some of which, perhaps, are not fit or safe for me to communicate.

CROMWELL. —I pray, my Lord, what are they ? You may trust me with them. There shall no prejudice come to you by any private discourse betwixt us. I shall never betray my friend ; you may be as free with me as with your own heart, and shall never suffer by it.

WHITELOCKE.—I make no scruple to put my life and fortune in your Excellency's hand, and so I shall, if I impart these fancies to you, which are weak and perhaps may prove offensive to your Excellency,—therefore my best way will be to smother them.

CROMWELL.—Now, I prithee, my Lord Whitelocke, let me know them, be they what they will ; they cannot be offensive to me, but I shall take it kindly from you. Therefore, I pray, do not conceal those thoughts of yours from your faithful friend.

WHITELOCKE.—Your Excellency honours me with a title far above me, and since you are pleased to command it, I shall discover to you my thoughts herein, and humbly desire you not to take in ill part what I shall say to you.

CROMWELL.—Indeed I shall not, but I shall take it, as I said, very kindly from you.

WHITELOCKE.—Give me leave, then, first to consider your Excellency's condition. You are environed with secret enemies. Upon your subduing of the public enemy, the

officers of your army account themselves all victors, and to
have had an equal share in the conquest with you.   The
success, which God has given us, has not a little elated their
minds.   Many of them are busy and of turbulent spirits,
and are not without their designs how they may dismount
your Excellency, and some of themselves get up into the
saddle,—how they may bring you down and set up themselves.   They want not counsel and encouragement herein,
it may be from some members of the Parliament, who may
be jealous of your power and greatness, lest you should
grow too high for them, and in time overmaster them.   They
will plot to bring you down first, and clip your wings.

CROMWELL.—I thank you, that you so fully consider my
condition.   It is a testimony of your love to me and care of
me, and you have rightly considered it.   I may say, without
vanity, that in my condition yours is involved and all our
friends', and those that plot my ruin will hardly bear your
continuance in any condition worthy of you.   Besides this,
the cause itself may possibly receive some disadvantage by
the strugglings and contentions amongst ourselves.   But
what, Sir, are your thoughts for the prevention of those mischiefs, that hang over our heads ?

WHITELOCKE.—Pardon me, Sir, in the next place, a little
to consider the condition of the King of Scots.   This prince
being now by your valour, and the success which God has
given you to the Parliament and to the army under your
command, reduced to a very low condition, both he and all
about him cannot but be very inclinable to hearken to any
terms, whereby their lost hopes may be revived of his being
restored to the crown, and they to their fortunes and native
country.   By a private treaty with him you may secure
yourself and your friends and their fortunes, you may make
yourself and your posterity as great and permanent, to all
human probability, as ever any subject was, and provide for
your friends.   You may put such limits to monarchical
power, as will secure our spiritual and civil liberties, you may

secure the cause in which we are all engaged, and this may
be effectually done, by having the power of the militia
continued in yourself, and whom you shall agree upon after
you.   I propound, therefore, for your Excellency to send
to the King of Scots, and to have a private treaty with him
for this purpose, and I beseech you to pardon what I have
said on the occasion.   It is out of my service and affection to
your Excellency, and to all honest men.   And I humbly pray
you not to have any jealousy thereupon of my approved
faithfulness to your Excellency and to this Commonwealth.

CROMWELL.— I have not, I assure you, the least distrust
of your faithfulness and friendship to me and to the cause of
this Commonwealth.   I think you have much reason for
what you propound, but it is a matter of such high importance and difficulty, that it deserves more consideration and
debate, than is at present allowed us.   We shall therefore
take a further time to discourse of it."

Here the General broke off, joined other company and
proceeded to Whitehall.   He seemed displeased at what he
had just heard by his countenance and carriage, but never
objected to it on any subsequent occasion, when they met.
His manner changed, however, from that hour, his great
intimacy grew cool for a time, and he no longer consulted
his legal friend so frequently.   His daughter Claypole confessed at a later period, that her father had been studious of
an opportunity to send him out of the way on some honourable employment, that Whitelocke might be no impediment
to his ambitious designs, and for this purpose the embassy to
Sweden was contrived. Whitelocke retired to Fawley Court as
soon as the Chancery business was over, by which his mind had
been excessively fatigued, and on his return to town, increased
the temporary estrangement by urging Cromwell not to do
any thing ungrateful or ungenerous in the way of putting a
period to the existence of the Parliament.   It might be, as
indeed it was, a duty on his part to tender this advice, but
he must have known in his own secret thoughts, that the

present state of things neither could nor ought to continue. When once implacable dissensions break out and mutual intolerance gains the upper hand, the fear of the sword can alone cement such disorderly elements of civil society. The evidence of history was there to admonish him, and what we have witnessed in succeeding ages has been but a confirmation of a truth known long before, not only in the modern but in the ancient world.

On the 20th of April—Whitelocke and Widdrington attended a meeting at Cromwell's lodgings in Whitehall, the sole business of which was to discuss the expediency of dissolving the House. Many members besides themselves were present, and in the course of the debate he and his companion opposed the almost general opinion, that the time was come for preventing all prolongation of power by its present holders. The meeting broke up late, but on the following morning Whitelocke and the other returned by appointment to a second meeting, by no means so numerous as the first, at which Colonel Ingoldsby was present. The point was raised, whether forty persons, or about that number of old members and officers should be nominated by the Parliament and authorised to manage the affairs of the Commonwealth, till a new House should meet, and so the present parliament to be dissolved forthwith.

It must have been clear to every one there that the crisis had come, that it could not be postponed,—matters had gone too far for that,—that the nominally existing House of Commons was virtually dead, but still Whitelocke and his faithful Achates opposed this proposal. He feared lest he himself should be one of the forty, who he thought would soon fall into a desperate condition after the dissolution, but others were very desirous of seeing such a council created and of forming a part of it. Whitelocke was perfectly right in his apprehensions ; such a council was meant merely as a blind, to be a stepping-stone, a bridge for facilitating the General's ascent to sole and sovereign command, and he wisely, as far as his own fame was concerned, refused to play the puppet. It was during their conference that Cromwell had news brought to him, how the House was still sitting without coming to any resolution for dissolving themselves,—the step they ought to have taken from motives of self-respect,—and on receiving a further report from Ingoldsby, that the members were actually engaged on questions necessitating more sittings, he went furiously to the House with a party of soldiers, led in a file of musketeers, and did what possibly in cooler moments and on maturer reflection he may have deeply repented of. But he was hurried on by that passion, to which he was constitutionally prone, even on the eve of battle, and the past could not be recalled. Men of violent action are sure to drift at last into the vortex of their own passions, and while seeming to the vulgar eye to be themselves creating new phases of events, are in reality but obeying superior impulses, themselves the creatures of circumstances, prepared by the one sole ruling mind, the only mind that grasps the whole and regulates the world.

The "fool's bauble," as he termed it, the mace, was taken away, that symbol of club law, derived perhaps from our Saxon ancestry, the savage and coarse form of the more refined sceptre, but now insulted by the same strong hand that had lopped the latter asunder. Into Whitelocke's moral reflections it is needless here to enter, beyond expressing our assent to its closing observation, "how God makes use of strange and unexpected means to bring his purposes to pass."

Whitelocke was not one of the 120 persons summoned by Cromwell to take upon them the supreme authority, and hold it till the 3rd of November, 1654. The new council called itself a Parliament on the 6th of July, 1653, and strange to say, the old Serjeant-at-Arms, Birkhead, attended it with the mace as usual, and not one member perceived the silent irony of its presence.

On the 23rd of the next month they passed an Act touching marriages and the registration of them, as well as of

births and burials, but the new law could not, it is to be
hoped, affect Whitelocke, already married about two years.
He was apparently also no longer a Commissioner of the Seal,
for the little Parliament had voted, on the 5th, that the Court
of Chancery should be taken away, and that means should
be devised for future relief in equity.   Thus released from
labour and divested of power, the company that used to call
and pay their court to him completely absented themselves
for nearly a whole month, when hearing that Cromwell had
sent him, on the Lord's day,* a letter, appointing him ambassador—the news of which was probably divulged on coming
out of church—they all flocked back, and tenderly inquired
about the health of his family and himself.   It is astonishing
how soon a levee or a succession of visits is improvised by a
little news of this description !   The man, about whom they
were now so solicitous, was doomed to be again deserted, but
the lesson of adversity had been taught already, and what
dependence he had to place on those that flattered.

On the following day he waited on Cromwell, when the
following conversation ensued :—

WHITELOCKE.—" My Lord, I received your excellent letter
but yesterday, and am now come to wait upon you to return
my humble thanks for the great honour done me, in being
judged worthy of so high a trust.   But I beg your Excellency's consideration of my want of abilities, both of body
and mind, for this service, and of the season of the year.
Besides there are some things relating to my private family,
with which I have acquainted Sir Gilbert Pickering, which
are of no small concernment to me.

PICKERING.—That is, my Lord, his lady is near her time
of being brought to bed.

WHITELOCKE.—My Lord, I am very free to serve the Commonwealth in anything within my capacity, and hope they
will not expect from me, what will be of such great prejudice
to me and my family, as this employment now would be.

* This letter was dated September 2, 1653, but not received till the 4th.

CROMWELL.—I am very sorry that the letter came no sooner to you.

PICKERING.—I confess, it was my fault.

CROMWELL.—Sir Gilbert Pickering would needs write a very fine letter, and when he had done, did not like it himself. I then took pen and ink, and straightway wrote that letter to you. The business is of exceeding great importance to the Commonwealth, as any can be,—that it is. And there is no prince nor state in Christendom, with whom there is any probability for us to have a friendship, but only the Queen of Sweden. She has sent several times to us, but we have returned no embassy to her, only a letter by a young gentleman. She expects an ambassador from us, and if we should not send a man of eminence to her, she would think herself slighted by us, and she is a lady of great honour, who stands much upon ceremonies.

WHITELOCKE.—The business being of such great concernment, as indeed it is, there is the more need of a person qualified with abilities for so great a charge, which I have not, as your Excellency and all that know me will conclude ; and I know best my own defects. I want experience in foreign affairs and matters of State, in language and ceremony, of which the Queen is so great a judge, and a lady that will soon discern my abilities and take advantage of them, nor will she look upon me as a person of eminence fit to be sent to her. So that, with submission to the judgment of your Excellency and the council, I must conclude myself altogether unfit for this very weighty and high employment, of which divers others in the nation are far more capable than I am.

CROMWELL.—The council have pitched upon you unanimously as the fittest man in the nation for this service ; we know your abilities, having long conversed with you ; we know you have languages, have travelled and understand the interest of Christendom, and I have known you in the army to endure hardships, to be healthful and strong, of

mettle, discretion and parts most fit for this employment,—
you are so indeed,—no man is so fit for it as you are. We
know you to be a gentleman of a good family, related to
persons of honour, and your present office of Commissioner
of the Seal* will make you the more acceptable to her. I
do earnestly desire you to undertake it, wherein you will do
an act of great merit, and advantage to the Commonwealth,
as great as any one member of it can perform,—and which
will be well accepted by them. The business is very
honourable, and exceedingly likely to have good success.
Her public ministers here have already agreed upon most of
the material and main points of the business. If it had not
been such an appointment, we would not have put you upon
it. The business of trade, and of the funds, and touching
the Dutch are such, as there cannot be any of greater
consequence.

WHITELOCKE.—Your Excellency will pardon me, if I cannot subscribe to your favourable opinion of me ; and I should
be sorry that a business of so great concernment should
suffer under so weak a management as by my hand. Besides,
that which Sir Gilbert Pickering is pleased to tell you of my
wife's condition is, to my private comfort, of as high consequence as may be. I would not seem unkind or ungrateful
to such a wife, and this time of the year, it is hard for me
to be put upon so difficult and dangerous a journey.

CROMWELL.—I know my lady is a good woman, a religious
woman, and will be contented to suffer a little absence of her
husband for the public good. As for the time of the year,
really the life of the business consists in the dispatch of it
at this time. The Dutch are tampering with the Queen, but
she holds them off, expecting to hear from us.

WHITELOCKE.—I see your Excellency is staid for. I shall
have some occasions into the country, and about a fortnight

---

* Cromwell was fond of appealing to motives of interest; he knew very well that
there was no Commissioner of the Seal, but promised in this indirect way the restoration of the office.

hence I will wait on you again. In the meantime, you will give me leave to consider of this business.

CROMWELL.—I pray, my Lord Whitelocke, do not think of so long a time, but let me entreat you to accept of the employment, and to return your answer within a few days to me.

WHITELOCKE.—I shall attend your Excellency.

On returning home he consulted with his wife, who strenuously endeavoured to dissuade him from the enterprise ; his friends were divided in their opinions, some approving, others condemning, and in this doubtful frame of mind he went down to his house in Buckinghamshire. Early in the morning, on going abroad to take the fresh air and look over his grounds, he took with him his bailiff, William Cook, a man that had been in his own and his father's service for upwards of forty years. Not disdaining advice, he listened patiently to what this old and faithful servant had to say, what reasons he had to offer, and they seem to have decided the master by the coincidence with his own.

Early on the morning of the 13th he again waited on the General, and spoke first.

WHITELOCKE.—I was to attend your Excellency, but missed you.

CROMWELL.—I knew not of it ; you are always welcome to me. I hope you have considered the proposal I made to you, and are willing to serve the Commonwealth.

WHITELOCKE.—I have fully considered of it, and with humble thanks acknowledge the honour intended me. I am most willing to serve your Excellency and the Commonwealth, but in this particular I humbly beg your excuse. I have endeavoured to satisfy my own judgment, and that of my nearest relations, but can do neither, nor gain a consent, and I should be very unworthy and ungrateful to go against it.

CROMWELL.—You know that no relations use to sway the balance in such matters as this. I know your lady very well, and that she is a good woman—a religious woman, indeed I think she is, and I durst undertake in a matter of this nature, wherein the interests of God and his people are concerned, as they are in your undertaking this business.—I daresay my lady will not oppose it.

WHITELOCKE.—Truly, sir, I think there is no woman alive desires more the promoting of that interest; but she hopes it may be done as much, if not more, by some other person.

CROMWELL. —Really, I know not in England so fit a person as you are for it."

After some further manœuvring on both sides in a similar strain, the arbiter of his countrymen's destinies no longer delays the essential explanation :

CROMWELL.—" I will engage to take particular care of those matters myself; and that you shall neither want supplies, nor anything that is fit for you ; you shall be sent out with as much honour as ever any ambassador was from England. I shall hold myself particularly obliged to you, if you will undertake it, and will stick as close to you as your skin is to your flesh.   You shall want nothing either for your honour and equipage, or for power and trust to be reposed in you, or for correspondence and supplies when you are abroad.   I promise you, my Lord, you shall not.   I will make it my business to see it done.   The Parliament and Council, as well as myself, will take it very well and thankfully from you, to accept of this employment.   And all people, especially the good people of the nation, will be much satisfied with it. Therefore, my Lord, I make it again my earnest request to you to accept this honourable employment."

This extraordinary earnestness prevailed, and Whitelocke saw he could no longer decline the proffered honour with prudence or safety, without converting the most powerful man in England into his open or secret enemy.   As the choice lay between two evils, as the danger at home would be greater than abroad, no alternative was left him, and accordingly, after a short pause, he replied :

WHITELOCKE.—"I see your Excellency is inexorable towards my excuse, and much set upon it, with more than
ordinary earnestness, for me to undertake this service, for
which, though I judge myself insufficient, yet your judgment
and that of the council is, that I am capable of doing some
service to the Commonwealth, to the Protestant interest
herein, and to the honour of God, which is above all other
motives.   Hoping that this may be so, and to testify my
regard and duty to your Excellency, who have honoured me
with your personal request for it, the council having unanimously pitched upon me, and to manifest that I am not self-
willed, how much-I value your Excellency's commands, and
can submit my own to better judgments, I am resolved to
lay aside further consideration of wife, children, friends,
fortune, all objections and fear of danger, so as to conform
myself to your Excellency's desires and to the votes of the
council, by accepting this difficult and hazardous * employment.   I do rest confident of your Excellency's care and
favour towards me, who undertake it by your command, and
hope that such allowances and supplies will be afforded me,
such memory had of me in my absence, as shall be agreeable
to the honour of the nation, of yourself, the business, and
your servant.

CROMWELL.—My Lord, I do most heartily thank you for
accepting the employment, whereby you have testified a very
great respect and favour to me, and affection to the Commonwealth, which will be very well taken by them.   I assure
you it is so grateful to me, who upon my particular request
have prevailed with you, that I shall never forget this favour,
but endeavour to requite it to you and yours.   Really, my
Lord, I shall, and I will acquaint the council with it, that we
may desire further conference with you."

And away he went.   Whitelocke's friends considered he
had done what was rational ; but, on the other hand, there

---

* No idle word, when we remember that two of Cromwell's agents or envoys had
been already assassinated ; one at the Hague, the other in Madrid.

was much weeping and sorrow at home. The council reported his consent to the Parliament, when one of the members objected. He knew not, he said, whether Whitelocke was a godly man or not, for although he might be otherwise quali- fied, yet if not godly, it was not fit to send him out ambas- sador. He alluded perhaps to the charge of Erastianism once brought by the Presbyterians against Selden and his friend, and to be suspected of being an Erastian, was tantamount to a charge at the present day of embezzlement, fraud, perjury, or other offences still more heinous. But another godly man, more charitably disposed, declared that the good tree could only be known by its fruit; and at length the vote was passed unanimously that he should go in the way proposed. A strict censure was passed at the same time on the "young gentleman" and his retinue, who had previously carried out letters from the late Parliament to Sweden, and when there had been guilty of excess in drink- ing healths. Hence Whitelocke's strict determination not to offend in the like manner, and the abstinence was not caused by fanatical notions. Cole, in his huge manuscripts, pre- served in the British Museum, impeaches our new ambassa- dor of fanaticism. He had private prayers there, it is true, and preached himself on one or two occasions an extemporary homily—a great sin I admit on the part of a layman, in the opinion of some clergymen.

After some negotiation the council of state, which sat on the 24th of September, 1653, at Whitehall, made an order providing for all his necessities, and making him an allow- ance of 6000*l.* for the first six months, the same sum that the Lord Viscount Lisle was to have had, in case he had gone instead. The half of this sum was to be paid in advance, and should the embassy, consisting of one hundred persons, be detained for a longer period than half a year, the stipend was then to be at the rate of 600*l.* a month, as Lisle was also to receive under the like circumstances. The glaring insufficiency of this sum, when all the expenses of both the sea voyage, and the land-journey in Sweden were taken into consideration, occasioned much perplexity, but the decision was made, the council deemed the amount competent, and to add to the prospective dilemma to which White-locke now found himself exposed, Captain Bishop, the secretary of the close committee, presented him with what may be truly called a paper of intelligence, received from some pensioners, as spies were then denominated, of the King's party.

" September 17, 1653.

" At a meeting of some of the King's chief agents, part of their discourse was this. One said : What will be your advantage, when you have taken off Cromwell and Lambert, seeing the present men in power are but a company of giddy-headed men ; some of the old men, as Bradshaw, St. John, Whitelocke, Rolles, Vane, would take the opportunity to bring themselves into power again, and if one of those get it into their hands, we shall never get it out again, they being the men that turned the wheel of the nation formerly, and what Cromwell did was by force to take it out of their hands, lest he should be turned out himself. For Bradshaw, said another, I hear he is going into Wiltshire · I warrant you we shall take a course with him,—you need not fear his return ; he is left to himself now, and out of his army guard ; he will not be walking on his battlements at Whitehall. For Whitelocke, said another, it was the wisest act that ever these men did to send him to Sweden, for he has a long journey to go, and before he comes to his journey's end may meet with divers good friends. They were all of them of the opinion," the letter went on to say, " that those men must be taken off, as well as Cromwell, for the reasons aforesaid, and that it was so concluded, without which, they said, their ends could not be effected."

Whitelocke did not pay any very serious attention to this warning, having heard from another source that Charles, on receiving an offer to murder Whitelocke, had strictly forbidden the deed, to which, he said, he would give no countenance, nor be a party to it by the least connivance.

In an interview with Lagerfeldt, the Swedish resident, Whitelocke discoursed about the assassination of Ascham in Spain, and Dorislaus in the Low Countries, both of whom were public ministers of this country, but the Swede assured him, there was not the least danger of any such attempt in his country, where the Queen and her subordinate officers were extremely careful to prevent any act of so barbarous a nature, that neither her subjects nor any strangers durst commit, or presume to attempt, any such thing in her kingdom, and if they should, the law was extremely severe in those cases.   He further assured his auditor, that assassination was a crime never yet perpetrated by any of his countrymen.

On the 1st of October, Cromwell induced the council to increase their grant by a niggardly 500*l.* for the whole term, and not per month, as it ought to have been, when such a retinue had to be maintained in a foreign country.   And now, having arranged with the council the solemn and weighty affair of chaplains, he began to think of a physician, the selection of which was far more arduous in those days, than it would be even now.   But he fortunately possessed a true and tried friend in Doctor Winston, an old man of eighty years, not long returned from voluntary exile, and whose estate he himself, when chancellor, rescued from the harpies of Parliament, who had sequestrated by a mandate from the speaker whatever land they found unoccupied or could by any pretext lay their talons upon.   This venerable man, to whose memory he had subsequently cause to be so grateful, had encouraged Whitelocke, from the first, to undertake the mission, and he now recommended Doctor Whistler. Shortly after this, Whitelocke, with his wife and some of his children, removed to his brother-in-law's house, Mr. Samuel Wilson, the wives being sisters, and whilst here Whitelocke applied for his salary still due to him as late Commissioner of the Seal, no less a sum than 1050*l.*, knowing well that if he did not get it paid to him then, he should run the greatest risk of never getting it at all.

He had no lack of books for his guidance and instruction. In addition to his own stock, his noble friend, Sir Thomas Cotton, lent him several valuable manuscripts, such as were pertinent, from his rare treasury, the general access to which is now open not to a friend alone, but to every literary man; and Mr. Bushel, formerly a servant to the great Lord Chancellor Bacon, sent him a noble present: a curious rich cabinet of green velvet with silver lace, containing twenty-four quart glasses of the most rare and best distilled hot waters, prepared from a receipt of Bacon's own. Each glass was properly tipped with Welsh silver, the greater part of which metal had been discovered by the donor, and the whole proved a most acceptable and opportune gift.

CHAPTER XVIII.

—◆—

1653.

Sails for Sweden in the *Phœnix* Frigate—Sets Free a captured Dutch Skipper—Details of the Voyage—Landing of the Embassy at Gothenburg—First Impressions—A Ceremonious Welcome followed by rough Accommodations on the way to the Capital—Whitelocke receives a Letter from Thurloe—Meets with a Son of the famous Salmasius—Mutinous Conduct of his Retinue—Receives from Thurloe a further Intimation as to his threatened Assassination—Account of Swedish Laws and Customs—Arrival at Upsala—His reception by the Queen—His description of her—Oxenstierne and his sons—Piemontelle—Private Audience with the Queen on the subject of his Mission—Their Conversations at various times—Delivers the Articles of the Proposed Treaty of Alliance, and confers with her on the supposed Designs of France and Holland—Hugh Peter's Present to the Queen accepted.

ON the 24th of October, 1653, Blake and the well-known Monk, who was now a general at sea as well as on the land, gave orders to Captain Nicholas Foster of the Phœnix frigate, to make all ready together with another frigate, the Elizabeth, and receive the ambassador on board, the chief command to be vested in that high officer of state, and on the same day Whitelocke sat in Chancery, which by this time seems to have been restored in conformity with what Cromwell had spoken, though it may be the Act not long since passed by the late Parliament had never been carried out, in consequence of its unpopularity with the lawyers.* After giving the rule in two or three motions, the Chancellor rose and took leave of his brethren, of the gentlemen at the bar, and of the officers, who gave him all testimonies of civility and respect, "as is usually done to men in authority." He had the like courtesy from the other courts in West-

---

* During the civil war, as well as in the reign of James II., we sometimes find both lawyers and clergymen resisting the execution of personally disagreeable enactments.

minster Hall, whom he saluted as he passed, and however
truly his philosophy might estimate these honours, his
vanity found the common courtesies of life by no means
displeasing.   Cromwell's farewell gift was highly charac-
teristic: a sword and a pair of spurs, richly inlaid with gold,
of a noble work and fashion.   And lastly, an old and faithful
servant, who had served both father and son for forty years,
no doubt the same bailiff Cook that had tendered him such
conscientious advice on a recent occasion, came up himself to
town in his cart, that he might see his master once more.
He brought with him meal and other homely products of a
farm, but on his return dropped dead upon the road, and
" became a saint in heaven," as his master affirmed, who
best knew his worth and the best tribute due to his honest
affection.

Whitelocke's wife, though so passionately averse to his
journey, yet when she saw he must go, took pains in her own
person to buy necessaries and make provision of wine, beer,
meal, baked meats, butter, cheese, fruits, sweetmeats, &c.,
all provisions and household-stuff, hard to be met with in
Sweden, but necessary for his accommodation.   He had
divers good horses of his own for the coach and saddle, and
he bought more, the best that he could meet with, though
at high prices, resolving to have, as far as he could, the best
of every thing, for the honour of his country.

Then he hired two transports, one called the Adventure,
for a floating stable, and the other, the Fortune, for a tender,
and now all things being ready, he made a farewell homily,
excusable at any time, but doubly so on that occasion and at
that period; then receiving his commission, credential letters
and instructions, both public and private, with final leave-
taking of Cromwell and another long-winded colloquy, one
long tearful and sobbing agony from the wife, whose confine-
ment was hourly imminent, he put off from the bank under
a salute from the Tower, and as his flag floated down the
stream, ship after ship took up the same rough melody, until

he passed the Fort at the Hope, where the great guns boomed out their complimentary adieu. He went directly to the Phœnix, then riding in that road, and was received by its captain with pennons all hung out, "his waist-cloathes" to the cabin-door, and a welcome of one-and-twenty guns. The men were in good order, stout and able mariners; the captain and officers not inferior to any of the sea-commanders; the ship as well-built and fitted for sailing or fighting as any in the fleet. Here were fourteen cabins for his company, and here he left some of them. Then he rowed away to the Elizabeth, whose captain, Winnes, was equally courteous, and here there were thirteen cabins for his gentlemen, some of whom he left behind him likewise, whilst he himself proceeded to Gravesend, receiving unexpectedly, and to a new ambassador's ears not disagreeably, a salute of three guns from a Dutch frigate, that lay there at anchor. There was war between the two nations at the time, and the enemy had a large fleet at sea, but a Dutch ambassador had lately arrived, and as this was the ship that brought him, she enjoyed all freedom from molestation.

His own ship carried forty-four guns and her consort thirty. In conformity with naval usage, and by advice, our new and constitutional commander ordered the Phœnix to carry her flag in the main-top, and then led the van. Other orders he gave, all under advice, about their firing, anchoring, weighing, sailing, and the like. The Phœnix was to carry the lanthorn, and every morning each ship was to come up, report condition, and then fall into order again. He ordered prayers to be constantly offered up twice a day, upon the deck in fair weather, and at other times in the steerage-room. Whoever "took" tobacco must do it behind the mainmast, where a tub of water was placed to receive the ashes, and thus prevent all risk of fire. I forgot to say, that when he landed at Gravesend, he had travelled back incognito to town, that he might take a second leave of his disconsolate wife and children.

It was managed so quietly, that the Council and Cromwell never knew it.

The wind being fair, and the anchors up, they hoisted sail, and by the evening reached the Nore at the mouth of the Thames, where a buoy gave warning of the sands. It was a place he gazed at with great interest, for there the English and the Dutch had fought a bloody fight, and the gallant Deane, the English commander, had lost his life. Queenborough castle was in sight, on the Isle of Sheppy, a name derived from the numerous sheep that fed there, and shortly after the evening sermon, the breeze veered round to the north, and blew so dead against them, that they had to drop anchor. It seemed to him providential, for on that very day his wife gave birth to her second son, afterwards named Carlton, and two bold watermen undertook to convey the joyful tidings. They rowed all night, but on reaching the spot where the ships were tossing, could not leave the shelter of the shore and get through such a heavy sea in their small wherry. So they made fires on the coast to give notice of an express, and a large boat was sent to fetch them on board. The news inspired him with fresh confidence, and he believed that the prayers of the congregation, of which his wife was a member, had been instantly granted from Heaven, and hence the reason why the wind had veered and retarded the progress of the ships. Such was the pious faith of our forefathers, a faith that armed the timid with courage not their own, and made the brave still braver.

At daybreak a gun was fired as signal to weigh, the fair breeze having returned, and they ran that day some five-and-twenty leagues. As night came on, and the towing cable having parted with a mighty crack, so that the Adventure fell adrift, the Phœnix carried two lanthorns, but there was much tossing and rolling all night, and the two tenders were not fleet in sailing. At sunrise the frigate pursued some strange vessels "with incredible swiftness," and fired off her chase-pieces at them, as a warning to strike sail. The argument was yielded to with a good grace by one of them, and she came to leeward, but while the English captor was intent on getting the skipper on board, the other Dutchman, seeing the wind so fair, the frigate's crew so busy in another direction, rehoisted all his sails, and got clear off.   At this affront Captain Foster was very angry, and prayed leave to renew the chase.   But Whitelocke, who had no desire to ruin by capture poor fishermen attempting to gain their honest livelihood on the high seas, was against this, and he had shortly after the following conversation with the enemy :—

WHITELOCKE.—"Skipper, whence art thou ?

SKIPPER.—A Flushinger.

WHITELOCKE.—What brought you to sea this weather ?

SKIPPER.—My trade ; though the weather be foul, we must fish, or our wives and children must starve.

WHITELOCKE.—Hast thou a wife and children ?

SKIPPER.—I hope I have a wife and seven children.

WHITELOCKE.—What right have you to fish in these seas ?

SKIPPER.—I thought any one might fish in the broad sea.

WHITELOCKE.—Not without leave of those who have the dominion of those seas.

SKIPPER.—I know not who have the dominion of the sea, but they that have the best fleet.   I have been thirty years a fisherman, and never asked leave yet.

WHITELOCKE.—Indeed a good fleet is the best argument for the dominion of the seas, but though you never asked leave to fish on the seas of our Commonwealth, your predecessors have asked leave to fish here.

SKIPPER.—My father and grandfather were fishers on these seas, but I never heard them say they asked leave.

WHITELOCKE.—It may be so, but others have.

SKIPPER.—I must not contradict you.

WHITELOCKE.—Thou mayest speak freely to me.

SKIPPER.—No, I thank you ; I know to whom I speak.

WHITELOCKE.—Dost thou know me ?

SKIPPER.—I think you are the English ambassador for Sweden.

WHITELOCKE.—Why dost thou think so?

SKIPPER.—Because you carry your flag in the main-top, and some of your men told me so.

WHITELOCKE.—What do they say in your country of my going to Sweden?

SKIPPER.—Our lords don't like it, but their subjects think you do wisely to get the Swedes for friends."

After a further parley upon political and religious topics, Whitelocke thought it time to keep the poor man no longer in suspense, and said:

WHITELOCKE.—"Well, Skipper, thou seemest to be an honest man, and to love the English, and thou sayest thou hast a wife and seven children; therefore, I shall do more for thee than thou expectest: thou shalt have thy ship again.

SKIPPER.—What did you say, sir? Shall I have my ship again?

WHITELOCKE.—Yes, Skipper, thou shalt have thy ship again. Captain Foster, give order that the ship be restored to the poor man.

SKIPPER.—Sir, your men took a world of goods when they boarded me. If I might have them too?

WHITELOCKE.—Skipper, thou shalt have them too. Captain, I pray see that your men restore both ship and goods, whatsoever they have taken from this poor man.

CAPTAIN.—Your Excellency's command shall be obeyed."

Whitelocke is hardly fair to himself and the native goodness of his heart, when he says he did this by design to create a favourable impression in Holland, and "amuse" the lords "upon his going to Sweden" by this action.

At the end of six days, after a continuance of stormy weather, they took the elevation, and found they were in fifty-four degrees and some odd minutes, so that they had come only a third part of their voyage. On the 14th, hoping

they were now near the coast, Whitelocke promised a bottle
of sack to the mariner, who should first descry land, which
carried many of them to topmast and top-gallantmast head.
About eight in the morning, there were so many descriers,
that all his bottles were claimed and given, and one hour
later, he made out land himself, which proved to be the
coast of Jutland in Denmark. With this good news he went
to his sick people to comfort them, jested with them, cheered
them as well as he could, and, after eating some of their
mess, a most appropriate name in those days of crude
cookery, he took a gulp with impunity of the water, and
encouraged them with the promise of a speedy end to their
sufferings. On the 15th, whilst at anchor on the weather
side of the sands in the Skaw, they had a raging storm,
which happily did not last long. On the following day they
reached the Pater-Noster rocks, off the coast of Norway,
rocks so called because they remind seamen of their prayers,
and here we learn, for the first time, that he did not attach
" much credit " to the stories they tell about witches and
monstrous giants, who in reality, though not in shape, are
monstrous fishes, that rise to the top of the water and
snatch men off the deck. " By twelve o'clock at noon,"
they reached the port of Gothenburg, saluted the castle with
eleven guns and a slight moving of his flag, but obtained no
sort of return, an omission of courtesy that proceeded from
the absence of the governor in the town. Here our ambassador's messengers found him, and met with a sort of civility
sufficient to warrant the landing of the whole embassy, who
as they passed the castle were honoured with two guns, an
example strictly followed by all the men-of-war and merchant-
men lying in the river. He had an interview with the
governor, received his apologies for the apparent discourtesy
of two guns, was assured that this was the invariable Swedish
custom, called by them a " Swede's leasing," for the sake of
sparing their powder, and that the Queen's orders were to
treat him with all respect. He carried on the greater part

of his conversation, while here, with the civil authorities in
Latin, which the syndic spoke well, and in the evening of his
second day at the inn, where he was staying, about twenty ·
men and boys, bearing lanthorns, came and sang in parts.
They were choristers, and either the music or their voices,
perhaps both, produced a lugubrious effect, and a present of
eight rixdollars, for which their own ears were much better
attuned.   The place in which he was stowed was a common
"cruise," inferior to an ordinary English inn, being meanly
furnished, without hangings or wainscot, with only bare walls
in the best rooms, but excellent in comparison with many of
those they had to lodge in subsequently.   He, himself, slept
between two feather-beds, after the fashion of the country,
found the arrangement light and warm, but preferred that of
rugs and blankets.   As for the stoves, these were not "sweet,"
but close and suffocating, and so he only used the chimneys ;
the beef and mutton was very lean, and there was no great
variety of fish or fowl.

At parting with his fellow seamen on the 18th, our
ambassador made them valuable presents,—to Foster a silver
basin and ewer, to Winnes a silver tankard, and on the
following day like a good centurion caused Stapleton, his
gentleman of the horse, to read his orders.   None were to
pledge or drink healths, none to swear or blaspheme, nor to
quarrel, nor stay out late in the evenings after six o'clock
upon any pretence whatever, without leave from himself or
his steward, upon pain of dismissal.   He made the discovery
here, that although the Swedes were Lutherans, they had
pictures, images, and many ceremonies in their churches, but
whether the sight gave rise to iconoclastic fancies or the
reverse he does not say.   He grew weary of his sojourn by
the last day but one of the month, and desired his steward
to call for the bill.   It was found to be of a most unscrupulous ambassadorial length, but mine host would not abate
one penny of it he said, and then there was mine hostess,
she too must have her gratuity.   They gave her twenty rix-

dollars, at which she turned up her nose, but took the money.
One hundred carts assembled on the 30th before his door ;
they all had four wheels, were very small and drawn by one
horse a-piece, or else by two cows abreast.   Only one large
trunk or two little ones could be stowed in one cart, and a
good many of the waggoners were women.   One hundred
saddle-horses were also brought in, and though small, turned
out to be hard trotters; the bumps were very severe at first,
as the saddles were French as to their size and shape,
but without covers or stuffing, of bare wood only, but then
they were well made, and that was some comfort.   The
bits were fashioned from pieces of ram's horn, the bridles
were small hempen ropes, the stirrups twisted withies.   He
sent on his quarter-master, cooks and butlers, to make provision at the "dorp" or village where they intended to sleep,
and after mutual valedictory courtesies between himself and
the authorities, both civil and military, set forth on horseback.   He was mounted on his best horse, a creature of
excellent shape and mettle, accoutred with a rich saddle and
pistols, and he himself wore a suit of plain grey English
cloth ; his other steed, a very beautiful entire horse, furnished
also with saddle and pistols, was led "leer," and then came
his suite, all armed with swords and pistols.   After the
horsemen came his travelling coach, of blue velvet and blue
silk, with silver fringe and richly gilt.   It was large enough
to hold eight persons, and was drawn by six of those bay
horses, of which Hengist himself would have had reason to
be proud.   Two more of the same set were led.   Two
gentlemen were all that rode inside, one was Mr. Ingelo the
chaplain, because he was sickly, and Colonel Potley, a nonde-
script, because he was unwieldy.

As the cavalcade went on, there was no longer any
pretence about economy of powder and a "Swede's leasing,"
for guns and musketry roared and rattled away "a great
while," and some complimental bullets came rather near, but
as the magistrates were still in attendance, he did not

suppose the cavalcade was purposely fired at.   One Swedish mile was their stage, and fresh carts and horses were in readiness.   Each horse cost three pence and the cart about nine pence for the stage, and the money had to be paid invariably in advance, without which the boors would not move forwards one step.   All they could accomplish that day was two of these stages, equal to fourteen English miles, and it was generally considered a great journey for that time of the year, when they only had four hours of daylight.   They halted at Seerum, where he lay in his field-bed, and most of his people in straw, but they had good lusty fires with their own cheerfulness to warm them, and so they put up with the bad beer, which was very strong and thick.

Thus the journey went on from day to day, with rest on the Lord's day, until they reached a city called Scara, where he had heard they should find beds, and was not disappointed. Here he saw in the cathedral many pictures of saints and other images, a high altar at the east end of it with a rich carpet of gold-embroidered velvet, and a stately crucifix.   In the vestry he gazed on chalices and pixes with pieces of the wafers in them, and for his life could not see any difference between this church and a popish one.   Then he paid a visit to the free-school hard by, that held from three to four hundred scholars; some of the senior "boys" were thirty years of age with great beards, but just as subject to the discipline of the ferula and the rod as the youngest urchin in the room, as far as the principle was concerned.   The origin of the city was attributed by the schoolmaster to a Goth, a servant to Abraham, who married one of his master's maids, and brought her home there with his acquired riches, and the Oriental lady had called the place Scara in honour of her mistress Sarah.   The visitor was rather sceptical as to the credibility of this myth, but as he himself in his history of England had traced us all back to the Trojan "Brute," he listened in silence and found later that the word "Scara" was only old Gothic for "shire."

Cows'-beef, lean, and " extreme bad," fried, roasted, boiled, and more than once whispered into his ear to be rotten, and to have died in the field, such was their daily fare with a keen appetite for sauce, until they got into the region of pork, bacon, white hares, and the yerpen, a superior bird to the partridge, all of which meat was firm, juicy and good, and though the travelling would have been dreary without company they were able to exchange their old snail-pace of two for five stages a day. One mile of this road was close beneath a rock. It had been cut by men's hands, and was only two feet broader than the track of his coach. On his right hand there was nothing but huge craggy rocks, some twenty or thirty fathoms high in beetling array above them, whereas to the left was a steep precipice, between fifty and sixty fathoms sheer down to the Lake Meler beneath. In this wide expanse of fresh water he heard there were 4444 islands, the least of which was one English mile in girth, and all inhabited, nor did he find in that unstatistical age the number exaggerated, on learning that the lake was one hundred miles in breadth. The people here were singularly honest. The only thing he lost was a great glass of tobacco ; but on the other hand, when his iron trunk of money broke and the dollars dropped out upon the road, they were all restored with scrupulous fidelity. On quitting an almost interminable forest, filled with the wild beasts of the north, they found they had only half a mile to go to their journey's end of that day. Mr. Lillycrone, a gentleman of the Queen's chamber, was here to greet them and escort them into Arsburg, the best and largest town they had yet met with. Here he received a packet of letters, one of them being from Thurloe, the secretary of the council, from which we extract one passage : " I have herein sent a character by which your Excellency may correspond with the council in things of secrecy, or signify your commands to your servant, which I hope will come safe to your hands unseen." Lager-feldt, the Swedish envoy, just come from London, had left

this packet with one of Whitelocke's servants, and as Thurloe
entrusted the letter to him, it is only fair to conclude that
the art, so well known now at some post-offices, of opening
letters was not deemed possible, and had not formed part of
a secretary's education. The son of Salmasius, Milton's
renowned adversary, happening to be the captain of the
company, was invited to dinner in the latter capacity. On
his broaching the subject of politics and his father's "*Defensio
regis*," Whitelocke, who was a great admirer of Milton, and
indeed had some of his works with him in his trunks, informed
the young man that the subject he was now starting was too
high for either of their judgments, and thus by declining to
listen, prevented so unpleasant a discussion. Shortly after
this a mutiny broke out amongst his own people ; they were
tired and sore, they said, with their hard horses and saddles,
and grumbled deeply at the wretched accommodation. He
quieted this, by causing the chief grumbler to change seats
with him in the carriage, whilst Whitelocke mounted the
vacated saddle, and so rode on with ready jest and harmless
banter. At Capin another scene of a different kind awaited
them. The "prætor" of the town refused to assist in finding
quarters for the people, abused the Parliament, said they had
killed their king and were a company of tailors and cobblers.
It turned out, that he was hardly sober when he uttered the
reproach, and he shed maudlin tears of sorrow on being
threatened with further consequences. "He use such words!"
he exclaimed, "not he ; what he had said was : What lies
these Holland gazettes do tell us, when they say, the Parliament are a company of tailors and cobblers, when you see
what gallant fellows they are by their ambassador,—what a
brave gentleman he is, how nobly attended, what a company
of gallant persons waiting upon him, above one hundred in
his company,—he loved and honoured the Parliament of
England—and London—with all his heart !"

Having seen what a "prætor" was, he made the
acquaintance of a consul, or major, at Westraas, a fine

city on the confines of Gothland. Several of the magistrates spoke French as well as Latin, and all were well-bred gentlemen, but the boors of the district proportionally churlish. It was here he learned the derivation of the English word "lord;" it is derived from "lagevard," *alias* "lovard" or "loverd," and means a warden or keeper of the law, a judge; and he recollected that in Bede and in many Saxon manuscripts, this very word "loverd" was used for lord. So lord and *dominus* are after all not synonymous, and we may congratulate both the Lord Mayor and the bench on the Gothic antiquity of their title. He learned also at the same time by another letter from Thurloe, how Cromwell was going to hang the brother of the Portuguese ambassador for murdering a man at the Exchange; much too respecting the Dutch treaty, the orders of the council about the Swedish ships taken as prizes, the liberation of some, and generally a good summary of foreign affairs. Then again he had valuable intelligence of designs laid by certain members of the King's party to kill him, and it came from no slight hands : "Whitelocke must have great fortune if he escape Dorislaus's and Ayscham's fate, for there are three in Sweden already, two of whom have been used to such sport, that will attempt and have designed to kill him. If they miss, there are those that will go over in the ships with him, that may do W. that friendly office."

Now it so happened that a man really had come with them, whose intentions seemed very suspicious from the first. He was a proper lusty fellow enough, that had obtained a footing in the vessel fitted up as a stable, and who tended the horses while the grooms were sea-sick. This man, being promoted and very kindly treated, was so touched with compunction, that he made a confession to one of his fellows and absconded on the journey.

Whitelocke did not fail to be struck with the fact, that the lands in Sweden were divided among the children; that each child of either sex received a share, and that it was not unlike the custom of gavelkind in England. As emigration did not exist at that time in his own country, it seems remarkable that the justice of the law in question did not more strike him, coming as it did without the palliation, with which some writers of the present day are wont to bolster up the practice in vogue with us of leaving the eldest son all the real estate, and the rest of the children comparatively nothing. He admits, however, that by this Gothic course of succession "much quiet and freedom from suits is gained," that there was "little occasion for conveyances, few or no questions touching descents or wills, because the law ascertains the course of them in all men's cases alike; whereas, in England, every possessor of an estate having a right to make private laws for the disposal of his property by conveyance or will, multitudes of questions and suits do arise upon the exposition of them, which are prevented by the partible law of Sweden. The like partible law takes place generally in Germany, Denmark, and other neighbouring countries, both for goods and lands," where all estates are comprised under the name of goods. As with these, so with titles and honour, with regard to which "their laws are more liberal than in England."

They did not get snow till the 20th of December, but happily they were now within half a league of Upsala, where the Queen's chamberlain, Vanderlin, as master of the ceremonies, was sent to reconnoitre what sort of animal the republican ambassador was like. He came in uncourtly garb, his bearing was supercilious, and after a hasty delivery of his mistress's greeting, he retired to his own coach. Shortly after, there followed sixteen other coaches, and those senators who came in them were civil. Whitelocke made his entry into the city with multitudes of people to line the way, and was conducted to a fair brick house provided and furnished by the Queen for his entertainment, nor was there a better in the place with the exception of the royal castle itself. A tedious but prompt initiation into the usages and etiquette of the country ensued, and a dinner equally tedious was discussed. The following description of the audience may serve to show what little prospect Spartan simplicity has of corrupting Englishmen who go to Court.

At his gate stood his porter in a gown of grey cloth, laced with guards of blue velvet between edges of gold and silver lace, two in a seam. He held his long staff with a silver head in his hand.

The liveries of his coachmen and postilions were buff doublets, laced with the same lace, the sleeves thick and round laced; their breeches and cloaks of grey cloth with the like laces.

His twelve lacqueys, proper men, had their liveries the same with the coachmen, and the wings of their coats very thickly laced as before.

The liveries of his four pages were blue satin doublets, and trunk breeches of grey cloth, thickly laced; the cloaks were also laced up to the cape, and lined with blue plush; their stockings long, of blue silk.

His two trumpeters in the like liveries.

The gentlemen attendants, officers and servants of his house most handsomely accoutred, and every man with his sword by his side.

The gentlemen of the first rank and his secretary very richly habited.

He himself, the ambassador, quite plain, but his habit extraordinary by its richness, though without any embroidery, being a suit of black English cloth, of an exceedingly fine sort; his cloak lined with the same cloth, but then the suit was set with fair rich diamond buttons, and his hatband with diamonds answerable, the whole worth a thousand pounds.

In the great court of the castle, at the entrance on the bridge, was a guard of 100 musketeers with their officers, and these formed a lane across the court. Whitelocke alighted at the foot of the stairs, where the Grave Gabriel Oxen-

stierne stood with his silver baton of court-marshal, with
many officers and servants in his rear. He was civil and
well-fashioned, complimented the stranger, bade him welcome
to court, and promised readily to do him service. All
Whitelocke's suite preceded him up the two pair of stone
stairs, excepting his secretary, chaplains, pages, and so on,
in the graduated scale of order, who all followed in his rear.
The Queen's lacqueys carried torches, and on reaching a
large ante-room, Prince Adolphus, brother to the hereditary
prince, as grand master or high steward was posted, and,
after some mutual courtesies in French, both marched abreast
into the room of reception, he being on the right and the
prince upon the left. He perceived the Queen sitting at the
upper end upon her chair of state, and saw it was of crimson
velvet with a canopy over it of the same substance. The
room was filled with lords and ladies, senators and courtiers,
and all were bare-headed. As soon as he entered he " put "
off his hat, and the Queen put off her cap, advancing two or
three steps ; this act revealed her rank, which otherwise it
might have been difficult to detect, for she wore a habit of
plain grey stuff, and over her petticoat, that reached to the
ground, a man's jacket descending to her knees. On her
left side, tied with crimson ribbon, descended the jewels of
the Amaranth order ; her cuffs were ruffled *à la mode*, but
she had on no gorget or band, only a black ribbon such as
common soldiers and seamen used ; her hair was braided
and hung loose ; her cap was of black velvet lined with
sable, it was turned up, and she used it as a hat. Her
countenance was sprightly, but somewhat pale ; her demeanour, he thought, possessed much majesty, and her
carriage noble, small as her person was.

Whitelocke made her three " congees," came up to her and
kissed her hand, that being a royal privilege to which all
ambassadors were entitled, the grace of doing which he had
learned in his youth, both at Whitehall and Saint Germains.
Then she put on her cap, and he did the same with his hat ;

when calling to his secretary and taking his credentials he pulled off his hat again, at which the Queen pulled off her cap once more. He addressed her in English; M. de la March interpreted it into French, and the burthen of it was, that the Parliament had commanded him to present those letters to her Majesty. She received them civilly, looked at their superscription, and then laid them by unopened. After a pause he continued speaking as before, and the Queen was very attentive, came close up to him, and by her looks and gestures tried to daunt him. But, as he very truly says, those who had been looking at the stern scenes at home so long, were not to be easily appalled by the presence of a young lady and her servants. He made her a long speech, and whenever he bowed during its delivery, she dropped him a courtesy in return. Her answer was quite as delicate and complimentary as his address, and he made so good an impression, that she excused her garb; she had been ill, she said, which caused her to put herself into the dress of her chamber, in which she chose to appear thus publicly, rather than disappoint him of his audience at the time appointed; she hoped she should have opportunity and time for further converse more at large. Upon this Whitelocke took his leave, returned to supper, and to be regaled with the Queen's band, without which the former, encumbered with senators and a most censorious master of the ceremonies, would have proved insufferably dull.

He had now to look about him, and find some one both capable and desirous of imparting to him the local knowledge of which he stood in so much need. As Denmark was at enmity with his country, his eyes were directed to that quarter, and how the Danish ambassador was to be " counterworked." There was a Danish gentleman staying at court, who was an exile and in disgrace at home; his friendship therefore must be gained. Then there was the French resident, with whom he must be on civil terms, but learn his transactions through some other person that possibly might comprehend them.   A Swedish gentleman turned up for this occasion.   Intelligence was likewise requisite of what the Dutch resident was doing ; and as the two nations were at war, he could have no personal intercourse with him, but he found a third party at last, whose name he suppresses as he did the Swede's.   As for Russia and Poland, they were not of that relative importance, and he did not much trouble himself about their envoys.   Not so with regard to Pie-montelle, the Spanish envoy extraordinary, whose intimate acquaintance he gained, and found in him a man of talent and address, in great favour at the Swedish court, his master not inimical to the English commonwealth, though very much so to Holland.   There still remained the Queen's favourite, Grave Tott, a gallant young gentleman, full of civility, and besides him he made the acquaintance at once of the senators Bond, Vanderlin, Erick Oxenstierne, and his father, the renowned chancellor himself, as soon as the old man came to town from his country seat.   Piemontelle called upon him on Christmas-eve, and they had a kind of good understanding together in a very short time, as may be seen by the following discourse :—

PIEMONTELLE.—" I have been some time at this court, and enjoyed much of the Queen's favour, and if thereby I may be serviceable to your Excellency, or to your business, I shall be glad of it.

WHITELOCKE.—I rejoice much that her Majesty's favours are so worthily placed, and hope that it may be of advantage to me.

PIEMONTELLE.—What course do you intend to take for procuring your audiences ?

WHITELOCKE.—The Master of the Ceremonies advises that I must go by way of memoir to the Secretary of State.

PIEMONTELLE,—With submission to him, to whose office it belongs, I think that way circuitous, and not so agreeable as to desire a private audience from the Queen herself.

WHITELOCKE.—Did your Excellency use that way ?

PIEMONTELLE.—I took that course in all my business; it succeeded well and was best liked by the Queen.

WHITELOCKE.—When does your Excellency suppose I may with civility desire one?

PIEMONTELLE.—I am confident, that if your Excellency desires a private audience to-morrow, though Christmas-day, the Queen will give it you."

Now this day was very strictly kept in Sweden, and by himself with every solemn observance. He records another discovery or two on the day in question. The first was, the great resemblance of their liturgy and service, their responsals and the administration of the sacrament, to his own, as it all used to be in Laud's time. The next was, that their ministers, in country parishes, were generally neither very learned nor studious; that many of them used one set of ready-made sermons year after year; then again, that the Archbishop of Upsala's stipend was not more than 500*l.* per annum, being ten times greater than the country parson's; and lastly that their parishes, though very large, yet not being populous, were not " much manured." That the parson was a right jovial fellow at feastings and times of jollity he took for granted from hearsay, having himself seen something similar in Wales, about five-and-twenty years before. He was amazed at the crucifixes, images, copes, surplices, and the chantings or intonations, all which had been retained as "*adiaphora*" from the first, by primitive Lutheranism, and which, had he been brought up in an English cathedral town, might possibly have less surprised him.

On the following day he procured a private audience through the medium of the Master of the Ceremonies. They spoke in French, and the chief points have been preserved:—

WHITELOCKE.—" Madam, I desired this audience for an opportunity of returning my thanks to your Majesty for the honour you have been pleased to show me, and for the favours I have received from your Majesty on my journey, in my entertainment and public audience here.

z

QUEEN.—Your accommodations on your journey and your entertainment here have not been such as I desired, nor could these places afford what was fit for you. I desire you to excuse it, and to be assured of a hearty welcome to my court.

WHITELOCKE.—Madam, what I intimated at my public audience in a general way, I am ready to give your Majesty a particular account of, and I hope it will be for the good of both nations.

QUEEN. —I believe the same, and am ready to entertain an alliance with the Commonwealth of England. The business is of very great weight and consequence, requiring good consideration and advice. I am at present in a condition of quiet and peace, and how far I should involve myself in troubles is of considerable moment.

WHITELOCKE.—Your Majesty is best able to judge whether an alliance with England will not add to your security, there being designs abroad against your Majesty as well as others.

QUEEN.—I believe there are, and that an alliance with England will be of advantage to us; but Sir, have you any other authority for such a business, besides the letters you brought to us ?

WHITELOCKE.—Madam, I have a commission under the Great Seal of England, which I have brought with me to show to your Majesty.

QUEEN.—I pray let us read it together !

WHITELOCKE.—I see your Majesty understands the Latin perfectly, and will find here sufficient authority given me for this business.

QUEEN. —I have Latin enough to serve my turn, and the authority given to you is very full. Upon what particulars will the Parliament think fit to ground the alliance between the two nations ?

WHITELOCKE.—If your Majesty please, I shall present you with the particulars in writing, in French or Latin, as you shall command

QUEEN.—It will be best in Latin, because I shall take advice in it.

WHITELOCKE. —I shall do it as your Majesty directs.

QUEEN.—Your General is one of the gallantest men in the world ; never were such things done as by the English in your late war. Your General has done the greatest things of any man in the world. The Prince of Condé is next to him, but short of him. I have as great a respect and honour for your General as for any man alive, and I pray let him know as much from me.

WHITELOCKE.—My General is indeed a very brave man ; his actions show it, and I shall not fail to signify to him the great honour of your Majesty's respects to him. I assure your Majesty he has as high honour for you as for any prince in Christendom.

QUEEN.—I have been told that many officers of your army will themselves pray and preach to their soldiers ; is that true ?

WHITELOCKE.—Yes, Madam, it is very true. When their enemies are swearing or debauching, or pillaging, the officers and soldiers of the Parliament's army use to be encouraging and exhorting one another out of the word of God, and praying together to the Lord of Hosts for His blessing, who has shown His approbation of this military preaching by the successes He has given them.

QUEEN.—That's well. Do you use to do so too ?

WHITELOCKE.—Yes, upon some occasions, in my own family, and think it as proper for me, being the master of it, to admonish and speak to my people when there is cause, as to be beholden to another to do it for me, which sometimes brings the chaplain into more credit than his lord.

QUEEN.—Does your General, and do other great officers do so ?

WHITELOCKE. —Yes, Madam, very often and very well. Nevertheless, they maintain chaplains and ministers in their houses and regiments. Such as are godly and worthy ministers have as much respect, and as good provision, in England, as in any place of Christendom. Yet it is the opinion of many good men with us, that a long cassock with a silk girdle and a great beard do not make a learned or good preacher, without gifts of God's spirit, and labouring in His vineyard. Whoever studies the holy scripture, and is enabled to do good to the souls of others, and endeavours the same, is nowhere forbidden by that word, nor is it blameable. The officers and soldiers of the Parliament held it not unlawful, when they carried their lives in their hands, and were going to adventure them in the high places of the field, to encourage one another out of His word, who commands over all. This had more weight and impression with it than any other word could have, and was never denied to be made use of but by Popish prelates, who by no means would admit lay people, as they call them, to gather from thence that instruction and comfort which can nowhere else be found.

QUEEN.—Methinks you preach very well, and have now made a good sermon. I assure you I like it very well.

WHITELOCKE.—Madam, I shall account it a great happiness, if any of my words may please you.

QUEEN.—Indeed, Sir, these words of yours do very much please me, and I shall be glad to hear you oftener in this strain. But I pray tell me, where did your general, and you his officers, learn this way of praying and preaching yourselves?

WHITELOCKE.—We learned it from a near friend of your Majesty, whose memory all the Protestant interest has cause to honour.

QUEEN.—My friend! Who was that?

WHITELOCKE.—It was your father, the great King Gustavus Adolphus, who, upon his first landing in Germany, as many then present have testified, did himself in person on the shore, on his knees, give thanks to God for his safe landing, and before his soldiers himself prayed to God for His blessing on that undertaking, and he would frequently exhort his people out of God's word, and God testified his good liking thereof by the wonderful successes He was pleased to vouchsafe to that gallant king."

To this the Queen made no further reply, but as her manner was, fell out of one subject into another, "full of variety and pleasant intermixt discourses." Having satisfied her curiosity about the state of the war between England and Holland, the history of the civil war, the business at Worcester, where her narrator did justice to the personal gallantry and conduct of Charles, the King of Scots; and after two hours of walking up and down the room, which made him very weary, and his sick leg lame afterwards, he took his leave. Thence he returned to his own house, and gave an audience in his turn to the scholars of the university, who conferred upon him the titles of Jupiter and Mars, made a classical pun upon his names, and did not forget Neptune nor the three Kings of the East, all of which must have reminded him of a classical oration at home, when he studied that very essential subject, mythology, at Oxford.

To relate the various interviews he had with subordinate personages would be idle, and therefore let us hasten on to his next interview with royalty. On this occasion two stools were brought in, as the Queen had heard by this time of his lameness. He showed her a list of the Parliament's fleet; explained to her the number of men, the several officers, the burthen of the ships, how many pieces of ordnance each of them carried; the pay, diet, stores and ammunition,—not of his own mooting, but in answer to her questions, for she was very inquisitive :—

QUEEN.—"Do these ships belong to the Commonwealth, or to private persons, made use of by the State when they have occasion, as at this time ?

WHITELOCKE.—They are all the State's own ships, built and furnished at the public charge, and are set out for this winter guard only. The State has many more and still larger ships belonging to their navy, which are reserved and are to be fitted for the summer guard, besides many others, that are repairing and now building.

QUEEN.—This is a gallant navy indeed; I am exceedingly taken with the description of it. I thought no prince or state in the world had had so good a fleet, except the Hollanders, who, I believe, have more ships than England.

WHITELOCKE.—The Hollanders may have more ships and vessels than England, especially if fisher-boats be reckoned; but for ships of war England is not inferior to any other nation. The Hollanders take more care for ships of burden, than of force, but the English merchant ships may be easily converted into able ships of war. The Hollanders, till their present sea-war with England, had not much occasion for ships of war, being at peace with their neighbours, and the less, being on the Continent. But for carriage ships, their principal interest being trade, they had as much occasion, and for a greater number than any other people. As the dominions of our Commonwealth consist of islands, our chief defence is in our navy, so as to meet with an enemy before he lands, and our best bulwarks are these wooden walls.

QUEEN.—You have reason for what you say; some of these ships of yours would do good service to open the Sound. What do you think fit to be taken for opening and making free that passage?

WHITELOCKE.—That must needs be better known to your Majesty, who are a neighbour to the place, and much concerned in it, than to me who am a stranger.

QUEEN.—But I desire your opinion in it.

WHITELOCKE.—I do not think it convenient to permit the Dane and the Dutch to lay what exactions they please upon all the people of the world, who have occasion to pass that way.*

---

* This question has, after the lapse of two centuries, been laid finally at rest. The Sound dues are now abolished.

QUEEN.—It cannot be taken out of their hands but by force."

At this word the Queen drew her stool nearer to Whitelocke's, and said :—

QUEEN.—" Do you think that the Commonwealth of England will give assistance in that business ?

WHITELOCKE.—Madam, I think they will, upon such just and honourable terms as may be agreed.

QUEEN.—Do you think they will send any ships for that purpose ?

WHITELOCKE.—I believe upon fit terms they would.

QUEEN.—What would you propose as fit to be done in the business ?

WHITELOCKE.—I suppose your Majesty does not expect any proposal from me in the first place. But if you will be pleased to consider of some proposals to that effect, that I may have them in writing, I will send them to my superiors, from whom I shall speedily receive instructions, agreeable to the interest of both nations, a conclusion may be had here in this business.

QUEEN.—*Par Dieu!* This is worthy the consideration of both nations, and not only concerns them, but all the world besides. But what do you think of the Emperor's taking part with the King of Denmark?

WHITELOCKE.—The business will be chiefly at sea, where the Emperor has no strength. I believe his Imperial Majesty will have no opportunity of molesting your Majesty's territories in Germany, in regard to his own affairs with the princes and his neighbours.

QUEEN.— But he may assist the Dane with money.

WHITELOCKE.—I don't think he has much to spare.

QUEEN.—The King of Spain may lend him money.

WHITELOCKE.—Not against England or Sweden, especially if to advance the interest of Holland, though he should have money enough besides for his own many occasions, which I believe he has not.

QUEEN.—I presume the Dutch will come with all their power to assist the Dane, chiefly against England, and to hinder their having an interest in the Sound.

WHITELOCKE.—It concerns them so to do, the rather now, being in hostility against us, and in alliance with the Dane; but this is to be expected and provided for, and the business will come the sooner and the more certainly to an issue.

QUEEN.—Do you think your Commonwealth will send ships enough, sufficient to encounter the Dutch?

WHITELOCKE.—In all our affairs hitherto the blessing of God has been with our Commonwealth; so that I doubt not our ships joining with your Majesty's will suffice to bring to reason the Dane or Dutch, in these or any other seas.

QUEEN.—I believe the King of France will assist them.

WHITELOCKE.—His navy is not very formidable, nor frequent in the Baltic, and for land-forces, they will have a long march, after they have made an end with the Prince of Condé and their old enemy; nor has that king much spare money.

QUEEN.—You speak very fully and truly of the interest of the several princes and states of Europe. I like the affair extremely, and will prepare a memoir of some proposals concerning it, and give it you to send to England. But speed, vigour, and secrecy are requisite herein. I must enjoin you to acquaint nobody with this discourse, but only your General, Cromwell, whose word I shall rely upon; but I would not have this matter made known to any other whomsoever. I desire you not to speak of it to any of my own ministers, nor of anything else relating to your negotiation but what I shall give way unto.

WHITELOCKE.—Madam, I shall faithfully obey your Majesty's commands, and not reveal one tittle of these matters without your permission.

QUEEN.—Have you not heard in England that I was to marry the King of Scots?

WHITELOCKE.—It has been so reported in England, that letters have passed between him and your Majesty for that purpose, and that your Majesty had a good affection for the King of Scots.

QUEEN.—I confess that letters have passed between us, but this I will assure you, that I will not marry that king : he is a young man, and in a condition sad enough. Though I respect him very much, I shall never marry him, you may be well assured. But I shall tell you under secrecy, he lately sent a letter to the prince palatine, my cousin, and with it the order of a knight of the garter to the prince ; the messenger had the wit to bring it first to me. When I saw it, and had read the letter, I threw it into the fire, and would not suffer the George to be delivered to my cousin.

WHITELOCKE.—Your Majesty did very judiciously, testifying great prudence in yourself, and great honour and respect to the Commonwealth of England. I met in your court one of my countrymen, no friend to our Commonwealth, who, as I suspect, might be the messenger.

QUEEN.—Who was that ?

WHITELOCKE.—Sir William Balendine.

QUEEN.—He was indeed the messenger ; but do not communicate this passage to any save your General.

WHITELOCKE.—I shall fully perform your Majesty's commands ; and, Madam, I hope you will not trouble yourself to receive any public minister or message from the King of Scots or any of his party. Or if any should come, that your servant may have the honour to know of it.

QUEEN.—What would you do in case any such thing should be ?

WHITELOCKE.—I hope that, in reason and in right of friendship with our Commonwealth, I may prevail with your Majesty not to entertain any such minister or message. It behoves me in that duty and service which I owe to my superiors, to make my protest against any such message or messengers.

QUEEN.—That would be an act of stoutness in you, and I believe you may be commanded to do so ; but I suppose

there will be no occasion for it.   There is no such messenger
in my court; and as for Balendine, he is one of my servants.

WHITELOCKE.—I hope there will be no occasion for it.

QUEEN.—What are the particulars which you have to propose to me of this treaty?

WHITELOCKE.—Madam, I have them here in writing."

Having resolved on the best way of dealing with a princess
of honour, he presented her with all the articles at once,
reserving only three, the discussion of which could not take
place, till a decision on the others had been previously obtained.   Perhaps he would have acted differently with the
Dutch or others, and have proceeded by degrees; but with
this Queen, the frank method he thought would be the best.
And so it proved, for she said later to some that were around
her; "The English ambassador had dealt with her, not as a
merchant, but as a gentleman and man of honour, and that
he should fare all the better for it."

After he had finished his letters to England on the 30th,
which was the post-day, the Queen's favourite, Grave Tott,
came to fetch him; the Queen, as soon as he entered, offered
to send his letters, under her cover, to her commissary
Bonnele at London, and to give the latter orders to forward
Whitelocke's letters to him at Upsala in her own packet, for
which favour he thanked her, but did not think fit to make
any serious use of the permission, not wishing his correspondence to be looked into :—

QUEEN.—"I have intelligence by this post, that the treaty
between England and the Dutch is broken off.   Have you
heard so?

WHITELOCKE.—I have received no letters, but possibly it
may be so.   Yet if there should be a peace between them, I
do not apprehend any inconvenience from that to the alliance
of England and Sweden, which the Dutch could have no
pretence to oppose.

QUEEN.—As friends to the Dane they must.

WHITELOCKE.—Then it will be against their peace with England.

QUEEN.—Here are my letters in Dutch; you may have them translated, and take copies of them.

WHITELOCKE.—I most humbly thank your Majesty.

QUEEN.—I have considered of the discourse between us yesterday, and I think it would be very advantageous to our alliance to take the King of Spain into it. What do you think of that?"

It struck him, that the Queen had imparted to Piemontelle the conversation of the previous day, and that it was he who had put her on this overture.

WHITELOCKE—Madam, I know not how far the Parliament may hold off, in regard that no justice has been yet done upon those who murdered our public minister there.

QUEEN.—That is a just exception; but as the Dutch are now making an alliance, and are very near it, between themselves, France, and Denmark, it were good for us also to have a trinity* of Sweden, England, and Spain, in an alliance.

WHITELOCKE.—Probably some may object the difference in religion.

QUEEN.—That will be no hindrance to the force of the union. The Dutch and Danes, being Protestants, unite with the French, though Papists; I pray consider further of it. Methinks the Papists have not equal liberty with others, as they ought to have.

WHITELOCKE—Their tenets do not consist with the public peace of Protestant princes and states, whom they esteem heretics, and that it is a good service to God to cut them off.

QUEEN.—This opinion some have vented in former times, but now their interest leads them from it, and they do not hold it.

WHITELOCKE—I doubt they still retain it.

QUEEN.—I pray, what religion do you profess in England?

WHITELOCKE.—In regard your Majesty does me the honour

* Her own word. Hence perhaps the idea of the "Holy Alliance."

to catechise me ; I shall answer you very freely. We profess the true reformed Protestant Christian religion, &c. &c."

In the long discourse which followed on sects and the Anabaptists at Munster, Whitelocke gave utterance to many sensible observations, that were far in advance of the age in which his lot was cast. One passage I cannot pass by in silence :—

WHITELOCKE.—"But many with us consider it right for every one to be left to take care of his own soul, which concerns no one but himself; and that the magistrate ought not to confine or persecute another into his judgment for that which concerns the other only, so long as the public peace is preserved, to which the law of England has a strict regard ; and whosoever, by his opinion or practice, disturbs that peace, is to be severely punished."

Then the Queen, who indulged in the most rapid transitions and digressions, here suddenly changed the theme :—

QUEEN.—"How do you contrive to write to your superiors, that others may not know what you write, in case your letters should be intercepted ; do you write by cyphers ?

WHITELOCKE.—That is a way that may easily be uncyphered. I write to my General in such a way as no flesh can ever find out, unless by agreement beforehand.

QUEEN.—How is that, I pray ?

WHITELOCKE.—I leave with my General, or with the secretary of the council, two glasses of water. With one of the same waters I write my letters, having two glasses with myself also. The letter thus written no man can possibly read, no more than if it were written with fair water, but wash over this letter with the water in the other glass, and it turns it to black, just as if it had been written with ink.

QUEEN.—That is a curious way indeed, and have you of those waters here ?

WHITELOCKE.—Yes, madam, I make them myself, and have left some with my General, so that no creature can read his or my letters without them.

QUEEN.—What huge dog is this?

WHITELOCKE.—It is an English mastiff, which I brought with me, and he has, it seems, broken loose, and followed me even to this place.

QUEEN.—Is he gentle and well-conditioned?

WHITELOCKE.—The more courageous they are, the more gentle; this is both. Your Majesty may stroke him.

QUEEN.—I have heard of the fierceness of these dogs; this is very gentle.

WHITELOCKE.—They are very gentle, unless provoked; and are of a generous nature. No creatures have more mettle or faithfulness than they have.

QUEEN.—Is it your dog?

WHITELOCKE.—I cannot tell; some of my people told me, that one Mr. Peters sent it for a present to the Queen.

QUEEN.—Who is that Mr. Peters?

WHITELOCKE.—A minister, and great servant to the Parliament.

QUEEN.—Did that Mr. Peters send me a letter?

WHITELOCKE.—He is a great admirer of your Majesty, but to presume to send a letter or a dog for a present to a Queen, I thought above him, and not fit to be offered to your Majesty.

QUEEN.—I have many letters from private persons; his letter and the dog belong to me, and are my goods, and I will have them.

WHITELOCKE.—Your Majesty commands in chief; all ought to obey you, and so will I, not only as to the letter and dog, but likewise as to another part of his present, a great English cheese of his country making.*

QUEEN.—I accept them kindly from him, and see that you send my goods to me.

WHITELOCKE.—I will not fail to obey your Majesty."

* The exportation of English cheese being still prohibited, it was held to be a rare and precious gift.

CHAPTER XIX.

THE Queen had been misinformed about the Dutch treaty.
Whitelocke received his packet of letters a day or two later,
in which there was one from Thurloe, who told him it was
still going on, but *lento pede*. The constant and authentic
intelligence he received from this secretary was of the highest
value to him, and enabled him to make good his footing at
court. Having caused an abstract of his news to be translated into French, he took it himself to the Castle. It was
such a frosty and slippery night, that he was obliged to walk
the distance, having two of his servants to support him.
The Queen amongst other things began talking about the
late King James, who, she had heard, was poisoned, and his
son, Prince Henry, also. Although Whitelocke believed the
fact, he thought it very dangerous ground, and avoided
treading on it. But he gave her, at her request, a long
account of the first Duke of Buckingham, what his extraction
was, and how he rose to favour. His knowledge surprised
the Queen, until he informed her, there was a near alliance
between the Duke and Whitelocke's children, by his second
wife, about which she was very inquisitive. Then she asked

about the old **Earl of Arundel,** the Countess of Kent, and many of the nobility ; of Selden, Patrick Young, some of the bishops, and of various learned men ; and he acquired her esteem by giving every one of them his due, whether a political enemy or not. Then she commended the library at St. James's, and the rare manuscripts there, of some of which she desired to get copies, and as he was the keeper of that library, he promised on his return to England to fulfil her wishes.

No further interviews took place until the 4th of January, 1654, when, instead of business, her Majesty preferred gratifying her curiosity about Cromwell :—

QUEEN.—"Has your General a wife and children ?

WHITELOCKE.—He has a wife and five children.

QUEEN.—What family were he and his wife of ?

WHITELOCKE.—He was of a baron's, and his wife the like from Bourchiers.

QUEEN.—Of what parts are his children ? *

WHITELOCKE.—His two sons and three daughters are all of good parts, and liberal education.

QUEEN.—Some unworthy mention and mistakes have been made to me of them.

WHITELOCKE.—Your Majesty knows that to be frequent, but from me you shall have nothing but truth.

QUEEN.—Much of the story of your General has some parallel with that of my ancestor, Gustavus the First, who, from a private gentleman of a noble family, was advanced to the title of a marshal of Sweden, because he had risen up and rescued his country from the bondage and oppression, which the King of Denmark had put upon them, and he expelled that King. For his reward, he was at last elected King of Sweden, and I believe your General will be King of England in conclusion.

WHITELOCKE.—Pardon me, Madam, that cannot be, because

---

* A most politic question, and one which Whitelocke would have done well to have bestowed far deeper attention upon at an after-period.

England is resolved into a Commonwealth, and my General has already sufficient power and greatness, as General of all their forces both by sea and land, which may content him.

QUEEN.—Resolve what you will, I believe he resolves to be King, and hardly can any power or greatness be called sufficient, when the nature of man is so prone, as in these days, to all ambition.

WHITELOCKE.—I find no such nature in my General.

QUEEN.—It may easily be concealed till an opportunity serve, and then it will show itself.

WHITELOCKE.—All are mortal men, subject to affections.

QUEEN.—How many wives have you had ?

WHITELOCKE.—I have had three wives.

QUEEN.—Have you had children by all of them ?

WHITELOCKE.—Yes, by every one of them.

QUEEN.—*Par Dieu, vous êtes incorrigible !*

WHITELOCKE.—Madam, I have been a true servant to your sex, and as it was my duty to be kind to my wives, so I count it my happiness, riches, and strength to have many children.

QUEEN.—You have done well, and if children prove well, it is no small nor usual blessing."

After some further discourse in this palace of truth, her Majesty was pleased to exclaim with some abrupt earnestness :—

QUEEN.—" You are hypocrites and dissemblers.

WHITELOCKE.—For myself, I can have little of design, especially in your country, to dissemble. I always hated hypocrisy, as a thing unworthy of a Christian or a gentleman, nor has my General been charged with that odious crime.

QUEEN.—I do not mean either your General or yourself, but I think, that in England there are many, who make profession of more holiness than is in them, hoping for advantage by it.

WHITELOCKE.—I doubt there may be some such in England,

especially at this time, when through the goodness of God
religion is become the chief interest of the nation.   And
there are of these likewise in other countries.   But when
they come to be found out with us, as such cannot be
long undiscovered, they lose their aim and credit, and their
dissembling is scorned and punished.

QUEEN.—Is dancing prohibited in England ?

WHITELOCKE.—Some there do not approve of it ; but it is
not prohibited by any law, and many there do use it."

He then launches out into the question as to the propriety
of dancing on a Sunday, which the Queen must have secretly
found distasteful, as she had only given a state ball on the
previous Sunday.   As he did not apparently understand the
history or meaning of what the Puritans, like the ancient
Greeks and Romans, called the Lord's-day, and as he intruded
a purely English conception of it, the Queen reverted to the
question of the Sound, and learned from him, that he had
already written and sent off a despatch concerning it :—

QUEEN.—" In what way must this business of the Sound
be done ?

WHITELOCKE.—I only know of two ways, by sea and by
land, and both will be here necessary.

QUEEN.—How many ships do you think the Parliament
will lend me for this design ?

WHITELOCKE.—I believe they will send a considerable
number of ships upon this or any other design to be undertaken by them.

QUEEN.—I desire only twenty or thirty ships, and that
the Parliament with the residue of their fleet would attend
the Hollanders.

WHITELOCKE.—It is probable that the Hollanders, upon
such a design, might advance with their fleet upon the Sound.

QUEEN.—Then they will be between my fleet with twenty
English ships on the one side, and the residue of the English
fleet on the other side.   I do not desire above twenty or
thirty English ships and some money.

A A

WHITELOCKE.—England has great occasions for money for the pay of her armies and great navies, especially in this time of our wars both by land and sea. It will principally be your Majesty's business to open the trade into your seas, and I suppose you will not expect ships and money too from others to do your work.

QUEEN.—I am in great want of money, and England has money enough.

WHITELOCKE.—They have enough for their occasions.

QUEEN.—And some to spare, which I have not.

WHITELOCKE.—I do not see your Majesty to waste the revenues of your crown in gallantry of clothes for your own person.

QUEEN.—I am the least curious in clothes of any woman, especially now I am in the country.

WHITELOCKE.—Your wearing plain clothes makes your people rich.

QUEEN.—My Chancellor will be in town shortly.

WHITELOCKE.—Your Majesty is happy in a servant of such great wisdom, experience, and fidelity.

QUEEN.—He is a very able and honest man; he understands this business well; I will give you a memoir concerning the Sound."

Whitelocke was invited to a ball, and his starch manners, acquired by the force of circumstances and contagious example, seem somewhat to have oozed out of his fingers' ends, by his residence in a foreign country, where different modes of thought enforced a departure from that stern gloom and sombre severity he had been so long familiarised with, and compelled to adopt. His own reasons are so natural, that I cannot refrain from giving them. "Seeing the high esteem and pleasure which her Majesty had in balls, dancing, and music" (he had taken the same delight in them when young), "which recreations being modestly and moderately used, I hold to be indifferent things, and not unlawful in themselves, and that it was fit for me, being invited by the

Queen, to attend them at fit times, lest I should be judged too severe and morose, and too much to censure those who used and delighted in them, and desired my company at them ;—having been before invited to a ball, and refusing to come, because it was the Lord's day, being now again solemnly invited from the Queen herself to a ball this night at court, I thought, if I should again refuse to come to it, the Queen might be distasted, and think her favour slighted. I resolved, therefore, to go, and after nine o'clock the master of the ceremonies, as a special compliment, brought two of the Queen's coaches to attend me to the Castle.   When I came into the room where the Queen was, she bade me welcome with more than ordinary respect, and led me into a large room where she usually hears sermons, but at other times it is for music and dancing," Here he sat next to her on the right hand.   The orchestra was in a place behind her chair of state ; it consisted of seven or eight violins, with bass viols, flutes, and citherns,—perfect masters. The Queen with her ladies and courtiers, first danced the brawls, then French dances, in which the Lady Jane Ruthven took forth Captain Whitelocke. Several others of the English gentlemen were taken forth by the Swedish ladies, to dance English country dances, and the gentlemen taught their fair partners some new ones.

Shortly after this scene of merriment, which may have made our diplomatist rather uneasy, not knowing how the fanatical party at home might resent it, he was honoured with a visit from the renowned statesman and Chancellor, Oxenstierne. He came in state, and, being an old man, was led by his host into the steward's chamber, on the ground-floor, specially arranged for his reception with rich hangings of silk and gold. He desired to sit with his back on one side to the fire, as the glare hurt his eyes, he said. He was tall, straight, and still handsome, although seventy-one years of age ; he wore a suit of black, a close coat, lined with fur, a cloak over that, and his velvet cap was furred.

A A 2

His hair was grey, and his beard broad and long ; his countenance sober and fixed; his carriage grave and civil. They
conversed in Latin, for although the chancellor knew French,
he refused to recognise it as the language of official or ceremonial intercourse. The first topic was England, and the
illustrious visitor described at great length the mission of his
eldest son as ambassador to the late King Charles, and his
unpleasant reception. Then he spoke of Sir Thomas Rowe's
negotiations and Sir Henry Vane's doings in Germany, and
how, when the Swedish forces were lying still, the late King
would instigate them to recommence active hostilities, but
whenever the troops had any success would withdraw his
promised assistance. He mentioned that the *parvus archi-
præsul*, as he termed little Laud, the treasurer, Weston, and
others were of the Spanish faction, and that they had tried
to introduce Popery. By degrees the conversation drifted
into the right channel :—

WHITELOCKE.—" I come, my Lord, to offer that, which I
conceive will be for the honour and advantage of both
nations, and I desire a despatch as soon as conveniently may
be, having many affairs in England to attend to, by reason
of my charge there, where I have also left a great family.

CHANCELLOR.—The Commonwealth of England has testified a very great respect to the Queen, my mistress, and to
the nation of Sweden, in sending your Excellency here. The
Queen has told me that she never received more contentment
in conversing with any ambassador than with you; and for
my part, I have a particular affection to your person, which
I shall be ready to manifest. As for the business, I do not
doubt but that it will receive such a good issue as shall be
to the satisfaction of England and their ambassador. It is a
matter of very great moment, and as you in England have
considered of it beforehand, so is it necessary to be considered
by us here, but there shall be no unnecessary delay in it.

WHITELOCKE.—I am happy in the Queen's goodness, and
the respects of your Excellency to a stranger. I hope there

will not be need of much time for this business, because many
of the things offered by me are the same with those mentioned by the Queen's public ministers in England.

CHANCELLOR.—Many of these things are new and of great
consequence.　As you have had your instructions from your
superiors, so must I have my instructions from the Queen,
my mistress, and no long time shall pass before the matter
shall be brought to some ripeness.

WHITELOCKE.—In this your Excellency will do me a great
favour.　I have heard the Queen intends going a journey
shortly.

CHANCELLOR.—It is so reported, but uncertain.　But in
case she does go, the affair will be left in the hands of some
of her servants, who will proceed in it without delay, though
her Majesty be absent.

WHITELOCKE.—Your favour to me by its dispatch will be
acknowledged by your servant, and no person knows better
how to do it than your Excellency.

CHANCELLOR.—I have been conversant with business in my
time, but for many years I was under a cloud, and in some
displeasure.　Whereupon I thought fit to retire into private
life in the country, and there, after all my troubles and toiling
in the world, I found more content than ever I met with in
all my public employments.

WHITELOCKE.—How could you frame yourself to such a
solitary way of retirement, you who had before spent all
your days amid the throng of public and great affairs?
And, being old, unfit for study, how could you pass your
time in that privacy?

CHANCELLOR.—I had been so much wearied out with
public and great actions, that this retirement and quiet
proved the greater source of content.　Business was a burthen,
and much company irksome, yet I was able to spend some
of my time in study.　Chiefly, I may say solely, I applied
myself to the study of the Bible, in which there is all wisdom
and the greatest delight to be found, but much more in the

practice of that divine wisdom. You are a much younger man than I am, and possibly may have the like occasion for retirement that I had, but do not doubt of being in favour again. I counsel you to make the study and practice of God's word your chief contentment and delight, as this will be to every soul that savours God's truths, which do infinitely excel all worldly things.

WHITELOCKE.—I shall remember your words, and thank you for this good counsel of the truth. Of what you say, I have formerly had some experience, and I hope God will improve it to me in all conditions."

At another interview, after giving a summary of parliamentary history, the new doctrine in politics was propounded by Whitelocke, which shews him to have been the first Whig in this country :—

CHANCELLOR.—" Do you hold *kingly* government to be unlawful, that you have abolished it ?

WHITELOCKE.—Every government, which the people choose, is certainly lawful, whether kingly or other, and that to be accounted best, which they, by their representatives, do make choice of, as best for them and their condition.

CHANCELLOR.—You have given me a full and satisfactory account, that you are a fixed Commonwealth, with whom we may safely treat, and I would know what you *desire* of us.

WHITELOCKE.—I desire nothing from you. I do not come to you in a precarious way, *non ut cliens, sed ut amicus.* My business is to make you an offer of that, which is worthy of acceptance by any prince in Europe, the friendship of the English Commonwealth, which, if you please to embrace it on just and honourable terms, will be for your advantage as well as ours. If not, you yourselves will have as much prejudice as any other by the refusal.

CHANCELLOR.—You are quick at the apprehension of reflection on the honour of your nation.

WHITELOCKE.—My affection and duty to my country will plead in my excuse.

CHANCELLOR.—I am so far from censuring you for it, that I cannot but commend you. And your humour gains so much upon me, that though you will not be a suitor to us here, for which you have reason, yet I will be a particular suitor to you, that our acquaintance and friendship may be intimate and familiar, the which I have not been used to pray from public ministers, though I have had to deal with many of them.

WHITELOCKE.—You reprove me so fatherly, and put so great an obligation upon me, that I cannot with sufficient gratitude acknowledge it, or hold myself worthy of so much honour from you. But since your great judgment allows it me, I shall not question, but endeavour to merit it, and promise to be a faithful servant to so noble a friend, who takes care of a stranger at so great a distance from his friends and country. Though I cannot make a suit on the behalf of my superiors to this or any other state, yet for myself, to you I can and do make this suit : you have many sons, adopted as well as natural, and persons of great esteem,—if I might be held worthy of being ranked in that number ? You are the greatest and the eldest chancellor in Christendom ; I have something to do with the chancery in England ; give me leave to hold it under the title of your son, and I hope I shall not defame my father.

CHANCELLOR.—You deserve much more honour, than it is in my power to give you. If you account this any, as his royal highness is pleased to take it, I do most freely adopt you one of my sons, and, in so doing, take the honour to be done to myself. But I shall assure you, by real demonstrations, that I will have the care and affection of a father to you, and that not only in your present business, but in any other wherein you may be concerned."

No sooner was this remarkable conference ended, which made a profound and lasting impression upon Whitelocke, as Penn relates, who visited him when living in retirement at Chilton, than Berkman brought him news about the dissolution of the little Parliament, and the further elevation of Cromwell. Agitated by many emotions, and desirous of ascertaining how this novel intelligence was viewed at Court, he sent to desire an audience. Before his own messenger returned, the Queen, with similar impatience, had sent Grave Tott to congratulate him on the accession of honour to his General.

He went to her in the afternoon, and was admitted into her bedchamber : —

QUEEN.—" Have you received your letters of it yet ?

WHITELOCKE.—No, Madam, but have reason to believe the news, and to expect your Majesty's inclinations concerning it.

QUEEN.—*Par Dieu*, I bear the same respect, and more, to your General and to you, than I did before. I would rather have to do with one than with many.

WHITELOCKE.—I may very well believe it, and return thanks to your Majesty for the continuance of your respects to England, to my General, and to his servant. Your Majesty understands he has a new title, but his power was not mean before.

QUEEN.—It was very great before, and I think it greater now, therefore better for England, but subject to envy. I tell you, under secrecy, that my Chancellor would formerly have been so in Sweden, when I was young, but could not attain it. But if he was my enemy, yet I should say, that he is a wise and a gallant man, and if your General were the greatest enemy I have, yet I should give him his due, that he is a wise and brave man, who has done the greatest things of any man alive. I much desire his friendship, and am heartily glad of his present condition.

WHITELOCKE.—I shall not fail to acquaint him fully with your Majesty's great respect to him."

However, in the course of that evening, letters and new credentials from Thurloe were brought him by the post, and that very night a second audience was given him at the castle. ·

QUEEN.—" Sir, you are welcome still to me, and if possible, more than before the change.

WHITELOCKE.—Madam, it is your goodness and favour to a gentleman, a stranger in your country, who truly honours your Majesty, and you are pleased to shew much respect to my General.

QUEEN.—Your General is a gallant man, and you are fit to serve any prince in Christendom.

WHITELOCKE.—I may without vanity think the better of him, and of myself, through your Majesty's judgment.

QUEEN.—My judgment is, that your affairs in England are much amended, and better established by this change than before.

WHITELOCKE.—We hope that our God will give us a settlement. We have found much of his favour already, and doubt not its continuance.

QUEEN.—Is your new government by a *protector* different from what it was before under a monarchy, or is the alteration in all points ?

WHITELOCKE.—The government is to be the same as formerly, by successive representatives of the people in Parliament, only the Protector is the head, or chief magistrate, of the Commonwealth.

QUEEN.—He is a gallant man, and I pray let him know, that no person has a greater esteem and respect for him than I have.

WHITELOCKE.—I presume then, that his letters to your Majesty will not be unwelcome.

QUEEN.—They shall be most welcome to me.

WHITELOCKE.—I then present these new credentials to your Majesty from his highness my Lord Protector.

QUEEN.—What is the reason, that the Protector's name is put first in the letters ?

WHITELOCKE.—The Protector's name, signed by himself, is at the bottom of the letter, and the naming of him first is because he writes to your Majesty, that being the constant form in England, used to all other princes and states.

QUEEN.—If it be used to other princes I am satisfied, and expect no other. What is the substance of your new government ?

WHITELOCKE.—I shall shew your Majesty the instrument of our new government, a copy of which is sent me, and I shall read such parts of it to your Majesty in French, as may satisfy you."

This he did, but when she came to the title, she said :—

QUEEN.—" Why is the title Protector, when the power is kingly ?

WHITELOCKE.—I cannot satisfy your Majesty as to the reasons of this title, being at so great a distance from the inventors of it.

QUEEN.—New titles, with sovereign power, proved prejudicial to the state of Rome.

WHITELOCKE.—One of your Majesty's ancestors was not permitted to keep the title of Marshal of Sweden.

QUEEN.—He was afterwards King, and that will be next for your Protector.

WHITELOCKE.—That will not be so consonant with our Commonwealth as it was with your crown.

QUEEN.—It is an honour to our nation, that you have looked into the story of it.

WHITELOCKE.—It is the duty of an ambassador to study the history of that crown, to which he is attached.

QUEEN.—It becomes you well, but why is your new government so severe against the Roman Catholics ?

WHITELOCKE.—It is not more severe against them, than it was formerly, and in some things less.

QUEEN.—Methinks that you, who stand so much for liberty, should allow it to them, as well as to others, in a toleration of them.

WHITELOCKE.—Their principles are held to be contrary to the peace of the nation, and therefore they are not tolerated the public exercise of their principles; they hold your Majesty's profession and ours to be heretical, that a foreign power is above you, and above our Commonwealth.

QUEEN.—Those among them, who understand themselves, are of another opinion, and it is a pity they should be persecuted for their conscience sake.

WHITELOCKE.—We are not for persecution in any point of conscience, but we expect a submission to the civil magistrate, and that nothing shall be done to the disturbance of our peace.

QUEEN.—That is fit to be preserved with all care.   Is your Protector *sacré* as other kings are ?

WHITELOCKE.—He is not anointed and crowned ; those ceremonies were not used to him.

QUEEN.—His power is the same with that of king, and why should not his title have been the same ?

WHITELOCKE.—It is the power which makes the title, and not the title the power.   Our Protector thinks he has enough of both.

QUEEN.—He is hardly a mortal man then, but he has brought his business notably to pass, and has done great things.   I give you my hand for it, that I set a great value on him.

WHITELOCKE.—Madam, I kiss your hand with all gratitude for your favours, and do assure your Majesty, that the Protector has a high honour for your Majesty, and shall not want information of your very great respects to him."

Whitelocke's private opinion was, at the time, that Cromwell's usurpation was violent and unjust, but that he, who had no participation in it, and was at that great distance from the scene, when the General invested himself with regal powers, was bound to obey the constituted authorities.   Most of the sober people with him applauded his judgment, and had previously urged upon him not only his own, but the condition of them all.   Here they were, they said with great truth, in a strange country and far

away from home ; here none of them could have any credit
to take up money or to supply their wants, but as they were
enabled by the present power in England ; here they would
have no means of returning to their native land but by
acquiescence in the new order of things. He came to the
correct solution of the difficulty, as the reader has seen.
But it is not a little singular, that from this moment he
made a nearer approach to the French resident, and became
willing, as he prudently words it, to improve the friendship
between them, and all good understanding between the two
nations. His prescience foreboded the change of policy that
was so soon to follow.

If he found the Queen so contented with the new alteration,
it was slightly different in the Chancellor's case. Upon his
sagacious mind the change had evidently made no satisfactory impression. He came to Whitelocke's house in this
unsettled state of feeling, and the following colloquy ensued,
of which time has not impaired the interest :—

WHITELOCKE.—"I had thoughts of waiting upon your
Excellency this day, to have put you in mind of my business,
and to desire that a progress might be made in it. My
occasions in England, in respect of my charge there and of
my private family, require my return with all convenient
speed.

CHANCELLOR.—I doubt not but that your employments
in England are very considerable, and that you may
justly desire a speedy return to them and your family.
It is to further this that I have desired this conference
with you.

WHITELOCKE.—You will pardon my earnest desire of
returning home, especially upon the great alteration which
has happened since my being abroad.

CHANCELLOR.—Indeed, there has been a great alteration
among you, pulling down one and setting up another, abolish-
ing kingship, as you term it, and resolving yourselves into a
republic, but now again setting up another monarchy. Which

uncertainty in your government may occasion some doubt how the treaties made with you may be observed.

WHITELOCKE.—The government is not changed, though a new head be made. The body of the laws and the magistracy remain the same as they were before. And certainly the nation and people of England, on whose behalf treaties are made, do remain the same still. They will give due observance to foreign treaties, whosoever is the chief governor, or in whose name soever they are made. The same objection lies upon the death of every prince, as upon the late alteration in England.

CHANCELLOR.—How could your Parliament justify the deposing of your King, nay, the putting of him to death, and that by a public trial, he being a king, whatsoever faults you could charge him with ? Other nations have sometimes caused their kings to be made away with secretly, or have expelled them, but you, in the face of all princes, and of the whole world, proceeded against him as a common criminal, as a subject rather than as a king, and took away his life in this manner, unwarrantably by any law divine or human.

WHITELOCKE.—I suppose you do not expect from me here, where I am under the protection of a sovereign Queen, or elsewhere, a justification of that proceeding.* I had no hand in it; and those who had by the authority of Parliament, I believe held it more justifiable to proceed in an open trial, than by secret means to take his life away. Their reasons and grounds for the action concern themselves, and is not my present business, nor is the law the same for all countries in cases of the like nature and example.

CHANCELLOR.—It was exemplary with a witness, or rather minatory to all princes of the world. Yet I must confess, it was more honourable to proceed in an open avowed way, than by underhand dealing to have cut him off. And for

---

* Deposition, with banishment or imprisonment, was the proper penalty incurred by Charles for his misgovernment

the laws of every country, we must leave each to its own ordinances, and its actions are responsible to those alone.

WHITELOCKE.—If you are not so satisfied with our government, that it is such as you may safely proceed in the treaty with me, my stay here is to small purpose.

CHANCELLOR.—Truly I am satisfied, that we may safely proceed in the treaty with you, it being a national business, and not personal. I shall, therefore, not doubt the due observance of what shall be agreed between the two nations.

WHITELOCKE.—I am glad you are so clearly satisfied, and could not but assure myself, that a person of your wisdom and judgment could not be otherwise, upon your due consideration of our affairs.

CHANCELLOR.—It is your reason and full information to me, whereby I have the satisfaction more than by my own judgment. I like your settlement the better, because the power of the Protector is limited by your law. There remains nothing for him now to do, but to get him a back and breast of steel.

WHITELOCKE.—Without limitation in the power of a chief magistrate, it would be hard to distinguish him from a tyrant. But what does my father mean by a back and breast of steel ?

CHANCELLOR.—I mean the confirmation of his being Protector to be made by your Parliament, which will be his best and greatest strength.

WHITELOCKE.—For your further satisfaction as to the settledness of government, I have caused the instrument, agreed upon in our last change, to be translated into Latin, that you may peruse it.

CHANCELLOR.—Are the Protector and the people bound to observe this instrument ?

WHITELOCKE.—This is agreed upon, as to the government, to oblige both the people to obey it, and the Protector to govern according to it.

CHANCELLOR.—From whom is this power derived, and given to the Protector? And who had power to ordain it to be binding on the people?

WHITELOCKE.—The Parliament, then sitting, found the peace of the Commonwealth in danger of fresh disturbance, and the many divisions in the nations hardly to be cured. They therefore judged it the best and most expedient way to prevent the mischiefs threatened, to make choice of a head to the Commonwealth, and the General to be the fittest and worthiest person for that office and trust. By a solemn writing, therefore, they resigned their power and authority into the hands of the General, and desired him to accept of the government as chief magistrate, under the title of Protector. To this the officers and soldiers of the armies and navies, the magistrates of London, the principal judges of England, divers noblemen, gentlemen, and persons of quality, all faithful to the common peace and interest of the nation, assented and were present at a solemn meeting, where he was sworn to observe this instrument, and the people generally, by their acclamations, testified their agreement.

CHANCELLOR. — This seems to be an election by the sword and the prevailing party of the nation. Such precedents in other countries have proved dangerous and not durable.

WHITELOCKE.—God has thus ordered it. I hear there is a general acquiescence and submission to it, and the supreme law of *salus populi* seemed to require this change. And though he were the general that is chosen to be the head, yet the soldiers were not the sole but joint actors in this designation.

CHANCELLOR.—Such military elections of the Roman emperors, and in other nations, proved fatal to the public peace and liberty.

WHITELOCKE.—I hope this may prove a means for the preservation of our peace and freedom.

CHANCELLOR.—Do you hold this to be an election, and not rather a military imposition of your chief governor ?

WHITELOCKE.—It is certainly a very general agreement of persons in power and authority, and of principal interest in the nation, to set up this government, and therefore may be hoped to continue as firm as those elections of kings by a few great men only, such as was used in yours and the neighbouring countries by the senators.

CHANCELLOR.—Those elections by the senators, formerly made, raised great factions, occasioning much civil war and misery. Therefore our Ricksdagh judged it necessary to alter that electoral course with our kings, and to settle the crown in hereditary succession, which proves more peaceful and prosperous than those elections.

WHITELOCKE.—This was a great change; yet foreign treaties were still kept by you. I was born under hereditary kings, and do not disapprove that government. Yet I hope our Commonwealth, as now constituted, will also flourish, affording liberty and advantage to the people under it, and be as fixed as any other. If you, my noble father, have as good an opinion of it as I have, our treaty will have the better issue.

CHANCELLOR.—The great doubt will be of its permanency, you being so subject to changes; and then how will our treaties be observed ?

WHITELOCKE.—I suppose that the treaties you made with other states in the names of your elective kings remain still good, and are observed in the time of your hereditary Queen. I come not to treat with you concerning the interest of my General, now Protector, but the interest of England, and in behalf of its people and Commonwealth, to treat with the Crown of Sweden in behalf of the Swedish people. Whether the head of either people be called King or Queen, or Protector, and the nation a commonwealth or a kingdom, yet the people's interest is the same, and of equal force at one time or another.

CHANCELLOR.—Son, I am satisfied with your reasons, and convinced that we may safely proceed in a treaty with you."

Much negotiation ensued at that and a following conference between the two chancellors, and some progress was made towards a satisfactory issue ; but, on the 21st of the month, a new source of anxiety was opened to him.   The Queen, who had now returned from her journey, sent one of her secretaries to him, desiring him to come to the castle at three o'clock in the afternoon, which he did, and was presently admitted into her bed-chamber, where two stools were placed.   Her Majesty sat down on one, and caused him to sit by her.   After a few brief compliments, and a courteous inquiry or two (on her part respecting the progress of the treaty), she drew her stool close up to his, as if for the purpose of making to him a confidential and important disclosure.   And so it proved.

QUEEN.—"I shall surprise you with something which I intend communicating to you, but it must be under secrecy.

WHITELOCKE.—Madam, we that have been versed in the affairs of England are not used to be surprised with the discourse of a young lady.   Whatsoever your Majesty shall think fit to impart to me, and command to be under secrecy, shall be faithfully obeyed by me.

QUEEN.—I have great confidence in your honour and judgment ; and therefore, though you are a stranger, I shall acquaint you with a business of the greatest consequence to me in the world, and which I have not communicated to any creature.   Nor would I have you tell any one of it, no, not your General, till you come to see him ; and in this business I desire your counsel.

WHITELOCKE.—Your Majesty does me in this the greatest honour imaginable, and your confidence in me I shall not, through the help of God, deceive in the least measure, nor relate to any person, except my General, what you impart to me.   In what your Majesty shall judge my counsel worth

B B

receiving, I shall give it you with all sincerity, according to the best of my poor capacity.

QUEEN.—Sir, this it is. I have it in my thoughts and resolution to quit the crown of Sweden, and retire into private life, as much more suitable to my contentment than the great cares and troubles attending on the government of my kingdom. What think you of this my resolution?

WHITELOCKE.—I am sorry to hear your Majesty call it a resolution. If any thing would surprise a man, the hearing of such a resolution from a lady of your talents, power, and judgment would do it. But I suppose your Majesty is only pleased to be jocose with your humble servant.

QUEEN.—I speak to you the truth of my intentions; and had it not been for your coming here, which caused me to defer that resolution, it might have been probably done before this time.

WHITELOCKE.—I beseech your Majesty to defer it still, or rather to exclude it wholly from your thoughts, as unfit to receive any entertainment in your royal breast. And give me your pardon if I speak my poor opinion with all duty and plainness to you, since you are pleased to require it. Can any reason enter into a mind, so full of reason as yours is, to cause such a resolution by your Majesty?

QUEEN.—I take your plainness in very good part, and desire you to use freedom with me in this matter. The reasons which conduct me to such a resolution are, because I am a woman, and therefore the more unfit to govern, being subject to the greater inconveniences. The heavy cares of government outweigh the glories and pleasures of it; these are not to be embraced in comparison with that content which a private retirement brings with it.

WHITELOCKE.—As I am a stranger I have the advantage of speaking more freely to your Majesty, especially in this great business; and as I am one who have been acquainted with a retired life, I can judge of that. But as to the cares of a crown, none but those that wear it can judge of them.

Only this I can say, that the higher your station is, the more opportunity you have of doing service to God, and good to the world.

QUEEN.—I desire that more service to God and more good to the world may be done than I, being a woman, am capable of performing. As soon as I can settle some affairs for the good and advantage of my people, I think I may without scandal release myself from my continual cares to enjoy the pleasures of privacy and retirement.

WHITELOCKE.—But, madam, you that enjoy the kingdom by right of descent, you that have the full affections and obedience of all your subjects in every degree, why should you be discouraged at continuing the reins in your own hands? How can you forsake those who testify so much love to you, and liking of your government?

QUEEN.—It is my love to the people that causes me to think of providing a better governor for them than a poor woman can be. And it is somewhat of love to myself, to please my own fancy, that I design my private retirement.

WHITELOCKE.—Madam, God has called you to this eminent place and power of queen. Do not act contrary to this call, and disable yourself from doing Him service, for which end we are all here. Your Majesty, as queen, has far greater opportunities than you can have as a private person of bringing honour to him.

QUEEN.—If another person, who may succeed me, has capacity and better opportunity, by reason of his sex and talents, to do God and his country service, than I can have, then my quitting the government, and putting it into better hands, will fully answer this objection.

WHITELOCKE.—I confess my ignorance of better hands than your own in which the government may be placed.

QUEEN.—My cousin, the Prince Palatine, is a person of excellent parts and abilities for government, besides his valour and knowledge in military affairs. I have caused him to be declared my successor. It was only I that did it.

Perhaps you may have heard of the passages between him and me : but I am resolved never to marry. It will be much more for the advantage of the people that the crown be on his head than on mine. None fitter than he for it!

WHITELOCKE.—I believe his royal highness to be a person of exceeding great honour and abilities for government. You have caused him to be declared your successor : it will be no injury to him to stay his time. I am sure it may be to your Majesty, if persuaded, perhaps designedly, to give up your right to him while you live and ought to enjoy it.

QUEEN.—It is no design, but my own voluntary act. He being more active and fit for the government than I am, the sooner he is put into it the better.

WHITELOCKE.—What your Majesty likes best is best to you. But do you not think that Charles the Fifth had as great hopes of content by his abdication as your Majesty has, and yet repented of it the same day ?

QUEEN.—That was by reason of his son's unworthiness. But many other princes have, happily and with all content, retired to a private condition. I am confident my cousin, the prince, will see that I shall be duly paid what I reserve for my own maintenance.

WHITELOCKE.—Madam, let me humbly advise you, if any such thing should be, as I hope it will not, to reserve that country in your possession out of which your reserved revenue is to be issued. For when money is to be paid out of a prince's treasury, it is not always ready and certain.

QUEEN.—The Prince Palatine is full of justice and honour. But I like your counsel well, shall follow it, and advise further with you in it.

WHITELOCKE.—Madam, I shall be always ready to serve you in any of your commands, but more unwillingly in this than any other. Suppose, madam, as the worst must be cast, that by some exigencies or troubles your lessened revenue should not be answered and paid to supply your own occasions You that have been mistress of the whole revenue of this Crown, of so noble and bountiful a heart as you have, how can you bear the abridging of it, or, it may be, the necessary supplies for yourself and servants to be wanting to your quality?

QUEEN.—In case of such exigencies, notwithstanding my quality, I can content myself with very little ; and for servants, with a lacquay and a chambermaid.

WHITELOCKE.—This is good philosophy, but hard to practise. Give me leave, madam, to make another objection : you now are queen and sovereign lady of all the nations subject to your crown and person, whose word the stoutest and greatest among them obey, and strive to cringe to you, but when you shall have divested yourself of all power, the same persons, who now fawn upon you, will be then apt to put affronts and scorns upon you. How can your generous and royal spirit brook them, and to be despised by those whom you have raised and so much obliged ?

QUEEN.—I look upon such things as these as the course of this world; shall expect such scorns, and be prepared to contemn them.

WHITELOCKE.—These answers are strong arguments of your excellent temper and fitness to continue in your power and government : such resolutions will advance your Majesty above any earthly crown. Such a spirit as this shows how much you are above other women, and most men in the world. And as such a woman, you have the more advantage for government, without disparagement of the prince, not inferior to him or any other man, to have the trust of it."

The remainder of the interview was spent in discussing the treaty, the contemplated joint attack on Denmark, and her Majesty's declaration, that she would appoint him to the command of Zealand with the greatest pleasure, in case her scheme met with the Protector's concurrence.

CHAPTER XX.

—•—

FOR many successive days he saw various individuals of
note in the diplomatic world, and had two protracted conversations with the Archbishop on the recent events in
England, and the general state of religion in both countries.
He must have gained by this time the esteem of the Queen
to some extent, for on sending his son James in the early
part of February to inquire after her health, she had him
conducted into her bedroom and desired him to carry back
for her answer : *se non alio morbo laborare, quàm quod tres
integros dies non convenerit ipsam,* that she was sick of no
other disease, but that for three whole days he had not
come to see her.   He could do no less than go and give her
another lesson in the English language, for which a manuscript grammar had been hastily prepared by one of his
chaplains, M. de la Marche.   As she was an invalid, he took
with him also his own medical man, Dr. Whistler, who had
two questions put to him very shortly after his presentation :
1. Whether physicians knew anything by their art, or were

guided by adventure and chance ?   2. Whether good philo-
sophers were good Christians ?   Her Majesty was too hard
upon the poor doctor; as if he, who had vegetated at Oxford
nearly all his life, could answer such puzzling questions.
Whitelocke says his answers were full of ingenuousness and
learning.   No doubt they were.   But on the circulation of
the blood, Whistler was able to give her more than ordinary
satisfaction.   As soon as he had withdrawn, Christina returned
Whitelocke many thanks for his present of horses to her, and
particularly for his son's mare.

A few of the questions and answers between the ambassador and the Archbishop of Upsala, may possibly amuse
the reader.

ARCHBISHOP.—" It is related here, that you have not only
abolished the distinction between the clergy and the laity,
but even hierarchy itself.

WHITELOCKE.—We have now no prelacy in England or
Scotland ; our bishops were their own destruction.   But with
you the authority and dignity of bishops continues as it was
in former times.

ARCHBISHOP.—The state ecclesiastical with us, blessed be
God, is still preserved. . . . .

*   *   *   *   *   *   *

WHITELOCKE.—It is a happy condition to live together in
unity, but you suffer no dissent in opinion.

ARCHBISHOP.—No man must vent his private fancies, or
new opinions, contrary to the doctrine of the Church.   If he
does, we severely punish it.

WHITELOCKE.—That is somewhat strict, and may be construed to a kind of assumption of infallibility.

ARCHBISHOP.—We take no such thing upon us, but
desire to preserve peace and unity in the Church, and its
members.

WHITELOCKE.—Those are good things, but I doubt hardly
to be settled in this world, where offences must come.

ARCHBISHOP.—But woe to those by whom they come !

WHITELOCKE.—They may possibly come by imposing too much on men's consciences, as well as by new opinions.

ARCHBISHOP.—We impose no further than is warranted by the word of God.

WHITELOCKE.—And who interprets that word?

ARCHBISHOP.—The Church of God.

WHITELOCKE.—The Holy Scriptures interpret one another.

ARCHBISHOP.—That is true, and learned men are the best interpreters of those scriptures."

Some days after this, the audience of the Muscovite envoy came off. The first person who presented himself was a tall big man, with a large rude black beard, pale countenance and ill demeanour. His habit was a long robe of purple cloth, trimmed with small gold lace, the livery of his master. On his right hand was a companion in the same livery, and resembling the envoy in features and behaviour, He carried on high the grand duke's letters, set in a frame of wood, with a covering of crimson sarsenet over them. On the left hand of the envoy was his interpreter. As soon as he had made his uncouth reverences, he began to speak in his own language, but fairly broke down half way. After a short pause he recovered himself with the assistance of a paper. When he had quite done the interpreters commenced, and as soon as they had completed their duties, the envoy threw himself flat upon the ground, seemingly kissing it. Then rising to the erect posture, he came and kissed the Queen's hand, holding his own hands the while behind his back. His fellow observed precisely the same etiquette, and then presented his master's letters. The Queen handed Whitelocke, who was standing at her right hand, one of these letters to look at. The characters he found to be like the Greek, but some like the "Persick." After this ceremony the Russians returned to their *aqua-vitæ*, and he to his own dinner at home.

We have just seen by the few items of a discourse introduced above, what a Protestant Lutheran Archbishop was in

those days of intolerance, when even Presbyterians, so persecuted themselves before, were unwilling in their turn that
any man should have license to think for himself in opposition to their doctrines and code of ethics, when any independent thought on the part of a layman was so dangerous
throughout the length and breadth of all Europe. Turn we
now to the Chief Justice of Sweden, whom our chancellor
visited about the beginning of March. He wore a coat, a
furred black cap, a sword and belt, but no cloak. Two
soldiers were stationed as sentries at his door, a privilege
possessed by him, a subject, alone. Whitelocke knew beforehand that this great legal functionary was no friend to
England and her sons, but he found him for the nonce full
of affection for the Commonwealth. They spoke in Latin,
for although the Swede knew French, like Oxenstierne the
Chancellor, he refused to use it in ordinary discourse. One
of the observations he made was so precisely similar to what
the modern English traveller is sure to hear abroad, that I
cannot refrain from inserting it. He had been Governor
of Finland, he said, for ten years, a province larger he
insisted than all France, and as for the Swedish dominions,
they were bigger than France, Spain, Italy—all put
together !

My omission of the endless negotiations, apart from their
want of intrinsic interest at the present day, may be justified
by the ambassador's own note in his diary : " Thus was
March passed over, full of trouble, yet nothing effected in
this business."

At the end of the first week in April, he waited on the
Queen, who was already anticipating the delights of freedom.

QUEEN.—" I am resolved on retiring into Pomerania, and
mean to go to the Spa this summer, and there drink the
waters for my health.

WHITELOCKE.—Give me leave, madam, to put you in mind
of two things to be specially taken care of ; one is the security of your own person, the other is the settling of your

revenue. Your Majesty, being of a royal and bountiful spirit, cannot look into such matters so much beneath you, as expenses or accounts; so if care be not taken for good officers, your majesty may be disappointed and deceived.

QUEEN.—I thank you for this counsel. I intend to have Mons. Flemming with me, to take charge of my revenue. He is a discreet, wise man, fit for that employment, and to order the expenses of my house. I believe he will neither deceive me himself, nor permit others to do it, for he is faithful to me.

WHITELOCKE.—Such a servant is a jewel. I hope care is taken that your Majesty's revenue is secured in such a manner, that you shall not depend upon the pleasure of any other for the receipt of it, but to be in your own power as mistress of it, not as a pensioner.

QUEEN.—It shall be settled according to the advice you gave me, and I thank you for it.

WHITELOCKE.—Madam, I account it a happiness, if in any thing I may be serviceable to your Majesty. Whom does your Majesty take with you besides Mons. Flemming of that quality?

QUEEN.—I desire the company of M. Woolfeldt and his lady, if they will go with me.

WHITELOCKE.—I suppose they will be very serviceable to your Majesty, and I hope it will not be long, after the business here effected, before you transport yourself into Pomerania, lest any designs should be against your liberty, for, Madam, in this age, there are few persons to be trusted.

QUEEN.—That's too great a truth, and I thank you for the caution. I could freely trust yourself with any of my concernments, and if you will come with me into Pomerania, you shall be as welcome as any man living, and we will be merry together.

WHITELOCKE.—I humbly thank your Majesty for your great favour to your servant, who has a wife and children enough to people a province in Pomerania, and I shall bring them all there to do your Majesty service.

QUEEN.—If you will bring your lady and all your children and family to settle there, you shall want nothing in my power, and shall be very welcome to me."

On the 28th of April, the treaty was concluded, and Whitelocke penned down the hopes he entertained of it. "Thus, after a long and intricate, it might be said vexatious transaction of this great affair, for near five months together, all bitter opposition, cunning practices, and perplexed difficulties being removed and overcome, through the goodness and assistance of the only wise counsellor, the Prince of Peace, it pleased Him to give a good issue and happy success in the conducting of this treaty by him, who accounts his great labour and hazards in this transaction well bestowed, and who humbly prays that this treaty may prove to the honour of God, the interest of the Protestant cause, and the good of both nations therein concerned."

He waited on the Queen the next day, and after settling the day for the audience of leave, she said :—

QUEEN.—"I had some cloths in a ship coming hither, the ship is taken and my cloths detained in England, so that I cannot get them to wear.

WHITELOCKE.—If your Majesty want cloths, I have a piece of English stuff at my house which cost two shillings a yard ; if that were not too dear for your Majesty's wearing, I would send it you.

QUEEN.—Two shillings a yard is dear enough for me ; I pray send your stuff hither, I shall willingly accept it and thank you for it.

WHITELOCKE.—Will your Majesty be pleased on Monday next to go into England?

QUEEN.—Hardly so soon, yet perhaps I may one day see England. But what is your meaning in this ?

WHITELOCKE.—Madam, Monday next is the first day of May, a great day in England ; we call it May-day, when the gentlemen use to wait upon their mistresses abroad to bid the spring welcome, and to have some collation or entertainment for them. Now your Majesty, being my mistress, if you will do me the honour that after the English custom I may wait upon you on May-day, and have a little treatment for you after the manner of England—this I call going into England, and shall take it as a very great favour from your Majesty.

QUEEN.—If this be your meaning of going into England, I shall be very willing as your mistress to go with you on Monday next and see the English mode."

She came accordingly, cold as the weather was, bringing with her Woolfeldt, whose wife was the king of Denmark's sister, Tott, and five of her ladies. The collation was ready, and the Queen took her place at the table with the "beautiful countess," the countess Gabriel Oxenstierne, Woolfeldt, Tott, and Whitelocke ; the other ladies sat in another room. "Their meat was such fowl as could be gotten, dressed after the English fashion, and with English sauces, creams, puddings, custards, tarts, tansies, English apples, *bon-chrétien* pears, cheese, butter, neats' tongues, potted venison and sweetmeats brought out of England, as his sack and claret also were. His beer was also brewed and his bread made by his own servants in his house after the English manner. The Queen and her company seemed highly pleased with this treatment ; some of her company said, "she did eat and drink more at it, than she used to do in three or four days at her own table."

The entertainment was as full and noble as the place would afford, or as Whitelocke could make it ; so well ordered and contrived, that the Queen said she had never seen any like it. She was pleased so far to play the good housewife, as to inquire how the butter could be so fresh and sweet, and yet brought out of England. From his cooks he satisfied her inquiry, that they put the salt butter into milk, where it lay all night, and the next day it would eat fresh and sweet as this did, or any new-made butter ; he commended her Majesty's good housewifery, who, to express her contentment with this collation, was full of pleasantness and gaiety of spirit, both at supper-time and afterwards. Amongst other frolics, she commanded White-locke to teach her ladies the English salutation, which, after some pretty defences, their lips obeyed, and Whitelocke " most readily."

The air of Sweden was decidedly doing him good.

The Queen was pleased to commend his music of trumpets, which sounded all supper-time, and the whole party cast the cares of state away, until the hour arrived when he had to escort his royal guest back to her castle, and as she seemed so struck with the novel tastes of his cates, he sent the whole of them next day as a present to her, not forgetting the sack and claret. Generous as he had been with his horses, cabinets, and other matters, his mistress of May-day was not to be outdone, for she ordered 200 ship-pounds of copper to be taken by a ship to his address in England, and then sent her master of the ceremonies to himself with a handsome jewel. It was a case of gold, fairly enamelled, with an admirable likeness of herself in the midst of it. It was set round about with twelve large diamonds and several smaller ones between each of the larger. To each of his two sons she sent, by the same messenger, a chain of gold of five links, with her picture at the end of each chain in gold, worth 400 ducats a-piece. And as he had bestowed largesses on the Queen's servants, so did she on all the members of his embassy. In return for the salutation he had taught the Swedish ladies, he was invited a few days later to a wedding at court, and was conveyed there between ten and eleven at night in one of the Queen's coaches. His sons accom-panied him. Having an eye for everything, he admired the costume of the newly-married couple. They were both clothed in white tabby ; the bridegroom's dress was em-broidered with very broad gold and silver lace ; the bride bore on her head a coronet set full of diamonds, with a diamond collar having lappets, a diamond girdle, and a rich jewel at her breast. On entering the great hall, the Queen took her chair of state, and dancing commenced. The Queen rose and came to Whitelocke to take him out, but he excused himself.

WHITELOCKE.—"Madam, I am fearful I shall dishonour your Majesty as well as shame myself by dancing with you.

QUEEN.—I will try whether you can dance.

WHITELOCKE.—I assure your Majesty I cannot in any measure be worthy to have you by the hand.

QUEEN.—I esteem you worthy, and therefore make choice of you to dance with me.

WHITELOCKE.—I shall not so much undervalue your Majesty's judgment as not to obey you herein, but wish I could remember as much of this, as when I was a young man."

After they had done dancing, and Whitelocke had waited upon her to her chair of state—

QUEEN.—"*Par Dieu!* These Hollanders are lying fellows!

WHITELOCKE.—I wonder how the Hollanders should come into your head upon such an occasion as this is, who are not usually thought upon in such solemnities, nor much acquainted with them.

QUEEN.—I will tell you all. The Hollanders reported to me a great while since, that all the *noblesse* of England were of the King's party, and none but mechanics of the Parliament party, not a gentleman among them. Now I thought to try you, and shame you if you could not dance, but I see that you are a gentleman, and have been bred one; that makes me say the Hollanders are lying fellows, to report that there was not a gentleman of the Parliament's party, when I see by you chiefly, and by many of your company, that you are a gentleman."

Queen Christina's abdication arrived, and Whitelocke was present at the ceremony. She made her speech; the Archbishop of Upsala, as marshal of the clergy, made his, and then

in due order the two marshals of the nobility and the burgesses.   What they said matters little, but this was not the
case with the marshal of the boors, for he gave utterance to
truth, nature, and the honest purposes of his heart.   As he
stepped out, it was seen that he was a plain country fellow,
in his clouted shoon and corresponding accoutrements ; he
made no " congees," and spoke bluntly to the point :

" Oh, Lord God !   Madam, what do you mean to do ?   It
troubles us to hear you speak of forsaking those who love
you so well as we do.   Can you be better off than you are ?
You are queen of all these countries ; and if you leave this
large kingdom, where will you get such another ?   If you
should do it (as I hope you won't, for all this) both you and
we shall have cause, when it is too late, to be sorry for it.
Therefore, my fellows and I pray you to think better on't,
and to keep your crown on your head ; then you will keep
your own honour and our peace.   But if you lay it down, in
my conscience, you will endanger all.   Continue in your
gears, good madam, and be the fore-horse as long as you
live, and we will help you the best we can to bear your
burden.   Your father was an honest gentleman and a good
king, very stirring in the world.   We obeyed him and loved
him as long as he lived, and you are his own child, have
governed us very well, and we love you with all our hearts.
The prince is an honest gentleman, and when his time comes,
we shall be ready to do our duties to him, as we do to you ;
but as long as you live we are not willing to part with you,
and therefore, I pray, madam, don't part with us."

When the boor had ended his speech, he waddled up to
the Queen without any ceremony, took her by the hand,
shook it heartily, and kissed it two or three times ; then
turning his back to her, he pulled out of his pocket a dingy
handkerchief, wiped the tears from his eyes, and in the
same posture he had come up returned to his own place
again.

By the side of this noble-hearted boor the ambassador

was soon able to place the conduct of one of his own servants at home, for about that time, a day or two later, he received some letters from his friend, Mr. George Cockain, in one of which was the following passage :

" Your old servant Abell is much courted by his highness to be his falconer in chief, but he will not accept it, except your excellency had been here to give him your explicit leave to serve his highness.   He told me, without stuttering, he would not serve the greatest prince in the world, except your excellency were present to make the bargain, that he might wait upon you with a cast of hawks at the beginning of September every year into Bedfordshire.   It is a pity that gallantry should hurt any ; certainly it is a noble profession that inspires him with such a spirit."

I think we had better have falconers back again.

May the 12th was the day appointed for Whitelocke's last public audience.   It arrived and found him habited in a plain suit of very fine English cloth, the colour of which was musk, with buttons of enamelled gold ; in each button there was a ruby, and the points and ribbons were of gold.   The ceremony of going was much the same as on the first occasion, and the queen's dress not altogether so different as might have been expected.   Her habit was black silk stuff for her coats, and over them was a black velvet jippo, such as men wear ; she had upon her breast the jewel of the Amaranth ; her hair hung loose as it used to do, and this time she had on a man's hat.   Two days later he was admitted to her bed-chamber, as usual, and the discourse turned on recent events :—

WHITELOCKE.—" I humbly thank your Majesty for admitting me to be present at the Ricksdagh.

QUEEN.—How did you like the manner and proceedings of it when you were there ?

WHITELOCKE.—It was with the greatest gravity and solemnity that I ever saw in any public assembly, well becoming persons of their quality and interest.

QUEEN.—There are among them very considerable persons, and wise men.

WHITELOCKE—Such an assembly requires such men, and their carriage showed them to be such. But, Madam, I expected that your chancellor, after he spoke with your Majesty, should, according to the course in our parliament, have declared, by your direction, the causes of the council's being summoned.

QUEEN.—It belongs to the office of the chancellor with us to do it, and when I called him to me it was to desire him to do it.

WHITELOCKE.—How then came it to pass that he did not, when his place and your Majesty required it?

QUEEN.—He desired to be excused, and gave me this reason, that he had taken an oath to my father to use his utmost endeavour to keep the crown on my head, and that the cause of my calling this diet was to have their consents for me to quit the crown; that if he should make this proposition to them, it would be contrary to the oath he had taken to my father, and therefore he could not do it.

WHITELOCKE.—Did not your Majesty expect this answer?

QUEEN.—Not at all; but was wholly surprised at it. And when the Ricksdagh were met, my chancellor thus excusing himself, there was nobody appointed by me to declare to them the cause of their meeting. But rather than the assembly should be put off, and nothing done, I plucked up my spirits the best I could, and spoke to them on the sudden as you heard, although much to my disadvantage.

WHITELOCKE.—Indeed, Madam, you were much surprised. And I cannot but wonder that you should have had no intimation given you beforehand of your chancellor's resolution. But your Majesty will pardon me, if I believe it proved no disadvantage to you, when I had the honour to see and hear with how excellent a grace and how princelike your Majesty, in so great an assembly, and on a sudden, delivered your mind and purpose.

QUEEN.—You are apt at putting the best construction on it. You see I did adventure upon it, remembering that they were my subjects and I their Queen.

WHITELOCKE.—Madam, you spoke and acted like yourself, and were highly complimented by the several marshals, but above all the rest, by the honest boor.

QUEEN.—Were you so taken with his clownery?

WHITELOCKE.—It seemed to me as pure and clear natural eloquence, without any forced strain, as could be expressed.

QUEEN.—Indeed, there was little else but what was natural; and by a well-meaning man, who has understanding enough in his country way.

WHITELOCKE.—Whosoever shall consider his matter more than his form, will find that the man understands his business. The garment, or phrase, in which he clothed his matter, though it was rustic, yet its variety, plain elegancy, and reason, could not but affect his auditors.

QUEEN.—I think he spoke from his heart.

WHITELOCKE.—I believe he did, and acted so too, especially when he wiped his eyes.

QUEEN.—He showed his affection to me in that posture, more than greater men did in their spheres.

WHITELOCKE.—Madam, we must look upon all men to work according to their present interest, and so I suppose do the great men here as well as elsewhere.*

QUEEN.—Here I have had experience enough of such actings. I shall try what they do in other places, and content myself, however I shall find it.

WHITELOCKE.—Your Majesty will not expect to find much difference in the humours of men, as to seeking themselves, and neglecting those from whom they have received favours.

QUEEN.—It will be no otherwise than what I am armed to

---

* As the Queen in a former interview had called the English hypocrites and dissemblers, she could not carp at this indirect and gentle reproof of her own countrymen

bear, and not to regard. But your particular respects I shall always remember with gratefulness.

WHITELOCKE.—Your Majesty shall ever find me your faithful servant. Do you intend, Madam, to go hence to Pomerania?

QUEEN.—My intentions are to go presently after my resignation to the Spa. But wheresoever I am you have a true friend in me.

WHITELOCKE.—There is no person alive more cordially your Majesty's servant than I am.

QUEEN.—I do believe it, or else I should not have communicated to you such things as I have done.

WHITELOCKE.—Your Majesty expressed by this much confidence in me, which I hope shall never deceive you, however my want of abilities may not answer your Majesty's favours to me.

QUEEN.—I have no doubt of your faithfulness, and you have sufficiently manifested your abilities. Give me leave to trouble you with the company of a gentleman, my servant, whom I purpose sending over to England with you, to take care for those things which I desire to have from there.

WHITELOCKE.—He shall be very welcome to me and my company, and I shall give him my best assistance for your Majesty's service.

QUEEN.—I shall thank you for it, and command him to obey your directions.

WHITELOCKE.—Madam, if you please to accept a set of black English stone-horses for your coach, I shall take the boldness to send them to your stables, and pray your Majesty that the Master of your Horse may furnish me for my journey to Stockholm.

QUEEN.—I thankfully accept your kindness, and all mine are at your service.

WHITELOCKE.—I have interrupted your Majesty too long. I desired the favour of this opportunity to present my most humble thanks to your Majesty for all your noble favours to me and my company.

QUEEN.—I entreat your excuse for the meanness of my presents. I could not do therein what I desired, nor after your merit.

WHITELOCKE.—There is nothing of my merit to be alleged, but your Majesty has testified much honour to the Protector and Commonwealth, whom I serve.

QUEEN.—England is a noble country, and your master is a gallant man   I desire you to assure him, on my part, of all affection and respect towards him.

WHITELOCKE.—Your Majesty may be confident of the like from his Highness, and your humble servant will heartily pray for your Majesty's prosperity wherever you are.

QUEEN.—I wish you a happy voyage and return to your own country."

He had after this a long interview with the Prince, who was so soon to become the King of Sweden, and nobly did he endeavour to impress his illustrious visitor with the sincerity of the dominant party in his own country. Nor were his efforts less commendable to restrain the spirit of persecution, so long the disgrace of Sweden, and to this day somewhat more than theoretically and legally carried out. Take the following remarks as a proof of the Englishman's enlightenment on this question :—

PRINCE.—"I do very well approve that course, and your profession and practice in matters of religion. But we hear of too much difference of opinion among you on those matters.

WHITELOCKE.—We have indeed too much difference of opinion amongst us on matters of religion, and yet the public peace is not broken, but carefully preserved.

PRINCE.—But if there be not uniformity among you in those matters, your peace will be endangered.

WHITELOCKE.—We do not yet find that danger, and we look upon it as a liberty, due to all Christians, to take what way of worship they think best for the good of their own souls."

And so on to the end of the chapter. But here he pleaded in vain for the cause of toleration and the rights of private conscience. The Prince thought not differently from Clarendon, or the Oxford divines at a later date, from their restoration to it may be this day. With what success the world has seen, perhaps has yet to see, for that dream of unity still lingers in this land, where men may yet be found so blind that they believe the human race, under all climates and in various stages of knowledge, can be brought to adopt their articles of faith. To this day crowned heads and mitred priests are striving to turn Nature out of the door from their stable, while she as constantly is descending again from the loft, and ready to create another Hercules so soon as the Augæan filth becomes intolerable.

During his whole stay in Sweden the ambassador had exercised the utmost hospitality, and his table had been open to most of the nobility, but he never received a single invitation to dinner in return, except from Grave Eric and General Douglas, the latter of whom was not merely Scotch by name, but birth, and had not forgotten during his long sojourn abroad those little acts of festive kindness, which the Gothic or German race is found even by modern travellers to ignore so grievously.

On the 20th of May his travelling party reached Stockholm, and set sail in a Swedish ship, the Amaranth, from a place called the Dollars, on the 1st of June. It was the first sea-trip of this new vessel, but after a perilous voyage of eight days, she reached Lubeck in safety.

He was much pleased with the inhabitants and the town, but soon left it on his route to Hamburg, where he also found much to admire and praise. At a collation given him here by the English resident, a strange waiter, whom he never saw before nor after—and doubtless he was rigidly sought for—played the part of cupbearer, and poured him

out a glass of small beer.   It seemed to him of a bad taste
and colour, but as none of his own servants were present,
good breeding kept him silent and he made no inquiries,
nor indeed had he any suspicion of foul play.   He had eaten
very little, and only drunk· one glass of Spanish wine during
the whole meal.   On returning to his lodgings he was taken
extremely ill, grew worse and worse, and felt sick with
agonising pains like strokes of daggers.   In this state he
remained for thirteen hours, till about five o'clock in the
morning, when his physician, Dr. Whistler, suspecting poison
had been given him, administered a powder with a great
quantity of sweet almond oil.   Emetics were then prescribed,
and their effect restored him in a short time.   While still
confined to his bed, the senators of the city, who had previously entered his bed-room to condole with and then felici-
tate him, sat down to his hospitable table in a neighbouring
apartment, at which they continued with unflinching devotion
from noon to six in the evening.   They then returned to
cheer their entertainer in his sick room, and a short time
after went back to the viands and their joyous converse till
nine at night.   These jovial senators, in short, were aldermen,
as the reader has already divined, nor were they to be
outdone in civility, being quite as ready to confer gifts as to
receive them.

On quitting the German coast, the English frigate that
conveyed him encountered such imminent danger on the
28th of June, that he considered it ever after to have been
the day of his greatest deliverance.   His own description
will represent it best.

"After midnight, till three o'clock in the afternoon, there
was a great calm, and though the President was taken with
it, yet the Elizabeth had a good wind.   Notwithstanding
that the day before she was left behind a great distance, yet
this morning she came up near to him and got before him.
So great is the difference sometimes, and at so small a distance, on the sea, that here one ship shall have no wind at

all, whilst another ship a few yards off shall have her sails filled.

Notwithstanding the calm, yet the wind being by flashes large, they went the last night and the day before twenty leagues up and down, sometimes in their course and sometimes out of it. In the morning, sounding with the plummet, the pilot judged that they were about sixteen leagues from the Texel, and twenty-four from Orfordness, but he did not certainly know whereabouts they were. Between three and four o'clock in the afternoon, the wind came to north-north-west, which gave them hopes of finishing their voyage the sooner, and it blew a fresh gale.

About five o'clock in the evening there rose a very great fog and thick mist, so that it was exceedingly dark, and they could not see their way a ship's length before them. Whitelocke came upon the decks, when seeing the weather so bad with night coming on, that all their sails were spread and that they ran extraordinarily fast, he did not like it, but called together the captain, the master, the pilot, and others, to consult what was best to be done. He asked them, why they spread all their sails, and desired to make so much way in such ill weather so near to night. They said, they had so much sail because the wind favoured them, and that, notwithstanding the bad weather, they might safely run as they did, having sea-room enough. He then asked them, if they knew whereabouts they were. They confessed they did not, because they had been so much tossed up and down by contrary winds, and the sun had not shone, whereby they might take the elevation. He replied, that having been driven forward and backwards as they had been, it was impossible to know where they were; that the ship had been and was now running fast, and if she should run so all night, perhaps they might be in danger of the English or the Dutch coast; that by Norfolk there were great banks of sand, by which he had passed at sea formerly, and which could not be unknown to them; that in case the ship should fall upon those sands, or any other dangers of that coast before morning, they should all be lost. He thought fit, therefore, to take down some of the sails, and slacken their course, till by daylight they might come to know more certainly in what part they were.

The officers of the ship continued earnest to hold on their course, saying, they would warrant it, there was running enough for all night, and that to take down any sail, now the wind was so good for them, would be a great wrong to them in their course. But Whitelocke was little satisfied with their reasons, and less with their warranties, which among them are not of binding force. His own reason showed him, that not knowing where they were, and in such weather as this, to run on as they did they knew not whither, with all their sails spread, might be dangerous; whereas, to take down some of their sails and slacken speed could not be dangerous, and but little prejudicial to their course this night. He thought this better to be borne than to endanger all.

Upon a strange earnestness in his own mind and judgment he gave a positive command to the captain to cause all the sails to be taken down, except the mainsail only, and that to be half-furled. Upon the captain's dispute, he told him with quickness, that if he did not presently see it done, he would cause another to do it, whereupon the captain obeyed, and it was a great mercy that the same was done, which God directed as a means to save their lives.

After the sails were taken down, Whitelocke also ordered them to sound and try what water and bottom they had; about ten o'clock they found eighteen fathoms, at the next sounding but fifteen, and so lessening till they came to eight. This startled them, and made them endeavour to tack about, but it was too late, for within less than a quarter of an hour after they had eighteen fathoms of water, the ship struck on a bank of sand, and there stuck fast.

Whitelocke was sitting in the steerage-room with some

of the gentlemen when this happened. He felt a strange motion of the frigate, as if she had leaped, not unlike the curvetting of a great horse, and the violence of the shock threw several of the gentlemen from their seats into the midst of the room.

The condition they were in was quickly understood; both seamen and landsmen discovered it by the wonderful terror and amazement that had seized on them, and more upon the seamen than the others, who knew less of the danger.

It pleased his good God to keep up the spirits and faith of Whitelocke in this great extremity. And when nothing would be done but what he in person ordered, God gave him in this frightful confusion extraordinary fixedness and assistance, a temper and constancy of spirit beyond what was usual with him. He ordered the master-gunner presently to fire some pieces of ordnance, after the custom at sea, to signify their being in distress. But the gunner was so amazed with the danger, that he forgot to unbrace the guns, and shot away the main sheet. Had not the ship been strong and staunch, the guns being fired when they were close-braced, they had broken the sides of her. He caused them to be unbraced and divers of them fired, to give notice to the Elizabeth, or any other ship that might be within hearing, to come in to their assistance, but they heard no guns again to answer theirs."

After a few hopeless efforts, in which it was found that the water was very shallow to windward and very deep to leeward, that there was no hope of help in short, "the captain went up to the quarter-deck, saying, there he lived and there he would die." All the officers, sadly enough, concluded there was not the least show of any hopes of preservation, but that they were all dead men, that upon the return of the tide, the ship would questionless be dashed in pieces. "Some lay crying in one corner, others lamenting in another; some, who vaunted most in time of safety, were now most dejected ; the tears, and sighs, and wailings in all parts of the ship would have melted a stony heart into pity; every swelling wave seemed great in expectation of its booty ; the waters raged, as if their prey was too long detained from them , every billow threatened present death, who every moment stared in their faces for almost two hours together."

Having comforted his sons, he walked on the deck to see his orders executed for throwing the ordnance overboard, when the boatswain met him and spoke to him in his language :

BOATSWAIN.—" My Lord, what do you mean to do ?

WHITELOCKE.—Wherein dost thou ask my meaning ?

BOATSWAIN.—You have commanded the ordnance to be cast overboard.

WHITELOCKE.—It is for our preservation.

BOATSWAIN.—If it be done, we are all destroyed.

WHITELOCKE.—What reason have you to be of this opinion ? Must we not lighten the ship, and can we do it better than by beginning with the ordnance ?

BOATSWAIN.—It may do well to lighten the ship, but not by throwing overboard the ordnance, for you can but drop them close to the ship's side, and where the water is shallow, they will lie up against the side of the ship and fret it, which with the working of the sea will make her spring leaks presently."

He listened to this sound advice, and turned to his chaplain, Mr. Ingelo.   While conversing with him, a mariner came running up to him from the head of the ship and crying out :

MARINER.—" My Lord ! my Lord ! my Lord !

WHITELOCKE.—What's the matter ?

MARINER.—She wags ! she wags !

WHITELOCKE.—Which way does she wag ?

MARINER.—To leeward.

WHITELOCKE.—I pray God it be true ; it is the best news I ever heard in my life.

MARINER.—My Lord, upon my life the ship did wag; I saw her move.

WHITELOCKE.—Mr. Ingelo, pray stay awhile before you call the people; it may be, God will give us occasion to change the style of our prayers. Follow, seaman, and show me where thou sawest her move.

MARINER.—My Lord, here, here, at the head of the frigate, I saw her move, and she moves now: now she moves! you may see it.

WHITELOCKE.—My old eyes cannot discern it.

MARINER.—I see it plain, and so do others."

" While they were thus speaking and looking, within less than half a quarter of an hour, the ship herself came off the sand and miraculously floated on the water.

The ship being thus, by the wonderful immediate hand of God, again floating on the sea, the mariners would have been hoisting of their sails, but Whitelocke forbade it, and said he would sail no more that night. But as soon as the ship had floated a good way from the bank of sand, he caused them to let fall their anchors, that they might stay till morning to see where they were, and spend the rest of the night in giving thanks to God for his most eminent, most miraculous deliverance."

The reader, who has read the voyages of Cook, will remember a similar event, and how seemingly inevitable death was prevented by a sudden and instantaneous veering of the wind. An equally remarkable occurrence is recorded in the life of Columbus, and in each instance the beholders deemed their preservation due to a special intervention of Providence.

CHAPTER XXI.

—— • ——

1654—1656.

Whitelocke lands at Gravesend—His Friendly Reception by the Protector—Their
Conversation respecting Christina and Swedish Affairs—Formal Attendance with
his Retinue at the Council Chamber, when he is officially thanked by Cromwell
—Is returned Member for Oxford City, and appointed First Commissioner of
the Great Seal—His Popularity at this time—The House gives him a Vote of
Thanks and authorises the Payment of his Arrears—The Protector again Dissolves
the House—Death of Selden—Whitelocke intercedes on behalf of Lauderdale
and his Brother—Refuses Compliance with some of Cromwell's Measures—
Resigns the Seal, and resumes Private Practice—Appointed a Commissioner of
the Treasury—Extracts from his Notes touching the Mission of the Swedish
Ambassador at this period.

On the 1st of July, 1654, Whitelocke landed at Gravesend.
His faithful servant, Earle, was sent on to Greenwich to
acquaint his mistress with his master's arrival, but he there
learned she was at Chelsea. The weather although cold,
wet, and windy, as if it had been still winter, was cheerfully
endured as the conclusion of a bad voyage. Having staid
some little time at the "Bear," he proceeded to Whitehall,
where not finding the Protector, who had gone to Hampton
Court, he drove straight to Chelsea, to embrace his wife and
family. He had been absent eight months, and after such
long wandering, was glad to find rest for his weary feet once
more. The children were all well, and his youngest son,
born as its father was quitting his native shore, was not the
last, although the least, to be caressed.

He then sent Captain Beake to Hampton Court to acquaint
the Protector with his return, to present his duty and receive
commands, when he should wait upon his Highness to kiss his
hand, and give him an account of his negotiation.

Beake came back the same evening with Cromwell's best wishes. He looked on Whitelocke's arrival as a mercy, that he did, and blessed God for it; he hoped to see him at Whitehall on Monday next. A little while after this first message, two of the Protector's gentlemen came to bid him welcome home, inquire after his health, and to say, how glad his Highness was, who hoped on Monday next to see him. And on Sunday evening, the Protector sent yet again the same message and compliments by Mr. Strickland, one of his council.

On Monday accordingly, about nine in the morning, Thurloe, the secretary, Whitelocke's sincere and tried friend, escorted him to the presence. Cromwell received him with every outward sign of warmth, led the way into his cabinet, and conversed with him for nearly an hour.

PROTECTOR.—" How have you enjoyed your health in your long journey, both by sea and land, and how could you endure those hardships you were put to in that barren and cold country ?

WHITELOCKE.—Indeed, Sir, I have endured many hardships for an old crazy carcass as mine is. But God was pleased to show much mercy to me in my support under them by vouchsafing me competent health and strength to endure them.

PROTECTOR.—I have heard of your quarters and lodging in straw, and of your diet on your journey. We were not so hardy nor so often put to it in our service in the army.

WHITELOCKE.—Both my company and myself endured cheerfully all our hardships and wants, being in the service of our God and our country.

PROTECTOR.—That was also our support under our hardships in the army, and it is the best support, indeed it is ; you found it so in the very great preservations you have had from dangers.

WHITELOCKE.—Your Highness has had great experience of God's goodness to you; the same hand has appeared wonderfully in the preservation of my company and myself from many imminent and great dangers both by sea and land.

PROTECTOR.—The greatest, I hear, was at your return home upon our coast.

WHITELOCKE.—That indeed, Sir, was very miraculous.

PROTECTOR.—I am glad to see you safe and well after it.

WHITELOCKE.—I have cause to bless God with all thankfulness for it, as long as I live.

PROTECTOR.—I pray, my Lord, tell me the particulars of that great deliverance."

Here Whitelocke gave him the particulars.

PROTECTOR.—"Really, these passages are full of wonder and mercy, and I have cause to join with you in acknowledgments of the Lord's goodness herein.

WHITELOCKE.—Your Highness testifies a true sense thereof, and your favour to your servant.

PROTECTOR.—I hope I shall never forget the one or the other, indeed, I hope I shall not. But I pray, tell me, is the queen a lady of such rare parts as is reported of her?

WHITELOCKE.—Truly, Sir, she is a lady excellently qualified, of rare abilities of mind, perfect in many languages and in most sorts of learning, especially history, and beyond compare with any person whom I have known, understanding the affairs and interest of all the states and princes in Christendom.

PROTECTOR.—That is very much; but what are her principles in matters of religion?

WHITELOCKE.—They are not such as I could wish they were; they are too much inclined to the manner of that country, and to some persuasions from men not well inclined to those matters, who have had too much power with her.

PROTECTOR.—That is a great deal of pity! Indeed, I have heard of some passage of hers, not well relishing with those that fear God. This is too general an evil among those people who are not so well principled in matters of religion as were to be wished.

WHITELOCKE.—That is too true, but many sober men and good Christians among them hope, that in time there may be a reformation of those things. I took the boldness to put the queen and the present king in mind of the duty incumbent upon them in that business. This I did with becoming freedom, and it was well taken.

PROTECTOR.—I think you did very well to inform them of that great duty, which now lies upon the king. And did he give ear to it?

WHITELOCKE.—Yes, truly, Sir, and told me he acknowledged it to be his duty, which he resolved to pursue as opportunity could be had for it. But he said it must be done by degrees with a boisterous people, so long accustomed to the contrary. The like answer I had from the Archbishop of Upsala, and from the chancellor when I spoke to them upon the same subject, which I did plainly.

PROTECTOR.—I am glad you did so. Is the archbishop a man of good abilities?

WHITELOCKE.—He is a very reverend person, learned, and seems very pious.

PROTECTOR.—The chancellor is the great wise man.

WHITELOCKE.—He is the wisest man that ever I conversed with abroad, and his abilities are fully answerable to the report of him.

PROTECTOR.—What character do you give of the present king?

WHITELOCKE.—I had the honour divers times to be with his Majesty, who did that extraordinary honour to me as to visit me at my house. He is a person of great worth, honour, and not inferior to any in courage and military conduct.

PROTECTOR.—That was an exceedingly high favour to come to you in person.

WHITELOCKE.—He never did the like to any public minister; but this and all other honour done to me was only to testify their respects to your Highness, the which, indeed, was very great, both there and where I passed in Germany.

PROTECTOR.—I am obliged to them for their very great civility.

WHITELOCKE.—Both the queen, the king and his brother, the archbishop, chancellor, and most of the grandees gave testimony of very great respect to your Highness, not only by their words, but their actions likewise.

PROTECTOR.—I shall be ready to acknowledge their respects upon any occasion.

WHITELOCKE.—The like respects were testified to your Highness in Germany, especially by the town of Hamburg, where I endeavoured in your Highness's name to confirm the privileges of the English merchants, who, with your resident there, showed much kindness to me and my company.

PROTECTOR.—I most heartily thank them for it. Is the court of Sweden gallant and full of resort to it?

WHITELOCKE.—They are extremely gallant for their clothes. As for company, most of the nobility and the civil and military officers make their constant residence where the court is, and many repair to it on all occasions.

PROTECTOR.—Is their administration of justice speedy, and have they many law-suits?

WHITELOCKE.—They have justice in a speedier way than we, but more arbitrary, and fewer causes, in regard that the boors do not dare contend with their lords. They have but few contracts, because they have but little trade. There is small use of conveyances or questions of titles, because the law distributes every man's estate after his death amongst his children, which they cannot alter, and therefore have the fewer contentions.

PROTECTOR.—That is like our gavelkind.

WHITELOCKE.—It is the same thing, and in many particulars of our laws, in cases of private right, and of the public government, especially in their parliaments, there is a strange resemblance between their law and ours.

PROTECTOR.—Perhaps ours might, some of them, be brought from there.

WHITELOCKE.—Doubtless they were, when the Goths and Saxons and those northern people planted themselves here.

PROTECTOR.—You met with a barren country, and very cold ?

WHITELOCKE.—The remoter parts of it from the court are extremely barren, but at Stockholm, Upsala, and most of the great towns, they have store of provisions. Fat beef and mutton in the winter time is not so plentiful with them as in the countries more southerly. Their hot weather in summer as much exceeds ours as their cold does in winter.

PROTECTOR.—That is somewhat troublesome to endure, but how could you pass over their very long winter nights ?

WHITELOCKE.—I kept my people together in action and recreation by having music in my house, by encouraging that and the exercise of dancing, which held them by the ears and eyes, and gave them diversion without any offence. And I caused the gentlemen to have disputations in Latin, and declamations upon words which I gave them.

PROTECTOR.—Those were very good diversions, and made your house a little academy.

WHITELOCKE.—I thought these recreations better than gaming for money, or going forth to places of debauchery.

PROTECTOR.—It was much better, and I am glad you had so good an issue of your treaty.

WHITELOCKE.—I bless God for it, and shall be ready to give your Highness a particular account of it, when you shall appoint a time for it.

PROTECTOR.—I think Thursday next, in the morning, will be a good time for you to come to the Council, and make your report of the transactions of your negotiations. And you and I must have many discourses upon these arguments.

WHITELOCKE.—I shall attend your Highness and the Council."

On the Thursday he came accordingly with the whole of his company, and being presently brought into the council

D D

chamber, where the Protector sat, covered, in his great chair
at the upper end of the table, and the rest of the council,
with their hats off, on each side of it, he made a long speech,
in which he recounted the various events of his mission.
After a little pause, the Protector pulled off his hat, then put
it on again, and desired Whitelocke to withdraw. At the
end of a quarter of an hour he was called in again, and after
the same ceremony of uncovering and recovering the head,
his Highness returned. him his great thanks, and made many
promises to his retinue, who at his command had been all
called in. They were very much elated and thought they
should all be great men, little knowing that the great man
in power had been long in the habit of holding out great
promises to his instruments, whom he would cast aside when
useless ;—that he looked to the future, not to the past. He
had risen, indeed, by using the necks and backs of his
countrymen for stepping-boards as he climbed to power, but
once ascended, some of the boards were no longer needed

On the 12th of July, 1654, Whitelocke was returned to
Parliament for the city of Oxford, the borough of Bedford,
and the shire of Buckingham ; and his influence in Oxfordshire was so great, that the electors returned his son James
as one of their knights ; and after waiting patiently he was
appointed First Commissioner of the Great Seal. On the
4th of August he was named one of the eight Commissioners
for the Exchequer. He was now at the zenith of his popularity, for, on returning from Bristol, of which place he was
the recorder, the mayor and aldermen of London came out
to meet him with five hundred horse, and conducted him into
the city to the public entertainment awaiting him. Two days
later, when the Protector rode in state to Westminster Abbey,
he carried the purse after Lambert, who bore the sword. It
was on this celebrated day that Oliver made, in the Painted
Chamber, the ever-memorable speech which, Whitelocke
terms " large and subtle," to the new Parliament. His old
colleague, Lenthall, was chosen Speaker, and to him he

addressed a long speech, recounting what he had already
related to the Protector.   The House voted him its thanks,
and at the same time the arrears due to him, amounting to
nearly 2000*l.* Whoever reads the debates and votes of this
assembly will see that it could not last.   Its mutinous spirit
was transparent from the first, and one clause in their
" Articles of Government," " that if the Protector consent
not to bills presented to him, within twenty days, they shall
pass as laws without his consent," must have stung him to
the quick.   It was followed by many rash and ill-timed
resolutions, some of them being a direct interference with
the Executive, such as this : " that a new Parliament should
be summoned to meet upon the third Monday of October,
1656 ;" or as this, " that the Protector for the time being
should not have power to pardon murder and treason."
They were playing the Long Parliament over again, but
forgot that vacillation, weakness, and administrative incapacity were not qualities possessed by their new master.

And now that Cromwell had lost his mother, whose fearful
apprehensions as to the fate of her son had palsied him for
a time, the energies of the Protector were roused by these
repeated attacks on what he deemed his sovereign rights,
and to do his memory justice, on the spiritual freedom of the
people at large.   They dictate to him, indeed, that he might
have a negative to bills touching liberty of conscience, but
not to bills for suppressing heresies, which damnable heresies
shall be enumerated in the bill !   No wonder that Whitelocke
saw the gathering storm ; and although he attended in his
place, found he could do no good.   The dissolution was
prompt, and the Protector needed not to have made a speech
extending over fifteen folio columns, before he pronounced it.
His resolution had been taken with the concurrence of a
majority in his council ; but Whitelocke, although he disap-
proved a great part of the proceedings of the House, most
earnestly attempted to dissuade him from the step, foreseeing
greater evils by the absence than the presence of this legis-

lative body, and well knowing what odium would be incurred by the Executive.

His private feelings had been deeply wounded about this time by the loss of his most valued acquaintance and friend, the learned Selden. He received this letter from him on the 10th of November, 1654.

" My Lord, I am a most humble suitor to your Lordship, that you would be pleased that I might have your presence for a little time to-morrow or next day. Thus much wearies the most weak hand and body of

> " Your Lordship's most humble Servant,
>
> " J. SELDEN."

His friend went to him as desired, and was consulted by him respecting the settlement of his estate, the alteration of his will, and a change of executors; but Selden's weakness increased so rapidly that his intentions were prevented. Whitelocke's eulogy, though short, is as good as a more laboured panegyric : " his mind was as great as his learning; he was as hospitable and generous as any man, and as good company to those whom he liked."

The new year commenced auspiciously for Whitelocke, by enabling him to do good. At the urgent request of Lord Douglas, whose hospitality he had known in Sweden, he urged on Cromwell to spare two of his victims, Lord Lauderdale and his brother Laundie ; and having conjointly pleaded for them, he did them other considerable services.* When the times changed, these men remembered nothing of the benefits conferred, made no return, and gave no sign of gratitude. I cannot coincide with the fallen statesman in his sweeping condemnation of their conduct by branding it as "Scotch-like ;" the fact is, like nearly all Englishmen of his day, he had a secret dislike of Scotchmen and Irishmen—a dislike that must be regarded, if we analyse history, as one

---

* According to the "Memorials" it was owing to Douglas's direct intercession on behalf of these two men, his kinsmen, and to the recommendation of the King of Sweden, that Cromwell spared their lives.

of the grounds, more perhaps than the religious discord, of England's opposition to the dynasty of the Stuarts.   Before the month was over, Whitelocke and his colleague Widdrington refused to comply with what they considered an arbitrary and illegal interference on the part of Cromwell with the court they presided over.   They refused to be made his passive instruments for depriving several persons of their freehold without offence or legal trial, in violation of the principles laid down by the Great Charter, and for many technical reasons as well.   Both these judges regarded the " uncertainty of the laws," so far from being "glorious," as nearly equivalent to a denial of justice altogether, yet this would be dangerously augmented if they yielded obedience to the injunctions of his Highness   One of their reasons may displease the profession, but it deserves to be written in letters of gold : that the proposed changes would increase motions to the advantage of lawyers and solicitors.   He had been to Sweden, where he, doubtless, found the Norway rat to infest the houses, but no common lawyers to plague and harrow the country.   Travel, we see, had enlightened him, as it does most men.

For this disobedience he was summoned to resign the Great Seal, though not till many indirect applications had been made to him, with a view to induce submission, and his compliance with the new regulations.   When the Commissioners attended the Council Chamber, the Protector gravely told them, he was sorry *some* of them, excluding Lenthall by this partitive expression, could not satisfy their own consciences, and had refused to execute the new ordinance ; to which Whitelocke in virtue of his seniority replied, that they scrupled about the execution of this ordinance as a law, which they believed would be of great prejudice to the public, and contrary to what they had formerly promised on their oath.

Laying down the Seal, he departed, and in after years in his old age, blessed God, that he had never had cause to

repent of that action. His fortunes and interest seemed so
impaired, or rather altogether ruined, by this second depriva-
tion, that many of his dear friends and frequent visitors, by
whom it was not expected, repeated their old trick of ceasing
to come near him, or even owning him, and knowing him,
when he happened to pass near them. He thought them
dirty worldlings, loaf-friends, and hypocrites, and valued
their averted glances at the same price, with which he had
previously estimated their looks of devotedness and studied
gestures of good will.

On returning to private practice the retaining fees began
to pour in, but before the month of June had come to an
end, the Protector, who really was good-natured and constitutionally prone to be tolerant, and who felt in his own
conscience the right of its free exercise by others, resolved
to make amends for his past harshness, and appointed the
ousted Keepers of the Seal to be Commissioners of the
Treasury. In those days the Exchequer seems to have been
intimately connected with the former, and a Mr. Sherwyn,
an able man of business in the latter department, became
their secretary. In this new employment he displayed his
usual zeal and activity ; a systematic course of book-keeping
was introduced, and precautions taken, so that the State
could not be cozened ; no sum could be paid out but under
the sanction of their hands, and although the forms of the
Exchequer were retained, their hard ways were not perse-
vered in. But his principal services were those connected
with our foreign policy, and so useful was his superior knowledge of continental affairs, that the Protector found he
could not do without him. Thus the duty of receiving the
new Swedish ambassador devolved chiefly on him ; to him
was mainly confided the task of negotiation, and whenever
the head of the government became entangled, he uniformly
applied to the man, on whose discretion and sober advice he
knew he could depend. This advice was sometimes less
pleasing to him, than what had been tendered by his council,

but the Protector was already beginning to see they flattered him, assented too obsequiously to his own expressed wishes, that they rarely differed from him in his judgment, and he gave accordingly greater heed to Whitelocke's counsel than perhaps to his own biassed convictions. From the hour of the Swedish ambassador's arrival to the last day of Cromwell's life, the ascendancy acquired by the treasurer was never forfeited, and it gained strength as it advanced.

Unfortunately most of his private notes and minutes of his interviews at Whitehall or Hampton Court were destroyed by his wife a short time previous to the Restoration, to the great regret of her husband, who was away somewhere, lying concealed from anticipated arrest, and the insane vengeance of the Rump. A few fragments however escaped the flames, and some of these I now present for the first time to the reader, who will pardon their mutilated state :—

" I was very constant in attending the business of the Treasury, gained very much experience in those matters, in the way and course of the Exchequer, whereof we had the supervision. All the chequer officers were very obsequious to us, were ready to attend and give us information of what was required of them. Mr. Sherwyn, our secretary, was very diligent and understanding in that business. We had from him upon view all the books, accounts, a constant weekly sum of all the receipts and disbursements in all the offices, and all receipts whatsoever ; so that not a penny was received or issued out but what we had an account of every week.

" March 31.   51st year.—I attended the business of the Treasury with my best care and diligence, and gained much experience in the matters of the public revenue. We had a constant weekly account of all the receipts and disbursements of that great revenue, which, being so often taken, made it the more easy, giving us the more opportunity of ordering the same to the best advantage of the Commonwealth. And as we received this account from the officers under us, so we

gave information to the Protector how it was from time to
time, together with our advice concerning the same, wherein
he would afterwards consult with me particularly.

"August.—I and the master of the ceremonies usually
dined and supped with the Protector. He was very cheerful.
His gentlemen, pages, lacquays, and all his people, were very
civil and well pleased. I being named first in all the orders,
and Strickland giving me the precedence. . . . By the
Protector's order, I accompanied the ambassador to Hampton
Court, where he was feasted. I sat on his right hand. His
gentlemen of the embassy sat at another table in the same
room, and the feast was sumptuous at both tables. The
Protector was pleasant, very civil, and discoursed at dinner-
time of Sweden and their customs. After dinner, his
saddle-horses were brought forth, when himself, with the
ambassador and the rest of the company, rode into one of
the parks, where they saw abundance of deer. They coursed
and killed a fat buck, which was sent to the ambassador's
house. The ambassador would not adventure to leap ditches
after the Protector, but was more wary. Afterwards the
Protector carried the ambassador up to see his lady and
daughters, who were in great state to receive him, with
many ladies waiting on them ; and when it grew late the
ambassador took his leave, and came by night to London.
The week after this, I visited him at his house in Salisbury
'Court, dined with him, and not long after that, he came to
my house at Chelsea to do the same, but his entertainment
was chargeable. I could not go my intended journey into
Wales* by reason of my attendance upon the business of this
ambassador, which the Protector desires me to take particular care of, and to accompany the ambassador, as I did
often to my cost.

"September.—I attended the business of the Treasury
with my best diligence and care ; was often with the
Protector, who advised with me in many things of the

---

* Where his sister, Lady Mostyn, and a daughter of his, Lady Price, resided.

greatest importance. He had me often with him at bowls, and in his diversions at Hampton Court and other places. I had at this time more than ordinary leisure for my studies, being out of all professional business or public employment, save that of the Treasury, which was nothing cogent and troublesome, like that of the Seal. In this time of leisure, I bless God I applied myself to the study of the Bible, and of its expositors, out of which, as God put it into my mind, I collected many notes and observations, which I wish may be of some advantage to the souls of my children, and of any others.

" In the latter end of this month, the Swedish ambassador, who came often to me at Chelsea, did in his discourse, amongst other things, much commend the sports in England of hawking and hunting. He intimated the great desire of himself, and of several of his gentlemen, to see some of those sports. As I was invited by Sir Humphrey Forster to his house at Aldermarston, where I knew the entertainment would be noble, and no great addition of charge if the ambassador should come privately with me ; and as it was so gallant a seat, so noble a house, richly furnished, and the place so fit for country sports, I thought it would be a kindness to the ambassador, who was then very solitary in London, and an honour to the gentry and country of England for foreigners to see such a place and such noble treatment from a private gentleman. I therefore told the ambassador that I was to go to a friend's to hawk and hunt ; that if he pleased to bear me company as a private friend and incognito, not as Lord Ambassador but as my particular friend, I would assure him a hearty welcome, and show him some of our field-sports. He quickly accepted the invitation, and went with me and my wife in our coach, wherein I had then six good horses. He was only accompanied on this journey by the Marshal du Val, a gallant Swede, three or four more of his gentlemen, one page and two of his lacquays. Sir Humphrey gave us noble entertainment for three days

together, in which time we had hunting, hawking, and
fishing, with excellent sport.   Within doors the ambassador
played at cards with the ladies.   All were full of mirth,
which the place and treatment much increased, and the
sports abroad afforded great delight to the Swedes, who had
never seen any before.   I supplied the party with horses of
my own.   On the fourth day we returned, after giving great
and due thanks to Sir Humphrey."

I am anticipating scenes and events, but think this the
best place for introducing another fragment.

"April 2, 1656. I went in the morning to Whitehall,
where Sir Oliver Fleming, Master of the Ceremonies, told
me, that yesterday the Swedish ambassador had been there,
and much discontented, because he waited above an hour,
that occasioned great impatience in his excellency.   I told
him I was very sorry the ambassador had so much cause for
his discontent, and that I should have been quite as angry
myself, if I had been so used in Sweden, that I would go
and speak with the Protector about giving a despatch to the
Swedish business, and should he intimate anything to me
respecting the ambassador's discontent, that then I would
speak my mind plainly to him about it, but the master
desired me not to let the Protector know, that he had informed me of anything in this matter.   I went up to the
long gallery, where the Protector was with Lambert, Strickland and another, whom he left, and came to me.   He discoursed freely with me about the Swedish business, and told
me of the ambassador's discontent at his long stay before he
had his audience.   I spoke plainly in reply, and told him
how distasteful it was to public ministers and their masters,
that they should be put to such attendance.   I told him,
that when I was his servant in Sweden, being once used in
that manner, I took great exceptions to it in his right, and
that it was excused and amended.   I entreated his Highness
to give a command to his servants, that he might have
notice, when an ambassador came to his audience, so that he

might not be put to wait long, and I imputed these neglects to his Highness's servants. He heard me, as he used to do, very patiently, and told me that he would take order to have this amended. I said to him, that if he pleased, I would go this day and dine with the ambassador, endeavour to excuse yesterday's affront, and bring him to a better temper. The Protector desired me to do so, and to assure the ambassador from him, that he had a very great affection for his person, and as great a respect for the King, his master, as for any prince in Christendom. He then communicated to me the discourse, which had passed between him and the ambassador the day before, and that when the matter of a nearer alliance was mentioned, he had given his answer plainly, that he was willing in case of a nearer alliance, or of a closer union, concerning the Protestant interest, to have our neighbours and allies, the Low Countries, included therein ; that he thought it did behove him to have a particular care of them and to take them into any such treaty or alliance, and that he was not willing, that he was not, to do any such thing without them. I said, I thought such plain dealing to be most honourable, and that it was both fit and just to have a care of our neighbours, the Low Countries, but I believed that those expressions of his Highness would a little startle the ambassador, and I offered to his Highness's judgment, whether it were not fit in all things, that might stand with our interest, to give contentment to the King of Sweden, who had shown such great respect to his Highness in my person, and in other ministers of his there, and by his sending his ambassador now here. I told him he knew the King of Sweden was a wise and potent prince, and that God had given him great successes, that the Dutch were greatly for their own interest as well as other states, and in case there be not a nearer alliance betwixt us and Sweden, it was not impossible for the Dutch to step in and make a nearer alliance between Sweden and themselves, without taking much care to have us included in it. This caution the

Protector seemed to relish, and said that the Dutch would
not stick to do what was for their own advantage.   He told
me also there was a flying report, he believed it came from
Holland, as if the King of Poland had given a great defeat to
the King of Sweden, but he wished me not to mention this to
the ambassador as coming from him, for he would not be
thought to be the author of any such thing, but should be
very sorry if it were true.   I told him I hoped and believed
it was not true, especially if it came by that way of Holland.
I parted from the Protector, and took with me the master of
the ceremonies to the Swedish ambassador's house.

" The ambassador discoursed with me alone an hour together before dinner, and expressed great discontent at his
long attendance for the audience the other day, that it was
often so, and that it was as much to him as his head to permit
any dishonour to his master, who was jealous of nothing
more than his honour,—that he could say nothing for the
fashion of this court, but in other courts he was sure it was not
so, that the Protector's ambassador was not so used in Sweden,
that the King, his master, had put upon him the highest
character that could be of ambassador extraordinary, that
he represented the King's person, that it was not fit for one
sovereign to attend upon another, especially when the time
of audience was appointed by himself, who was nevertheless
the occasion of that attendance, and that he could not in
honour to his Majesty bear it.   I let him run on till he was
out of breath, and then told him that I came now from the
Protector, and by his command I was to excuse that neglect
to his excellency.   I affirmed to him, there was not the least
intention of reflecting on the King's honour, or of any dis-
respect to himself, that it was solely the omission of the
Protector's servants in their duty, wherein care should be
taken for the future that it be amended.   I delivered the
compliments of his Highness, with the best expressions I
could of civility and respect, and with this the ambassador
seemed fully satisfied, desired me to return his service to the

Protector, and his most humble thanks.   Then he communicated to me the discourse betwixt him and the Protector the other day to the same effect as I had just heard before, and said he perceived at his last audience, that his Highness's mind was somewhat altered from what it seemed to be formerly, that now there was nothing to be done with the Dutch, he much wondered why the Protector should seem so forward heretofore for a nearer alliance and conjunction with his master, and now seemed to be more cold in that matter ; he wished he had known his mind at first, for he had already given the King an account of the Protector's willingness to have a nearer alliance with his Majesty, who thereupon had dressed his counsels accordingly, and now he must acquaint the King, that he perceived his Highness's mind to be changed on that point, which would cause the King very much to marvel, and put him to inconvenience.

I answered, that I believed the Protector's inclinations to be unchanged, and told him that in this he might see an evidence of the Protector's sincerity, which all who had to do with him knew to be very great.   I put my host in mind that at a private audience when I was present, his Highness expressed to him, the ambassador, his willingness to a nearer alliance with the King of Sweden, and to a union of the Protestant interest, whereby his excellency had from the Protector's own mouth the honour, he desired, of laying the foundation of that great business for the glory of God, the settlement whereof would require more time than his excellency proposed to himself for his continuance in England.   The ambassador replied, it was true the Protector had so expressed himself formerly, but now his mind seemed to be altered on that point, which was the matter that did so trouble him ; that as for the Dutch his master was very willing that they might be admitted into the nearer alliance and common union, but that it would be impossible for all the Protestant princes and states to be brought in at one time, that to have their several deputies to meet in one place and conclude upon particulars would demand a long time ; that it would be better to have a beginning between the King of Sweden and the Protector, for them to unite first, and then by degrees to bring in the other Protestant princes and states into the same league with them—which would be sooner and best done this way, —that in case England should not enter into a nearer union with Sweden, but break off, perhaps the Dutch would provide for themselves, and presently make a nearer alliance with the King of Sweden, without taking much care to have the Protector included with them, if they could gain any advantage by leaving him out,—which matter of advantage the Dutch do very well like,—that they were now upon very good terms with his master, and he did not believe they had any design against him, and in this strain he continued *ad finem orationis.* I let him go on, and wondered at his freedom, resolving to make use of it for the service of my country, but without prejudice to him. I answered his arguments, and we had much other private discourse together, wherein I laboured to satisfy him as to the reality of the Protector's intentions, as likewise the great affection of the English people towards the King of Sweden and his subjects."

CHAPTER XXII.

It was in consequence of the extraordinary favour and
influence he was now gradually acquiring, that the members
of the council, of whom the Lord Deputy Fleetwood was the
most influential member, formed so early as in January,
1655, the scheme of sending him out again to Sweden as
ambassador ; they even went so far as to appoint him and
Sir Christopher Pack as the joint envoys, and Fleetwood
was pitched upon to communicate the intelligence and gain
his consent.   Colonel Sydenham, a brother commissioner of
the Treasury was similarly employed, and exhausted his
powers of persuasion, as Fleetwood had done.   Blunt refusals
do not seem to have been in vogue in those days, and therefore time was asked and granted, as in the former case, but
the definitive answer was to be given next day at dinner ;
they said the Lord Deputy would expect the happiness, not
only of his company, but his assent to their wishes.   And
then Lord George Fleetwood took him aside, hoped he would

undertake the journey, no man could or would be so acceptable to the King, that he, George, had been working at this
a good while. "I wish I had known it before you proceeded
so far," was the reply of the man whom these shallow personages sought to dupe. The flimsy network of intrigue was
easily broken through. He represented to Fleetwood, and
Fleetwood knew that what was said would come to Cromwell's ears, that to send him now to the same court from
which he had so recently returned, would give an alarum to
all the Popish princes and hasten a league among them, an
act so prejudicial, that no good man could possibly desire its
accomplishment. The Lord Deputy was compelled to admit
that the Pope was even then at work to unite and cement
his interest amongst all the Popish princes, particularly
between France and Spain, and Whitelocke pointed out to
him that the union so projected would only be hastened and
furthered by so impolitic a step as sending out another
mission to Sweden, whereas by arranging the business here
with the Swedish ambassador, no notice would be taken of
it. Shortly after this interview, Sir Charles Wolsey (or
Wolseley, for the name is written both ways) of the council,
who was one of those staunch friends on whom Whitelocke
could rely, assured him the scheme had been propounded
and the vote taken during his absence, that he thought the
plan neither opportune nor desirable, and what was more—
the King of Sweden had issued a proclamation, desiring all
public men to forbear for a time and abstain from coming
to his camp, where he was too much engaged with military
affairs at present. Without giving a positive refusal, the
treasurer escaped in this way the honour intended him, and
it is singular, that at the close of these negotiations, Cromwell should have yielded so readily to these reasons, but, in
fact, he was secretly rejoiced at the decision his confidant
had adopted.

It was in November, 1655, that the council, the Protector
being present, appointed a Board of Trade, whose duty it

would be to consider how to improve, order and regulate
the trade and navigation of the Commonwealth. Whitelocke
was appointed one of the committee, and his attendance
required in the Painted Chamber at Westminster on the
27th of the same month.

Whitelocke observes, that this was a business of much
importance, but unfortunately the details of the transactions
are too scanty. The prevailing sentiment in those days
was to obtain profit and advantage at the expense of the
particular country with which we traded, and if we could
obtain or retain the sole manufacture of any article, this
would be the most desirable ideal. The advantage of free
competition and the inexhaustible resources of new inven-
tions, contrivances, and appliances, being utterly ignored,
could have had no influence with any board, as then constituted. The Swedish ambassador himself seems to have had
a gleam of truth, a dawning consciousness of how desirable
it was to economise human labour by introducing machinery
as a substitute, wherever practicable. He told a pleasant
story of the Czar and a Dutchman, and how the latter,
observing the boats passing upon the Volga to be manned
with three hundred men in each boat, who in a storm and
high wind held the bottom of the sails down with their hands,
offered to the former a mode of manning each boat quite as
efficiently with thirty men instead of the three hundred, by
which the cost of transport would be lessened. But the
Emperor called him a knave, and asked him if a boat that
now went with three hundred men should be brought to go
as well with thirty only, how were the other two hundred
and seventy men to get their living? The Board of Trade
comprehended but little the spirit of this anecdote, and could
not have made the true application of it. It has been reserved
for a wiser age to take off the shackles, and leave to com-
merce the free employment of her wings. In fact, a passage
of Whitelocke's, which I have just perceived amid the lumber
of these old negotiations, shows that he was imbued with

the current notions of the age. His observation, which I am about to quote, was partly based on the fact, that England possessed, or was thought to possess alone the *lapis calaminaris*, which smelted with Swedish copper formed brass, and hence he exultingly observed to the Protector, with whom he was closeted at the time, that the manufacturers of copper and brass would by this means be solely in England, that " hereby we should much increase our brass ordnance, which were of great consideration as to his Highness's navy, and as to the furnishing of such of our neighbours *only* therewith, as we should think fit." Such maxims as these were deemed unimpeachable at the time, but are now thought to be opposed to all the true principles of political economy.

The jealousy and envy lately adverted to, now found a vent in a more offensive manner. On the 3rd of May, 1656, Lord General Fleetwood thought proper to tell Whitelocke that he had some enemies at court, who were willing to keep him out of the council ; the objections, he said, were two : the first was, that in the treaty he had made at Upsala, he had consented to acknowledge passes for ships, which the council regarded as detrimental, especially now that England was at war with Spain ; that he had consented to the specification of contraband goods, which would also be very inconvenient in relation to the same war. The second was, that Whitelocke was a lawyer, and the council wished to show the world, that their counsels might be carried on without the wisdom of lawyers, which would but trouble and interrupt their proceedings by telling them what was law upon every occasion, and their affairs would not permit them to tie themselves up to those rules of law. Whitelocke' conceived it right to vindicate himself at great length on both these charges.

About the 13th of August he received the following letter:

" HONOURED SIR,—The 20th of August being appointed at Bucks for the election of members to serve in Parliament for our county, out of that long experience we have had of your suitable qualifications for that purpose, we are emboldened earnestly to desire, that you would vouchsafe your presence at the 'George,' in Aylesbury, the day before the election, where we shall be ready to perform our due respects and service, by which you will engage among many others, sir,

"Your most humble Servants."

This was subscribed at the sessions by the justices of the peace, the grand jury, many gentlemen and freeholders of quality. On the day of election his friends marched into Bucks 1000 horse, and were in the field above 3000 strong, so that he was first and unanimously elected; he had four colleagues, and by this we learn that the county then returned five members. But such a Parliament as this, where no member was permitted to sit without a certificate from Nathaniel Tayler, clerk of the Commonwealth in chancery, was sure from the first to prove an utter failure. As the council of his Highness claimed the right of approval, a large number of the returned members were excluded, who protested against such a tyrannical infringement of their rights as Englishmen, by a remonstrance, which they published. Cromwell must have surely seen that he would be beaten in the long run, that such victories as these were fatal to himself, and that he was alienating the hearts of his countrymen. One of nature's laws was being called into play against him by his own violence, and this was more to be dreaded than the speeches of the most gifted lawyers, if any such were made. Whitelocke himself at all events was content to play a very insignificant part in common with those that sat. They should have refused to do so, but the spirit of resistance slumbered in their bosoms. If Cromwell was a necessity, if dictatorial power was essential for healing the wounds of civil war, their deliberative counsels as popular representatives under such humiliating circumstances were worthless, and the sooner the dissolution came, the better for the nation and their own respectability. But his mind at this time, when not engaged on foreign policy, was too much bent on

money-making, for which his large family affords the sole
excuse.   Thus he was appointed Speaker during the illness
of Sir Thomas Widdrington ; and it so chanced, that he had
the passing of several private bills—that stigma and dishonour
on the legislation of this country—and on each bill his fee
was to be 5*l*., provided Sir Thomas were not back in his
place   At the hazard of his life, his old colleague, though
very feeble and ill, did come back, since the collective fees
proved much too strong a temptation.   And his doing so, one
can easily see by the context, annoyed the deputy speaker
not a little.   It so far did good, he thought, that the House
besides returning him its thanks, decreed, as the former
House had ineffectually done, that Whitelocke should have
the 500*l*. still due to him as arrears, and they voted likewise
a further grant of 2000*l*. to be paid to him in respect of
his great and faithful service to the public in that embassy,
Moreover, the sum was paid on this occasion to the great
dissatisfaction of certain "ill-willers" about Cromwell. Legal
the vote may have been, but the recipient would have better
consulted his fame by altogether declining the gift.   It looks
like one of those little jobs that we occasionally find denounced by members when in the opposition.

As a set-off to this thirst of gold, which most men, be it
admitted, find little compunction in slaking, there are a great
many of his acts displaying private benevolence and charity
recorded, some of which are in print, and one amongst them
may well be mentioned here, from its singularity.   The
reader may remember, that when he went out ambassador,
Sir Thomas Cotton lent him some of his rare manuscripts,
thereby conferring a great obligation.   To such a man, in
what way could he make an honourable return, and testify
his thanks ?   Fortune favoured him : he was enabled to get
Sir Thomas excused serving as sheriff for Bedfordshire, and
so he repaid with interest the favour he had received.

Plots were now thickening, and insurrections threatened.
The settlement of the kingdom was yet to be effected, but

how ?   It seemed as remote as ever ; the Lord Protector
felt himself secretly the inutility of his title ; it was neither
sanctioned nor hallowed by time.   An event transpired, that
by the association of ideas it created in Whitelocke's mind,
and by leading his memory back to a remarkable conversation with Christina, in which that queen, as the reader may
remember, expressed her satisfaction at Cromwell's assumption of power and the hope he would make himself king,
suggested to him the true remedy required.   The event
itself occurred about the time when Cromwell was in the
habit of shutting himself up three or four hours at a
time with Lord Broghill, Pierpont, Whitelocke, Sir Charles
Wolseley, and Thurloe.   Perhaps they were making verses,
whilst the chief himself was smoking his pipe of tobacco ;
perhaps they were all discussing some secret despatch from
Breda, at the moment Christina's messenger was announced
to her English friend.   His name was Signor Philippi
Passerini, an Italian by birth, and he brought he said his
credentials for his Highness, but private letters for Whitelocke himself from the Queen.   They referred to that dark
and mysterious transaction, which history has never been
able to clear up, the death of the Marquis Monaldeschi, her
Italian favorite, by her command at Fontainebleau, and
contained the solution of the enigma.   On receiving them
he read their contents to the Protector, being so instructed
by the Queen to do, but their revelation to these two men
has never transpired, and her secret was inviolately kept
by them both.   They were written in French, and he communicated them word for word in that language, but when
he had done, the Protector, who did not know the language,
requested him to translate them to him, and then said, he
would, upon consideration of the business, let him know
whether he would grant the private audience required by
Passerini or not.   Upon advice with his council about it,
some of them, to show their extraordinary care of his person,
suggested, that this messenger, being an Italian, must be

skilful nationally in the art of poisoning, and ready for any
engagement of that nature, that he might be bringing a
poisoned letter, and consequently advised His Highness not
to receive him.   The Protector, with a smile upon his lips,
but with some doubt in his secret thoughts, acquainted our
mediator with this cautious counsel, but heard the instant
refutation of such an hypothesis, and was told how offensive
to the Queen so groundless a refusal would be.   The Protector
rejoined, that the messenger desired to deliver his errand in
private, and none to be by save one, whom he should appoint.
This very comment would seem to argue how shattered his
nerves had become at last through the incessant plots and
attempts at assassination he had had of late to baffle.   In
this instance, however, to calm his mind, Whitelocke offered
to take upon himself the danger of being poisoned, for he
would be by and take the letter first from the Italian gentleman, and Cromwell allowed him to do so.   The letter when
presented contained the expected revelation, with some
additional matter of a political nature, but though narrating
this circumstance, Whitelocke has jealously shrouded it in all
its original secrecy.   How well the Queen must have understood the character of these two Englishmen ?   She never
confided her secret to any other human being.

This circumstance, therefore, from the discussion it provoked as to the existence of danger to the Protector's person,
directed Whitelocke's mind to what he conceived would alone
furnish the true settlement of these three kingdoms, and he
labored in the matter with zeal.   His idea, however, to be
successful at all, would require time for its realisation.   At
present the title of Protector was by petition and advice
from the Parliament to be changed into that of hereditary
Lord Protector, and one of the arguments used was unhappily
well-founded.   " We consider likewise the continual danger
which your life is in, from the bloody practices both of the
malignant and discontented party, (one of which through the
goodness of God you have been lately delivered from), it

being a received principle among them, that no order being settled in your life-time for the succession in the government, nothing is wanting to bring us into blood and confusion, and them to their desired ends, but the destruction of your person." Cromwell, who could no longer laugh and sing in his heart, as he said he could when he dissolved the late Parliament on the 31st of January, 1654, who could no longer declare that he had no melancholy thoughts, who knew that he *had* begotten a fool and not a wise son, was willing enough now to make his power and dignity hereditary, and to guard his throne with "another" house of Parliament.

On the 11th of December Whitelocke received a writ of summons under the great seal to sit as a member of that "other house." The form of the writ was the same with those, which were sent to summon the old peers in Parliament, and therefore he became to all intents and purposes, in accordance with the ancient laws of this kingdom, a peer. There were only sixty of them, a number quite large enough for the discharge of their duties, provided they did not use the privilege that peers possess of voting for and against a measure by proxy. It was large enough to form what Cromwell and his adviser, Whitelocke, wished,—a still and small voice,—a voice "enough to hold forth a certain and distinct sound, but not to make so great a noise as to drown all other voices besides," as the jubilant and again hopeful Protector through Fiennes his spokesman said in the speech to both the assembled Houses. In another part of it, he was made to say : "This constitution of a chief magistrate and two houses of Parliament is not pageantry, but a real and well-measured advantage to itself, and to the Commonwealth ; so consonant to reason, that it is the very emblem and idea of reason itself, which reasons and discourses by a medium between two extremes. If there be two extremes, and the one vary from the other, how shall they be reconciled, if there be no medium to bring them together ? "

One step more, and monarchy would be restored. So

Whitelocke designed, and so he desired, but whence this
change in the heart, and why did he no longer turn in his
secret aspirations to the dynasty of the Stuarts ?   Why had
he forgotten all he had once wrought for them, the advice
he had himself tendered to Cromwell in St. James's Park ?
As a man of the world, he could not fail to see the impaired
health of the Protector, the uncertainty of his life, the no-
distant accession of Richard, whose boorish and inapt nature
none knew better than himself; as a politician, he must
have known the bias of the gentry in favour of the old
dynasty, and he himself loathed revolutionary ideas, such as
those entertained by the levellers and Fifth Monarchy Men.
What made him thus changed, that he even preferred con-
sorting with the latter subsequently, rather than go over
to the Cavaliers ?   Was it because he had now married a
Puritan according to the new marriage law then in force,
and which would assuredly be repudiated by the return of
the Stuarts with the old established and intolerant church ?
It was not alone this sad conviction, but his private knowledge, that Charles Stuart and James Stuart were Papists as
well as libertines.   Not that he ever divulged his secret
knowledge to the world, he was too great a lover of fair play
to do that.   Queen Christina told Charles at Breda, that
when conversing about him with Whitelocke in Sweden, she
had never heard the ambassador say a single dishonourable
word against his Majesty, as Charles after the Restoration
spontaneously informed him.   He learned in Sweden, that
Christina was secretly a Papist, and that she abdicated for
the purpose of enjoying her religious convictions without the
necessity of concealment, but his sense of honour forbade
his revealing it even to Cromwell, when the latter questioned
him so inquisitively on his return, and although trusted,
perhaps through the medium of the sympathetic water of
which he possessed the receipt, with the great, and to all
the rest of the world, impenetrable secret, why she had murdered her Italian favourite at Fontainebleau, and with many

other state secrets, he never used them for any temporary
purpose

But the knowledge of these things influenced to a great
extent his own future conduct, and it forms one of the keys
for enabling the world to understand much that otherwise
would appear inexplicable and often contradictory. His going
over to the Royalists, sooner or later, would have been easy.
It would have cost him little, provided his conscience had
not opposed the step, to abandon a cause which he had long
foreseen could not always be triumphantly maintained with
such tremendous odds against it—the growing indifference
and hostility of the nation, more especially of the aristocracy,
so powerful in their respective districts. Nearly every one
of his relations had long since quitted the Parliamentary or
Cromwellian service, and were now hostile to the existing
state of things. He had saved Lord Willoughby with great
difficulty ; he had now to procure the liberty of Sir Roger
Mostyn, with permission for the fiery Welshman to reside in
his own house, after giving his word to do nothing prejudicial to the existing government, and among scores of other
cases, he obtained favour for the Duke of Buckingham,
another kinsman, and the profligate husband of the daughter
of Fairfax. He even carried his kindness to the Duke too
far, for when president of the council at a still later date,
and compelled by duty to commit to prison several lords, as
Delaware, Oxford, and Falkland, the Duke was spared and
alone liberated.

I have been anticipating much, and I return to the petition and advice. Before its final presentation, Whitelocke,
with other lawyers, had urged Cromwell to assume the title
of king. When the Protector saw and heard him speak as
an advocate of the measure, he could not but have reflected
on the very different advice once tendered in a private conference by his friend. But time has effected a change of
views in each. The statesman had learned much of the *de
jure* monarch during his absence from England ; the suc-

cessful warrior had studied more impartially the capacity of
his son Richard to wear the crown after his own decease.
Both of them now knew many secrets of state, with which
they had on the former occasion been unacquainted.   The
antipathy of Cromwell's officers could not have been the real
barrier ; he, the conqueror, could not have dreaded a revolt
on the part of such men as Harrison or even Lambert.
Great despondency as to the future must have determined
Cromwell to a refusal, that in reality sealed England's destinies and paved the way for the overthrow of his party.

Cromwell's illness, and its speedy fatal termination does
not seem to have been wholly unforeseen.   Life was more
precarious in those days than even now, but independently
of the general sense of its insecurity, there was much going
on at that period to inspire unusual apprehension and alarm,
such as are not felt in ordinary times.   Just before the
illness in question Buckingham was committed to the Tower,
and his lenient friend could not prevent the arrest on this
occasion.   This proves that the Royalists were actually at
work in hatching a conspiracy.   Conspirators, if constantly
baffled, are apt to become gradually indifferent to the means
they employ for the accomplishment of their purpose.   Open
warfare at first, but if arms fail, then the dagger or the
poisoned wine-cup.   Many of the deaths, that occurred about
this time, were of a nature to excite suspicion.   Two speakers
in rapid succession, Chute and Sir Lillisbone Long, were
carried off, and the Earl of Mulgrave died suddenly on his
return from Hampton Court to London.   Many persons considered Cromwell's end to be unnatural, and they had some
grounds for their belief.   Secret poisoning was rife on some
parts of the continent at that time, and was not unknown in
this country.   But, on the other hand, not wishing to consider
Charles a more unprincipled villain than he really was, we
think there is much incidental evidence to favour the conviction of natural death in the case of Cromwell.   In the absence
of scientific evidence, the question must be left undecided.

The Protector's failing health, it is fair to presume, had been seen by his friends. Two months before his death he had offered the governorship of Dunkirk to Whitelocke, who had declined it. What the civilian desired was the provost-ship of Eton, where he hoped he might spend the remnant of his days in learned calm, but his request was similarly declined by the Protector. The one saw that the powerful hand was about to be removed, the other knew that his son and successor would require a sustaining hand when his own became powerless.

Family tradition has it, that at the interview between the two men on the 26th of August, five days after Cromwell had signed a patent for raising Whitelocke from the rank of a simple peer to the dignity of a viscount, but which the latter did not think it advisable to use, they discoursed together on the affairs of state, and the minister gave a solemn pledge to uphold Richard to the best of his power. In this he followed the example set him by Oxenstierne, who had promised the great Gustavus to support Christina. All this shows that the termination of Cromwell's malady was foreseen by himself and friend, and it certainly entitles us to presume that foul play had not been practised, recently at least, upon him by the adherents of Charles.

Cromwell's death put an end to the investigation, upon which Whitelocke with other learned men was engaged, to examine and report whether our present translation of the Bible was correct or not. This labour was stopped, and men's thoughts were diverted into other channels. All that had transpired on the subject was, that the translation was held to be the best existing at that time. The subject has since been suffered to sleep, but will inevitably be revived.* Should the task be eventually accomplished, as there is every reason to suppose, the world may have reason to

---

* A new version of the Bible is being now published in German by Chev. Bunsen, the well-known historian of ancient Egypt.

congratulate itself that the new version had been so long deferred, to a period when scholars, through the various discoveries of modern times in languages and science, had become so much better fitted to discharge the duties of faithful and competent translators.

CHAPTER XXIII.

1658—1660.

Distracted State of the Country—Incompetency of Richard Cromwell—Parliament dissolved, and another elected on the old System—Whitelocke nominated a Member of the New Council of State—Is called upon by Parliament to draw up an Act for the Union of Scotland with England—Falsely accused of corresponding with Hyde—Chosen President of the Council—His great Labours, and Confidence reposed in him by Parliament—Success of his Endeavours—Angry Disputes between the Army and Parliament—Hostilities averted by the Council of State, and Monk applied to—The Seal again confided to Whitelocke—He is invited by sundry Officers to form one of the "Committee of Safety"—Monk's Communication to him—Detects Monk's Designs to restore Charles II.—Advocates a Negotiation with Charles, and offers to go to Breda for that purpose—His Advice thwarted by Fleetwood's Indecision—Cabal against Whitelocke—He returns the Seal to the care of the Speaker—Precipitate Destruction of valuable Papers, through the Apprehensions of his Wife.

THE death of the great Cromwell, a man distinguished quite as much by the liberality of his mind and generosity of his noble nature, as by the signal success of his arms and vigour of his administration, must have rendered the sagacious and veteran statesman more than usually solicitous as regarded the future condition of his country. Had his valuable Annals been preserved, which recorded this portion of England's history and his own career, they would have thrown full light on what is felt to be very obscure. His own reflections as a lawyer were at this time of so desponding a character, that he resolved as if in desperation to make the best of what ordinary common sense could not but point out as hopeless and irretrievable. Every act during the existence of the Long Parliament, after its breach with Charles I., and that of the first Protectorate, was illegal and not recognised by any loophole of the English statute-book. The case of an interregnum without some usurper or another, as a *de facto* king, to fill the vacant throne, was not contemplated by the English laws.

The idea of the possibility of a republic without king and lords had never entered the minds of Englishmen from the time of the Heptarchy downwards. Men were born with the idea of king in their heads as camels with indurations on their knees. But here our statesman of the new school, at first sanguine in the success of novel institutions, hoping or believing that they had struck deep and ineradicable roots in the soil, had ample opportunity of contemplating their inability to resist the gathering storm, his own inability to surround them with an adequate defence. He knew the aristocracy of the country, at that time the comparatively enlightened portion of the community, to be implacably averse to the new system. He knew the clergy, who then might be regarded as the exclusive teachers of the people, and who used their pulpits as political rostrums, to be, with the exception of the Independents and perhaps one or two other sects, opposed likewise to the new system. The army and the mass of the citizens remained it is true, but the former had lost the strong controlling hand, and the latter were gradually returning to their old habits of reverence for old constituted power and the forms they had been taught to love and honour from their cradles. As for the army, their enemies being vanquished in the field, much of their stern enthusiasm had already cooled down, the veterans were diminishing in numbers, and even they, when their mighty chief lay low, must have looked for some goal, some profitable object worth fighting for, and have looked in vain.

Wherever Whitelocke gazed, his looks must have been disconsolate at surveying the waste around him, and there was nothing but the dim uncertain future to awaken and sustain his hopes.

His optimism could not delude him as regarded the prospects of the second Protector, whose feeble capacity was wholly incapable of sustaining the tottering Commonwealth. The house of the government was divided against itself, and could not stand. There was a fatal dualism of power, which the Royalists were not the last to perceive, and seeing how well their adversaries were doing their work, they stayed their hands and remained passive for a brief time. Fleetwood, Lambert, Desborough, and the Republican party were doing all they could to ruin Richard, were holding him up to the contempt of the world, and shaking his credit among the citizens, so that plain policy taught the monarchical party the expediency of some repose. This comparative quiet, novel, and indeed portentous to the few men accustomed to scan the political horizon in that age, served like an ambuscade to insure the destruction of their enemies. All warning given by wisdom to imbecility becomes in such circumstances futile. Whitelocke, now again seated on the woolsack, was, on one of these dispiriting emergencies, summoned by Richard to council. Lord Broghill, Fiennes, Thurloe, Wolsey, and some others, had been also convoked. The question proposed to them for solution was, whether it would be fitting or not to dissolve the present Parliament. The majority was in favour of so doing; the minority, consisting of Thurloe and the Chancellor, doubted the success of such a measure, which they considered inopportune. They thought the House should be permitted to sit a little longer, especially now that they had begun to consider the necessity of raising money—" the sole means of keeping the soldiery in order." What a sad confession is this! There is no thought taken of the legislative functions of the House. But the reasons are not yet at an end. Most of the councillors, he goes on to observe, "were for the dissolution [of that House], where the party of Haselrigge, Nevil, and others excited as much apprehension as if they had been Cavaliers;" these too had flocked to London, and were now, he thought, fomenting secretly the distractions of the hour.

Richard had many enemies, not only to his government,

but to himself in this very council; he was, moreover, cheated
and betrayed by some of his nearest and dearest relations,
who, if he had possessed even latent energy, would not have
dared at such a juncture to kindle it; and as for the common
soldiers, the only men to whom he could have appealed for
support, they had been taught by their officers to scoff at
him, because, amongst other offences, he wore silk-stockings,
though his father had been satisfied with worsted ones.

All matters, in consequence of this unfortunate dissolution,
having come to a stand, the soldiers being left without their
pay, Fleetwood with the rest of the officers invited the
members of the Long Parliament to return to the exercise
and discharge of their trust. The Cromwellian glory had
expired, and with it all permanent stability.

The reassembling of the Long Parliament gave hopes to
many, that the peace and liberty of the nation would now be
restored by this means; men could not forget what great
things it had done, and a momentary calm ensued. As
soon as the members met, their first act was to appoint a
council of state, consisting of thirty-one members, animated
with very different political tenets, entertaining adverse
social views, and if dissonance be desirable, most admirably
qualified at this juncture for promoting harmony among the
King's party. By the side of Fairfax and Whitelocke sat
Vane and Scot : the two former, monarchists ; the other two,
levellers ; contiguous with the arrogant and insolent Sidney,
the subtle, crafty, and scheming Sir Anthony Ashley Cooper.
Their next act was to decree the formation of a new Seal,
equivalent to a deposition of Richard, and to loss of office on
the part of the present Commissioners. They then voted the
pay of the army and navy, anticipating by one day the
receipt of a most loyal address from Monk and his brother
officers. In this tender effusion, that general, who was at
that time corresponding with Charles, laments the departure
of God from " our Israel," but sees when God's hour is come,
and how He cometh skipping over all the mountains of sin

and unworthiness that Monk and others daily cast in the way. Then beseeching God to heal the backslidings of his people, he congratulates the House on its happy restoration to the governor of these nations, and hopes it will make some honourable provision for the family of Cromwell, that the blackest of designs may never be able to cast dirt in the faces of the members any more, and that they will be pleased to countenance godliness, assert the native rights and liberties of the Free State, and provided they act in this manner assures them, that he (in common with the rest, whose names were appended to his own) will vindicate their authority against the opposition of all arbitrary power whatsoever.

This dutiful and pious address was followed by an order of the House for the Council of State or for any five of its body to prepare an act for the union of Scotland and England. Whitelocke was desired by the council to take charge of this business.

His hereditary enemy, Scot, upon the authority of a letter from an Irish friar abroad, as he pretended at least, from a man whom he asserted to be a spy in his own pay, came forward now with an accusation against both Cooper and Whitelocke. Scot declared, that they had kept up a correspondence with Sir Edward Hyde, but he utterly failed to prove his assertion. Subsequent events revealed the truth, —Sir Anthony was guilty, the other innocent. Not that Scot made his accusation openly ; on the contrary his denunciation had been private, and but for an equally private intimation from Fleetwood, the accused member might never have known the name of his accuser, for when he desired the House to bring forward their informant and let him see who he was, they declined doing that, but absolved him from all complicity and dismissed the charge.

Cromwell the Second has now tamely and submissively acquiesced in the sole and supreme authority of the senate ;

F F

he disappears from the scene, and finds happiness in travel and rural solitudes.

Whitelocke on the other hand declines going on a mission to the Sound, in order to mediate a peace between the kings of Denmark and Sweden ; old age and infirmities pleaded for him, and the overbearing temper of Colonel Sidney was too inauspicious, too much opposed to his own conciliatory spirit. Nor had he quite regained his ancient influence, as many little circumstances show, to warrant even a temporary absence from his post ; his situation may even have been critical, or thought to have been so by his friends, since they went so far as to propound, towards the latter end of June, that all should take out a general pardon, meaning especially the various commissioners of the great Seal. The bill of indemnity did not pass till about the middle of the next month, and until then his policy was to remain quiet and passive, and devote himself to his task of accomplishing the union by an act of the legislature.

Fresh conspiracies and unexpected dangers soon roused them all from their dream of fancied tranquillity. Although Buckingham escaped through the interest of Fairfax and himself, the ungracious task devolved on him, as President of the Council, of committing several to prison, amongst whom were Lady Mary Howard, daughter of the Earl of Berkshire, and several others, doubtless of both sexes. His time was taken up both day and night for a long time, and letters poured in from several parts of the kingdom, describing insurrections, announcing new conspiracies, fresh risings here and there. Perplexity besieged, but did not bewilder him for an instant. Lambert was despatched with great care and vigilance to put down the rebellion of Sir George Booth in Cheshire and Lancashire, and an ample force was placed under the orders of the parliamentary general. Letters of ill tidings still came in, many at midnight ; he read them in his bed, dictated the answers to his secretaries, sent couriers in hot haste away, and then turned to court sleep upon his pillow till roused again. The House gave him full powers to commit any person brought before him for one fortnight by virtue of a warrant under his hand and seal, and he issued proclamations in the name of the Parliament and Council. But if he committed many, and some were powerful noblemen, to such temporary durance, the inevitable consequence of their own acts, he lost not the opportunity of procuring Sir William Davenant's discharge from his long and wearisome imprisonment.

This short but turbulent episode was soon brought to a close by the total defeat of Booth, the capture of the Earl of Derby, the surrender of Chirke Castle, of Chester and Liverpool, the suppression of the movements in Staffordshire, Worcestershire, and Surrey. The congregational churches had raised three regiments in aid of the government ; the Presbyterian ministers had generally favoured the insurrectionists ; but order being restored at last, our president lost his sternness, and took compassion on his prisoners. Through his mediation Lady Howard and her father obtained at first indulgence, then release, and ungratefully was his kindness requited by both at a later date.

The true functions of this extraordinary Parliament were now again at an end. In the first stage of their existence they had prospered, so long as confusion was paramount, as civil war was raging, and until they had consummated their triumph by the decapitation or banishment of their principal antagonists. When this was accomplished they quarrelled with the army, and seemingly ended their career by having the doors of their own house closed and locked against them. They were now passing through a scene not altogether dissimilar ; they had been once again victorious, once more made happy by sequestrations, fines, banishment and imprisonment, with the prospect of more heads on the scaffold, when they fell to their old game and quarrelled with the officers of the army as before. "Pride's purge" and the subsequent humiliations were forgotten ; they disgraced Fleet-

wood, Lambert, Desborough, Berry, and seven or eight more
discontented superior officers, nor cared to inquire beforehand whether such violent measures were likely to obtain
obedience.   The sergeant-at-arms was desired to convey to
them the commands of the House, and so much, thought
the jubilant majority, " for the petition and representation"
of those mutineers.   With their own Evelyn, their own life-
guards to defend them, they would have no Fleetwood to
be lieutenant-general any longer ; he should be a commissioner of the forces if he liked, with Ludlow, Monk, Haselrigge, Walton, Morley, and Overton, but nothing more.   The
very day after these wild proceedings, Lambert walked
quietly out alone to meet their Evelyn at the head of his
life-guards, on their daily march to the House, and on
coming up to him commanded him to halt and dismount.
Evelyn obeyed, the troops obeyed, and other forces being
rapidly collected, Lambert placed them along King-street
and near the Abbey, with orders to stop the Speaker or
others, and turn them back.   These were carried out to a
certain extent, and the House did not sit that day ; the
soldiers had stopped the Speaker in his carriage, and turned
the heads of the horses in an opposite direction, but several
members eluded their vigilance and got into the House.   A
collision was imminent, bloodshed might occur ; one word,
and the soldiers might storm the sanctuary—a word which
they expected, and were only too eager to obey.   In this
emergency the Council of State stepped in ; messengers
were sent to the forlorn members sitting in the House, like
those senators at Rome before the entry of Brennus, but not
like them resolved to sit and brave the worst ; the message
implored them to come to an accommodation, to save the
effusion of blood, and they hearkened to good counsel.   An
arrangement was effected ; the members promised on their
part not to sit, and the officers on theirs to withdraw their
troops ; a council, partly military, partly civil, would provide
for the preservation of the peace, draw up a form of govern-

ment, and shortly summon a new Parliament to settle all things.

The new council met seldom, and when it did, to debate about what it called the settlement, and it appointed Fleetwood the Commander-in-chief. In the mean time Haselrigge and his friends deliberated on what was to be done to effect their own restoration to power, and how they could curb the revolted officers. They turned their eyes to Monk, whom they hoped to secure as their champion. Both parties indeed were active to obtain the concurrence of the forces in Scotland and Ireland, but in the meantime the officers nominated a committee of ten from the old Council of State to carry on the government. Of this ten Whitelocke was one, Vane another; the rest appear to have been officers, with Fleetwood at their head. It was this nomination of Fleetwood to the chief command, that discontented Monk (so Whitelocke thought) and paved the way for the return of Charles. There was another committee of six for the nomination of officers, to which Vane belonged, the other civilian not; and as soon as these little arrangements were completed, they kept—what was indeed most needful to some of them—a day of humiliation, in Whitehall Chapel. All this was done without asking Whitelocke's consent; he was then absent, however, and was not desirous of such dangerous employment, especially at such a time. But he could not well refuse now that the original committee of ten was increased by thirteen new members, one of whom was Ireton, the Lord Mayor, and that a wholesome title was given it— The Committee of Safety. Upon appointing him to this post, twelve officers, whose names are recorded, addressed to him the following letter :—

"For our honoured friend Bulstrode Lord Whitelocke.

Sir,— Upon consideration of the present posture of affairs in this Commonwealth, the general council of the officers of the army have thought fit to appoint a committee of safety

for the preservation of the peace, and management of the
present government thereof; As also for the preparing of a
form of a future government for these nations, upon the
foundation of a government or free state.   And yourself
being one of the persons nominated for that purpose, we do
by their direction hereby give you notice thereof, and desire
you to repair to-morrow morning at ten of the clock, to the
horse-chamber in Whitehall, in order to the service aforesaid.
We rest,

Your faithful friends and servants."

" WHITEHALL, 27th October, 1659."

He tells us, that on receiving this letter, he was in some
perplexity what to do upon it, and had much discourse with
his friends about it ; that Desborough and some other great
officers of the army, actors in this business, came to him
and earnestly requested him to undertake this trust, and
told him, that some of the committee, as Vane, Salwey and
others, had a design to overthrow magistracy, ministry, and
the law; that to be a balance to them, they had chosen him,
with some others, to oppose such design, to support and
preserve the laws, magistracy, and ministry in these nations.
Their further arguments were a mere amplification of this
appeal, and under those circumstances he thought it his duty
to comply, there being a strict understanding, that a new
Parliament was to be convoked as speedily as possible.   He
acted quite rightly in complying with the request.   Looking
at Vane on the one hand, at what Anabaptists had done and
might do over again: on the other hand at the fact, that the
law was at that time, however bad intrinsically, the only
safeguard against the brutal violence of savage men, who
hardly wanted a pretext for any act of insolence or rapine,
Whitelocke, so long at the head of the law, could do no less
than accept.   He was not morally bound to respect the
wishes or feelings of the Long Parliament, of this or that
party in the state, but he was morally bound to preserve

social order if he could, and prevent the excesses of fanatics.
Besides this, as Whitelocke reasoned rightly, there was no
constituted or visible authority in existence, no power but
what was latent, save that of the sword ; legal it might not
be exactly, but unquestionably the basis of power under all
forms of government with which he was acquainted, from
theocracy to democracy inclusive. It would be better for
him to temper the sharpness of that sword, and gradually
cause it to be sheathed. As for Vane, there was no ambiguity
in him, no doubt respecting his purpose; give him sway, and
he would make a clean sweep of every thing, for the introduction not of superior institutions but of some visionary
absurdities, like those which disgrace the pages of German
history at Munster and elsewhere. The new councillor went
accordingly to the appointed place, and was cordially received.
His influence had to be developed ; for the present, Vane,
Fleetwood, Titchburn, and two others were named as a sub-
committee to consider of a form of government, and efforts
were made to come to a better understanding with Monk.

Whitelocke received back into his custody the Great Seal.
No one but he seems to have penetrated the true designs of
the refractory general in Scotland ; it is true he had cor-
responded with him, had received from him several applications, and one singular invitation so far back as the 21st of
June ; in that mysterious letter Monk complimented him
highly, was glad that he had the conduct of the Union, and
hoped to see him at his head-quarters in Scotland. A modern
writer of lives, in describing this particular, considers Whitelocke was prevented from accepting this offer by his unlucky
star. I think, with a similar astrological figure of speech,
that some lucky star detained him, that star which prevents
men from turning traitors to their country. But although he
made no response to the invitation, his eyes were gradually
opened to Monk's projects, and on the 8th of November, he
publicly declared to the Common Council of London, what
these were. Nothing could be stronger than his language,

and no prophecy was ever more literally fulfilled. He
said, that the bottom of Monk's design was to bring in the
King upon a new civil war ; then he showed the danger of
it to the city and the nation, counselled them to provide for
their own safety, and to join for that of the whole nation,
for the preservation of the peace. The common-councillors
returned him thanks, and resolved to follow his advice.

By the end of the first week in December, discontent
having been previously perceived among the troops about
London, intelligence arrived, that Colonel Zanchey with his
Irish brigade had placed himself under the orders of Monk.
Now Zanchey was one, and indeed the first, of those very
officers, that had invited him so formally to become a member of the Committee of Safety, and the news appeared to
him so disastrous, that he fell into a state of great perplexity.
Fleetwood's character he knew to be weak, vacillating and
fickle, so he resolved to further with all his influence the
convocation of a new Parliament, the proclamation of which
was solemnly published on the 15th of the month, one week
after hearing the news of Zanchey's defection. Every day
increased his gloom, and as Fleetwood's party was rapidly
melting away, his old brother-in-law Lord Willoughby, Sir
William Fleetwood the brother of the commander-in-chief,
Alderman Robinson, Major General Browne, Mr. Lowe and
others came to him, confirmed his suspicions about Monk,
advised him to take council with Fleetwood, get the start of
the other by sending forthwith to Breda, and as the King
must be brought in, to bring him in on the best terms.
After serious consideration, this seemed the only plan to
pursue under the circumstances, growing more and more
desperate with every fresh post from the provinces. He went
to Fleetwood, related what had passed, and stated the reasons
for his advice. There was no need of pointing out to him
the helpless and hopeless condition of his party, how Lambert
had all but fallen, how the troops in London were wavering
and ready to desert him, how the garrisons at Portsmouth

and elsewhere were not to be depended on for one instant,—
Fleetwood knew all that already ; what he required to see
in the true light was Monk's conduct and intentions, which
Whitelocke pointed out to him clearly, to the end that he
should not be deluded, as Haselrigge, Scot, and other old
parliament men would assuredly be by Monk, who intended
bringing in the King without making any terms for the
country, whereby the lives and fortunes of the parliamentary
party would be at the mercy of the cavaliers, and exposed
to the vengeance of the monarch.   Fleetwood therefore
should do one of two things : the first was to draw all his
forces together, put himself at their head, borrow money
from the city, and strike a blow for victory.   Upon this
Fleetwood asked, whether Whitelocke would go with him
into the field and to the Tower, and the answer was, yes.
Then he asked, what the other alternative was.   To send
some person of trust to Breda, and offer Charles the crown
upon satisfactory terms, and on being again asked, whether
he himself would go, his answer was again, yes.   The same
biographer, already alluded to in the course of this work,
has related this affair in such a way as to induce the reader
to believe, that Whitelocke made the offer to go himself, and
then compares what Whitelocke's future fortunes might have
been, had Monk been so anticipated or forestalled.

To compare the two men, to make out a hypothetical
parallel between them is not justified by the text in the
" Memorials," or the true state of the two cases.   So far from
there being any similitude between them, there is the widest
conceivable distance.   One was a traitor to the nation of
England, an officer who had been intriguing for months, aye,
for years, with profound dissimulation, contrary to his duty,
his oath, and own conscience, supposing him to have had one;
who had been plotting against the existing order of things
upon his own authority, unknown to every one ; whereas the
other merely suggested, in hopeless extremity, from the only
visible chief in authority, the expediency of so acting in a

fair, open, and warrantable manner, of going as an ambassador
for the good of his country, the healing of discord and civil
war, the obtaining of fair terms by negotiation and treaty for
all classes, but more especially for those, who might through
Monk's unconditional surrender be sacrificed in a variety of
ways.   One would have thought that an English judge,
accustomed to sum up impartially and able to distinguish
truth from misrepresentation, would have remembered the
career of Charles, the arbitrary death of Vane and others,
the fines and extortions ; though to be sure, being a *laudator*
temporis acti, an approver of those good old days in bluff
Harry's time, when a thousand men or so were strung up per
annum, he may think those executions of Charles quite just
and proper, and that the restoration, as effected by Monk,
was quite satisfactory.   So thought not the nation, when it
was found necessary to expel a second time the dynasty of
the Stuarts, and have a Bill of Rights passed to protect the
people from chief justices and others in time to come.

Fleetwood decided on sending him to the King, desired
him to go and prepare for the journey, said that he and his
friends would in the meantime prepare his instructions, and
that no time should be lost.   So ordered this doughty chieftain, and retired to the next room, where Vane, Desborough,
and Berry, were awaiting him, but on perceiving them, he
hastily begged Whitelocke to stay a moment; Whitelocke,
who knew how little he could be depended on in any great
crisis, foresaw what the issue of their consultation would be.
The general returned in a quarter of an hour, and exclaimed
in an excited state : "I cannot do it, I cannot do it."
Upon asking Fleetwood the reasons of this change, the
leader replied . "These gentlemen have remembered me ;
and it is true—I am engaged not to do any such thing
without my Lord Lambert's consent.   The other rejoined
that Lambert was at too great a distance to have his
consent to this business, which must be instantly acted.
Fleetwood said, "I cannot do it without him."   "You will

ruin yourself and your friends," was the prompt rejoinder; "I cannot help it," came out piteously but doggedly, and the two separated.

But how came Whitelocke, while Lambert and Fleetwood were being duped into procrastinating negotiations with the man they ought to have crushed at once, if they could, by vigorous action, to know what Monk's real designs were, or rather to suspect them to that degree as to be enabled to predict so accurately the course taken by him? His brother-in-law, Lord Willoughby, was one source of that knowledge. This nobleman, who had fought by sea and land on behalf of the second Charles, had good intelligence, and was now in a position both to requite benefits and to redeem some wrongs he had himself committed. By an act of piracy, which his loyalty construed at the time into fair retaliation, he had, only a few short years before, made prize of a ship containing bullion to a very large amount, and which property belonged to the third wife of his kinsman, *ergo*, by the law of England, which treats the wife as a chattel to the husband, the father of nine children, by that lord's own sister. He could do no less than try and save his old benefactor in return. So clear was the future to many others, that Colonels Ingoldsby and Howard came and begged Whitelocke, as the holder of the Great Seal, to take it over to the King, which he now refused to do; but he did send out some writs for a new Parliament: one to the Lord Mayor, for instance, and another to the sheriffs of London.

As soon as Lenthall found out that Fleetwood's and Lambert's troops were in a state of revolt, he took courage, ordered those quartered near London to come to his house, gave them the word, and, as a matter of course, the Long Parliament came together again for the third time. From them Whitelocke could expect little favour: he had sinned against them by having served in the Committee of Safety, and issued writs for a new House of Commons. Scot declared, that he should be hanged with the Great Seal about

his neck ; and the Haselrigge party, of whom Nevil was the
most violent, breathed nothing but vengeance and the exter-
mination of their adversaries.   Lenthall appears to have
summoned all the members with great impartiality ; and
Whitelocke went to him, explained his objections, and stated
his belief that he should be sent to prison.   The Speaker
assured him that no such thing would be moved ; and they
would take it as an owning of their authority if he came and
sat with them.   Upon this he went to the House, and found
many of his old acquaintance,—such men as Reynolds and
Nevil,—very reserved to him ; whereupon some of his friends,
perceiving the general irritation that prevailed among the
ranks of the republican party, advised him not to be in the
House on the day they had appointed for considering the case
of the absent members.   Strange to say, he had too deeply
involved himself with Fleetwood and the rest of the committee to expect himself much mercy at the hands of men completely subservient to the new dictator on the one hand, or
to the desperate gang of Nevil and the rest on the other.
He therefore retired to a friend's house in the country ; but,
before he left, directed his wife to carry the Great Seal to
the Speaker, which she did, locked up in a desk, and gave
the key to him as its new possessor.   Unfortunately, in her
state of trepidation and alarm, she committed several papers,
connected with recent events, to the flames, to the irreparable
loss of posterity, as well as to her husband's lasting regret,
for it prevented him giving a perfect account of what had
been done during the Protectorates, and subsequently.   Nor
has this been the only calamity.   A great portion of his
Annals, containing an immense amount of suppressed passages, not suffered to appear either in the first or second
edition of the " Memorials," has seemingly been lost in some
inexplicable way.   The probability is, that one of his descendants has mislaid them ; and hence my hope, that time
may reveal the spot where they lie neglected and forgotten.

CHAPTER XXIV.

—◆—

1660.

Whitelocke's Public Career closed by the Restoration—His Interview with the King,
who compels him to pay a grievous Price for his Pardon—Compelled thereby to
sell one of his Estates, and to raise a Mortgage on Fawley Court—Returns to his
Estate at Chilton—Writes, at the King's suggestion, a Treatise on Parliaments,
subsequently Published under the Title of "The King's Writ"—Also composes
his "Annals" and various Religious Tracts—Extracts quoted from some of the
latter—How the Manuscript of "The King's Writ" came to the British Museum,
and was published in 1766—Dedication of this Work to the King quoted, with
Whitelocke's Views on a Codification of the Laws—List of his Letters contained
in the Thurloe Collection of State Papers

THE King being now virtually restored, Whitelocke was
not sent to the Tower, like Lambert and others, as he himself
expected, nor was anything done before the day of Jove, as
Thursday began again to be called, on the 14th of June,
1660. On this day his humble petition was presented and
read. On the question being propounded, that Bulstrode
Whitelocke, esquire, as they now called him, should be one
of the twenty persons exempted out of the act of general
pardon and oblivion, for and in respect only of such pains,
penalties, and forfeitures, not extending to life, as shall be
thought fit to be inflicted upon him by another act intended
to be hereafter passed for that purpose, it was rejected by
what may be called a considerable majority, when we take
into consideration the wonderful turn affairs had taken, and
the complete infatuation of the nation at large respecting the
happiness they anticipated from the restoration of monarchy
in the person of Charles. Resistance against this universal
delusion would have been madness. Even Milton, no common republican, no friend of English parliaments, and still

less of the Stuarts, was fain to rest in mute though indignant silence ; nor did even he ever again give vent to his ineradicable hostility, save under the garb of profound mystery, as the learned reader may perceive by studying the "Samson Agonistes."   In the same spirit of prudence, dictated by necessity, but with more sincere submission to the voice and declared will of the nation, himself a friend to a monarchical government, provided it were conducted on principles of law, moderation, and merciful justice—no friend to the civil war nor the death of Charles—no friend to anarchy and disorder—the now fallen statesman resigned himself with decent submission to the new order of things, and prepared to lay aside ambition and greatness for the whole remainder of his life.   To his own county of Buckingham, where his former influence was gone, it would have been too humiliating to retire ; and as the fortune of his third wife had been partly employed on the purchase of an estate called Chilton Park, or Chilton Lodge, near Hungerford, in Wiltshire, once the property of a near relative, where his aunt had lived and died, thither he decided on finally retreating, there to spend the greater part of his solitude in study, meditation, and prayer.   But, before he went, he waited on the King.   If no one else saw through and appreciated this man, his forbearing and charitable subject did, who now appeared before him, not to "beg his pardon," as all the biographers and historians have erroneously represented, but to pay for his pardon, engrossed on parchment in due form, which Charles, in violation of his promises, in defiance of the majority that had decreed otherwise, in contempt of law and justice, was determined to sell.   As this magnanimous personage had caused the bones of Cromwell, Bradshaw, and others, to be hung in chains at Tyburn—as he possessed the power and the will to have any one prosecuted on the charge of treason —his victim, who now stood helpless before him, had no resource left him but compliance.

He had been fined by his Majesty's autocratic decree to an

enormous amount; had sold one of his estates, that of
Greenland in Hambleden, which he had purchased in 1651
from Sir John Doiley; had raised pecuniary help by mortgage on Fawley Court, and now brought the money to his
Majesty. This act restored him to favour, and he withdrew
to Chilton with even a token of good will from his master,
his coronation bible and prayer-book. Charles told him on
this occasion what the ex-queen Christina had reported of
him, how he had invariably abstained from saying one word
to the prejudice of his liege lord, the present gracious com-
memorator, and to show how highly he thought of his legal
experience desired him, it is said, to compose in his retirement a work upon parliaments for his Majesty's especial use.
To which command he yielded obedience, and commenced his
labours as soon as he had settled down in his country abode.

Too great a sufferer from an incurable malady, that of the
stone, to indulge in much out-of-door exercise, he devoted
much of his leisure time in composing his Annals, a gigantic
work, of which the "Memorials" are a mere fragment, introduced by himself at the end of each year, to explain to his
children what his motives had been, and why he had acted
in this or that way, as the circumstances of the time or case
imperiously demanded, and as they, indeed, now and ever
will demand of all great statesmen. He wrote, too, a great
number of religious books, many of which have been preserved, and are now lying before me. They have never
been published, nor were they intended to be. They breathe
resignation, piety and submission, but contain not a passage
of a sectarian or polemical nature, and accordingly would be
considered unfit, in the opinion of many, for our religious
libraries, or the generality of readers in the scriptural department. A great deal of learning is displayed in them, as
might be expected, and as he used the original Hebrew or
Greek text for his authority, many of his observations would
appear quite novel to most of my countrymen, who on
hearing them for the first time, might conceive he was

occasionally mistaken in his illustrations.   Here and there I
have met with an isolated sentence or group, that I think
ought not to be consigned to oblivion.

One of these MSS. has for its title, " A Father's Lectures
upon particular occasions to his family," with this text from
Joshua, " As for me and my house we will serve the Lord."
He composed these in the year 1667 upon the new buildings
at Chilton Lodge, and at the 34th page has this remarkable
passage, which I hope may not prove applicable to England
with respect to her possessions in India :—

" If you take the building of a house, as this word signifies
a family or nation in that sense, you will find in like manner
that such as go about to build it in pride, whose aim is only
to raise it up in wealth, power, and worldly greatness, such
builders also will labour in vain, such families or nations are
not built by God.   The same judgment is on the building
of a nation by oppression, seeking to enlarge the territories
or dominions thereof by injustice, ambition, or violence, such
building is not of God.   Whosoever goes about to build
his dwelling-house, or his family, or a nation, by oppression,
God will make their houses desolate, his judgments will
overtake such builders ; He does not build such houses ;
they labour in vain that build them."

About half way through the book I find a legal allusion
that goes far to redeem the Saxons from the contempt
thrown on them by many Norman writers.   " Our ancestors
did so detest lying and falsehood, that very many and severe
laws in divers ages were made against them, some of which
are still in force, though not put in execution, yet I doubt
there is now as much cause as ever to continue the force of
them.   The most ancient that we find among those laws was
in the Saxon times, by which he that was guilty of falsehood,
or told a lie, was to lose his tongue or to pay his wereguild."
An income-tax on such a basis, were it practicable, would
yield a large revenue to the state, and be popular.   It is the
only income-tax that is ever likely to be so.

The following is a phrase equally beautiful as new, considering that era, in favour of religious forbearance, tolerance, and unity among men, things little understood at the time he wrote it. It may serve to show also, why Paul, the converted Jew, laid such stress on unity, and what he meant by it:

" This unity may be remembered from the name of brother, which in the Hebrew means *one*, as brothers ought to be. The Latin word for brother signifies almost the same, for *Frater*, as Aulus Gellius says, is *fere alter*. Brethren ought to be, however, not almost, but wholly the same, which will much strengthen and beautify a family by this furniture of their unity."

In another work, " Upon the new gardens and plantations at Chilton Park, in 1666," we learn, by the following passage, the condition of his mind at that dreadful epoch, when even Milton despaired and thought of quitting his native country, all blind, aged, and helpless as he was:

" Privacy frees you from all this, and every other glorious misery. There you may sleep, and eat, honestly disport and enjoy yourself. To live in continual sight of evil, to a well-disposed mind, is next to hell. Certainly to live among toads and serpents is a paradise to this. One jests pleasantly with his Maker, another makes himself sport with scripture ; one fills his mouth with oaths of sound, another scoffs at religion ;—one speaks villainy, another laughs at it, a third defends it ;—one makes himself a swine, another a devil ;—who, that is not earth, can endure this ? Every evil we see doth either vex or infect us, but retiredness avoids it. The desert is too wild, the city too populous; the country is only fit for rest. The court is for honour, the city for gain ; the country for quietness, a blessing that need not, in the judgment of the wisest, yield to the other two."

He became enamoured of his rural occupations, and eulogised them in his peculiar way, as incitements not to evil, but to good. He says :—

" Man is the farmer, the soul is the field to be tilled

Christian duties are the good seed to be sown ; sins are the tares or cockles to be weeded out ; the grace of God is the sweet shower distilling holy motions into the heart, causing the good seed to spring and grow up ; temptations are the winds which purify and fix the seed ; the spirit of Christ is the heat of the sun, which ripens and makes the soul fruitful ; the reward of eternal life is the harvest ; but sorrow for sin and the other graces are the labourers."

I would not introduce the subjoined extract, but that it seems to show who the "fool in the forest" was that Jacques met :—

"A person met him, whom the Popish authors term St. Francis, and who had been banished because he hearkened to his conscience, walking alone in a sequestered grove, and asked him how he could spend his time in that solitary place, he that had no books there, though a great student with a large library at home ?

"The holy man answered :—'I want no books in this place ; I have here a larger library than I had at home ; every tree, leaf, plant, and briar is a book of God, declaring his power and goodness. These books I study all the day, and spend my time in contemplation upon the wonderful works of God ; that too with more content and profit to my soul, than I did when I was at my own house, and in my greatest prosperity.'"

That he should have composed many lectures on Job will not surprise anyone. Milton identified himself with the eyeless Samson, and although our aged husbandman, our contented tiller of his own grounds, did not go so far as to compare himself with the patient patriarch, he studied the text that records the sufferings of the Eastern sage, believing him to have been great in spiritual as well as worldly wisdom, and a good model for himself.

The voluminous manuscript of his work on Parliaments, written, as we have previously stated, by desire of Charles II., is in the British Museum ; it consists of six volumes octavo,

and is entitled : "Notes upon the King's Writ for Choosing
Members of Parliament, ann : 13 Charles II., being disquisitions on the Government of England by King, Lords, and
Commons." This work was published in the year 1766 by
Dr. Morton, the librarian of that noble institution, an institution that would be perfect, were it only a little more liberal,
by allowing no work of learning or genius to stand in its
black book, its *liber expurgatorius*. The Doctor gives an
entertaining account of the way the manuscript came into
the possession of the Museum, and of which it was intended
that he should be the editor. The last owner had been
Thomas Carew of Crocombe, Esq., in the county of Somerset, a member in the ninth Parliament of Great Britain for
the borough of Minehead in the same county. Its presentation had been procured at the instance of Sir John Cust, Bart.,
who was then Speaker of the House of Commons, and of the
Right Honourable Arthur Onslow, Esq., the late Speaker.
Mr. Carew had bought this manuscript at the sale of the
library belonging to the late Duke of Chandos in the year
1747. It was knocked down to the purchaser as lot No. 1849
of the manuscripts, on the 26th of March, being the thirteenth
night's sale of the library, as shown by the auctioneer's
catalogue, at page seventy-seven. It was supposed by some
to have once been in the hands of the first Earl of Clarendon, but the Doctor thought this doubtful, because that
nobleman's library was not dispersed till about the year
1756. The Doctor himself believed the copy in question to
have been the original, and that which had been presented
to King Charles by the author. He was quite right in his
first conjecture, and may be well excused for his error in the
second, having been deceived by the author's preface, addressed
to the King, and possibly with the intention of presenting it
to his Majesty on some fortunate opportunity, that subsequent events never conferred. Knowing how heavy his fine
had been, and how he had paid, or been commanded to
pay, 90,000*l.* for his pardon, a sum which he never could

raise, so that the monarch was fain to content himself with
50,000*l.*, my own impression is, that the author wrote that
preface merely to shield his son William or his other son
Bulstrode, both of whom were brought up to the profession
of the law, from any charge of constructive treason, in case
the work, advocating as it does constitutional opinions, might
happen to be seen by some such limb of the law as Jeffreys
or Scroggs. It is not credible, that such a profligate tyrant
as Charles, who hated parliaments, no matter how slavish or
how constructed, would desire to know more than he knew
already respecting them.

Now, when Sir William Whitelocke died at Phyllis Court,
the Duke of Chandos may have purchased this manuscript
at the sale of his library, as he did another, which I know
came likewise into the possession of the British Museum, and
which work is in praise of limited monarchy.

Morton says : " The time when Whitelocke began the present treatise, seems to have been soon after the King's return
to England, and issuing the writ of summons, for at page
44 of vol. ii., he mentions, that the bishops were not then
restored to the House of Lords, which was effected in the
13th of Charles II. And it must have employed him
several years, as we find him cite an Act in the 16th of
Charles II."

The author's dedication is here subjoined, and no better
proof can be desired of how tyranny acts, when a victim
still bleeding from the oppression of a tyrant, felt himself
compelled by prudential motives, for the sake of his children
and for preserving the small estate still left to him, heavily
mortgaged as it was for the payment in part of a most
exorbitant mulct, to use such loyal language, expressive of
sentiments, that could not have been conscientiously felt, and
which could only have been uttered from the dictates of
arbitrary necessity, and from a conviction of what the dreadful state of the law was concerning treason, until his son
Sir William, at a later period, brought in a bill to amend it.

"To my Lord the King.

Sire,—When it was in the power of your Majesty and in the purpose of some men to have taken my small fortune, liberty, and life from me, you were pleased most graciously to bestow them on me,* and to restore me to a wife and sixteen children, who all join in our humble and thankful owning of your mercy. And God hath pronounced you blessed, and to receive mercy, for you have been merciful to many thousands of your offending subjects. In which number I rank myself with penitence, and with study how to express a gratitude, whereof my present mean and yet troubled condition allows me no larger evidence, than this present of a free-will offering of the first fruits of my labours to your Majesty ; not exposed to others' view, but gathered purposely, and tendered most humbly to your Majesty, not in a presumption of anything worthy your acceptation, but in a grateful sense of your goodness to him, who desires to own it, with his own conviction and endeavour to convince others.

" He hopes these Analecta in his own profession will not be improper for his Prince's view, the subject thereof being that government, whereof yourself is the head, and therein concerned more than any other, and that if somewhat herein occurs in vindication of your Majesty's government from calumnies, and scandalous invectives, cast upon it by ignorance and malice, and to shew its dependence upon the sacred polity, the unparalleled justice and equality of it,† with its approbation under so many conquests, changes and ages as have passed under your royal ancestors, with some resemblances in other governments, it will not be displeasing to your Majesty. To whom if any syllable here may be useful or acceptable, I have my end ; if not, I shall hope for my pardon, from your accustomed goodness, because my design

---

* Quite true—for a consideration—for the lion's share of it.

† The irony of this sentence must strike every one. Where persecution or censorship exists, truth can only be expressed by some figure or under some veil.

could be nothing else, but to give a particular testimony of
the duty and gratitude of

Sire,

Your Majesty's most humble, most obliged, and most
obedient servant,

B. WHITELOCKE."

The work commences with a most ridiculous etymology
about the name of Charles, and all that can be said is, that
it was the fashion of that age to indulge in etymologies. It
was not more absurd, than to call a constellation *Cor Caroli*
or a newly-discovered planet, the *Georgium Sidus*. The
introduction of loyalty or the political feelings of the day
into science or any branch of knowledge is happily of rare
occurrence, now that better taste prevails ; when investiga-
tions of such a description are regarded as arid and unprofit-
able in the extreme. With regard to the sources from which
the materials are drawn, the worthy editor informs us, that
they were chiefly Selden's works, "which he seems to have
transferred wholly into his common place, and uses, with
the same freedom, as if they were his own. Not but that
very frequent recourse is had to many other authors, amongst
whom the names of Mr. Lambard, Lord C. J. Coke, Sir Roger
Owen, and Sir Henry Spelman, are very conspicuous. Our
author appears also to have thoroughly searched the rolls
and journals of Parliament, the patent and close rolls with
other records, also the Royal and Cottonian libraries, of the
former of which he condescended to be keeper."

The motto to the work is the fourteenth verse of the
eleventh chapter in Proverbs : "In the multitude of counsellors there is safety."

In consequence of what Morton the editor says, I must refer
the antiquarian to the work itself, for were I to quote any
passage that strikes me, it might eventually turn out to be
after all a mere extract from something written by Selden or
Fortescue, or Spelman. And in truth, on poring over its

pages, I agree with Hallam, that the work is deficient in critical discrimination. But one passage is so unquestionably original and genuine, that I cannot deny myself the satisfaction of introducing it. The reader will find it more applicable at the present day, than it was when written.

"Now the volume of our statutes is grown or swelled to a great bigness. 1 remember the opinion of a wise and learned statesman and lawyer, the Chancellor Oxenstierne, that multiplicity of written laws does but distract the judges, and render the law less certain ; that where the law sets due and clear bounds betwixt the prerogative royal and the rights of the people, and gives remedy in private causes, there needs no more laws to be increased, for thereby litigation will be increased likewise. It were a work worthy of a parliament, and cannot be done otherwise, to cause a review of all our statutes, to repeal such as they shall judge inconvenient to remain in force, to confirm those which they shall think fit to stand, and those several statutes which are confused, some repugnant to others, many touching the same matters, to be reduced into certainty, all of one subject into one statute, that perspicuity and clearness may appear in our written laws, which at this day few students or sages can find in them."

The idea of a Code has recently been revived, but does not appear to deserve the support of the nation. A code is apt to fossilise the legislative mind, and the attempt to form such a digest of our laws might transform our Parliament into a constituent assembly, whose new laws, fashioned in too great haste, might undermine the reverence of the people for all law, the fall of which would be tantamount to the ruin of the state. Notwithstanding the acknowledged evil, it seems best to go on as we have begun, and only simplify by slow degrees.

There is another treatise mentioned by the quaker Penn in his Introduction to Whitelocke's "Memorials of English Affairs." It had for its title ; "A treatise upon the power of princes, especially in ecclesiastical affairs." I regret to say, that the manuscript appears to be irrecoverably lost. Doubtless it found its way, like the preceding work, into the hands, not of the Duke of Chandos, but of some other purchaser, and it may, at this moment, lie neglected in the library of some nobleman or gentleman, who, should he read this notice, may perhaps kindly make known the fact in the proper quarter.

Whitelocke composed also in French. The fragment of a religious work, written by him in that language, is in my possession. He taught the language to his children. In his third wife's manuscript, there is a passage in proof of this: "And in a very short time, he (Samuel, their son,) learned so fast, that he could almost discourse anything with his father in French, and could interpret a French letter, if it were read unto him, which was a very great delight unto his father to hear." This was at Chilton, where a French teacher would hardly be procurable in those days.*

* For many of Whitelocke's letters the reader is referred to the state papers of John Thurloe, Esquire, volumes 1 and 2, in which there are about fifty. In vol 1 *vide* pp. 59, 69, 249, 470, 480, 500, 575, 601, 602, 645 *seq.*, 627, 646, 652, 654, 656. In vol 2 *vide* pp 22, 40, 42—44, 80—83, 103, 111—113, 126, 131, 134, 155, 157, 202, 203, 217 *et seq.*, and yet more, as registered in the index.

CHAPTER XXV.

—◆—

1660—1675.

Whitelocke's Arrangements respecting the Inheritance of his Property—His Narrative
of the Death of Dr. Winston, and what thence ensued in connection with this
Matter—Death of Bulstrode Whitelocke—Estimate of his Character.

WHITELOCKE had, long before his death, the inestimable
blessing of knowing, that all his children were provided for
in such a manner, as to secure them from want, but his
dream of being a constitutional peer was at an end.   His
estate at Fawley, mortgaged it is true at the Restoration,
went to his heir at law, James, the only child of Rebecca
the first wife.   Phyllis Court descended to William, the
eldest of three sons by the second wife, Miss Frances
Willoughby, who was married to Sir Bulstrode on the
10th of November, 1634.   The next son in order was named
Willoughby, and the fourth, after his father, Bulstrode,
respecting whom there is a manuscript fragmentary leaf in
the British Museum.   It is a part of the father's Annals, and
deposited there for some reason that I cannot divine, seeing
how much of the entire work has been secreted or suppressed,
and is to the following effect :

" October 24 [1655].

"I had much company at dinner with me at Chelsea of
Swedish and German Lords and Gentlemen, and before we
had quite dined a messenger from my brother Wilson
brought me this letter : 'To the Right Honourable Sir
Bulstrode Whitelocke, one of the Lords Commissioners of
his Highness's Treasury, these present—Chelsea : May it

please your good Lordship and my good Lady! Just now,
coming from the Exchange, I met with a messenger, who
acquainted me that he came from hearing Dr. Winston's
will, who departed this life about two hours since, and telling
me he hath left part of his land to the Lord Portland, but
the greatest share after Mr. Lawrence and his son's death to
your Lordship's child, which he could not tell me for very
certain, but tells me that Mr. Lawrence and the rest charged
those who were there with secrecy.   I thought it my duty
to acquaint you herewith, which will be an excuse for my
not waiting on you this day, and a great rejoicing it is to
me to understand the prosperous condition of you and yours,
which the Lord long continue to his glory.   I conceive it
requisite somewhat may be done speedily herein, for I like
not their willingness to have things secret.   I need not
acquaint you my house is yours, and that I am your
Lordship's most humble servant,

SAMUEL WILSON.'

" 'BISHOPSGATE-STREET, *October* 24, 1655.'

" Upon the receipt of this letter, and shewing it to my wife,
we supposed it might be our son Carleton, on whom the
Doctor had settled his land, because he had been very kind
to that boy, and my wife having been his former acquaintance, and I a stranger to him before she brought me
acquainted with him.   We could not imagine but that his
kindness was intended for one of my children by her.   I
found out excuses and business to dismiss my great company
the sooner, and my wife and I hastened to my brother
Wilson's house.   And after conference with him I sent for
the scrivener, who drew Dr. Winston's will, to come to me
and bring the will with him, which he did, and related the
passages to me there.—That the Doctor being extremely ill
sent for him this morning and gave him instructions to draw
a new will for him and to cancel the old one : That he drew
the new will as he was directed and read it to the Doctor,

who caused him to alter some things and to interline other matters in several places, whereby the will became blotted, and therefore the Doctor, after he had sealed it, ordered the scrivener to write it over again, fair, and he would sign it. That he wrote it all over again, except two or three lines of the latter end of it, and then the Doctor died about twelve o'clock this day,—that those who were with him when he died would have had the new will from the scrivener to have burnt it, but he refused to let them have it, because he thought it to be a good will, and because it concerned one of my children, and he professed a great respect for me, his wife being of kin to my wife, and he was a very honest man, as this action testified, with many other of his dealings. I read the will, and found it to be of lands in Essex called Blunt's Hall, which he gave to the Earl of Portland and his son for their lives, and the reversion to my son Bulstrode, and his heirs, and his other lands in Northamptonshire he gave to my son Bulstrode, and his heirs. We wondered at his giving the land to Bulstrode, but supposed that he took him to have been my son by this wife, and therefore was so kind to him. I asked the scrivener, if he could prove what he had informed me ; he said he could prove every word of it. I then told him, that the will would prove a good will, and gave it again into his hand before witnesses, desiring him to keep it safely, until it should be required of him legally. About two days before the Doctor died, my wife went to his lodging in Gresham College to visit him, and he was very kind to her, and desired to speak with her in private, but she did not bid one of the children who was with her to withdraw, and so the Doctor probably did forbear to say to her what he intended concerning the settlement of his estate, neither did he at any time advise with me about it. But he was always exceeding kind to me, my wife and children, as when I was out of England he took daily care of them. Indeed he was the kindest friend that ever I had, but those passages of his constant love are formerly mentioned. Captain Hinde, a hosier in London, whom Doctor Winston made his executor, came to me, and offered his assistance to me in the business of my son Bulstrode by the will, for which I thanked him, and promised my assistance to him touching the personal estate due to him as executor, and advised him in all that business. Both of us had reason to . . . ."

So far the fragment, and by a manuscript book still extant, I am enabled to complete the history of this transaction.

"The 30th of October, 1655, being Tuesday, in the evening, was the funeral of Doctor Winston, at which a great number of his friends and acquaintance were present. The executor, Captain Hinde, entertained them with burnt wine, and gave them gloves and gold rings, with this posy : "

The writer forgot to insert it.

"None had mourning given them but his two men-servants and the old woman that waited on him. I and my son Willoughby and my people were at his burial, but I could not send for my son Bulstrode to be here time enough. No women were there, it being, as his friends said, at his own desire in his lifetime, that no woman should be present at his burial.

"There were good store of torches, and things ordered handsomely and decently. We all went on foot after the corpse from Gresham College unto Basinghame Church, where his father was buried, and he desired to be laid in the same vault, which was done accordingly.

"The minister of the parish preached his funeral sermon, and according to custom gave him his due commendations. The poor flocked in great numbers about the church and people, and were very unruly, some of them speaking disgraceful words of him, but it was thought best to take no notice of such passages, and to bestow something upon them for custom's sake and to stop their mouths."

Of course the Lord Portland would not allow a will of this

description, wanting the signature, to pass unquestioned, as may be gleaned from the extracts beneath:

"Nov. 1655.—After much debate and consideration had by ourselves of the several propositions, and advice with our friends, at another meeting we came to this agreement:

"That within two days I shall pay to the Earl of Portland 1000*l.*, and that I should pay to his son, Lord Weston, during his life, 200*l.* a year, he being then to go to travel, and this to be for his maintenance; that I should have the present possession, and receive the profits of the Northamptonshire lands, as well as of those in Essex; that the Earl would presently pass over unto me his own estate and right in all the lands of Dr. Winston, and that his son should do the like for his estate and right, when he should come to the full age of twenty-one years.

"According to this agreement, writings were drawn and sealed between us, bearing date the eighteenth day of this month."

"Dec. 1655.—I understood that one Mr. Winston, a prisoner in the Fleet, husband to Mrs. Winston, a great acquaintance of my sister Mostyn, and who lived near Wales, had given out in speeches, that he was heir to the doctor, and would try to have the estate. I employed Mr. Starkey, my deputy steward at Windsor, who was of counsel with Mr. Winston, and from whom I heard this, to speak with Mr. Winston about it, and he did so accordingly. Mr. Winston came to me and alleged that he was the doctor's heir. I desired to know his pedigree, which he could not make out to me, but after a long discourse he told me that he was acquainted with my father, who was his friend, and my uncle Edward Bulstrode, and my sister Mostyn, and for their sakes he would show respect to me, saving his own right, and so we parted."

"May, 1656.—My sons, Willoughby and Bulstrode, being brought from Grandon by reason of their schoolmaster's death, Mr. Shelborne, who was a very honest good man, and

an excellent schoolmaster, by whose death I and my family
have a great loss, I caused the boys to be brought from
school to Mrs. Cokaine's house, in Bedfordshire, being but
twenty miles from Grendon. I thought it not good to remove
them further, because Bulstrode had then an ague, and the
ways were bad. But I thank God his ague left him at Mrs.
Cokaine's, and I purposed to have gone down there this
month to have seen the land in Northamptonshire, and to
have brought up my boys to London, but the treaty with
the Swedish ambassador hindered me. Mr. George Cokaine
and his wife went into Bedfordshire and brought up the boys
with them two days before Whitsuntide, to Chelsey, where
they were with me the Whitsun week, I thank God, in
good health, and the same time I had with me in my house
twelve of my children all together, for which mercy and
comfort I pray God to make me thankful, and to give his
grace and blessing to all my children, that they may be
instrumental to do him service. The boys were very wild,
by reason of their long being from school, but I brought
Mr. Harrison to be acquainted with them, with whom I
intend to place them at school."

"1659.—I being under some trouble from the Long Parliament, upon their return after the Portsmouth business,
had not the Lord Weston's rent so ready as formerly, which
caused the Earl to rant very high what he would do, and
this is according to the usual course to insult upon such as
we think to be under a cloud. But I made a shift to procure
the money, and so as to his Lordship the cloud was then
dispersed."

The ensuing passage will serve to show how mistaken
Whitelocke's biographers have been, in supposing that he
was banished to his estates in the country by Charles II.,
upon his return.

"1661.—I met in the beginning of this year with my
Lord of Portland at the Chancellor's house, where we had
some discourse about Dr. Winston's estate. The Earl was

very grave and reserved, and said that he must be better informed concerning that business. I told him that I supposed he was fully informed thereof before he set his hand and seal to the agreement made between us. He replied, that he knew well enough what was done, but was not satisfied therewith, and would look further into it. I told him that I was satisfied with his Lordship's hand and seal to the agreement, from which I supposed he would not depart, and so I took leave of him."

The estate was finally settled in 1663, by Act of Parliament, on Bulstrode, the fourth son ; his cousin Dixon's estate on Willoughby, the third son ; and Lilly, the astrologer's, on Carlton, the sixth son. The last-named property had been originally intended for Bulstrode, as the following note testifies :

" 1654.—My kind friend, Mr. Lilly, propounded to me about August this year, that he would settle upon my son Bulstrode in reversion after his (Mr. Lilly's) life, his house and lands in Hersham, at Walton, in Surrey, and a fee farm rent, and several houses in the Strand, all of the yearly value of above 100*l.*, and moved me to take off a mortgage of those lands and houses, that they might be clearly settled, which I willingly paid, and he settled them accordingly. The redemption sum came to 350*l.* The interest for six months on this sum was 9*l.*"

It was not till many years after the death of Sir Bulstrode that his son Carleton came into the possession. He immediately sold the land and house for 500 years, bought a commission in the army, and rose to the rank of a major.

As for Samuel Whitelocke, the eldest son by the third wife, Chilton Lodge, or Park, in the parish of Chilton Foliatt, was settled upon him and his heirs in the twenty-fourth year of Charles II., A.D. 1671, by an indenture made on the 22nd of February. In this deed Bulstrode is called " Knight," but he could only have been so entitled by courtesy, being nothing more than a knight of Queen Christina's order of

the Amaranth.   Dr. Morton, in his editorial introduction to
the "King's Writ," lays some stress on the fact, that the
title of "Sir" was acknowledged by Lord Sunderland, when
secretary of state under Queen Anne, in the privilege pre-
fixed to the second edition of the "Memorials of English
Affairs," printed in the year 1709.   The worthy and good-
natured doctor apparently valued the title far higher than it
intrinsically merited.

Bulstrode Whitelocke died in the year 1675 of that cruel
disease the stone, from which he had suffered very many
years, and was buried privately in some vault, it is now
supposed, beneath the parish church of Chilton.

In estimating the character of any great man it is requisite,
before we can obtain a correct analysis, to take into account
the cosmical perceptions of the age in which he flourished,
for on these the social conditions and the religious convictions
greatly depend, by which his conduct in life is repeatedly
determined.   This is self-evident when dealing with any
great personage belonging to antiquity, though even here the
modern historian too often forgets to inquire whether the
life to be investigated was that of a profane or initiated
person, the historian being too generally himself incompetent
to decide.   But when we come to a period of time comparatively near to our own epoch, we are apt to lose sight of this
necessity.*   We fancy the difference between our ancestors,
removed from us by four or five degrees, and ourselves cannot
be very great.   In reality, however, it is as great, when contemplating any truly great man, as between us and the times
of a Cicero, an Aristotle, and a Ptolemy.   The mental influence of those ancients still prevailed, and even Bacon was

---

* Thus King Robert Bruce appears to have been a Culdæan, and Melancthon,
Cromwell, Napoleon Bonaparte are known to have been freemasons. But historians
have failed to study and explain the consequences of such a fact.

not free from it. Their perceptions were still instilled into
the minds of each succeeding generation of men scattered
over those regions once forming parts of the old Roman
empire.

In discussing, therefore, the public and private character
of this eminent man, whose life we have endeavoured to
represent, we must first quit the fields of modern thought
and transplant ourselves back to those that existed in
England during the Cromwellian period. Let us then
remember, by an abrupt act of the memory, that no Englishman of that day had a clear idea even as to the shape of
the world he inhabited ; the sun was still believed by him to
travel round the motionless brute earth, and in a word the
Ptolemaic system formed the key to the musings of every
refined mind in the hours of meditative repose during the
sublimer moments of its earthly existence. Astrology, white
and black magic, alchemy, dreams, omens and superstitious
fancies, entered more or less into the reflections and illusions
of every one ; kings regulated their course by them ; the
world at large, now called public opinion, was slavishly controlled by them. Education—that is to say, the power of
doing into English the authors of Greece and Rome—was
enjoyed by few, but the subjective truths in those authors
were understood by only a few among the few, when life was
subsequently engrossed by objective pursuits, and perhaps
there was not at that period a single soul living, that was
wholly emancipated from the love of arms, glittering armour,
barbaric show, sensuous enjoyments, and petty distinctions.
How could such minds be ennobled æsthetically and morally
even by the purest maxims of religion, when such ignorance
of nature's laws obtained, when a superstitious darkness so
obscured the eye of reason ? Men—the best, the wisest—
were fighting in the dark against unseen antagonistic powers,
against phantoms and imaginary foes; they wrestled in their
ignorance with an invincible, because to them invisible adversary ; they reverenced as truth nearly everything which

H H

modern reason, scientifically and properly educated, deems now incredible. On consulting the page of history, in order to refresh our memory, we see what crimes were committed in the belief that they were virtues. The legislators of that age endeavoured to conquer the hydra of vice with the club alone, and never thought of the sacred fire of reason, but merely of fire for roasting and burning witches, heretics, or books. They relied on violence wherewith to overcome violence. Death, fine, or imprisonment, was resorted to, after the crime had been committed; but of prophylactic and humanising legislation they had no conception, and thus by dint of legal murder, legal oppression, and legal cruelty, they fostered vice, as the ever-restless surges of the ocean promote the vitality and activity of the coral-worm.

Public opinion, poor substitute as it is for that moral development which continuous knowledge can alone impart to a nation, liable as it is to be turned to evil account by ambition and unprincipled power, or by mercantile interests, during periods of popular illusion, is still better than no opinion at all, during periods of popular stagnation. At the time of which we are treating there certainly was a popular opinion, still in an infantine state, but being without accumulated power sufficient to check corruption in high places it was unable to enforce, though it might demand, reforms. The masses were too simple and rude to penetrate the hypocrisy and perceive the criminality of the ruling powers, whose legislation was altogether partial. And because wisdom was so rare, so little impressed into the service of mankind, passion, imagination, blind faith, and wild hope, had the arena of life to themselves. The people formed a toy-machine to be pulled by wires, and the men who pulled them were themselves merely children of a larger growth, delighting in baubles and gew-gaws not accessible to the vulgar.

If then, amid this congregation of human beings with their innate faculties of nature so undeveloped, we see any

individual detached from the opaque mass, and shining with
his own light through the night of time after the lapse of
centuries, him we nominate great, and such a man the
subject of this biography appears to have been.   In an age
when action more than meditation gained the palm too
frequently, we find him advocating just ideas and ende-
vouring to realise them by his deeds.   As a public man he
displayed the most restless activity, and the maxims of state
he held up to himself as the guide to his conduct are now
being recognised by men of all parties.

No unnatural selfishness can be laid to his charge.   If as
a labourer he took more than his fair hire, the accusation
does not impeach him alone, but the whole body of his
profession, whose remunerative emoluments were calculated
on too high a scale by the Court requiring their services in
the administration of the country.   Taught to regard it as
one of his first duties to provide for his family, he did not
see the injustice of accepting a plurality of offices.   Nor was
it altogether an injustice, if competent holders of them were
scarce, and if his fellow-men did not then regard it in this
light.   It is certain, that he himself did not, and that he
considered he was thereby serving the interests of the State.

He thought of races yet unborn, when he saved from spoliation, and in one or two cases from destruction, some of our
best institutions, charitable and literary.   He felt sympathy
with the people, when he introduced and carried his measure
for having the laws of the land drawn up in the English
language, foreseeing what a boon it would be in future ages.

The dark passions of human nature, from which no one is
exempt at his birth, were gradually subdued by his educated
reason, and by those antagonistic qualities with which humanity is mercifully endowed.   Averse to our penal code,
more terrible at that period than Draco's, deeply repenting
his small share in Stafford's attainder, and in the punishment
that should have been mitigated by the extenuating circumstances of the case, he refused the honours of the criminal

H H 2

bench, and devoted himself rather to the so-called equitable branches of the law.

Partly the pains of conscience he felt in his early manhood when passing sentences as Recorder at Abingdon, partly the unexpected misery he endured at the same time in his domestic relations, awoke in his mind a certain train of philosophical reflections, that are now better understood by the name of optimism, subsequently professed and elaborated by Leibnitz. That the further experience of life may have partially shown him his error, during his retirement towards the end of his earthly career, is probable. Perhaps he may have asked himself then, why there should be a constant and not recurrent change for ever going on in the world, if that which is is best. It would have been better for his fame, if he had been a pessimist, for he then could have earlier looked up to a more exalted ideal.

As for the sincerity of his religious convictions—and which is all that we have any right to expect in matters of belief—this is best shown, not by his words or even public actions, but by the devotion of his old age to the incessant study of Scripture, when not engaged on the task of confessing to his children all the workings of his past life. Of his private charities we of course know nothing. But as his faith, so his horror of the infidelity and profligacy that reigned at the court of the restored monarch. So deeply did he distrust this man, that he, as it is presumed, desired his body to be buried with all possible secrecy, and it is only surmised now that it sleeps in some unknown vault beneath his parish church. The world was led to believe that it had been conveyed to the ancestral vault at Fawley, and the error was only discovered in the year 1830. He apparently dreaded the fate attending the remains of Cromwell and others, with whom he had served so many years after the death of Charles, that King whose grave had been likewise selected with great secrecy, probably under Whitelocke's auspices, with Cromwell's consent. It is certain that he viewed the reigns of Charles and James with feelings of dismay, but he never harboured a thought of revenge against them, although they had brought comparative ruin on his house.

His public life has been thought inconsistent, and would perhaps be such in ordinary times, but a statesman's life is ever dependent on the times.   His lot was cast in a period of volcanic and demoniacal agency, as well as in an age of transition, when men were contending with the fiercest passions for the overthrow or preservation of past institutions, as they are now ; when new ideas on every subject were being poured forth lava-like, and as unprofitably as they are now, upon the surface of this land, or other lands.   As we see, his line of conduct had to be selected by himself, at an early period of his manhood.   He might have lived in agricultural retirement.   For this he had little taste in his youth, being in want of sympathetic society, which could not be enjoyed in the country among boors, when very little difference of mind existed between the squire and his domestics. Even had he quitted his post in the Long Parliament, to which he had been sent by his constituents, and retired to his estate, this would not have saved it from the waste that ensued, nor him from being regarded as friend or foe by the contending parties.   Had he gone over to the King, as Clarendon and so many other lawyers did, this would have not satisfied his conscience, which acknowledged the majesty of constitutional law to be greater than the will of an arbitrary monarch, who refused so pertinaciously to abate one jot of his Divine pretensions.   Whitelocke could think as deeply on these matters as any modern statesman.   It required no scientific knowledge, but plain sense, to be able to perceive that the Divine right of kings was no longer a tenable doctrine.   He saw that the King had done much wrong, and that wrong was itself the refutation of the claim set up.

After making renewed but vain efforts to restore peace, the victories of his party settled the question, and the abuse by the Parliament of the power so acquired, as recorded in these pages, transferred it to the army. For the country at large had never given authority in the first instance to the Long Parliament (and consequently not to the army even) to convert the monarchy into a republic. A strong hand was necessary to restore order throughout the distracted country. The behests of the majority in the Parliament were obeyed by that army much longer than they deserved, for the House ought long since to have dissolved itself according to promise. Having usurped and exceeded its powers far beyond the necessity of the case, it now sat by no right, for he who by compulsion had delegated to them the right of sitting as long as they pleased—an option which could not with justice be conferred—had himself perished, and with him all his regal powers, real or imaginary. A parliament in this country is, in so far as the Commons are concerned, returned by the people, but it sits no longer than the sovereign thinks proper, that sovereign representing the people in its conservative, coercive, or permissive functions, as the assembly does in its deliberative or legislative.

The doctrine that executive power is vested in the people was never advocated by Sir Bulstrode, who could easily see that only general power is so vested. Historic precedent conferred on them the power of electing the person that should wield the former ; but precedent derived from barbarous epochs, or from national self-delusion, is not worth much. Supreme power ought to reside in knowledge alone, and virtually does so reside, however ignored occasionally by a people stirred up to madness through vicious administration or party intrigues. Such blind impulse may be instinctive, or, in other words, may be traced to Providence ; and when princes abuse power, the instinct is evoked in due ratio. Again, all power must proceed from the people as the source (the more remote, the more placid and majestic the derived stream), since it is from them that genius and talent are continually supplied. Such seems to have been the kind of reasoning by which Sir Bulstrode shaped his conduct, and

the more enlightened men become, the more will this doctrine
find favour, forming as it does a barrier to all absolute and
irresponsible power.

But unfortunately when a nation is distracted, when new
principles, true or false, are striving for the mastery, it is
only an armed force, visible or concealed, that can support
or overthrow the ruling power, can impart vitality or inflict
death.   Now, the Long Parliament, the instant it began to
abuse its functions, could possess no other than the usurped
right of holding the balance and the sword.   Its members
were told this in a speech recorded here, by their fellow-
member, who reminded them that they only held the purse,
to the correctness of which law they may have reluctantly
assented at the time.   But the vast bulk of the representative
body did not comprehend its deep truth, for they made
themselves absolute and irresponsible, which usurpation
evoked the hostility of knowledge, in which if Cromwell's
mind was deficient, the collective mind of the order to which
he belonged most assuredly was not.   Sir Bulstrode's dissatisfaction was not disguised, and when some of the members talked subsequently about hanging him with the great
seal about his neck, he must have smiled bitterly at the
vanity of the drama so tragically commenced, so unsatis-
factorily concluded.

The King being dead and hereditary right having been
violently put into abeyance, no other king having been proclaimed, and no coronation oath having been administered to
sanction the covenant between the throne and the people,—
without which Charles II. was only half a legal sovereign,—
Cromwell had as much right to reign as that Parliament
which he dissolved.   He was at the head of the army, and
this being in possession of the sword, may be said to have
represented the now latent monarchy.   It owed no allegiance
to the usurping members, it broke no oath of homage and
fealty to them.   What fidelity it did owe as born Englishmen,
it owed to the country, which at that time, in consequence

of the utter confusion in all its domestic relations, respected Cromwell more than the Speaker and his mace.

It has been usual with historians to apply the epithet of anarchy to the period immediately preceding the restoration of Charles; but, in truth, the entire period of the convulsion, called by some rebellion, by others revolution, from almost the commencement of the reign of Charles I., was anarchy. It might have been stopped by Cromwell's coronation, and a subsequent settlement of the dynastic question by legislation. But for the advice of his friend in St. James's Park, an advice Whitelocke modified when too late, Cromwell would have had time and opportunity to seize the vacant throne by using his influence over the minds of his officers—*and else-where.* It must have been practicable at that time, or Cromwell would not have entertained the design.

When Whitelocke, with other statesmen, did urge the Lord Protector to assume the title of King the favourable moment had in other respects passed away, the reaction had gathered accumulated strength, and men with their passions cooled, their thirst of vengeance slaked, were already by twos and threes returning slowly to those feelings of loyalty so ineradicably implanted by early training and education in the hearts of Englishmen.

There was, moreover, a very powerful motive, and that a personal one, that induced him to urge this step upon Cromwell. The marriage law had been twice altered by the Parliament, once on its sole authority by the Long Parliament, and again with the consent of Cromwell by the Barebones, or Little Parliament. It was not lawful to use the prayer-book or the ceremonies of what had been and has since been the Established Church ; its ministers, those at least who like the vicar of Bray did not conform to the dominant system, were rendered incapable of officiating. Sir Bulstrode, bound to uphold the law by his example, married his third wife in accordance with what was then the law of the land, by banns at some church in the city, probably that one

which was nearest to Bishopsgate Street. Of course an
Independent clergyman or minister, perhaps even a Presbyterian, married them, but the register was lost in the Great
Fire. Now had Cromwell assumed the title of King, all
would have been well. The law of this country recog-
nises every act performed under a King, whether he reigns
de facto merely, or *de jure*. As Cromwell finally refused
to assume the title, to the great disappointment and mortification of Whitelocke, the latter in despair supported
every and any form of government whatever, rather than
see Charles restored unconditionally to the throne. The
restoration destroyed at once the validity of his third
marriage, and rendered the issue illegitimate. Hence the
reason why he settled during his lifetime the estate of Chilton upon Samuel, that the question of legitimacy might not
be raised at his, Sir Bulstrode's, death ; hence the securing
of Lilly's estate to the other son, Carleton, at so early a
period by a special Act of Parliament. His virtually wedded
wife, as virtuous a woman as ever breathed, who had made
so many sacrifices for him, who had given up to him
without reserve a noble fortune on her marriage, never
knew to her last moments that her marriage was illegal
or worthless in the eyes of the law. But her husband did,
and this is why he made such deep submission to the tyrant
Charles, and why he stifled every feeling of indignation.
Is there any father, husband, or wife that will not comprehend his sacrifice of self, and why he preferred to offer
up his own fame, his consistency, his real principles with
a view to save his wife and younger children from what
was then considered so indelible a disgrace, but which now,
in a happier and more just age, can only be regarded as a
misfortune ? The legality of all social acts during the first
revolution and down to the Restoration has yet to be
established.

But although not insensible to the " divinity which doth
hedge in the name of King," Sir Bulstrode had been for

some time regarding despairingly the absent *de jure* monarch, of whose acts he, as Cromwell's trusted minister, was officially cognisant.   He knew that the exiled prince had committed wilful murder with his own hand, that he had connived at many crimes, that both he and his brother James were Papists by education, that the Prince professed opinions of an atheistical nature.

Lastly, he, Sir Bulstrode, had in his mature manhood, when the mind, no longer young, receives more solemn impressions, begun to entertain religious convictions which he knew would never be sympathised in by royalty, as royalty manifested itself in those days.   As a statesman, too, he possibly may have over-estimated the intensity and durability of the religious movement that had rendered the Puritans victorious ; and he may well be excused for having failed to foresee the intensity of vice and depravity that welcomed back the family of the Stuarts.

When Richard Cromwell succeeded to his father's chair, the lethargic people acquiesced, and the addresses of the various corporations may be reasonably supposed to have been sincere.   But the mind of the new Protector had been cast in too feeble a mould to sustain the part that required then peculiarly to be performed with energy and even dignity.   Richard was incapable of protecting, and so simple-minded, that even Monk felt pity for him, though forgetful of every other ancient tie.   The army in England, now much demoralised by a variety of causes, soon discovered the incapacity of their new chief ; the leaders grew disaffected ; and therefore no minister, however wise, could prevent the abdication that ensued.   Henceforth, no ability, no disinterestedness, no genius, could do more than delay the tide of loyalty flooding back to the old dynasty.   The only act that might have prevented it, would have been an appeal to the religious Protestant feelings of the community against the detected Papist sons of the beheaded King ; but Protestantism was at that moment less powerful than the social feelings of the nation, and the appeal was never made. The creed of the restored King was only discovered by our leading men a few hours before the succession of his brother James. It had not been suspected by the people ; and, if it had, would have been disregarded in the delirium of revived monarchy, so repugnant to Hudibrastic opinions.

With the Restoration the blessing of national order was obtained, but at the cost of all that noble minds hold dear. A scene of general profligacy and bitter persecution ensued. The conduct of the two Stuarts, of their courtiers and courts of law, is itself a vindication of Whitelocke's desperate though unavailing efforts to support his sinking party. Unhappily it was not he, but only Maynard, his old friend and colleague, who lived long enough to witness the retribution. Such catastrophes can hardly be renewed in this land ; but they serve as landmarks to show each party in the state those bounds beyond which it dares not trespass, unless with impious foot and the spirit of destructiveness.

The rest of Sir Bulstrode Whitelocke's claims, as a pioneer of our modern civilisation, to the favourable remembrance of all Englishmen, may be seen in the body of this work. His claim to be regarded as a prudent, humane, and temperate statesman will be universally allowed. If he had faults— and what man has not ?—they were, as far as his fellow-men are concerned, most amply expiated in his own person. Any evil he may have committed died with him, whereas the good lives after him, and demands the admiration of those who thoughtfully reflect on the obligations bequeathed to us by the great men of past ages.

THE END.

BRADBURY AND EVANS, PRINTERS, WHITEFRIARS.

Lightning Source UK Ltd.
Milton Keynes UK
UKHW021157271019
352395UK00009B/169/P

9 780530 613277